iOS Animations

by Tutorials

SECOND EDITION

By Marin Todorov

iOS Animations by Tutorials Second Edition

Marin Todorov

Notice of Rights

Notice of Liability

Trademarks

ISBN: 978-1-942878-09-4

Table of Contents:

Dedications

To my parents - ever so supportive and loving.

To Mirjam.

-Marin Todorov

Introduction

There's no denying it: creating animations is one of the most enjoyable parts of iOS development!

Animations are fun to create, they breathe life into your user interface, and most importantly, they make your interface a delight to use. Who doesn't love an app that gives you a little visual thrill when you open a menu or swipe right?

You've probably seen impressive animations in many third-party apps, as well as in Apple's own built-in apps such as Passbook:

When used properly, animations can convey information to your users and draw their attention to important parts of the interface.

To create responsive and attractive user interfaces, you'll need to use all kinds of animations, from very subtle effects, to extremely expressive ones that leap off the screen.

In this book, you'll learn about various iOS animation techniques, from simple view animations, to vivid 3D animations, to view controller animations that make the navigation in your app look *and* feel great.

By the end of this book, you'll have worked through the chapter content and you'll have hands-on experience solving the challenges at the end of the chapters — and you'll be well on your way to coming up with stunning animations for your own apps!

What you need

To follow along with the tutorials in this book, you'll need the following:

- **A Mac running the latest point release of OS X Yosemite (10.10.5) or El Capitan (10.11)**. You'll need this to be able to install the latest version of Xcode.
- **Xcode 7 or later.** Xcode is the main development tool for iOS. You can download the latest version of Xcode for free on the Mac app store here:

  https://itunes.apple.com/app/xcode/id497799835?mt=12
- **Basic knowledge of Swift and iOS development.** This book is about animations specifically; to understand the animation code and how the accompanying demo projects work you will need at least a basic understanding of Swift and Cocoa Touch.

If you want to try things out on a physical iOS device, you'll need a paid developer account. However, all the sample projects in this book will work just fine in the iOS Simulator bundled with Xcode, so the paid developer account is completely optional.

Who this book is for

This book is for iOS developers who already know the basics of iOS and Swift, and want to dive deep into animations.

If you're a complete beginner to iOS, we suggest you first read through the latest edition of *The iOS Apprentice*. That will give you a solid foundation of building iOS apps with Swift from the ground up.

If you know the basics of iOS development but are new to Swift, we suggest you read through *Swift Apprentice* first, which goes through the features of Swift using playgrounds to teach the language.

You can find both of these books at our online store: http://www.raywenderlich.com/store

How to use this book

Each chapter in this book includes a starter project and covers a small number of animation techniques in detail; this lets you work through the chapters in the book in any order.

However, for beginners, we do suggest that you work through the chapters in order, since the concepts build upon each other. Also, remember you'll get the most out of the book if you follow along with the tutorials and perform the hands-on challenges.

For advanced developers, there's still value in the early chapters since that cover the basics, since you might not yet be familiar with the Swift syntax for these familiar animation APIs. However if you're comfortable with that, feel free to jump ahead to the topics that interest you the most.

What's in store

This book is divided into six sections. You can find more details on each section in its introduction, which also includes a short description of its chapters. Here's a brief overview.

Section I: View Animations

The first section of the book covers **view animations** in UIKit. View animations are the simplest type of animations in iOS, but still very powerful; you can easily animate almost any view element and change things such as its size, position and color.

Section II: Auto Layout

Auto Layout is becoming more common in apps, and there are some special techniques to animate views that are sized and positioned with auto layout constraints. This section provides a crash course in Auto Layout and then covers the animation techniques that play nicely with Auto Layout.

Section III: Layer Animations

Views on iOS are backed by **layers**, which offer a lower-level interface to the visual content of your apps. When you need more flexibility or performance, you can use layer animations rather than view animations. In this section, you'll learn about layers and the Core Animation API.

Section IV: 3D Animations

In this section, you'll move beyond two dimensions and learn about **3D animations** and effects with `CATransform3D`. Although Core Animation isn't a true 3D framework, it lets you position things in 3D-space and set perspective – which leads to some very slick and impressive effects!

Section V: Further Types of Animations

There are two more animation techniques that are part of Core Animation and UIKit, but don't really fit into sections I and III. In this section, you'll get an impressive snowy effect working with particle emitters, and then learn about flipbook-style frame animation with `UIImageView`.

Section VI: View Controller Transitions

Animating views and layers is impressive, but you can dial it up to 11 and animate *entire view controllers*! In this section, you'll learn the techniques for transitioning between view controllers, as well as transitioning between changes in device orientations, all in the same view controller.

Section VII: Third-party Animation Libraries

Now that you've looked at all these animation APIs from Apple, it's time to take a step away and examine some open-source libraries. In this section, you'll learn about **Easy Animation** from your humble author, and **Pop** from Facebook. You'll learn about the additional features they offer to bring your animations and code to the next level!

Source code and forums

This book comes with the complete source code for each of the chapters. That includes starter projects, challenge solutions, and other required resources, so you'll definitely want to have these on hand as you go through the book.

You can get the source code for the book here:

- http://www.raywenderlich.com/store/ios-animations-by-tutorials/source-code

We've also set up an official forum for the book at http://www.raywenderlich.com/forums. This is a great place to ask questions you have about the book, to get feedback on developing your own animations, or to submit any errors or suggested updates.

PDF Version

We also have a PDF version of this book available, which can be handy to have the code there on screen or to search for a specific term through the book as you're developing.

Speaking of the PDF version, we have some good news!

Since you purchased the physical copy of this book, you are eligible to buy the PDF version at a significant discount if you would like (if you don't have it already). For more details, see this page:

- http://www.raywenderlich.com/store/ios-animations-by-tutorials/upgrade

License

By purchasing *iOS Animations by Tutorials*, you have the following license:

- You are allowed to use and/or modify the source code in *iOS Animations by Tutorials* in as many apps as you want, with no attribution required.
- You are allowed to use and/or modify all art, images and designs that are included in *iOS Animations by Tutorials* in as many apps as you want, but must include this attribution line somewhere inside your app: "Artwork/images/designs: from *iOS Animations by Tutorials* book, available at http://www.raywenderlich.com."

About the team

Marin Todorov is the author of this book, and is one of the founding members of the raywenderlich.com tutorial team.

He is an independent iOS consultant and publisher, and also has a background in web and desktop development.

Besides crafting code, Marin also enjoys blogging, writing books and speaking at conferences. He happily open sources code.

Richard Turton is the technical editor of this book. He is an iOS developer for a leading UK mobile agency, a prolific Stack Overflow participant and the author of a development blog, commandshift.co.uk.

When he's not in front of a computer, he is underneath one or both of his daughters as a horse, monkey or cushion.

Chris Belanger is the editor of this book. He has been a coder for over a quarter century, which makes him feel kind of old.

He's also a prolific writer, dabbles in electronic and organic music composition and occasionally manages to get real work done as a developer of real-time control systems.

Greg Heo is the final pass editor of this book, and has been part of the editorial team at raywenderlich.com since 2012.

He has been nerding out with computers since the 80s on his Commodore 64, and continues to this day on the web and on iOS. He likes caffeine, codes with two-space tabs, and writes with semicolons and the Oxford comma.

Vicki Wenderlich created many of the illustrations in this book. Vicki discovered a love of digital art four years ago, and has been making app art and digital illustrations ever since. She is passionate about helping people pursue their dreams, and makes free app art for developers available on her website, http://www.gameartguppy.com

iOS Animations by Emails

If you enjoy this book and are hungry for more, you can subscribe to Marin's free *iOS Animations by Emails* newsletter.

You'll get a monthly email featuring a cool iOS animation. It's a chance for us to share some of the animation ideas that didn't make it into the chapters and projects in this book. Think of it as a "Season 2" to continue the iOS animations experience!

You can find more information and sign up for the newsletter at:

http://www.ios-animations-by-emails.com

Section I: View Animations

These first five chapters will introduce you to the animation API of UIKit. This API is specifically designed to help you animate your views with ease while avoiding the complexity of Core Animation, which runs the animations under the hood.

Though simple to use, the UIKit animation API provides you with lots of flexibility and power to handle most, if not all, of your animation requirements.

Animations are visible, onscreen effects that apply to all of the views, or visible objects, in your user interface:

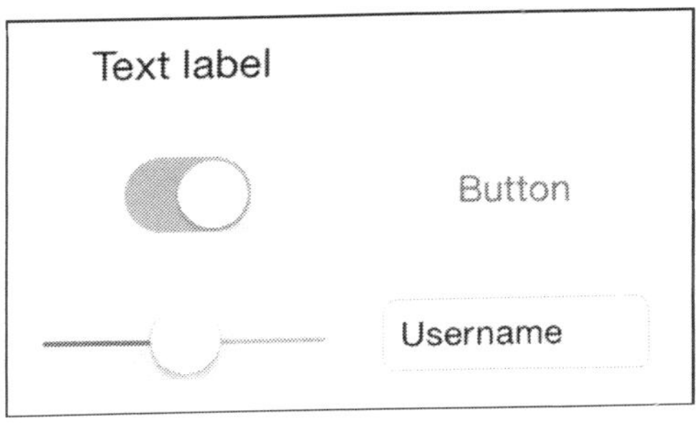

You can animate *any* object on screen that ultimately inherits from `UIView`; this includes `UILabel`, `UIImageView`, `UIButton`, and any custom classes you might have created yourself.

In the five chapters of this section on view animations, you'll learn how to use animation to improve a fictional airline app, **Bahama Air**, by adding various animations to its UI elements.

First, you'll add animations to the login screen:

You'll work on this screen in the following chapters:

- **Chapter 1, Getting Started with View Animations**: You'll learn how to move, scale and fade views. You'll create a number of different animations to get comfortable with Swift and the basic UIKit APIs.
- **Chapter 2, Springs**: You'll build on the concepts of linear animation and create more eye-catching effects using spring-driven animations. Boiiing! :]
- **Chapter 3, Transitions**: You'll learn about several class methods in UIKit that help you animate views in or out of the screen. These one-line API calls make transition effects easy to achieve.

Once you've completed your work on the login screen, you'll move on to the **Bahama Air** flight status screen. You'll work with the existing screen and make it more exciting by adding animations that follow on from the theme of the login screen:

You'll start with a visually static version of the screen and add a number of compelling, advanced animations to improve the user experience:

- **Chapter 4, View Animations in Practice**: You've learned most of what you need to know about animations in UIKit. This chapter teaches you how to combine techniques you're familiar with in creative ways to build up even cooler animations.
- **Chapter 5, Keyframe Animations**: You'll use keyframe animations to unlock the ultimate achievement of an impressive UI: creating elaborate animation sequences built from a number of distinct stages.

Once you've worked through all chapters in this section you'll have some in-depth experience on animation that you can carry forward to the rest of this book.

This section shows you how easy it is to add animations to your views – read on to Chapter 1 to get started!

Chapter 1: Getting Started with View Animations

In this chapter you'll dip your toes into the bottomless sea of view animations. Don't be misled by the chapter's title, however – getting started with such a powerful and rich API means there's a lot of interesting material to cover!

In this chapter and accompanying project, you'll learn how to do the following:

- Set the stage for a cool animation.
- Create move and fade animations.
- Adjust the animation easing.
- Reverse and repeat animations.

There's a fair bit of material to get through, but I promise it will be a lot of fun. Are you up for the challenge?

All right! Time to get started.

Your first animation

Open the starter project located in the Resources folder for this chapter. Build and run your project in Xcode; you'll see the login screen of a fictional-airline app like so:

The app doesn't do much right now – it just shows a login form with a title, two text fields, and a big friendly button at the bottom.

There's also a nice background picture and four clouds. The clouds are already connected to outlet variables in the code.

Open **ViewController.swift** and have a look inside. At the top of the file you'll see all the connected outlets and class variables. Further down, there's a bit of code in `viewDidLoad()`, which initializes some of the UI. The project is ready for you to jump in and shake things up a bit!

Enough with the introductions – you're undoubtedly ready to try out some code!

Your first task is to animate the form elements onto the screen when the user opens the application. Since the form is now visible when the app starts, you'll have to move it off of the screen just before your view controller makes an appearance.

Add the following code to `viewWillAppear()`:

```
heading.center.x  -= view.bounds.width
username.center.x -= view.bounds.width
password.center.x -= view.bounds.width
```

This moves each of the form elements outside the visible bounds of the screen, like so:

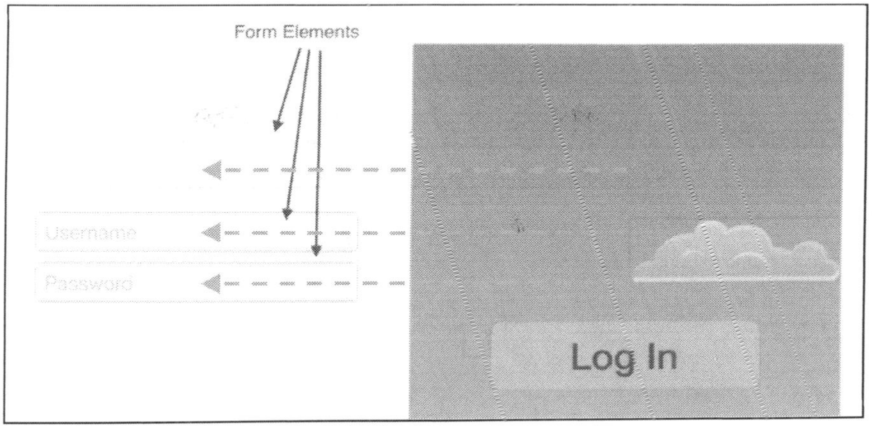

Since the code above executes before the view controller appears, it will look like those text fields were never there in the first place.

Build and run your project to make sure your fields truly appear off-screen just as you had planned:

Perfect – now you can animate those form elements back to their original locations via a delightful animation.

Add the following code to the end of `viewDidAppear()`:

```
UIView.animateWithDuration(0.5, animations: {
  self.heading.center.x += self.view.bounds.width
})
```

To animate the title in you call the `UIView` class method `animateWithDuration(_:animations:)`. The animation starts immediately and animates over half a second; you set the duration via the first method parameter in the code.

It's as easy as that; all the changes you make to the view in the `animations` closure will be animated by UIKit.

Build and run your project; you should see the title slide neatly into place like so:

That sets the stage for you to animate in the rest of the form elements.

Since `animateWithDuration(_:animations:)` is a class method, you aren't limited to animate just one specific view; in fact you can animate as many views as you want in your `animations` closure.

Add the following line to the `animations` closure:

```
self.username.center.x += self.view.bounds.width
```

Build and run your project again; watch as the username field slides into place:

Seeing both views animate together is quite cool, but you probably noticed that animating the two views over the same distance and with the same duration looks a bit stiff. Only kill-bots move with such absolute synchronization! :]

Wouldn't it be cool if each of the elements moved independently of the others, possibly with a little bit of delay in between the animations?

First remove the struck out line of code below that animates `username`:

```
UIView.animateWithDuration(0.5, animations: {
  self.heading.center.x += self.view.bounds.width
  ~~self.username.center.x += self.view.bounds.width~~
})
```

Then add the following code to the bottom of `viewDidAppear()`:

```
UIView.animateWithDuration(0.5, delay: 0.3, options: [],
animations: {
  self.username.center.x += self.view.bounds.width
}, completion: nil)
```

The class method you use this time looks familiar, but it has a few more parameters to let you customize your animation:

1. `duration`: The duration of the animation.
2. `delay`: The amount of seconds UIKit will wait before it starts the animation.
3. `options`: A set of animation options allowing you to customize a number of aspects about your animation. You'll learn more about this parameter later on, but for now you can pass the empty set `[]` to mean "no options."
4. `animations`: The closure expression to provide your animations.
5. `completion`: A code closure to execute when the animation completes; this parameter often comes in handy when you want to perform some final cleanup tasks or chain animations one after the other.

In the code you added above you set `delay` to `0.3` to make the animation start just a hair later than the title animation.

Build and run your project; how does the combined animation look now?

Ahh – that looks much better. Now all you need to do is animate in the `password` field.

Add the following code to the bottom of `viewDidAppear()`:

```
UIView.animateWithDuration(0.5, delay: 0.4, options: [],
animations: {
  self.password.center.x += self.view.bounds.width
}, completion: nil)
```

Here you've mostly mimicked the animation of the `username` field, just with a slightly longer delay.

Build and run your project again to see the complete animation sequence:

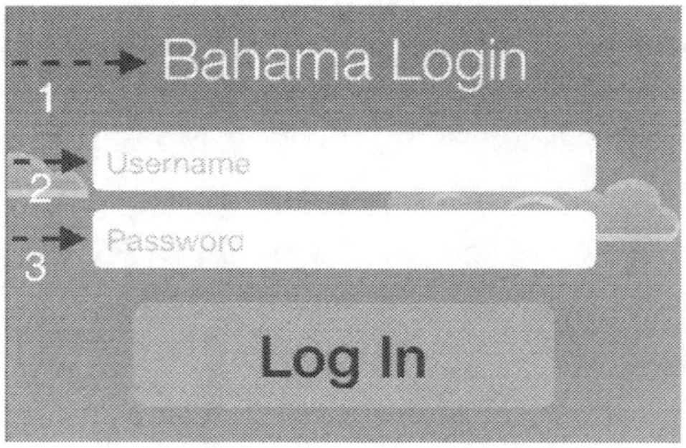

That's all you need to do to animate views across the screen with a UIKit animation!

That's just the start of it – you'll be learning a few more awesome animation techniques in the remainder of this chapter!

Animatable properties

Now that you've seen how easy animations can be, you're probably keen to learn how else you can animate your views.

This section will give you an overview of the animatable properties of a `UIView`, and then guide you through exploring these animations in your project.

Not all view properties can be animated, but all view animations, from the simplest to the most complex, can be built by animating the subset of properties on a view that *do* lend themselves to animation, as outlined in the section below.

Position and size

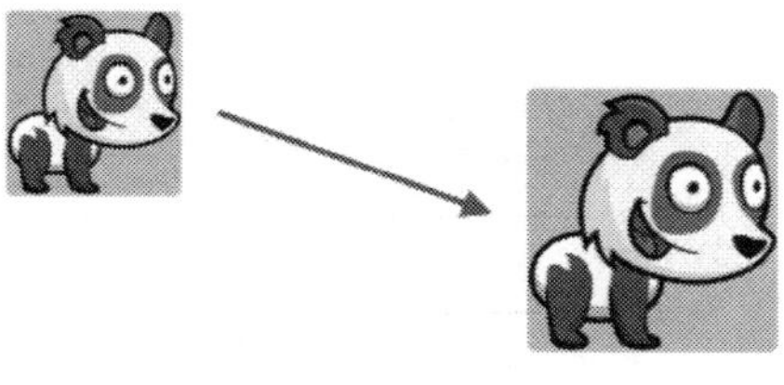

You can animate a view's position and frame in order to make it grow, shrink, or move around as you did in the previous section.

Here are the properties you can use to modify a view's position and size:

- **bounds**: Animate this property to reposition the view's content within the view's frame.
- **frame:** Animate this property to move and/or scale the view.
- **center:** Animate this property when you want to move the view to a new location on screen.

Don't forget that Swift lets you adjust single members of structures as well. This means you can move a view vertically by changing `center.y` or you can shrink a view by decreasing `frame.size.width`.

Appearance

You can change the appearance of the view's content by either tinting its background or making the view fully or semi-transparent.

- **backgroundColor:** Change this property of a view to have UIKit gradually change the tint of the background color over time.
- **alpha:** Change this property to create fade-in and fade-out effects.

Transformation

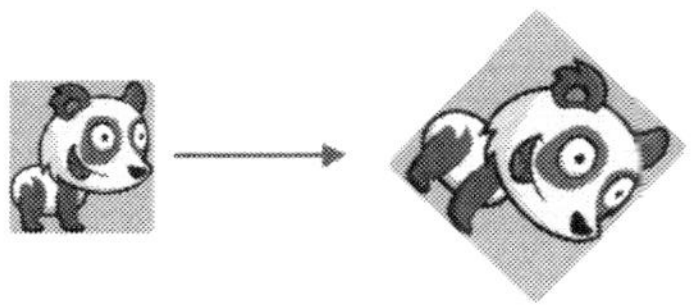

Transforms modify views in much the same way as above, since you can also adjust size and position.

- **transform**: Modify this property within an animation block to animate the rotation, scale, and/or position of a view.

These are affine transformations under the hood, which are much more powerful and allow you to describe the scale factor or rotation angle rather than needing to provide a specific bounds or center point.

These look like pretty basic building blocks, but you'll be surprised at the complex animation effects you're about to encounter!

Animation options

Looking back to your animation code, you were always passing in `[]` to the `options` parameter.

`options` lets you customize how UIKit creates your animation. You've only adjusted the `duration` and `delay` of your animations, but you can have a lot more control over your animation parameters than just that.

There's a list of options declared in the `UIViewAnimationOptions` set type that you can combine in different ways for use in your animations.

Repeating

You'll first take a look at the following two animation options:

- `.Repeat`: Include this option to makes your animation loop forever.
- `.Autoreverse:` Include this option only in conjunction with `.Repeat`; this option repeatedly plays your animation in forward then in reverse.

Modify the code that animates the password field `viewDidAppear()` to use the `.Repeat` option as follows:

```
UIView.animateWithDuration(0.5, delay: 0.4,
  options: .Repeat, animations: {
  self.password.center.x += self.view.bounds.width
}, completion: nil)
```

Build and run your project to see the effect of your change:

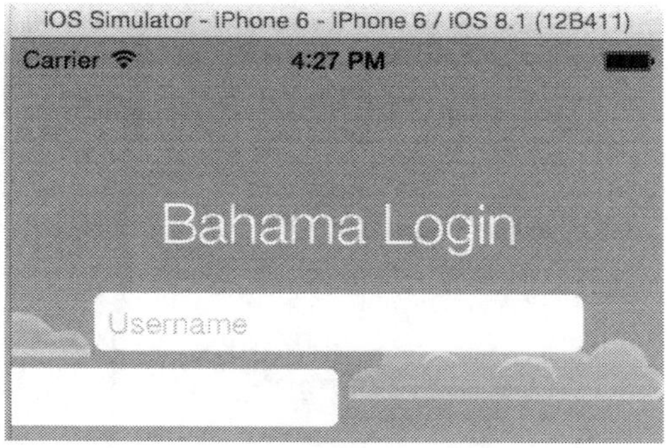

The form title and username field fly in and settle down in the center of the screen, but the `password` field keeps animating forever from its position off-screen.

Modify the same code you changed above to use both `.Repeat` and `.Autoreverse` in the `options` parameter as follows:

```
UIView.animateWithDuration(0.5, delay: 0.4,
  options: [.Repeat, .Autoreverse], animations: {
    self.password.center.x += self.view.bounds.width
}, completion: nil)
```

Note how if you want to enable more than one option you need to use the set syntax and list all options separated with a comma and enclose the list in square brackets.

> **Note**: If you only need a single option, Swift allows you to omit the square brackets as a convenience. However, you can still include them in case you add more options in the future – that means `[]` for no options, `[.Repeat]` for a single option, and `[.Repeat, .Autorepeat]` for multiple options.

Build and run your project again; this time the password field just can't make up its mind about staying on the screen!

Animation easing

In real life things don't just suddenly start or stop moving. Physical objects like cars or trains slowly accelerate until they reach their target speed, and unless they hit a brick wall, they gradually slow down until they come to a complete stop at their final destination.

The image below illustrates this concept in detail:

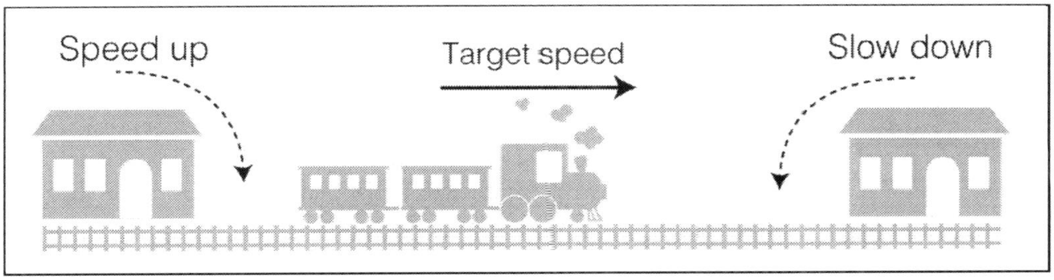

To make your animations look more realistic, you can apply the same effect of building momentum at the beginning and slowing down before the end, known in general terms as **ease-in** and **ease-out**.

You can choose from four different easing options:

- `.Linear`: This option applies no acceleration or deceleration to the animation. The only time in this book you'll use this option is in the final challenge of Chapter 3, "Transitions".
- `.CurveEaseIn`: This option applies acceleration to the start of your animation.
- `.CurveEaseOut`: This option applies deceleration to the end of your animation.
- `.CurveEaseInOut`: This option applies acceleration to the start of your animation *and* applies deceleration to the end of your animation.

To better understand how these options add visual impact to your animation, you'll try a few of the options in your project.

Modify the animation code for your password field once again with a new option as follows:

```
UIView.animateWithDuration(0.5, delay: 0.4,
  options: [.Repeat, .Autoreverse, .CurveEaseOut], animations: {
    self.password.center.x += self.view.bounds.width
}, completion: nil)
```

Build and run your project; notice how smoothly the field decelerates until it reaches its rightmost position, before returning to the left side of the screen:

This looks much more natural since that's how you expect things to move in the real world.

Now try the opposite: ease-in the animation when the field is still outside of the screen by modifying the same code as above to change the `.CurveEaseOut` option to `.CurveEaseIn` as follows:

```
UIView.animateWithDuration(0.5, delay: 0.4,
  options: [.Repeat, .Autoreverse, .CurveEaseIn], animations: {
    self.password.center.x += self.view.bounds.width
}, completion: nil)
```

Build and run your project; observe how the field jumps back from its rightmost with robotic vigor. This looks unnatural and isn't as visually pleasing as the previous animation.

Finally give `.CurveEaseInOut` a try - it combines the two options you already know into one very natural looking easing. `.CurveEaseInOut` is also the default easing function UIKit applies to your animations.

You've seen how the various animation options affect your project and how to make movements look smooth and natural.

Before you move on, change the `options` on the piece of code you've been playing with back to `[]`:

```
UIView.animateWithDuration(0.5, delay: 0.4,
 options: [], animations: {
  self.password.center.x += self.view.bounds.width
}, completion: nil)
```

Now that you know how basic animations work, you're ready to tackle some more dazzling animation techniques.

Animating views from point A to point B? Pshaw – that's so easy! :]

In the next chapter, you'll explore how to drive your animations using springs. (*Boing...boing...boing...boing...!*)

Challenges

If this chapter is the first time you've animated a view in iOS, your head might be spinning a little. Don't worry, though, because no matter your initial skillset, you'll be well on your way to animation mastery in just a few chapters.

For now though, there's one very simple challenge waiting for you where you'll create an animation of your very own.

Challenge 1: Fade in the clouds

In **ViewController** you have four outlets: `cloud1`, `cloud2`, `cloud3`, and `cloud4`. Your task is to fade those in when the application starts.

You can pretty much decide on the exact form your solution will take, but here's a list of the basic steps you'll need to fulfill:

1. Set the `alpha` property to `0.0` for all four cloud views in `viewWillAppear()`.

2. In `viewDidAppear()` make four separate calls to `animateWithDuration(_:delay:options:animations:completion:)`. You'll get a nice-looking effect if you use a duration of `0.5` for all four animations and delays of `0.5`, `0.7`, `0.9`, and `1.1` respectively.
3. In each `animations` closure change the `alpha` of the respective cloud view to `1.0`. This will fade the cloud in.

When you run the project you should see a nice transition effect that animates the clouds, one after another:

All views on the screen should animate nicely – but wait! The Log In button isn't animating!

Just wait - you'll fix that in the next chapter.

Chapter 2: Springs

In the previous chapter you learned how to create basic animations with UIKit, including how to provide start and end values along with a duration to UIKit, which automatically created an animation for you.

So far your animations have been fluid movements in a single direction. When you animated a view's position, it was a straightforward movement from point A to point B, like so:

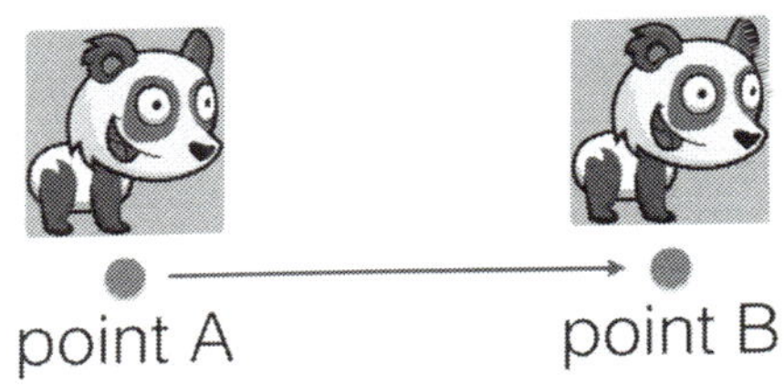

In this chapter you'll learn how to create more complex animations, which move views as if they were attached to a spring, as demonstrated below:

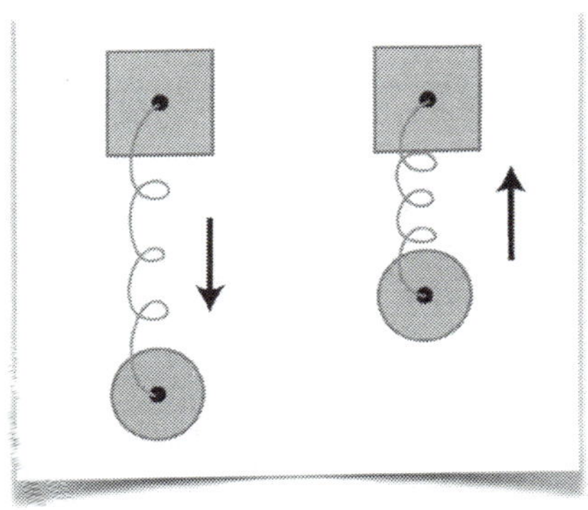

If you took the basic animation from point A to point B and added a bit of springiness to it, the motion of the animation would follow a path indicated by the red arrows below:

The view heads from point A to point B, but overshoots point B by a small amount. The view then heads back to point B and overshoots by a little less this time. This back-and-forth oscillation repeats until the view has come to rest at point B.

It's a nice effect; it adds a snappy, real-world feel to your animations. This chapter will show you how to use this effect to add a little bit of playfulness to your UI.

Spring animations

You'll continue on with the project from the previous chapter; if you didn't complete the exercises in Chapter 1 (including the challenge at the end of the chapter), then grab the starter project from the Resources folder for Chapter 2 and start from there.

Build and run your project; you should see the views on screen (except the Log In button) animate as soon as the app opens like so:

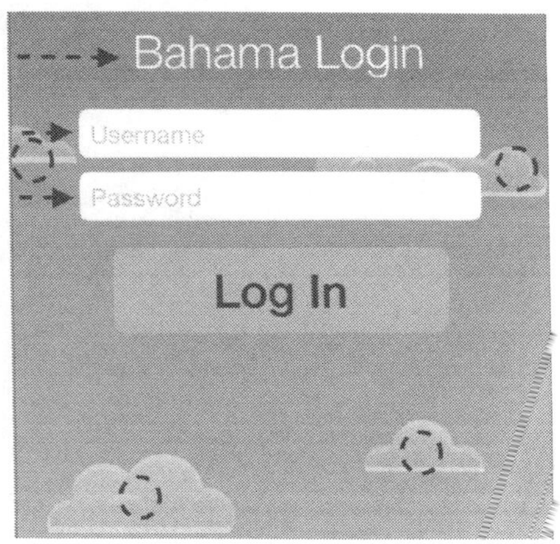

Your job is to take care of the last non-animated element on this screen: the Log In button.

Open **ViewController.swift** and add the following code to the bottom of `viewWillAppear()`:

```
loginButton.center.y += 30.0
loginButton.alpha = 0.0
```

Just as you did in the previous chapter, you set the start position of the button a bit lower on the y-axis and set its alpha value to zero so that it will start out as invisible.

Now move to `viewDidAppear()` and add the following code:

```
UIView.animateWithDuration(0.5, delay: 0.5,
 usingSpringWithDamping: 0.5, initialSpringVelocity: 0.0,
 options: [], animations: {
  self.loginButton.center.y -= 30.0
  self.loginButton.alpha = 1.0
}, completion: nil)
```

There are two key points in this piece of code.

First, you've animated two different properties at the same time! That was easier than you thought, right?

Second, you used a new animation method for the first time: `animateWithDuration(_:delay:usingSpringWithDamping:initialSpringVelocity:options:animations:completion:)`. Saying that method name too quickly just might injure your tongue! :]

The above method looks much like the ones you used in the previous chapter of the book, but it sports a couple of new parameters:

- `usingSpringWithDamping`: This controls the amount of damping, or reduction, applied to the animation as it approaches its final state. This parameter accepts values between `0.0` and `1.0`. Values closer to `0.0` create a bouncier animation, while values closer to `1.0` create a stiff-looking effect. You can think of this value as the "stiffness" of the spring.
- `initialSpringVelocity`: This controls the initial velocity of the animation. A value of `1.0` sets the velocity of the animation to cover the total distance of the animation in the span of one second. Bigger and smaller values will cause the animation to have more or less velocity.

Build and run your project; check out how the button moves now:

Since your animation has an initial velocity of `0.0` and a neutral damping of `0.5`, the animation doesn't look very eye-catching.

You should be able to dress up this animation a little by trying some different values for the velocity and damping.

Change the duration to `3.0` and the damping to `0.1`. This is just to let you observe the effect of your changes in slow motion instead of at normal speed.

Build and run your project again; note how the opacity of the button changes as it moves up. This is because the spring behavior affects **all** properties you animate; in your case, this affects *both* the vertical position of the button *and* its alpha value.

Now set `initialSpringVelocity` to `1.0` and build and run your project again:

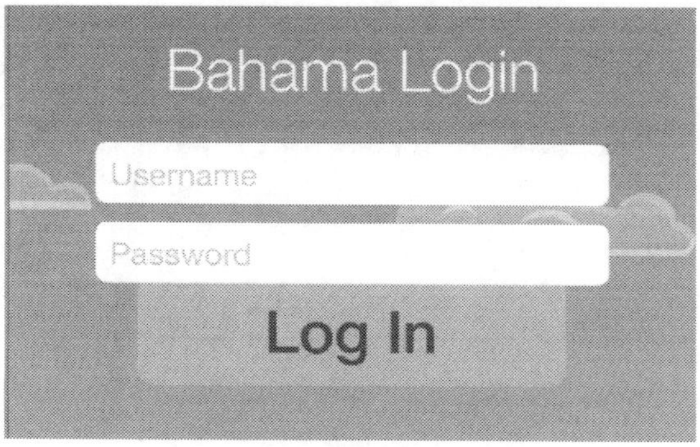

You'll notice that the button bounces a bit more when it animates and moves beyond the password field; this is because it has more momentum at the beginning of its movement and takes longer to settle down into its final position.

Play around with some different values for the damping and velocity parameters until you understand how changes in these parameters affect the look and feel of your animation.

When you're done, set the values for the velocity and damping back to their original values, like so:

```
UIView.animateWithDuration(0.5, delay: 0.5,
usingSpringWithDamping: 0.5, initialSpringVelocity: 0.0, options:
[], animations: {
  self.loginButton.center.y -= 30.0
  self.loginButton.alpha = 1.0
}, completion: nil)
```

Animating user interactions

You don't have to limit your spring animations to the initial placement of your views. In fact, animating views in response to user input can really make your interface come alive. In this section you'll animate the login button in response to a tap.

Add the following code to `login()` :

```
UIView.animateWithDuration(1.5, delay: 0.0,
usingSpringWithDamping: 0.2, initialSpringVelocity: 0.0, options:
[], animations: {
  self.loginButton.bounds.size.width += 80.0
}, completion: nil)
```

The above animation increases the button's width by `80` points over a duration of a second and a half. The button will bounce around a fair bit as well since the damping is set to just `0.2`. Increasing the `bounds` grows the frame on its left and right sides.

Build and run your project; tap the button to see your animation in action:

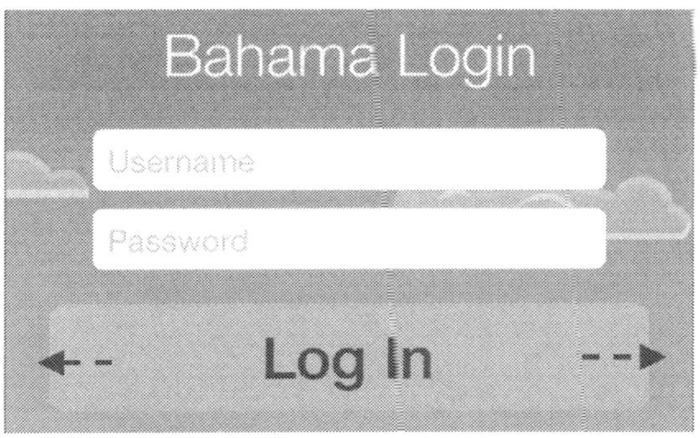

The button grows and bounces in a blobby fashion when you tap it – it's a neat way to provide tap feedback to the user.

Next you'll combine this animation with a few more spring movements to really bring the button to life.

Add the following code to the end of `login()`:

```
UIView.animateWithDuration(0.33, delay: 0.0,
usingSpringWithDamping: 0.7, initialSpringVelocity: 0.0, options:
[], animations: {
  self.loginButton.center.y += 60.0
}, completion: nil)
```

The above animation moves the button **60** points down when tapped. Notice that the duration for this animation is much shorter than the one that animates the button width.

This is intentional, since the desired effect is to make the button jump away from the tap and bounce a bit once it's settled into its new vertical position.

Build and run your project; tap the button and see how it moves in response to your touch this time:

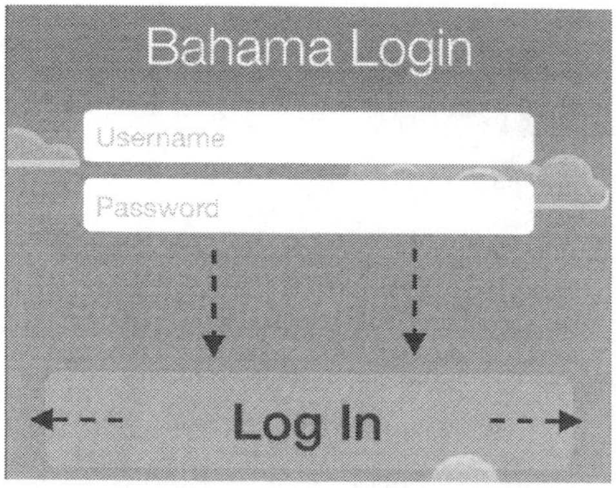

That looks really nice – but you're quickly becoming an animation master and you *know* that you can do even better!

Another great way of providing user feedback is through color change. You'll tint the button as it moves by animating the `backgroundColor` property of the button.

Add the following code to the last animation you added, inside the `animations` closure expression:

```
self.loginButton.backgroundColor =
  UIColor(red: 0.85, green: 0.83, blue: 0.45, alpha: 1.0)
```

Build and run your project again; you'll see the button move, change shape *and* change color – all at the same time:

There's one last bit of feedback to add here: an activity indicator. The Log In button is supposed to start a user authentication activity over the network, so it would be nice to show an activity indicator to the user to let them know that there's an action in progress.

Scroll up and have a look at `viewDidLoad()` and find the existing code for the progress indicator. `spinner` contains an instance of `UIActivityIndicatorView` that's all ready for your use. You haven't seen it on the screen yet because its `alpha` is set to `0.0`.

Head back to `login()` and add the following code to the last `animations` closure expression:

```
self.spinner.center = CGPoint(x: 40.0,
  y: self.loginButton.frame.size.height/2)
self.spinner.alpha = 1.0
```

This animation moves the spinner slightly to the left and fades it in. This should be enough to attract the user's attention and let them know their request is being processed.

Build and run your project; check out the final version of your spiffy new animation:

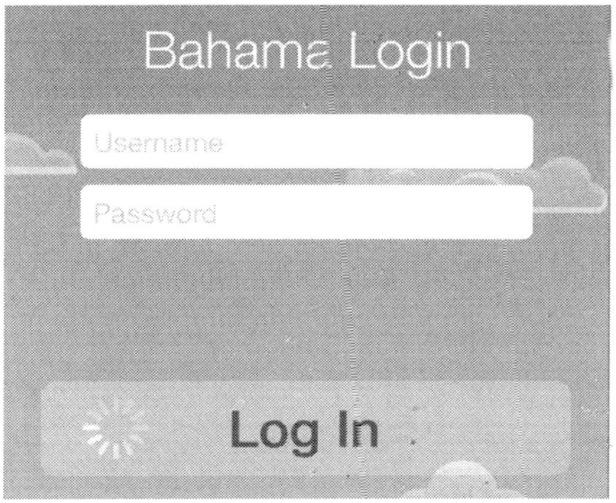

Take a moment to reflect on what you've accomplished here. You've added three simultaneous animations to the button view to make it grow in width, move down the screen, and change color.

You've also animated and faded in an activity spinner, which is itself a subview of the button view.

All animations are combined automatically by UIKit and run flawlessly to create one fluid visual effect.

There's no need for you to worry about the implementation details of your animations; you can instead focus on designing great animations and wowing your users thanks to UIKit!

Challenges

Challenge 1: Convert text field animations to spring-animations

The spring animation APIs in UIKit are quite similar in usage to their standard animation counterparts. Thus it shouldn't be much of a problem for you to convert the animations you have running on the `username` and `password` fields to spring animations.

To complete this challenge you will need to do the following:

1. Add the `usingSpringWithDamping` and `initialSpringVelocity` parameters to the animation for the `username` field. Use 0.0 for the spring initial velocity. Try out `0.2`, `0.6` and `0.9` for the spring damping and choose the value that looks most like a pleasant and subtle spring effect to you.
2. Repeat the same for the `password` field animation using the damping and velocity of your choice.

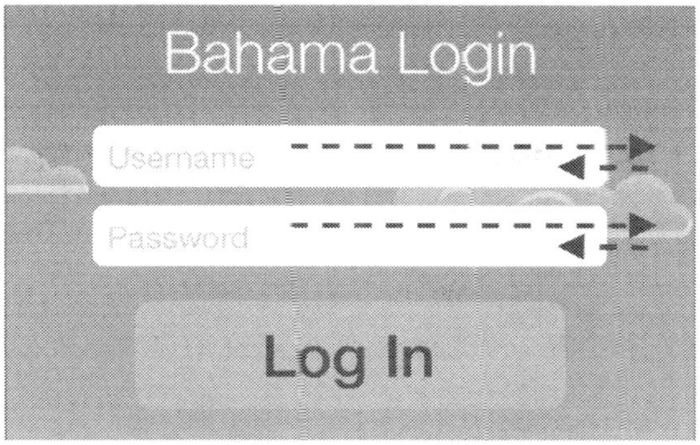

By this point in the book you've gained a solid foundation of spring animation. The more you play with this type of animation, and the more you experiment with different combinations of damping and velocity, the more comfortable you'll be designing the perfect spring animation for the views in your own apps.

Are you ready to *spring* into the next chapter? :] In Chapter 3, you'll learn about the next type of animation in UIKit: **transitions**.

Chapter 3: Transitions

In the previous two chapters you learned how to create animations based on the animatable properties of views such as `position` and `alpha`. But how would you handle the case where you want to animate the addition or removal of a view?

You *could* use the methods from the previous chapters and animate views in and out of your interface. However, this chapter will show you how to use transitions to animate *any* set of changes to your view.

Transitions are predefined animations you can apply to views. These predefined animations don't attempt to interpolate between the start and end states of your view. Instead, you'll design the animations so that the various changes in state appear natural.

Example transitions

To better understand when you'd use transitions, this section walks you through the various animation scenarios where you could make use of transition animations.

Adding a new view

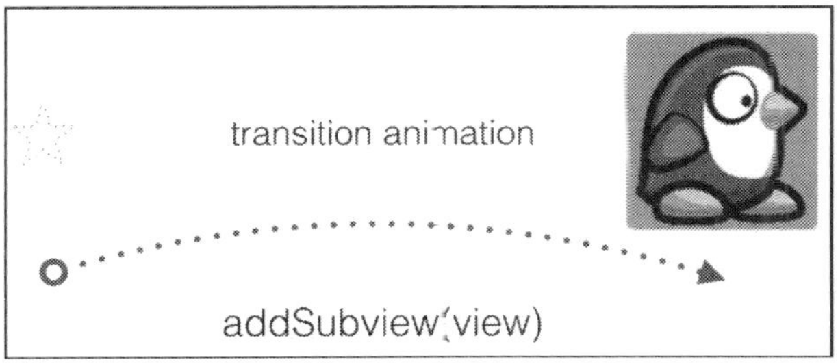

To animate the addition of a new view on the screen, you call a method similar to the ones you used in the previous chapters. The difference this time is that you'll choose one of the predefined transition effects and animate what's known as an **animation container view**.

The transition animates the container view, and any new views you add to it as subviews appear while the animation runs.

To better explain how you'd animate container views and when you'd execute the transition between subviews, consider the following code snippet:

```
var animationContainerView: UIView?

override func viewDidLoad() {
  //set up the animation container
  animationContainerView = UIView(frame: view.bounds)
  animationContainerView!.frame = view.bounds
  view.addSubview(animationContainerView!)
}

override func viewDidAppear(animated: Bool) {
  super.viewDidAppear(animated)

  //create new view
  let newView = UIImageView(image: UIImage(named: "banner")!)
  newView.center = animationContainerView!.center

  //add the new view via transition
  UIView.transitionWithView(animationContainerView!,
   duration: 0.33,
   options: [.CurveEaseOut, .TransitionFlipFromBottom],
   animations: {
    self.animationContainerView!.addSubview(newView)
  }, completion: nil)
}
```

In this hypothetical situation you create a new view named `animationContainerView` in `viewDidLoad()` of your view controller. You then position and add this container to the view.

Later, when you want to create an animated transition, you create a new view to animate – here it's named `newView`.

To create the transition, you call `transitionWithView(_:duration:options:animations:completion:)`. This is almost identical to the standard UIView animation method, but in this case you supply an extra parameter `view`, which serves as the container view for the transition animation.

There's a new animation option here, `.TransitionFlipFromBottom`, which you haven't seen yet. This is one of the predefined transitions discussed in the introduction of this chapter. `.TransitionFlipFromBottom` flips the view over with the bottom edge of the view serving as the "hinge" around which the view flips.

Finally, you add a subview to your animation container within your `animations` block, which causes the subview to appear during the transition.

Here's the full list of predefined transition animation options:

```
.TransitionFlipFromLeft
.TransitionFlipFromRight
.TransitionCurlUp
.TransitionCurlDown
.TransitionCrossDissolve
.TransitionFlipFromTop
.TransitionFlipFromBottom
```

Removing a view

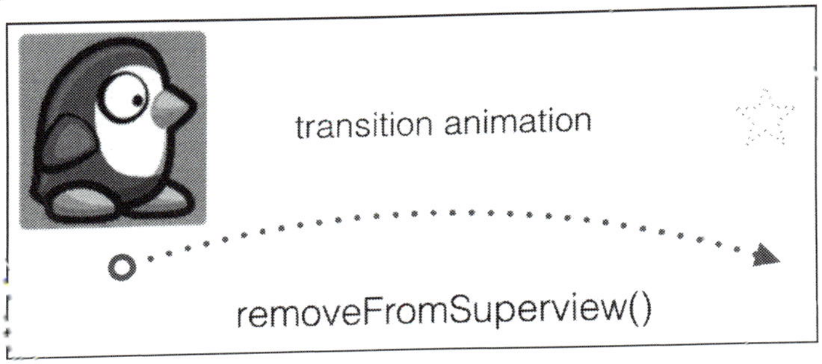

Removing a subview from the screen with a transition animation works much like adding a subview. To do this with a transition animation, you simply call `removeFromSuperview()` inside the animation closure expression like so:

```
//remove the view via transition
UIView.transitionWithView(animationContainerView!,
  duration: 0.33,
  options: [.CurveEaseOut, .TransitionFlipFromBottom],
  animations: {
    self.newView.removeFromSuperview()
  }, completion: nil)
```

As in the previous example, the wrapper transition will perform the flip animation and the `newView` will disappear at the end of it all.

Hiding/showing a view

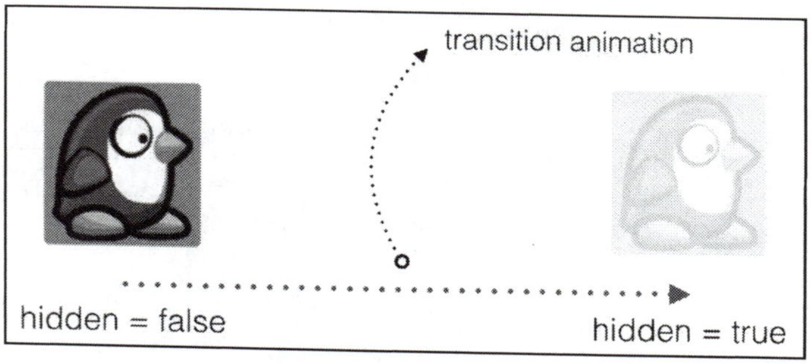

So far in this chapter you've learned only about transitions that alter the view hierarchy. That's why you needed a container view for the transitions – this puts the hierarchy change in context.

In contrast, you don't need to worry about setting up a container view to hide and show views. In this case, the transition uses the view *itself* as the animation container.

Consider the following code to hide a subview using a transition:

```
//hide the view via transition
UIView.transitionWithView(self.newView, duration: 0.33, options:
[.CurveEaseOut, .TransitionFlipFromBottom], animations: {
  self.newView.hidden = true
}, completion: nil)
```

Here you pass in the view you intend to show or hide as the first argument to `transitionWithView(_:duration:options:animations: completion:)`. All you do after that is set the `hidden` property of your view in the `animations` block and *voilà*, the transition animation kicks off.

Replacing a view with another view

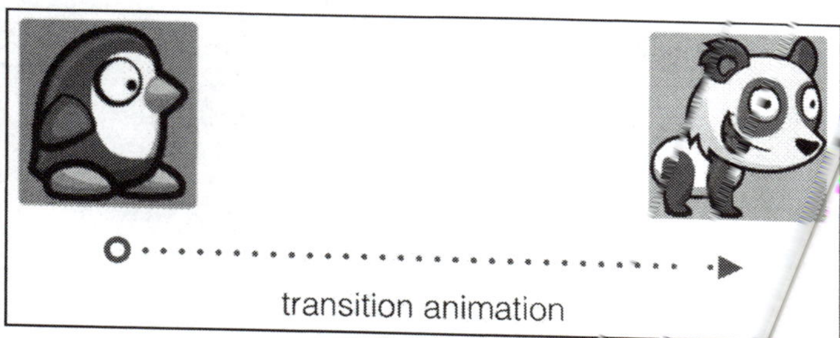

Replacing one view with another view is also an easy process. You simply pass in the existing view as the first argument and set the `toView:` parameter as the view you wish to replace it with as shown below:

```
//replace via transition
UIView.transitionFromView(self.oldView!, toView: self.newView!,
duration: 0.33, options: [.TransitionFlipFromTop],
completion: nil)
```

It's becoming quite apparent how much of the heavy lifting UIKit does for you! :]

In the remainder of this chapter, you'll work on showing and hiding UI elements via transitions – and learn some new animation skills you can bring into your own projects!

Mixing in transitions

You'll continue to work on the Bahama Air login screen project in this chapter; you've already created a number of compelling animations to the views on this screen to add a bit of pizzazz to the login form and to make the button react to being tapped.

Next, you're going to simulate a bit of user authentication and animate several different progress messages. Once the user taps the Log In button, you'll show them messages including "Connecting...", "Authorizing..." and "Failed".

If you haven't worked through the previous chapters, you can begin with the starter project in the Resources folder for this chapter. If you've followed the examples in the last few chapters in your own project, great job! :] You can simply continue working with your existing project.

Open **ViewController.swift** and look at `viewDidLoad()`. Part of this method adds a hidden image view stored in the class variable `status`. The code then creates a text label and adds it as a sub-view to `status`.

You'll use `status` to show the progress messages to the user. The messages are sourced from the `messages` array, which is another class variable included in the starter project.

Add the following method to `ViewController`:

```
func showMessage(index index: Int) {
  label.text = messages[index]

  UIView.transitionWithView(status, duration: 0.33, options:
  [.CurveEaseOut, .TransitionCurlDown], animations: {
    self.status.hidden = false
  }, completion: {_ in
    //transition completion
  })
}
```

This method takes one parameter called `index`; you set the value of `label` to the contents of `messages` based on `index`.

Next you call `transitionWithView(_:duration:options:animations:completion:)` to animate the view. To show the banner as it transitions you set `hidden` to `false` within the `animations` block.

There's another new animation option above: `.TransitionCurlDown`. This transition animates the view like a sheet of paper being flipped down on a legal pad and looks like the following:

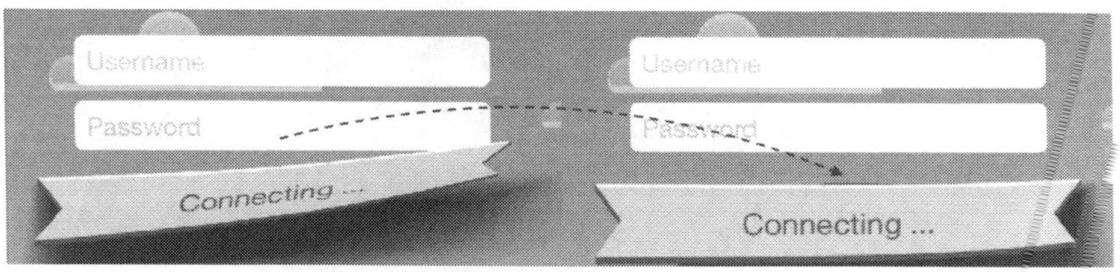

It's time to exercise your new `showMessage(index:)` method. Find the following block of code in `login()` :

```
animations: {
  self.loginButton.bounds.size.width += 80.0
}, completion: nil)
```

This is your existing `animations` block that makes the login button bounce when the user taps it. You'll add something new – a `completion` closure – to this animation that calls `showMessage(index:)`.

Replace the completion's `nil` argument value with the following closure expression:

```
completion: {_ in
  self.showMessage(index: 0)
}
```

The closure takes one Boolean parameter, which tells you whether the animation finished successfully or was cancelled before it ran to completion. In the above case you don't care whether it finished or not, so you skip binding the parameter by putting "_" in its place.

Inside the closure you simply call `showMessage` with index `0` to show the very first message from the `messages` array.

Build and run your project; tap the Log In button and you'll see the status banner appear with your first progress message:

Did you see how the banner curled down like a sheet of paper? That's a really nice way to bring attention to messages that are usually just shown as a static text label.

> **Note**: Some of your animations seem to run really quickly, don't they? Sometimes it's tricky to ensure the animation happens at just the right location, and in the correct sequence. Or maybe you just want things to happen slower so you can appreciate the effect!
>
> To slow down all animations in your app without changing your code, select **Debug/Toggle Slow Animations in Frontmost App** from the iPhone Simulator menu. Now tap the Login button in your app and enjoy the animations and transitions in vivid slow motion!

For the next animation, you'll first need to save the banner's initial position so you can place the next banner in just the right spot.

Add the following property to the `ViewController` class:

```
var statusPosition = CGPoint.zero
```

Then add the following code to the end of `viewDidLoad()` to save the banner's initial position:

```
statusPosition = status.center
```

Now you can begin to devise a mixture of view animations and transitions.

Add the following method to remove the status message from the screen via a standard animation:

```
func removeMessage(index index: Int) {
  UIView.animateWithDuration(0.33, delay: 0.0, options: [],
animations: {
    self.status.center.x += self.view.frame.size.width
  }, completion: {_ in
    self.status.hidden = true
    self.status.center = self.statusPosition

    self.showMessage(index: index+1)
  })
}
```

In the code above you use your old friend `animateWithDuration(_:delay:options:animations:completion:)` to move `status` just outside of the visible area of the screen.

When the animation completes in the `completion` closure, you move `status` back to its original position and hide it. Finally you call `showMessage` again, but this time you pass the index of the next message to show.

Combining standard animations with transitions is quite easy: you simply call the appropriate API and UIKit calls the corresponding Core Animation bits in the background.

Now you need to complete the chain of calls between `showMessage` and `removeMessage` to mimic a real authentication process.

Find `showMessage(index:)` and replace the comment `//transition completion` with the following code:

```
delay(seconds: 2.0) {
  if index < self.messages.count-1 {
    self.removeMessage(index: index)
  } else {
    //reset form
  }
}
```

Once the transition completes, you wait for `2.0` seconds and check if there are any remaining messages. If so, remove the current message via `removeMessage(index:)`. You then call `showMessage(index:)` in the completion block of `removeMessage(index:)` to display the next message in sequence.

> **Note:** `delay(seconds:completion:)` is a convenience function that runs a block of code after an elapsed delay; it's defined at the top of **ViewController.swift**. Here you're using it to simulate the usual network access delay.

Build and run your project once more; enjoy the resulting animation sequence, which updates the authentication progress messages like so:

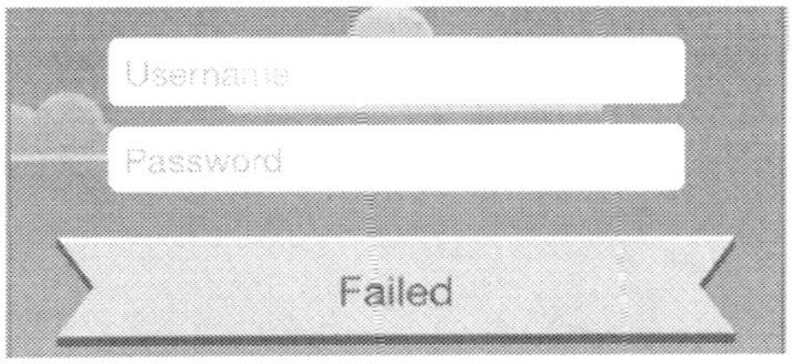

Transitions are a small but important subset of animation knowledge to keep in your figurative toolbox since they're the only way to create 3D-styled animations in UIKit.

If you're looking forward to learning more elaborate 3D effects, you'll have the opportunity to do that in Section IV: 3D Animations, which discusses Core Animation and 3D layer transformations in detail.

Before you move on to the next section, give the challenges in this chapter a try. Since you've learned so much about animation in the last three chapters, one challenge isn't enough – I've given you three!

These challenges give you the chance to wrap up development on your Bahama Air login screen – and also take on your first über haxx0r challenge. Woot! :]

Challenges

Challenge 1: Pick your favorite transition

So far you've seen only one of the built-in transition animations. Aren't you curious to see what the others look like?

In this challenge you can try out all the other available transition animations and use your favorite to animate the progress message banner.

Open `ViewController` and find the line in `showMessage(index:)` where you specify the transition animation `.TransitionCurlDown`:

```
UIView.transitionWithView(status, duration: 0.33, options:
  [.CurveEaseOut, .TransitionCurlDown], animations
```

Replace `.TransitionCurlDown` with any of the other transition animations available, then build and run your project to see how they look. Here's the list of available transitions:

```
.TransitionFlipFromLeft
.TransitionFlipFromRight
.TransitionCurlUp
.TransitionCurlDown
.TransitionCrossDissolve
.TransitionFlipFromTop
.TransitionFlipFromBottom
```

Which one do you think works best with the other animations on this screen?

In case you don't have a favorite, try my favorite transition: `.TransitionFlipFromBottom`. I think it fits really well with the banner graphic:

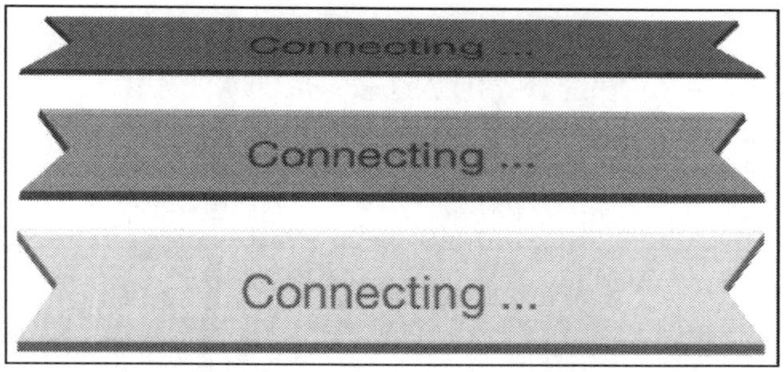

Challenge 2: Reset the form to its initial state

For this challenge, you'll reset the form to its initial state by undoing all the animations that run once you tap the Login button. That way, if the login fails the user would see all of the animations happen again when they tap the Log In button a second time.

Here's a list of the general steps you'll need to complete this challenge:

1. Create a new empty method `resetForm()` and call it from your code where the placeholder comment `//reset form` lives.

2. In `resetForm()` use `transitionWithView(_:duration:options:animations:completion:)` to set the visibility of `status` to hidden and `center` to `self.statusPosition`. This should reset the banner to its initial state. Use a `0.2` seconds duration for that transition.

3. It would be nice if the transition that hides your banner uses the exact opposite animation of the one that shows the banner. For example, if you show the banner via `.TransitionCurlDown`, then use `.TransitionCurlUp` to hide it. The reverse of `.TransitionFlipFromBottom` would be `.TransitionFlipFromTop` ...and so forth.

4. Next, add a call to `animateWithDuration(_:delay:options:animations:completion:)` in `resetForm()`. Make the following adjustments inside the `animations` closure block:

   a. Move `self.spinner` – the activity indicator inside the login button – to its original position of `(-20.0, 16.0)`.

   b. Set the `alpha` property of `self.spinner` to `0.0` to hide it.

   c. Tint the background color of the login button back to its original value: `UIColor(red: 0.63, green: 0.34, blue: 0.35, alpha: 1.0)`.

   d. Continue to reset all changes you made to the Login button and decrease the `bounds.size.width` property by `80.0` points.

   e. Finally, move the button back up to its original spot under the password field and decrease `center.y` by `60.0` points.

If you precisely reversed all of the animations in the authentication process, the screen should animate as below once all authentication messages have displayed:

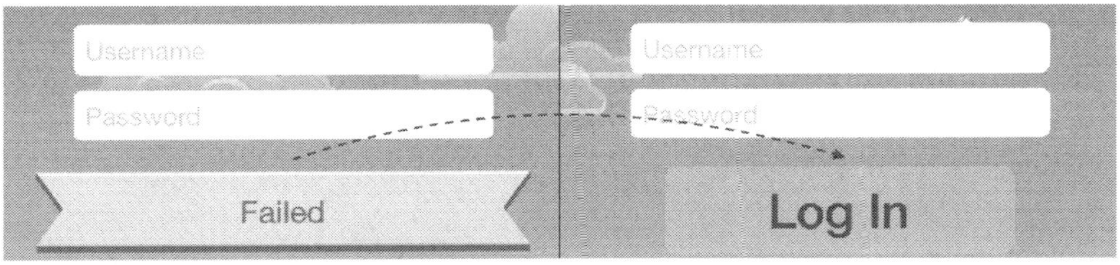

Well done! And now for this chapter's über challenge...

Über haxx0r challenge: animate the clouds in the background

Wouldn't it be cool if those clouds in the background moved slowly across the screen and reappeared from the opposite side?

Yeah, it would totally be cool – and that's your challenge!

The four cloud image views are already wired to four outlets in `ViewController` so you're good to go. You can try to make the clouds move on your own, using your newfound knowledge of transition animations, or you can follow the recipe below:

1. Create a new method with signature `animateCloud(cloud: UIImageView)` and add your code inside that.
2. First, calculate the average cloud speed. Assume the cloud should cross the entire length of the screen in about `60.0` seconds. Call that constant `cloudSpeed` and set it to `60.0 / view.frame.size.width`.
3. Next, calculate the duration for the animation to move the cloud to the right side of the screen. Remember, the clouds don't start from the left edge of the screen but from random spots instead. You can calculate the correct duration by taking the length of the path the cloud needs to follow and multiplying the result by the average speed: `(view.frame.size.width - cloud.frame.origin.x) * cloudSpeed`.
4. Then call `animateWithDuration(_:delay:options:animation: completion:)` with the duration you just calculated above. You'll need to create an instance of `NSTimeInterval` from it as the compiler won't have decided the correct type for you: `NSTimeInterval(duration)`. For the `options` parameter use `.CurveLinear`; this is one of the very few times you'll use an animation with no easing. Clouds are naturally quite far in the background, so their movement should look absolutely even-keeled.
5. Inside the `animations` closure expression set the `frame.origin.x` property of the cloud to `self.view.frame.size.width`. This moves the cloud to just outside the screen area.

6. Inside the `completion` closure block move the cloud to just outside the opposite edge of the screen from its current position. Don't forget to skip the closure parameter by using "_" as you did earlier in this chapter. To position the cloud properly set its `frame.origin.x` to `-cloud.frame.size.width`.

7. Still working in the `completion` closure, add a call to `animateCloud()` so that the cloud re-animates across the screen.

8. Finally, add the following code to the end of `viewDidAppear()` to start the animations for all four clouds:

```
animateCloud(cloud1)
animateCloud(cloud2)
animateCloud(cloud3)
animateCloud(cloud4)
```

This should make all four clouds traverse the screen slowly to create a nice, unobtrusive effect.

If you completed the challenges for this chapter – congratulations! They were tough! :]

There past few chapters had a lot of information to digest, but you took a stiff, static login form and turned it into an eye-catching and fun experience for the user:

It's time to take a short break from new material and put all your view animation knowledge to the test! In the next chapter, you'll use a wide assortment of the practical things you've learned to add some serious polish to the Bahama Air app!

Chapter 4: View Animations in Practice

You'll take a short breather in this chapter to learn a few techniques that combine the skills you've already gained to produce some new and impressive effects.

Having said that, please note that this chapter is *optional*. If you would like to keep on learning about new APIs, feel free to skip to the next chapter – no hard feelings! :]

However, if you want to flex your animation muscles and learn a few new tips and tricks, then you'll most definitely enjoy working on the project in this chapter, which takes the app for your made-up airline Bahama Air to a new level.

In this chapter you are going to add some cool animations to dress up a flight summary screen, like the one shown below:

There are a few new effects to be found in this chapter that build on the animation foundations you learned in the previous chapters:

1. **Crossfade animation:** An animation that blends one image into another.

2. **Cube transition animation:** A transition animation that creates a faux 3D transition effect.
3. **Fade and bounce transition:** A slightly different take on the combination of simple animations, auxiliary views and everything else you learned up to this point.

This chapter is juicy with code, so head on in to the next section to get started right away!

Crossfading animations

Open the starter project from the Resources folder for this chapter. Build and run your project to get acquainted with what you have to work with. The app currently shows the flight summary for a trip from London to Rome with a layover in Paris.

The flight summary screen alternates between the two connecting flights and shows items such as the destination, flight number and gate number:

Your first task is to smoothly transition, or **blend**, between the two background images.

Your first instinct might be to simply fade out the present image and then fade in the new one. But this approach would show the content behind the image as the alpha approached zero; you want the content behind this screen to remain hidden during the entire animation. Fading the images out, then fading them in again would result in an odd-looking transition like the following:

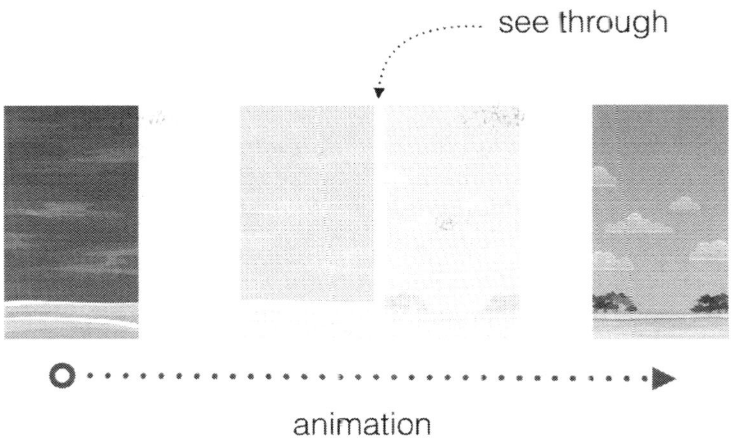

Obviously, you'll need a different approach to solve this problem.

Open **ViewController.swift** and add the following new method to handle your new crossfade effect:

```
func fadeImageView(imageView: UIImageView, toImage: UIImage,
showEffects: Bool) {

  UIView.transitionWithView(imageView, duration: 1.0,
   options: .TransitionCrossDissolve, animations: {
    imageView.image = toImage
  }, completion: nil)

  UIView.animateWithDuration(1.0, delay: 0.0,
   options: .CurveEaseOut, animations: {
    self.snowView.alpha = showEffects ? 1.0 : 0.0
  }, completion: nil)
}
```

The method takes the following three parameters:

1. `imageView`: This is the image view you are going to fade out.
2. `toImage`: This is the new image you want visible at the end of the animation.
3. `showEffects`: This is a Boolean flag indicating whether the scene should show or hide the snowfall effect. The snowfall animation should only run on the first connecting flight's screen, where presumably the airport is experiencing bad weather.

The transition animation you use this time is of type `.TransitionCrossDissolve` – this allows you to simply change the image view's image to the one supplied as a parameter and UIKit automatically creates a cross-fade transition.

> **Note:** If you want to have some fun you can try also some of the transition effects from the previous chapter; in the current project however transitions like `.TransitionFlipFromLeft` are simply too distracting. `.TransitionCrossDissolve` is a subtle "background" effect which only enhances the animations, which will happen in the foreground.

Additionally, you fade `snowView` in or out in parallel with the rest of the animation depending on the value of `showEffects`.

> **Note:** That snowfall effect looks pretty cool, right? You'll learn how to make a similar effect in Chapter 17, "Particle Emitters"!

Currently `changeFlightDataTo(_:)` switches all the data about the two connecting flights.

Since you are going to eventually animate all of the UI elements on this screen, update the signature of that method as follows:

```
func changeFlightDataTo(data: FlightData,
 animated: Bool = false) {
```

Above, you supply a default value of `false` for the new `animated` parameter so that existing calls to this method work as they did before, with no animation.

Next, find the code inside `changeFlightDataTo(_:animated:)` that updates both the image view and the snow view:

```
bgImageView.image = UIImage(named: data.weatherImageName)
snowView.hidden = !data.showWeatherEffects
```

Wrap it in an `if` statement as shown below:

```
if animated {
  fadeImageView(bgImageView,
    toImage: UIImage(named: data.weatherImageName)!,
    showEffects: data.showWeatherEffects)
} else {
  bgImageView.image = UIImage(named: data.weatherImageName)
  snowView.hidden = !data.showWeatherEffects
}
```

This method calls `fadeImageView` and passes in the proper parameters from `data` and the new `animation` parameter.

If you want to see what's inside of `data`, have a look inside **FlightData.swift**. The `FlightData` structure is the model that represents a single flight; there's two of those flights already pre-defined in **FlightData.swift**: `londonToParis` and `parisToRome`.

Back in **ViewController.swift** you still need to make one more change before you can see the crossfade effect on screen You need to add the `animated` parameter to the line where you call `changeFlightDataTo(_:, animated:)`.

In `changeFlightDataTo` change the call to `self.changeFlightDataTo` near the end of the method inside the `delay` call as follows:

```
self.changeFlightDataTo(data.isTakingOff ?
  parisToRome : londonToParis, animated: true)
```

Build and run your app; you should now see the image views transition smoothly:

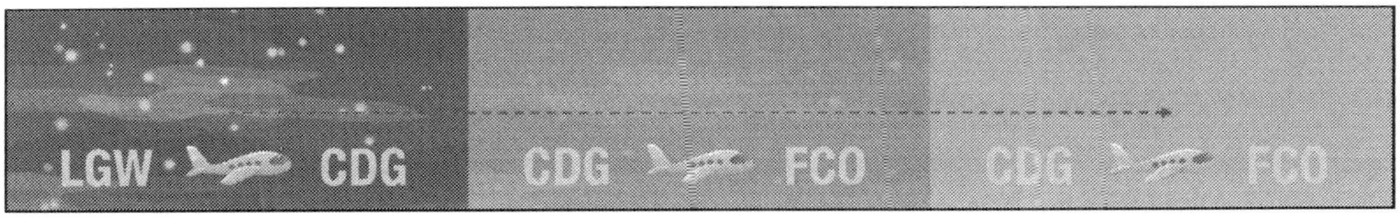

The images blend beautifully into each other, and since you fade the snow effect at the same time, the animation looks seamless. You can even see it snow in Rome for a split second! :]

You've learned an important technique here – transitions can be used to animate changes to non-animatable properties of your views.

That takes care of the image view, but the text labels for the flight number and gate number look like they could use some creative animation:

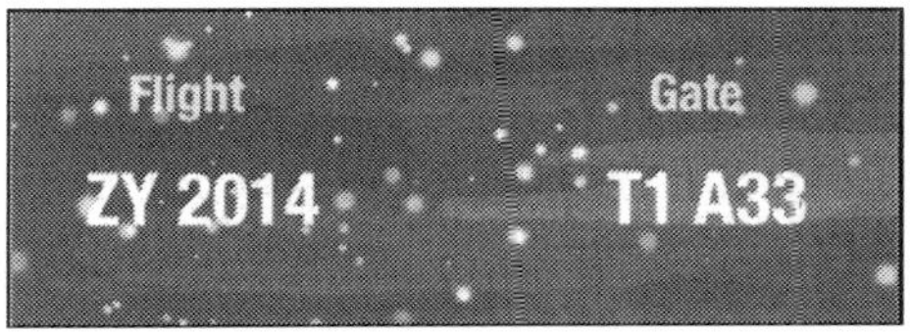

You'll take care of those next with a faux-3D transition.

Cube transitions

The effect you are going to build in this section makes it look like the flight and gate information is on adjacent sides of a cube that rotates around its center to reveal the next value. When complete, your animation will work as illustrated below:

This is not a real 3D effect, but it looks pretty close and it's a great opportunity for you to try animations featuring auxiliary views.

Your approach will be to add a temporary label, animate the heights of the two labels simultaneously, remove the temporary label and in the end clean up after yourself.

This will be also the first animation you create that has a **direction**, since you'll play it both forwards and backwards. The direction will determine whether the temporary label appears from the top or bottom.

Start by adding the following enumeration inside the `ViewController` class:

```
enum AnimationDirection: Int {
  case Positive = 1
  case Negative = -1
}
```

Your animation method will take a parameter that sets the animation direction.

Next, add the initial version of that method as shown below:

```
func cubeTransition(label label: UILabel, text: String, direction:
AnimationDirection) {

  let auxLabel = UILabel(frame: label.frame)
  auxLabel.text = text
  auxLabel.font = label.font
  auxLabel.textAlignment = label.textAlignment
  auxLabel.textColor = label.textColor
  auxLabel.backgroundColor = label.backgroundColor
}
```

The method takes three parameters:

1. `label`: The label that you want to animate.
2. `text`: The new text to display on the label.
3. `direction`: The location from where you animate the new text label; this is either the top or the bottom of the view.

To start, you'll create a new label `auxLabel` and copy all key properties of the existing label to it, including `frame`, `font`, and `alignment`.

The single difference between the two labels is the text they each contain: the auxiliary label will contain the new text.

Having the two labels appear at the same position is not what you want. Instead, you need to move the auxiliary label away from the existing view and make it really tiny.

Let's keep going with the transition! Add the following code to end of `cubeTransition`:

```
let auxLabelOffset = CGFloat(direction.rawValue) *
  label.frame.size.height/2.0

auxLabel.transform = CGAffineTransformConcat(
  CGAffineTransformMakeScale(1.0, 0.1),
  CGAffineTransformMakeTranslation(0.0, auxLabelOffset))

label.superview!.addSubview(auxLabel)
```

In the code above, you first calculate the vertical offset for the auxiliary label. The raw value of `direction` is either `1` or `-1`, which gives you the proper vertical offset to position the temporary label.

Next, you adjust the transform of the auxiliary label to create a faux-perspective effect. When you scale the text on its Y-axis alone, it'll look squashed like you're viewing the plane of the text on edge:

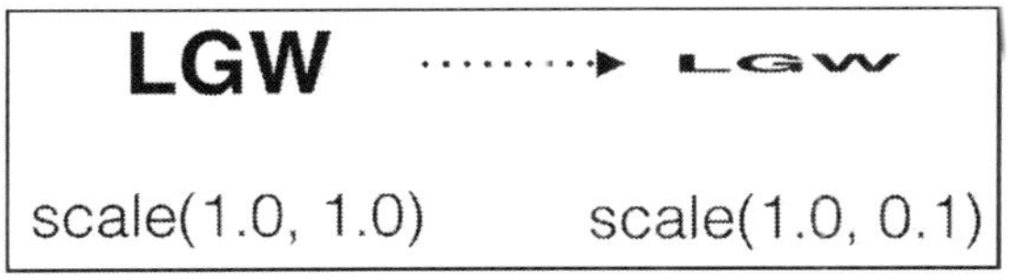

Finally, you add the newly created label at the same level in the hierarchy as the existing label.

Next add the following animation code to the end of `cubeTransition`:

```
UIView.animateWithDuration(0.5, delay: 0.0, options:
.CurveEaseOut, animations: {
  auxLabel.transform = CGAffineTransformIdentity
  label.transform = CGAffineTransformConcat(
    CGAffineTransformMakeScale(1.0, 0.1),
    CGAffineTransformMakeTranslation(0.0, -auxLabelOffset))
}, completion: {_ in
  label.text = auxLabel.text
  label.transform = CGAffineTransformIdentity

  auxLabel.removeFromSuperview()
})
```

In the `animations` block you reset the `transform` of `auxLabel`; this makes the new text grow in height and positions it exactly on top of the old one.

Speaking of the old text, you also apply a transform to `label` that scales it down and moves it in the direction opposite to where the new text appears.

Insert the following code to `changeFlightDataTo(_:animated:)` inside the `if` statement, just below where you call `fadeImageView`:

```
let direction: AnimationDirection = data.isTakingOff ?
  .Positive : .Negative

cubeTransition(label: flightNr, text: data.flightNr,
  direction: direction)
cubeTransition(label: gateNr, text: data.gateNr,
  direction: direction)
```

In the same method, **move the existing code** that sets the `flightNr` and `gateNr` text **inside** the `else` statement, otherwise those statements will change the label's text immediately and spoil your animation.

The completed `else` block should look now like this:

```
} else {
  bgImageView.image = UIImage(named: data.weatherImageName)
  snowView.hidden = !data.showWeatherEffects

  flightNr.text = data.flightNr
  gateNr.text = data.gateNr

  departingFrom.text = data.departingFrom
  arrivingTo.text = data.arrivingTo

  flightStatus.text = data.flightStatus
}
```

Build and run your project; enjoy the results of your labor as you watch the gate number and flight number animate via your fancy faux-3D transition:

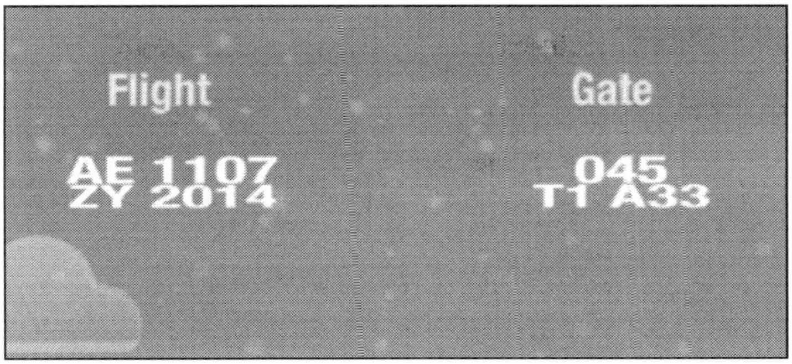

Notice how running the animation both forwards and backwards gives a real impression that you're switching between two alternate states. This screen is becoming more and more alive – thanks to you!

You're not quite done yet; you'll finish off this chapter by adding a composite animation to the three-letter airport codes on the screen to make the screen transitions feel organic and snappy!

Fade and bounce transitions

The final animation in this chapter makes use of labels, auxiliary views, and everything else you've learned up to this point. Consider it a chapter review, if you will! :]

Start by adding the following new method for the new transition animation:

```
func moveLabel(label: UILabel, text: String, offset: CGPoint) {
  let auxLabel = UILabel(frame: label.frame)
  auxLabel.text = text
  auxLabel.font = label.font
  auxLabel.textAlignment = label.textAlignment
  auxLabel.textColor = label.textColor
  auxLabel.backgroundColor = UIColor.clearColor()

  auxLabel.transform = CGAffineTransformMakeTranslation(
    offset.x, offset.y)
  auxLabel.alpha = 0
  view.addSubview(auxLabel)
}
```

The new method takes three parameters:

1. `label`: The label you want to animate.
2. `text`: The new text you want to display.
3. `offset`: The arbitrary offset you'll use to animate the auxiliary label.

The code above is pretty simple: just as you did in the previous section, you create an auxiliary label and copy all properties to it from the existing one. To create the label transform, you simply use the `offset` parameter.

Finally, just before you add the new label to the view controller's view, you hide it by setting its `alpha` property to `0.0`.

That sets the stage for your animations. Next you're going to exchange the places of the original and auxiliary labels. This time, instead of using the same animation for both labels, you'll create separate animations for each and move them independent of each other. This will result in an interesting, organic visual effect.

First add the following code to the end of `moveLabel`:

```
UIView.animateWithDuration(0.5, delay: 0.0,
 options: .CurveEaseIn, animations: {
  label.transform = CGAffineTransformMakeTranslation(
    offset.x, offset.y)
  label.alpha = 0.0
}, completion: nil)
```

This animation moves the label away from its original position and fades it out.

Next, add the following code to animate the auxiliary label:

```
UIView.animateWithDuration(0.25, delay: 0.1,
 options: .CurveEaseIn, animations: {
  auxLabel.transform = CGAffineTransformIdentity
  auxLabel.alpha = 1.0

}, completion: {_ in
  //clean up
})
```

You reset the auxiliary label's `transform` above, effectively moving it to its original location. You also fade the text in by animating its `alpha` value.

Note that this animation kicks off after a `0.1` second delay and it lasts only `0.25` seconds. This means that the two labels will overlap while exchanging places, creating a subtle yet pleasing "ghost" effect:

Before you can test your new animation, you need to add the code to remove the auxiliary label when the animation is complete.

Find the comment `//clean up` in the completion block of the code you just added and replace it with the following code:

```
auxLabel.removeFromSuperview()

label.text = text
label.alpha = 1.0
label.transform = CGAffineTransformIdentity
```

This wraps up the transition nicely, returns the label to its initial state and sets the new text of the label.

Now find `changeFlightDataTo(_:,animated:)` and add the following code to the bottom of your `if animated {` statement:

```
let offsetDeparting = CGPoint(
  x: CGFloat(direction.rawValue * 80),
  y: 0.0)
moveLabel(departingFrom, text: data.departingFrom,
  offset: offsetDeparting)

let offsetArriving = CGPoint(
  x: 0.0,
  y: CGFloat(direction.rawValue * 50))
moveLabel(arrivingTo, text: data.arrivingTo,
  offset: offsetArriving)
```

As before, **move the original non-animated versions** (the code that simply updates the text in `departingFrom` and `arrivingTo`) into the `else` statement to prevent your animation from being spoiled.

This new method takes an arbitrary offset as a parameter. This lets you create two different animations for the departure and arrival airports.

For the departure label, you create a horizontal movement; for the arrival airport, you create a vertical movement instead.

That's all the code you need! Build and run your app to see all labels animate via your snappy new transition effect:

Take a moment to appreciate that even in this impressive-looking animation, you've *still* only animated a few properties on any given view. You've worked with `bounds`, `frame`, `center`, `transform`, `backgroundColor` and `alpha` – but you've managed to create some very impressive animations with those properties alone!

Animating each property on its own might not always result in mind-blowing effects, but using a combination of a number of simple animations and using subtle yet powerful techniques such as adding auxiliary views and transitions can produce impressive visual effects.

Let your imagination... take flight! :]

Challenges

Challenge 1: Animate the flight status banner

So far there's still one UI element that doesn't animate when the screen switches between the two connecting flights – the flight status:

The piece of text on the banner saying "Boarding" is a `UILabel`; as such, you can use either of the two label animations you created in this chapter to show the alternate flight statuses.

I believe you can figure out how to animate the banner on your own; use the `flightStatus` outlet to access the label and `data.flightStatus` to get the new text to animate to.

Feel free to experiment and play around further with the project – the more experience you gain, the better understanding you will have of animations in UIKit!

Now that you're a pro at animations and transitions, it's time for the final topic on view animations – combining multiple animation steps together with **keyframes.**

Chapter 5: Keyframe Animations

Much of the time, you'll find that you need to support multiple, sequential animations for your views. Up until this point you've used the `completion` closure to **chain** multiple animations to each other.

This approach works in a pinch for chaining two simple animations, but it can lead to some incredibly messy and complicated code when you want to group three, four or more animations together.

Let's see how it would look like if you wanted to chain multiple animations together and move a view in a rectangular pattern:

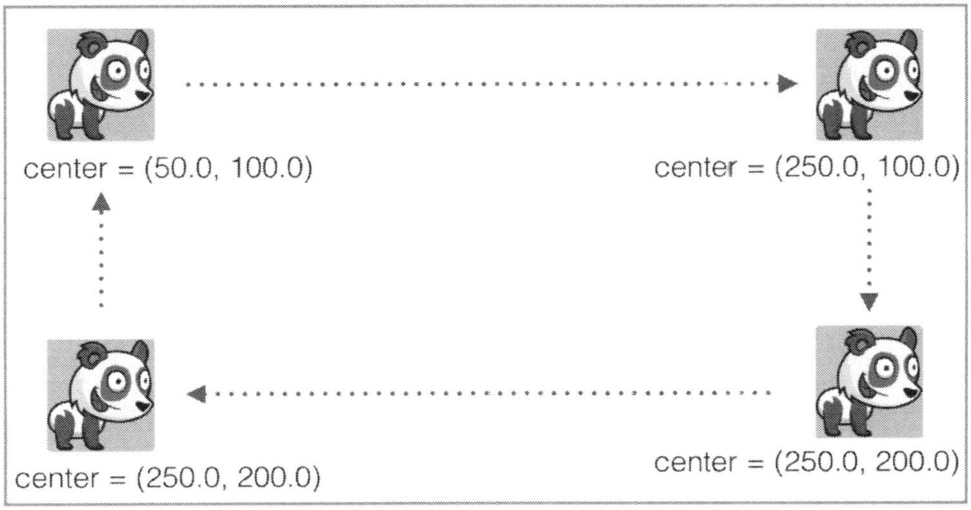

To achieve this you could chain several animations and completion blocks together like so:

```
UIView.animateWithDuration(0.5, animations: {
  view.center.x += 200.0
  }, completion: { _ in
  UIView.animateWithDuration(0.5, animations: {
    view.center.y += 100.0
    }, completion: { _ in
      UIView.animateWithDuration(0.5, animations: {
        view.center.x -= 200.0
        }, completion: { _ in
          UIView.animateWithDuration(0.5, animations: {
            view.center.y -= 100.0
          })
      })
  })
})
```

Look at all that nesting! And that's for a simple rectangle-shaped path; can you imagine what that would look like for a more complicated movement?

Instead, you can split the total animation into four distinct stages, or **keyframes**, and then combine the individual keyframes into a **keyframe animation**.

Keyframe animations

Consider another animation that depicts the take-off sequence of a plane. The distinct stages of this animation would look like the following:

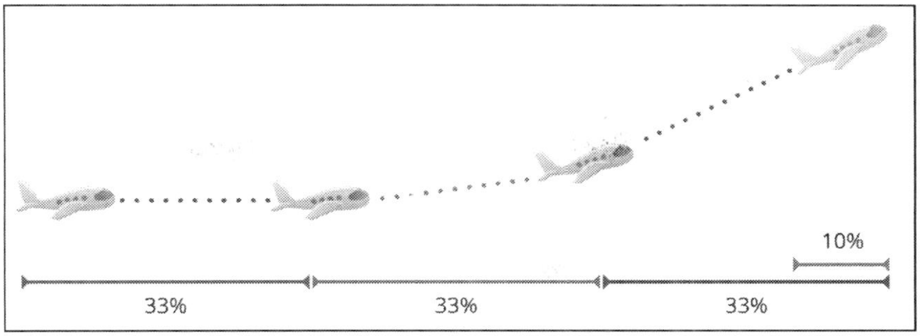

The first stage of the animation sequence accelerates the plane on the runway. The second stage gives the plane a little altitude and tilts it upward. The third stage continues to tilt the plane and boosts the plane skyward at a much faster rate.

There's a fourth and final stage in the final `10%` of the animation duration that fades the plane out of view, as if it were moving behind some low-hanging clouds.

The complete animation could be overwhelming to create, but breaking down the animation into the various stages makes it a lot more manageable. Once you've defined the keyframes for each stage, you've got the problem mostly solved.

You'll learn about keyframes and how to assemble them into a keyframe animation by creating an airplane animation similar to the above – but it will be far more complex. Don't worry – you're more than capable of handling this! :]

Setting up your keyframe animation

If you worked through the project in the last chapter you can use that as your starting point; if you didn't do that, or if you want to start fresh, you can use the starter project for this chapter.

Build and run your project; you should see the two alternating connecting flights:

You'll make the airplane take off from its starting position, circle around, then land and taxi back to the starting point. This animation will run each time the screen switches between connecting flights.

The complete animation will look something like this:

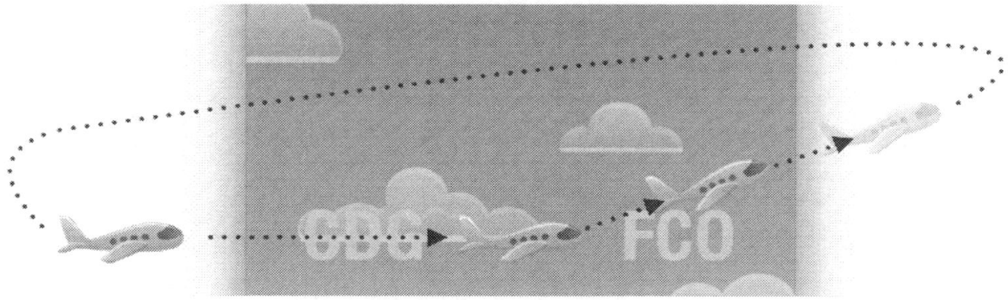

Open **ViewController.swift**; all the code for this animation will live in a new class method named `planeDepart()`.

Find `changeFlightDataTo(_:,animated:)` and you'll see an `if animated` statement near the top containing all of the animated changes. Add the following line to the top of the `if` block (be careful to place it inside the block):

```
planeDepart()
```

Now add the following initial version of your new animation method as shown below:

```
func planeDepart() {
  let originalCenter = planeImage.center

  UIView.animateKeyframesWithDuration(1.5, delay: 0.0,
   options: [], animations: {
    //add keyframes

  }, completion: nil)
}
```

You store the original position of the airplane in `originalCenter` so you'll know where your animation should finish.

You also use `animateKeyframesWithDuration(_:delay:options:animations:completion:)` to create your first keyframe animation. The parameter list is identical to the ones you've used all along in this book to create your view animations. You set the duration to `1.5` seconds, add no other options and add an empty `animations` closure.

The options for keyframes are different; they come from `UIViewKeyFrameAnimationOptions` enumeration instead of `UIViewAnimationOptions`. You'll learn about the fine details of keyframe options a little later in this chapter.

Adding keyframes

It's time to add your first keyframe. Replace the `//add keyframes` comment with the following code:

```
UIView.addKeyframeWithRelativeStartTime(0.0, relativeDuration:
0.25, animations: {
  self.planeImage.center.x += 80.0
  self.planeImage.center.y -= 10.0
})
```

This is the first of several calls to `addKeyframeWithRelativeStartTime` you'll be adding.

The animation keyframe above is little different than the animation methods you've used so far.

`addKeyframeWithRelativeStartTime(_:relativeDuration:animations:)` is the first time you've used relative durations in the animations in this book. The start time of the keyframe, as well as its duration, are expressed as percentages relative to the entire duration of the animation. For example, `0.1` would be `10%`, `0.25` would be `25%`, and `1.0` would be `100%` of the total duration.

Working with relative values lets you specify that a keyframe should last for a fraction of the total time; UIKit takes the relative durations of each keyframe and automagically figures out the exact durations for each keyframe, saving you a ton of work.

In the final bit of code above you set the start time to `0.0` – immediately – and the duration to `0.25`, representing `25%` of the total animation time:

Since you set the duration of the complete animation to `1.5` seconds, the first keyframe will last for approximately `0.375` seconds. Later on, if you decide to modify the total duration of the animation to a different value, the individual keyframe animations will recalculate their duration times accordingly.

Build and run your project and check out the first frame of your animation:

Running the first keyframe sets in motion the code in the `animations` closure: the airplane moves `80` points to the right and `10` points up.

This is, of course, only the first step in creating the complete animation sequence. To create the second keyframe, add the following code to the keyframe block, underneath the previous `addKeyframeWithRelativeStartTime` call:

```
UIView.addKeyframeWithRelativeStartTime(0.1, relativeDuration:
0.4) {
  self.planeImage.transform =
CGAffineTransformMakeRotation(CGFloat(-M_PI_4/2))
}
```

The second keyframe starts `10%` of the way into the animation and lasts for `40%` of the total duration. This keyframe rotates the airplane as it moves off the runway:

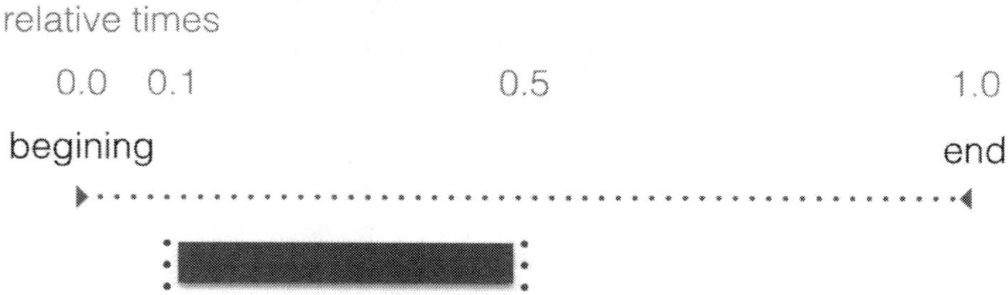

Build and run your project now and see how the two keyframes look when they run together:

Keep building your sequence by adding the third keyframe as follows:

```
UIView.addKeyframeWithRelativeStartTime(0.25, relativeDuration:
0.25) {
  self.planeImage.center.x += 100.0
  self.planeImage.center.y -= 50.0
  self.planeImage.alpha = 0.0
}
```

In this stage of the animation, you keep the airplane moving along but start to fade it out.

Build and run your project and see how the three keyframes in your animation look:

The plane flies out of sight and disappears. Now you'll need to bring it back and land it safely on the next connecting flight screen.

Before you show the airplane on the screen, you'll have to reset the orientation of the plane – that is, undo the rotation you've applied – and move it to the left of the visible area.

Since the airplane is invisible with its alpha set to 0 for the moment, you can move it around without the user seeing anything. Add the following keyframe to your animation:

```
UIView.addKeyframeWithRelativeStartTime(0.51, relativeDuration:
0.01) {
  self.planeImage.transform = CGAffineTransformIdentity
  self.planeImage.center = CGPoint(x: 0.0, y: originalCenter.y)
}
```

This keyframe runs after all three previous frames have completed and lasts just a small fraction of a second; it resets the plane transform and moves it to the left edge of the screen.

Now you can add the final keyframe and taxi the airplane frame and taxi back to the original location:

```
UIView.addKeyframeWithRelativeStartTime(0.55, relativeDuration:
0.45) {
  self.planeImage.alpha = 1.0
  self.planeImage.center = originalCenter
}
```

This keyframe fades the airplane back in while moving it to the original starting point of the animation.

Build and run your project to see the completed animation sequence as shown below:

Take a minute to review the code you wrote. It's easy to follow and decode; you can modify, rearrange or alter the timing of any of the sections above without too much work on your part.

It's a short step to imagine your animation as a series of separate animations with delays in between, or even as a set of animations triggered from completion blocks. Keyframes are an incredibly useful and flexible way to design and control your animations.

Calculation modes in keyframe animations

Keyframe animations don't support the built-in easing curves that are available in standard UIView animations. This is by design: keyframes are supposed to start and end at specific times and flow into each other.

If each stage of your animation above had an easing curve, the plane would jerk around instead of moving smoothly from one animation into the next. If you *could* apply easing to the entire animation, that would result in your animation durations being ignored – and that's not what you want.

Instead, you have several **calculation modes** to choose from; each mode offers a different method to calculate intermediate frames of the animation as well as different optimizers for smooth movement and even pacing. Check out the documentation by searching for `UIViewKeyframeAnimationOptions` for more details.

Now that you know how to group together any number of simple animations using keyframe animations, you can build just about any sequence that comes to mind. If you want to test your knowledge of keyframes and keyframe animations, give the challenge below a try before moving on to the next section.

Challenges

Challenge: Animate the flight departure times

There's still one UI element on screen that isn't animated: the black flight summary status bar at the top of the screen that shows the flight departure times:

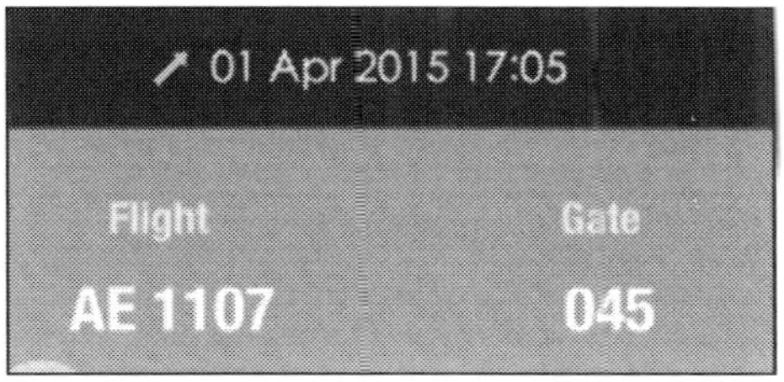

Your challenge is to add a keyframe animation to move the summary off-screen each time the connecting flight data changes. Then you'll change the text to reflect the departure time of the next flight animate it back on screen like so:

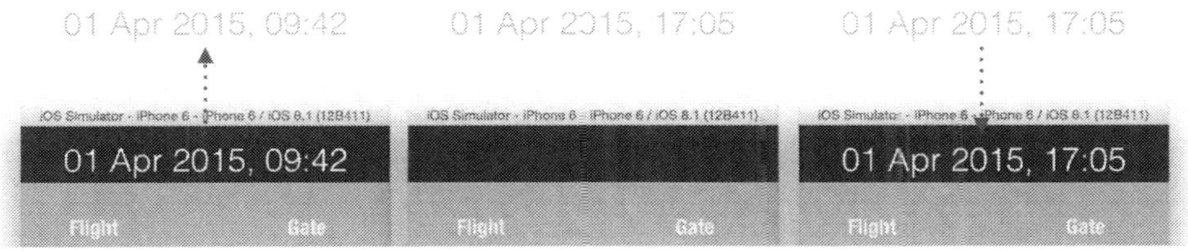

The departure summary label is already connected to an outlet called `summary`.

If you need a general structure for your solution, here's a basic recipe you can follow:

- Create a new method `summarySwitchTo(summaryText: String)` to animate the summary label.
- Inside the method define a keyframe animation with two keyframes – one to animate the text out of the screen and another to animate it back in.
- Finally, make a call to `delay(seconds:completion:)` outside of the keyframe animation and change the text of the summary label in the closure parameter. You need to time the text change to happen exactly when the label is off-screen.
- Call `summarySwitchTo(summaryText:)` from within the "animated" part of `changeFlightDataTo(data:,animated:)`
- Don't forget to move the existing non-animated call inside the `else` statement.

How did you do? If you succeeded, congratulations! You've managed to animate every single UI element in the project.

The next section of this book delves into the seemingly complex world of Auto Layout and animations; you'll learn that Auto Layout isn't nearly as mystifying as you might have thought, and you'll learn to animate constraints just as easily as you animate views!

Section II: Auto Layout

Auto Layout has been around for a while now – it was first introduced in iOS 6 and has gone through a series of successful iterations with each release of iOS and Xcode.

The core idea behind Auto Layout is incredibly simple: it lets you define the layout of the UI elements of your app based on relationships you create between each of the elements in the layout.

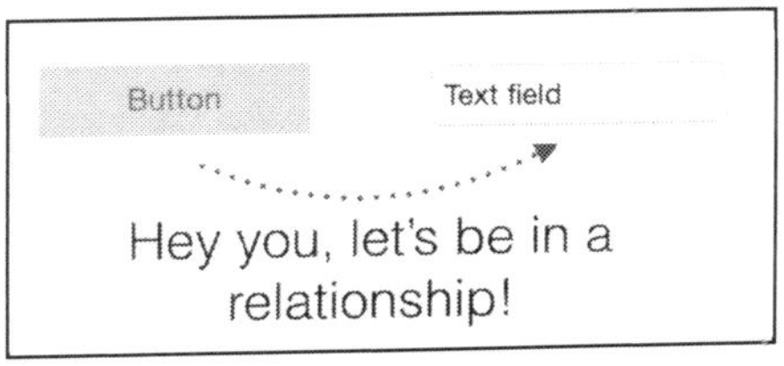

Although you may have used Auto Layout for static layouts, you'll go beyond that in this section and work with constraints in code to animate them!

You'll need a slightly better understanding of the Auto Layout paradigm than the average iOS developer in order to make your animations play nicely with Auto Layout.

Fortunately, you'll find working with Auto Layout constraints in code isn't as hard as it sounds at first, and it's a fairly straightforward process once you work through a few examples.

In this section of the book you are going to work on a little project named **Packing List**:

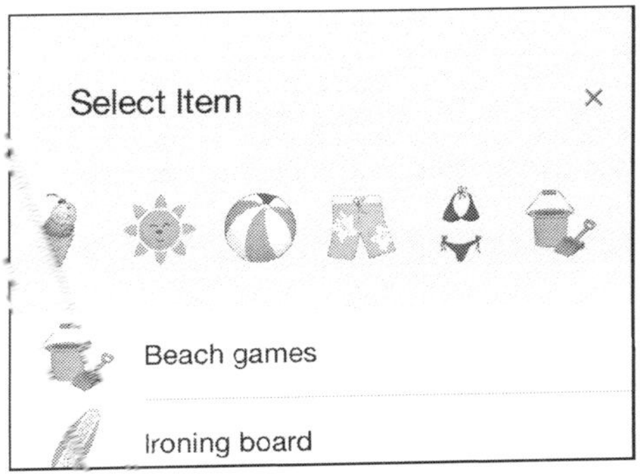

There are two chapters in this section that will guide you through creating animations that co-exist with Auto Layout:

- **Chapter 6, Introduction to Auto Layout** – This will be your crash course on Auto Layout; the great part is that you can carry these concepts on to other areas besides animation.
- **Chapter 7, Animating Constraints** – Once you've worked through the project in Chapter 6, you'll add a number of animations to it and put your newfound knowledge to good use.

By the end of this section, you'll have tamed Auto Layout and will know how to bend it to your will to create some really amazing animations.

Chapter 6: Introduction to Auto Layout

This chapter is for the readers that need an *iOS Animations by Tutorials* crash course on Auto Layout. You will need to have the skills taught in this chapter in order to proceed to the next one – where you learn about animations in Auto Layout.

If you are already well versed in building Auto Layout interfaces – you can skip ahead to **Chapter 7, Animating Constraints**.

For those of you out there still reading and eager to dive into using Auto Layout: imagine, if you will, a world *without* Auto Layout first...

You're in charge of creating a new app for your company. Your design, built with Interface Builder, would look like something like the following:

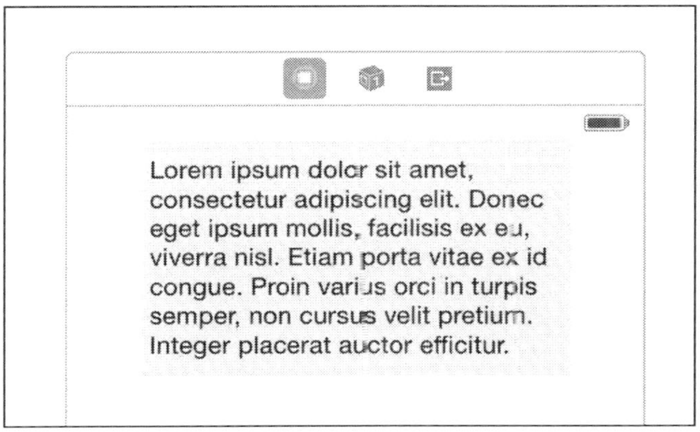

With the view positioned exactly as you want it you then check its frame in the Size Inspector:

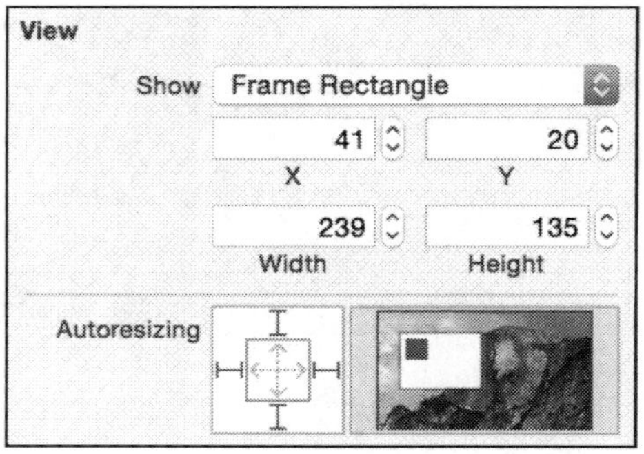

The position and size of your view are expressed in absolute values of points. That *looks* okay, so you launch the iPhone 6 Simulator to see your beautiful app in action:

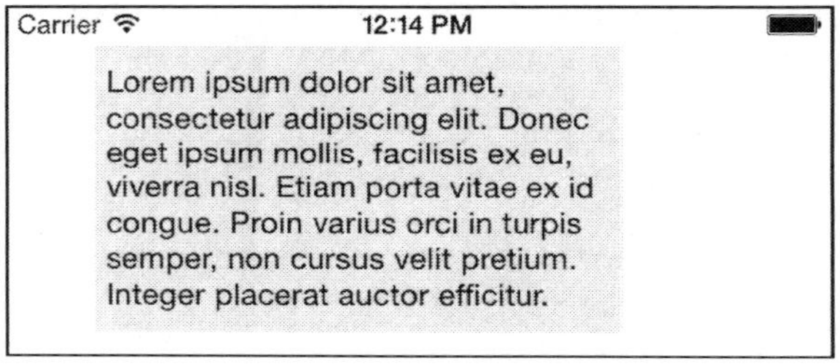

What happened? You view is no longer centered. The problem is that the view's position is expressed in points; you had designed your app in Interface Builder with the iPhone 5s in mind, but since the iPhone 6 has a different screen resolution, your view appears off-center.

When you press Cmd + Right arrow to rotate the Simulator, the situation gets even worse:

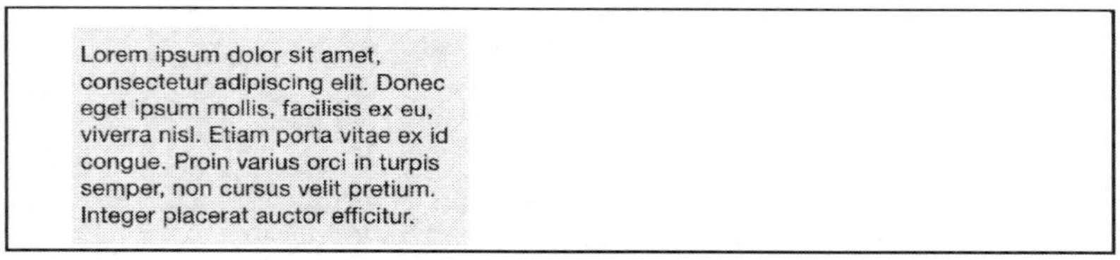

The auto-resizing and re-positioning system in Interface Builder provides a partial solution to these kinds of problems. However, if you're serious about creating dynamic and beautiful user interfaces that work with multiple device sizes and orientations, then you'll need to start using Auto Layout.

Auto Layout to the rescue

Enabling Auto Layout and size classes in Interface Builder creates view controllers with a default size of `600`pt x `600`pt. This neutral size forces you to think about your app in terms of the arrangement and relationship between UI elements, instead of the resolution or aspect ratio of a particular physical device.

Since you're no longer living in the Twilight Zone and Auto Layout is a reality, consider the same project from before, but this time using Auto Layout:

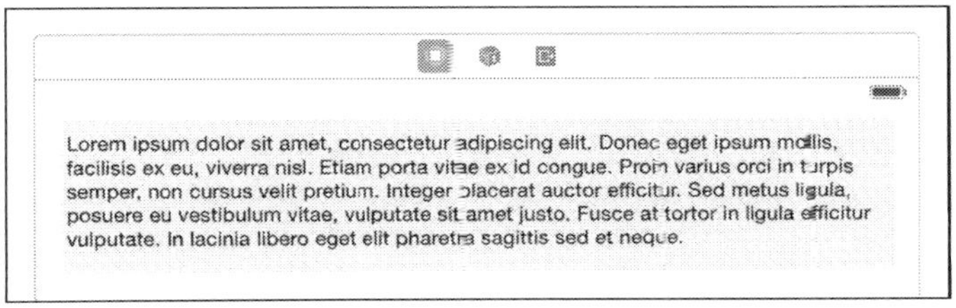

With Auto Layout it's easy to indicate that the `center.y` property of the text view should equal the `center.y` value of its superview. This means the text view will *always* be centered within its superview – independent of the screen on which the app runs.

You could also choose to set the width of the text view to `90%` of the width of its `superview`; this leaves a nice `5%` margin of white space around the text.

With this simple set of rules in hand, Auto Layout happily rearranges the elements in your UI to look good on any device, in any orientation:

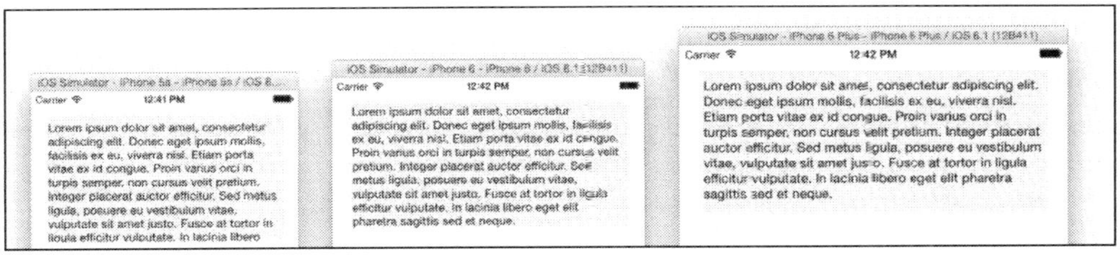

"So what's the catch?" you might be thinking. Well, there isn't a catch *per se*, it's just that you need to *think differently*.

Once you place your app in the hands of Auto Layout, you can't set the `bounds`, `frame` or `center` properties of a view, or Xcode will force a layout pass on your UI which will set everything back to the positions and sizes determined by your constraints.

Not being able to change these properties means that you can't *animate* those properties either! Therefore to move your views around or change their shape, you'll instead alter the Auto Layout rules – or *constraints* – that define where a view appears as well as its size.

But before you can animate constraints, you first need to learn how to create constraints, and more importantly, how they work.

Auto Layout Constraints

Open the Starter project for this chapter in Xcode, then build and run your project to see what it looks like:

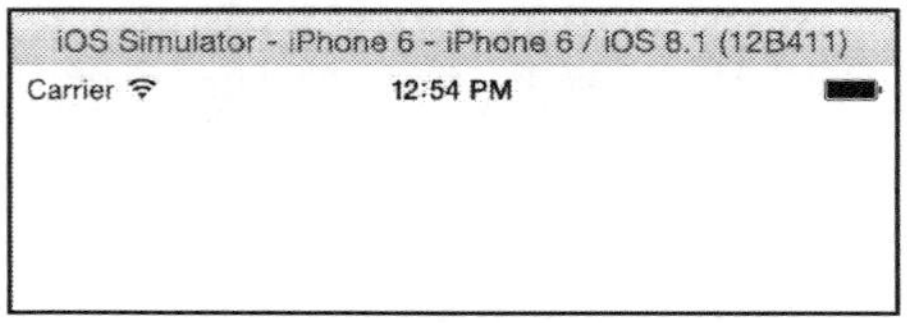

That's right – the project has no UI at all. Your job in this chapter is to build a simple interface with Auto Layout and learn how constraints work.

The project *does,* however, include some starter code:

- **ViewController.swift**: This class contains a few outlets to be connected to the views you'll create in Interface Builder. Further it contains table view delegate and data source methods, which you will use once you add a table view to the user interface.
- **HorizontalItemList.swift**: This is a scroll view subclass, which shows a scrollable list of images. You'll use this class in the next chapter.

Your goal is to build a very simple dynamic UI, which will have the following appearance on different devices and orientations:

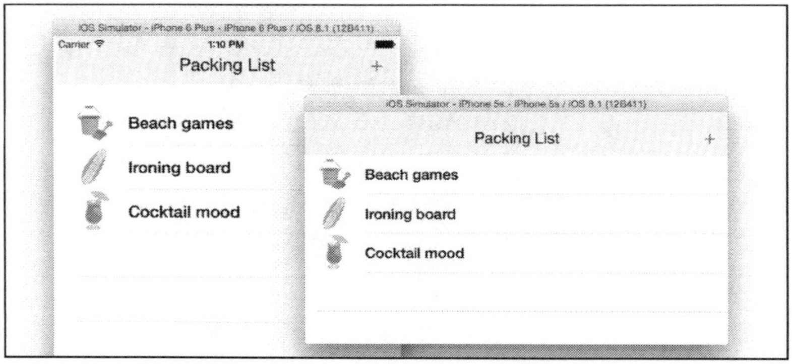

Adding the top menu

First you're going to add the top menu to the interface file. Visually the menu will resemble a bit a navigation bar:

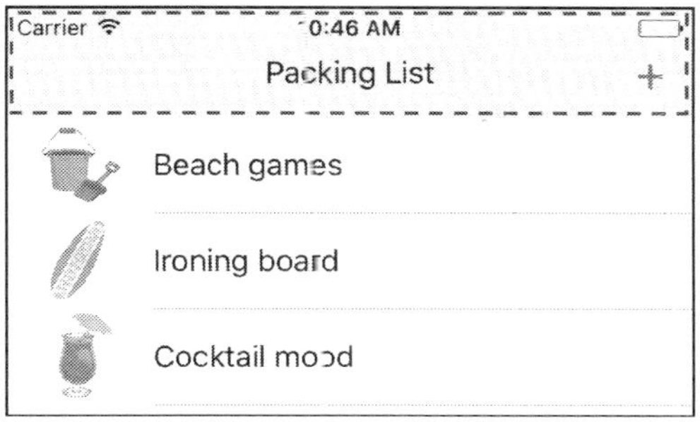

In the next chapter however you are going to make it expand and contract, and offer the user much more than a plain old navigation bar – stay tuned. :]

Open **Main.storyboard** and drag a custom view onto the existing view controller:

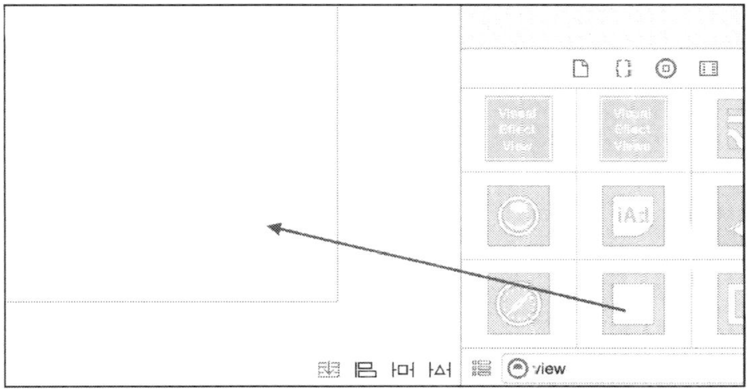

Use the Attributes Inspector to change the background color of the view to **Group Table View Background Color**:

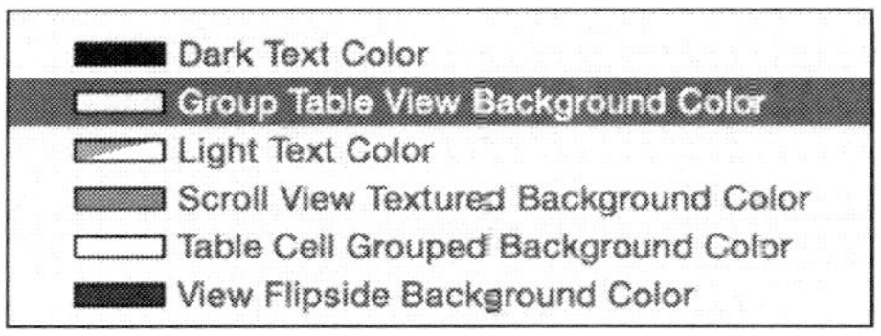

Resize the new view to more or less resemble a navigation bar in size (you don't need to worry about the exact dimensions right now).

Make sure to snap the view to the top, left and right edges like so:

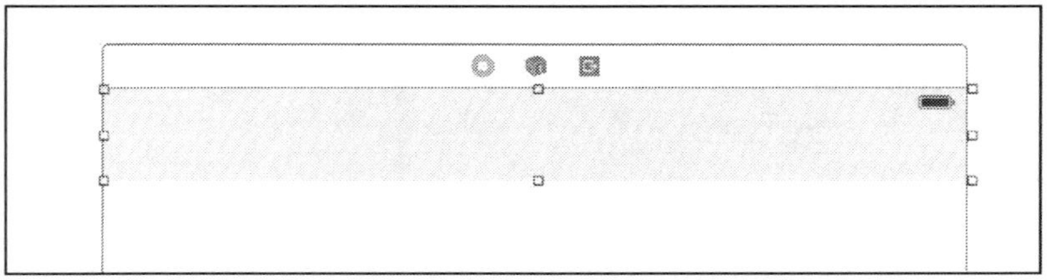

Now that you can actually see the view, you can constrain it to stay always in that top area where you mocked it up in Interface Builder.

Creating your first constraint

Select the view, and then click on the **Pin** button – the second button from the left – in the toolbar in the bottom right corner of Interface Builder (a.k.a. the square tie fighter button):

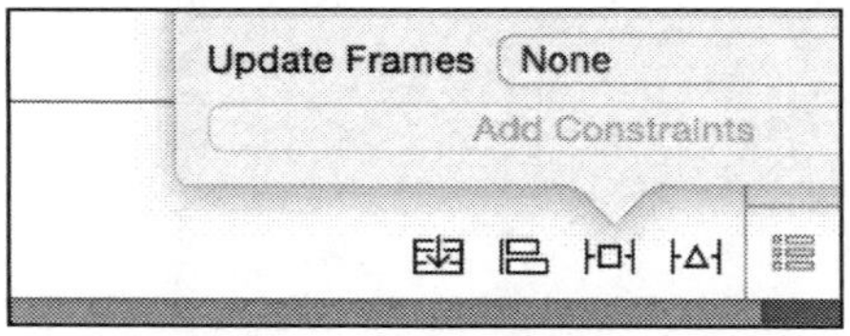

In the resulting popup menu, uncheck **Constrain to margins** and click the **left**, **top**, and **right** indicators to create three constraints as shown below:

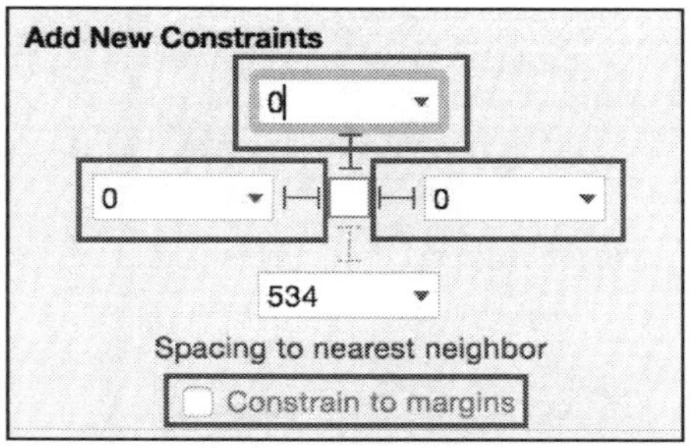

Click the **Create 3 Constraints** button to add them to your view and close the popup.

Each constraint is a relationship expressed as an equation; the top constraint you just created would be represented like so:

```
View.Top = 1 * Superview.Top + 0
```

The top position of your new view will always be `0`pt, because the top of the superview is also `0`pt.

Constraining the menu height

Select your view again and click again on the **Pin** button to get the constraints popup.

This time you want to create a constraint to fix the **Height** of the menu view to a constant value. In the popup you will see the height of the view you set while positioning the view – check the checkbox next to **Height** and then click **Create 1 constraint** at the bottom:

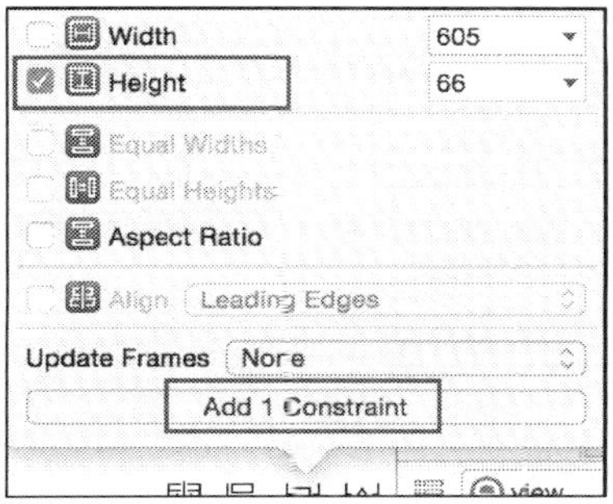

Now you've fixed the height of your menu bar forever. However, what if you wanted the height to be precisely `60`pt? Let's look into how to edit the already created Height constraint.

Deselect the current UI element and select your view once more then switch to the Size Inspector, the second tab from the right in the Assistant Editor:

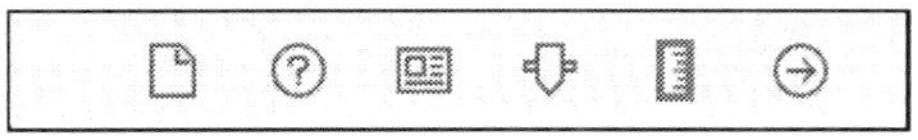

Here you'll see all the constraints for the selected view as shown below:

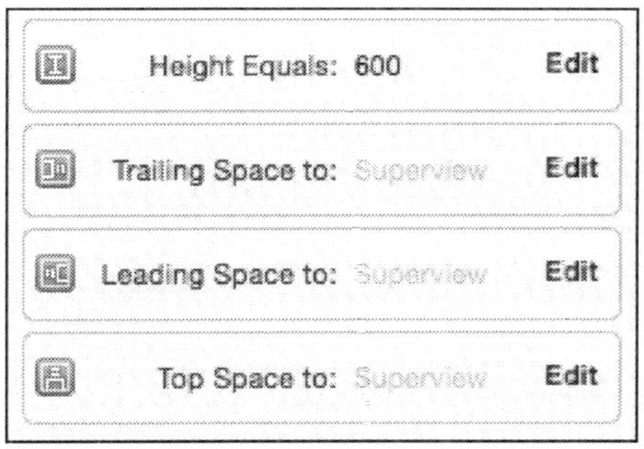

You probably don't have the Height fixed to `60`pt so let's fix that. Click the **Edit** button on the offending constraint and set it to **60pt**, like so:

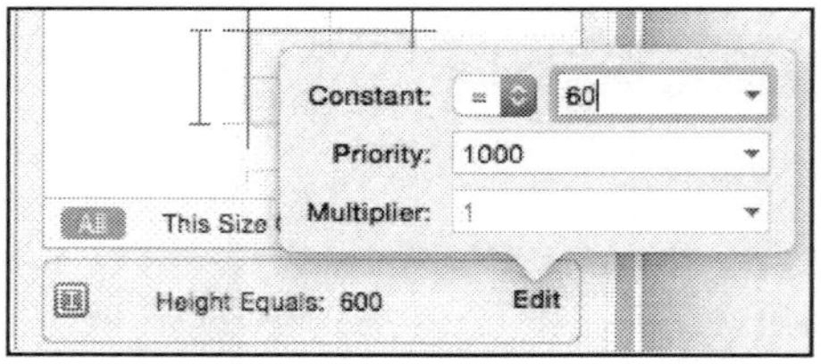

As soon as you do that you'll see the menu resize accordingly:

Build and run your project in any of the iPhone Simulators to see that the layout is preserved across different screen sizes:

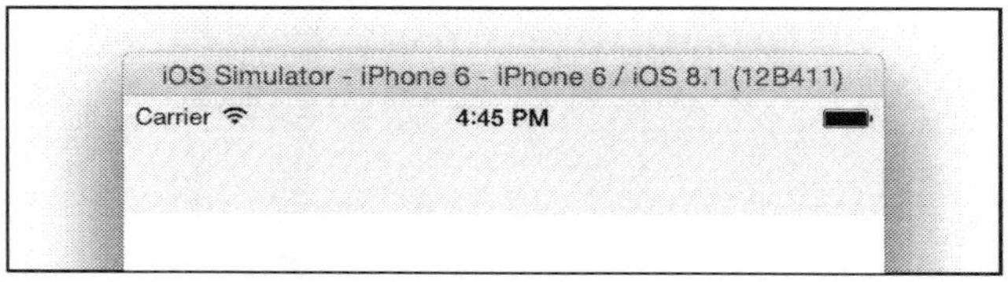

It works! The menu view is always pinned to the top and sides and has a height of `60`pt. And even better – you *understand* how it works. :] Now you can start to populate that menu.

Adding the menu title

Drag a label onto the menu view, set its Text to **Packing List**, the Alignment to Center (), and the Font size to **21.0** points. Your label should look as follows:

Now you need to center the label in its parent view. Select the label and while holding the Ctrl key drag with the mouse (in a diagonal direction) to the menu bar like so:

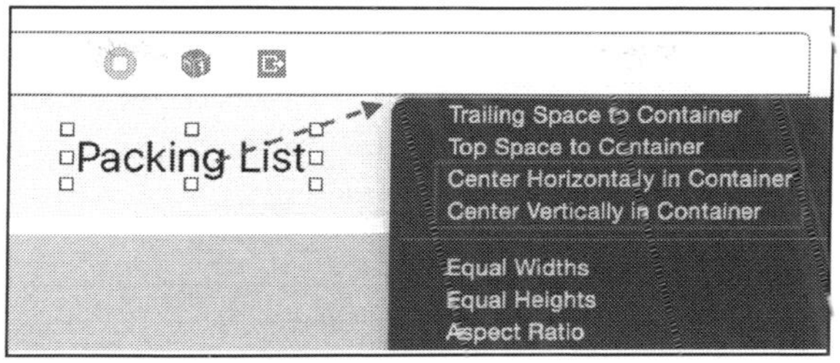

Click **Center Horizontally in Container** to center the label horizontally within the menu. Then while holding the Ctrl key drag again and click **Center Vertically in Container** to align the label vertically within the menu.

This creates to constraints that fix the label's `center` coordinate to the `center` coordinate of the menu:

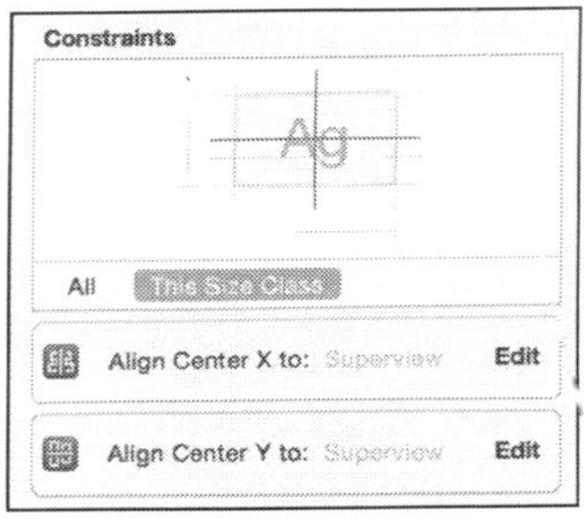

Things don't look quite right in Interface Builder; unless you placed the label precisely in the center of the menu view you'll probably see something like the following:

Resolving Auto Layout issues

While designing in Interface Builder it's possible that dragging views around can break your constraint equations (e.g. the view is positioned manually on a spot that doesn't reflect the applied constraints).

In the image above, the label just happens to be placed precisely in the vertical center of the menu, so Interface Builder notes this with a **blue guide** indicating the vertical constraint has been satisfied.

The **orange guide**, however, indicates that the horizontal alignment constraint is broken. Interface Builder shows you the current frame of your view in solid orange along with the frame that the constraint expects in a dashed orange line.

To fix this, ensure the label is selected, then click the **Resolve Auto Layout Issues** button in the bottom right corner of Interface Builder as shown below:

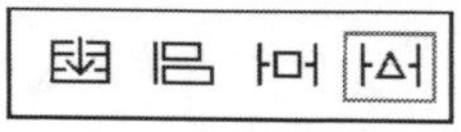

The menu popup presents you with lots of options, but all you want to do here is move the label to the position required by your constraint. Click **Update Frames** and your label will automatically jump to the correct position:

The two new constraints on your label translate to the following equations:

```
Superview.CenterX = 1.0 * UILabel.CenterX + 0.0
Superview.CenterY = 1.0 * UILabel.CenterY + 0.0
```

There's just a bit more tweaking required; you'll need to move the label down just a touch to leave a bit more headroom at the top.

Positioning elements with Auto Layout

Now, you can't just drag the label down without breaking your new constraints, so you'll have to work with the Auto Layout constraints to make it happen.

Select the label, switch to the Size Inspector in Assistant Editor, and then double click the constraint called **Align Center Y.** You should see the constraint displayed in a form like below:

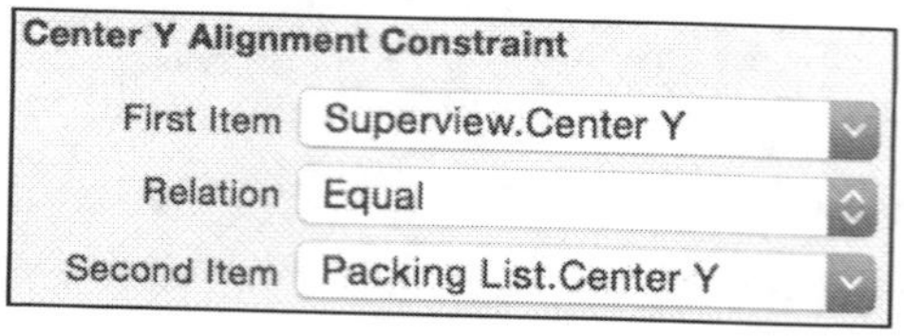

What's this First item/Second item business?

A relationship in Auto Layout, like any relationship in the world, has two sides to it. Constraint rules indicate the relationship between your two UI entities. For example, a rule could be: set the view's height (the first item) to half that of its superview (the second item).

Take a look at the constraint relationship above; the first item in the constraint is the Superview. That's not right – you want the constraint to be based from the point of view of your Label instead.

When creating a constraint, Xcode isn't always consistent with the order of the first and second item.

If you have the Packing List label as the first item, great! If not, that's a relatively easy thing to fix. Click on the drop-down menu under **First item** and select **Reverse First And Second Item**:

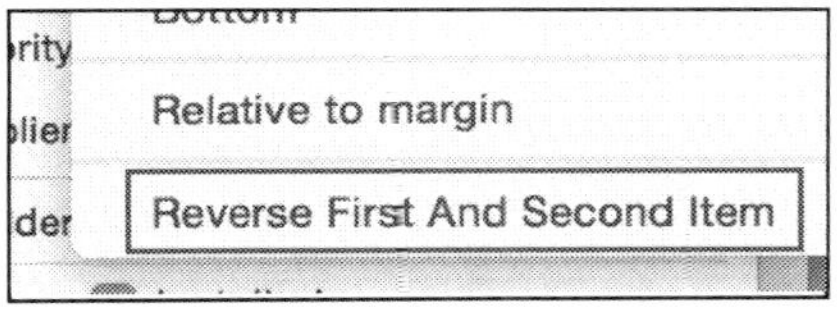

This switches the position of the first and second items. Now you can edit the equation from the point of the view of the label and move the label down a little.

Before going on double check that the label is your First Item:

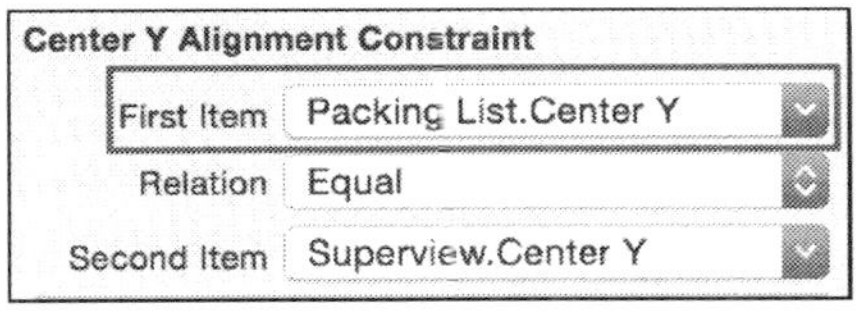

Set **Constant** to **5** as shown below:

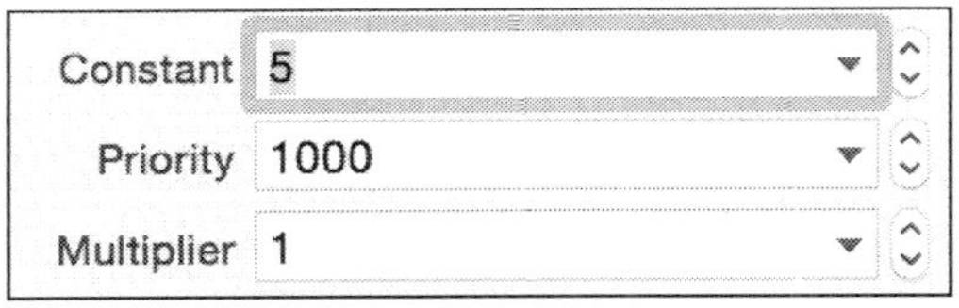

From now on the label will always be 5 points off the vertical center of its parent view.

Next you will add the + button on the right hand side of the screen.

Adding a menu button

Drag a button onto the menu view. Set its Title to **+**, Font Size to **27.0**, and align it as shown below:

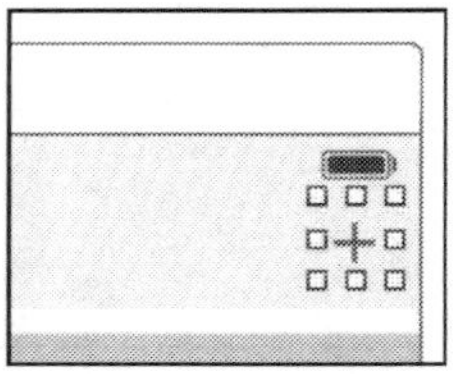

Click the Pin button and check the **Trailing Space** constraint. Click **Create 1 Constraint** to pin the button to the right edge of the view controller.

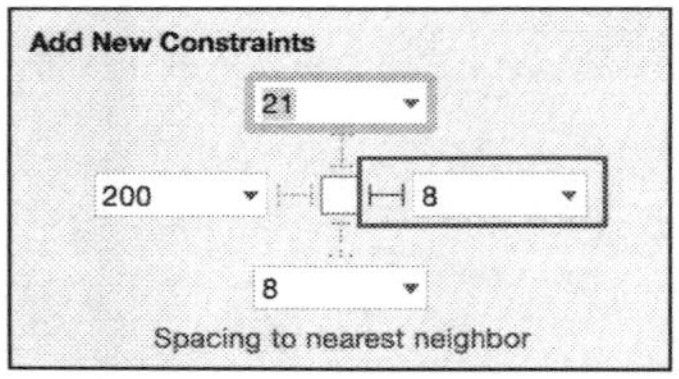

So far you've created only constraints between a view and its superview. But you don't have to *constrain* yourself in this way anymore – pardon the pun ! :] You can create relationships between views on the same level of the view hierarchy as well.

For example, it would be a good idea to vertically align the + button to the title label. This way if you change your mind about the `5`pt offset you added to the label and make it `10`pt instead, the button will automatically follow and stay aligned with the title.

Aligning views with Auto Layout

Select the button and hold **Ctrl** on your keyboard as you drag with the mouse from the button to the label. Release the mouse button when the label activates and you will see a popup menu like so:

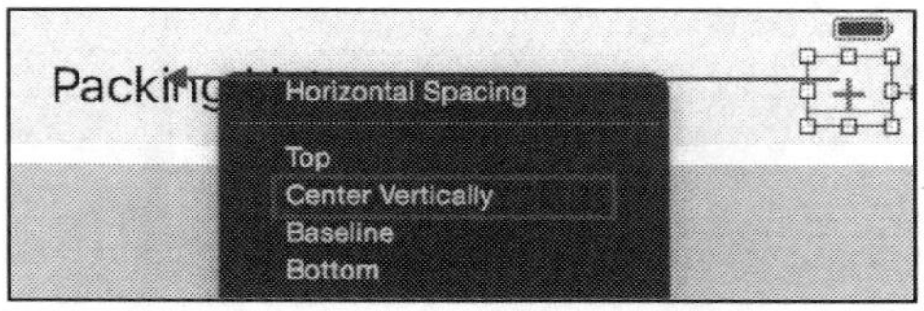

Click on **Center Vertically** to align the button vertically to the label.

Make sure the constant is **0** (zero) and the **First Item** of the new constraint is the **+** button, as shown:

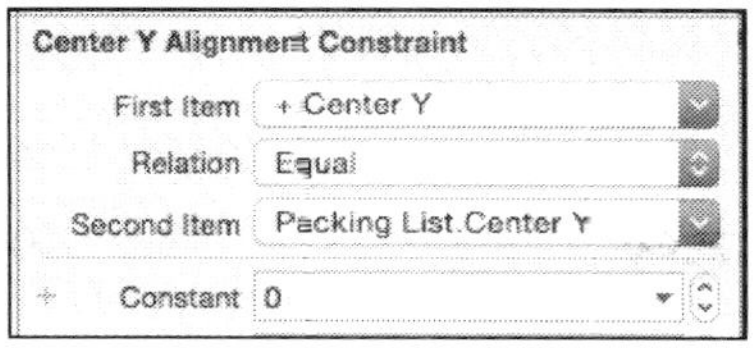

This is important because you want to attach the button the title, instead of vice versa. If you see **Packing List.Center Y** as the first item, click on the drop down next to it and then click **Reverse First and Second Item** to switch the two items.

Now select the button again and click on the **Resolve Auto Layout Issues** button, then from the popup menu select **Update Frames**:

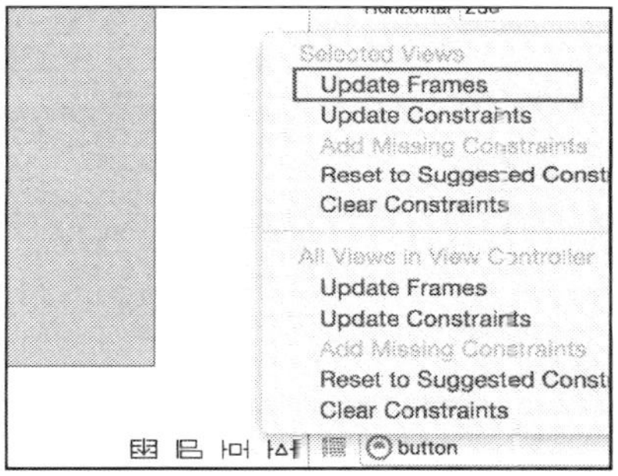

This ought to remove any warnings in Interface Builder. You are almost done with creating the user interface – the only missing element is the table view.

Adding and constraining a table view

Drag a table view and drop it in the empty view controller space:

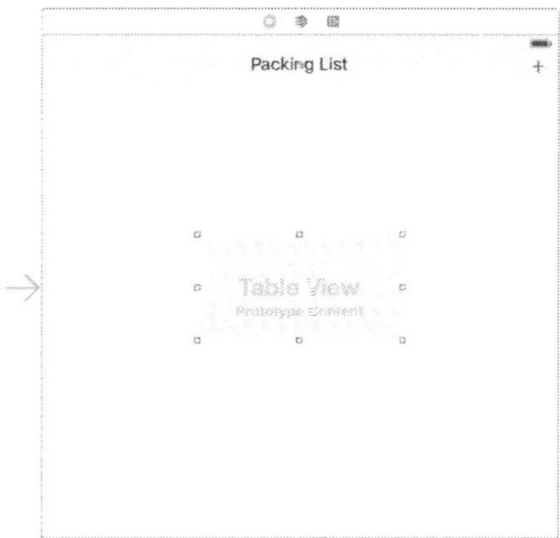

Since you're getting quite skilled at using Auto Layout in Interface Builder, you'll likely breeze through the steps to set up your table view.

Click the **Pin** button and uncheck **Constrain to Margins**, enable the **top**, **left**, **bottom**, and **right** constraints and set them all to **0** – just be careful *not* to press Enter prematurely before entering all values:

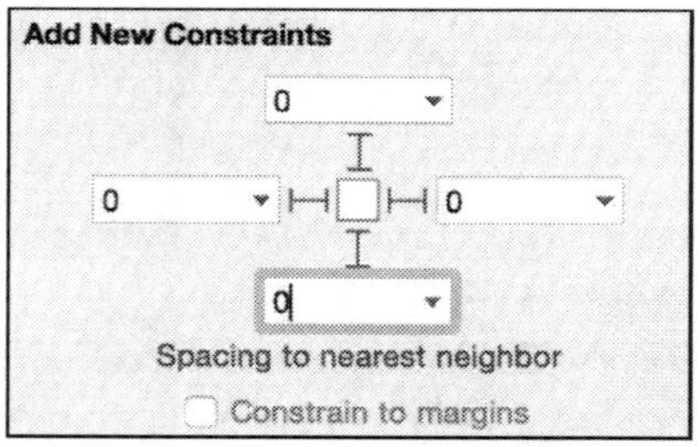

Click **Create 4 Constraints** to add the constraints to your view and close the popup:

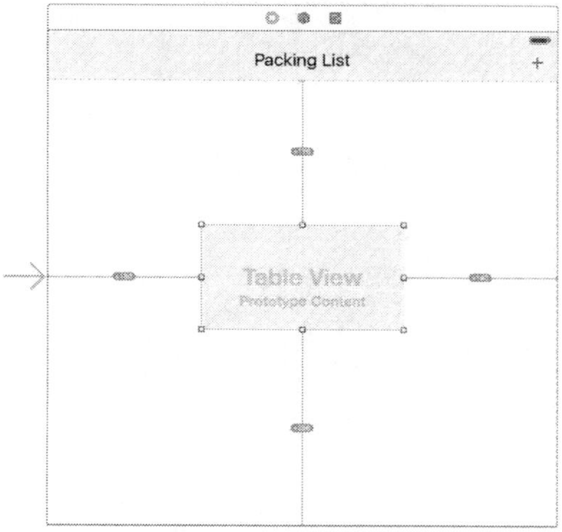

Note that the constraints you create via the **Pin** button popup relate to the table's nearest neighbor, not necessarily its parent view. In the case of the left, right, and bottom constraints above this is the superview – the view controller's view.

In the case of the top constraint above there's a neighboring view closer to the table's top – the menu. So Interface Builder automatically picks up that view for the top constraint.

There's one final step. Select the table view again, open the **Resolve Auto Layout Issues** popup and click **Update Frames**.

You should see the table align properly within the view controller's view like so:

You're done setting up the basic constraints for your app! You now have a good understanding of how Auto Layout works and how to setup constraints and relationships between views in Interface Builder. Thanks to these new skills of yours, you'll get to create some cool new animations for your Packing List project in the next chapter.

Finalizing the UI

There's just one more thing to take care of before you move on: you need to connect the existing outlets to their corresponding UI elements.

Ctrl-drag with the mouse from the view controller object to the table view, then select **tableView** from the popup menu:

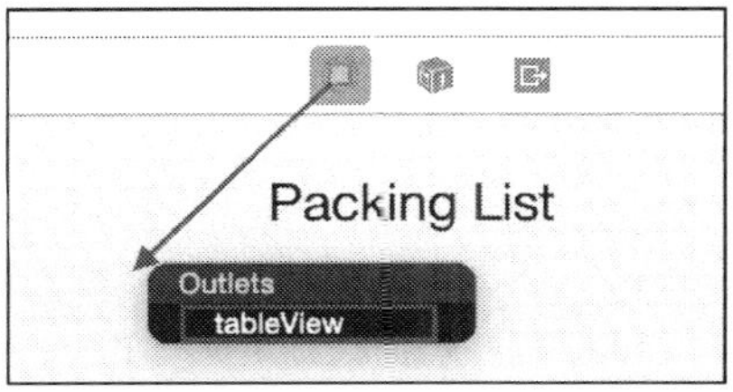

Then **Ctrl-drag** from the view controller to the title and select **titleLabel**:

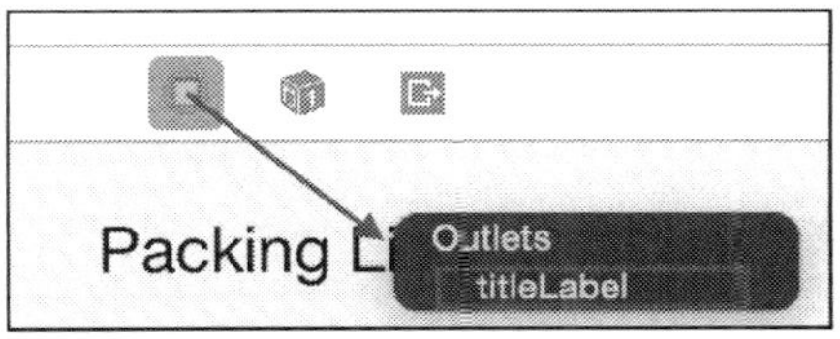

Do the same for the + button and select **buttonMenu**:

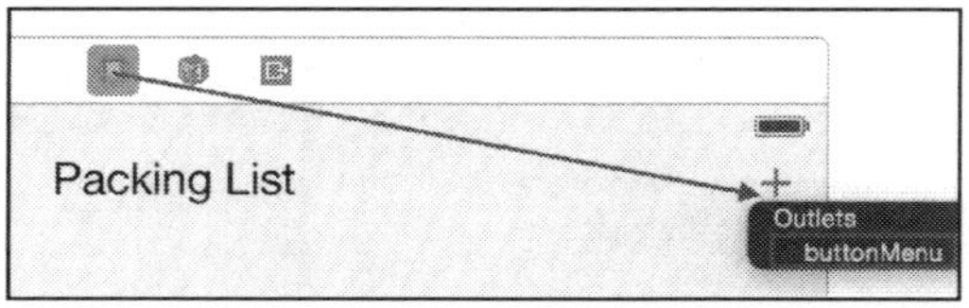

Now **Ctrl-drag** from the button back to the view controller and select **actionToggleMenu:** :

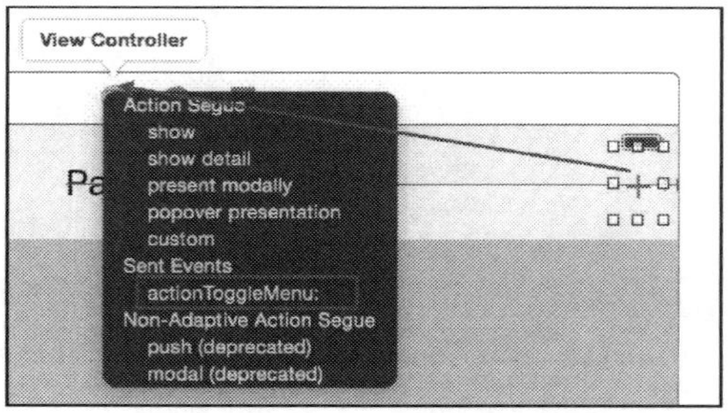

Next, drag from the table view to the view controller and select **dataSource**:

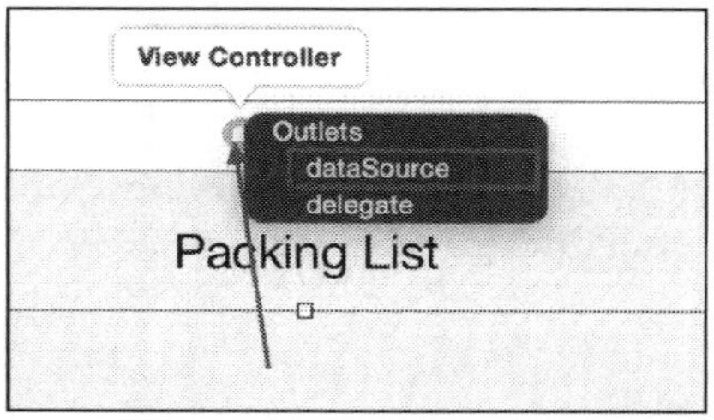

Once again, **Ctrl-drag** from the table view to the view controller but this time select **delegate**:

All that's left is to give your table a prototype cell. Drag a **table view cell** object onto the table view, like so:

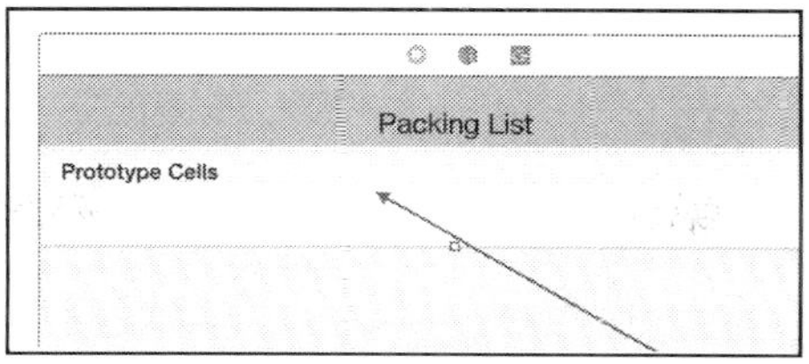

Then open the Attributes Inspector and enter **Cell** for the **Identifier**:

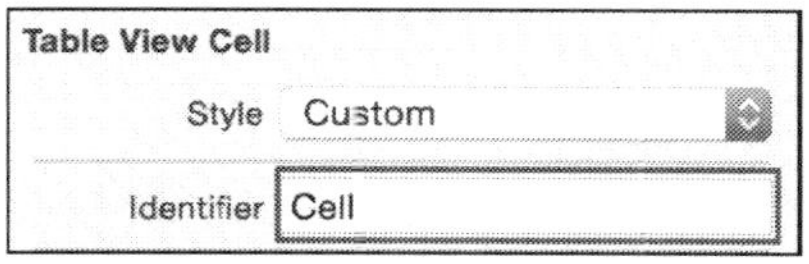

At long last, build and run your project; the existing table view code in **ViewController.swift** will pick up the newly connected outlets and populate the table with data:

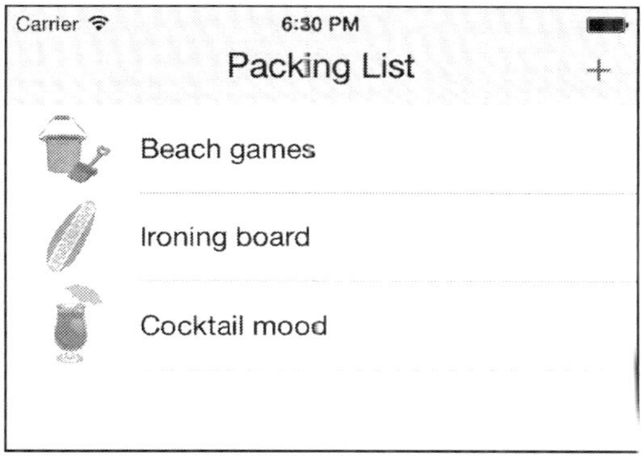

The app not only *looks* good, but it has a rock-solid layout, thanks to Auto Layout. Give the app a whirl in different Simulators – both iPhone and iPad – and change the orientation to check it out for yourself!

Challenges

Your challenge this time is simple – just head on in to the next chapter! By now you understand Auto Layout in some detail, which is an important prerequisite for the work you're about to do in the next chapter, which deals with animations and Auto Layout.

See you in the next chapter! :]

Chapter 7: Animating Constraints

In the previous chapter, you learned how to use Auto Layout to create a responsive user interface for your Packing List project. You'll take it up a notch in this chapter and add a number of bouncy animations to your project.

You've learned that in order for Auto Layout to work properly, you can't fiddle directly with the view's `frame` or `center` properties; instead, you have to work with the layout constraints to create your desired animations.

So far you've seen how to animate view properties: you can animate numeric properties, like `alpha`, from one float value to another. Instances of `CGPoint`, like in the case of the `center` property, can be modified progressively until the `center` value reaches the target position.

Naturally, your next question would be "That's great – but how do I animate a *constraint*?"

Animating constraints is no more difficult than animating properties – it's just a little different. Usually you simply replace an existing constraint with a new one and let Auto Layout animate the UI between the two states like so:

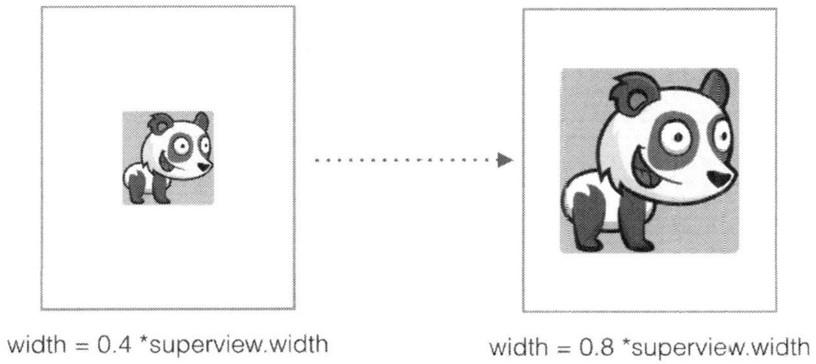

The sole exception is when you **only** need to change the *constant* in the constraint's equation: in that case, you simply modify the constraint directly from code and animate the change.

In this chapter you'll add an animation to expand the Packing List menu bar and reveal a list of items; the user can then tap an item to add it to their packing list as shown below:

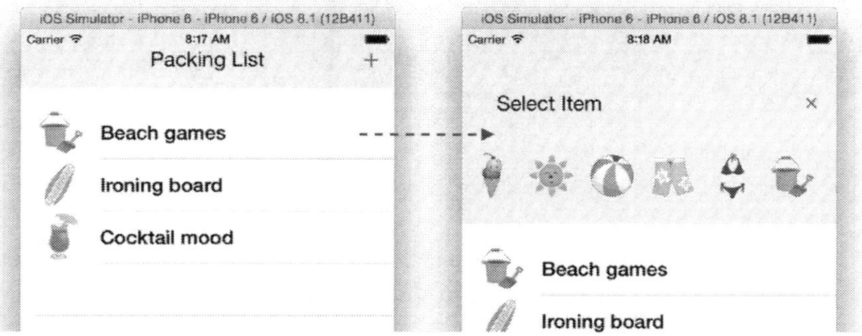

This interaction – as well as a few more visual treats – will be driven by fluid and eye-catching animations.

What are you waiting for? Time to get packing! :]

Animating Interface Builder constraints

If you completed the project from the previous chapter, you can carry on where you left off; otherwise, you can use the starter project from this chapter. Before you start, make sure the menu in your app looks like the images below across different iPhone simulators:

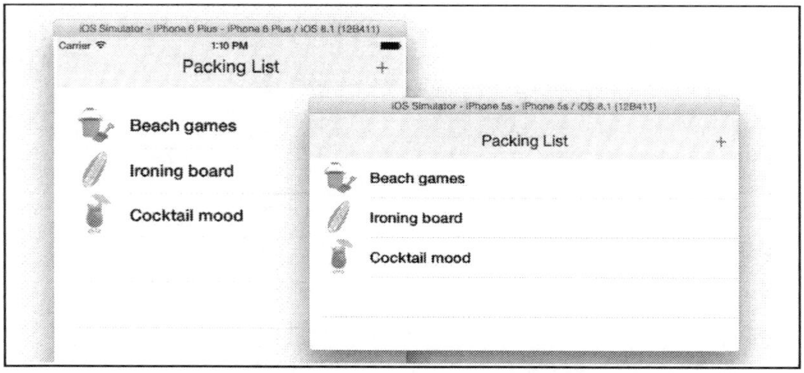

Your first task is to expand the menu when the user taps the + button. In order to do that, you'll need to change the height of the menu bar by animating its Height constraint.

Making the menu expand

Open **ViewController.swift** and scroll to the top of the class. Under the rest of the outlets add the following line of code:

```
@IBOutlet weak var menuHeightConstraint: NSLayoutConstraint!
```

`NSLayoutConstraint` is the class that represents the constraints you create in Interface Builder. Just like any other button, image view, or label, you can also create an outlet to a constraint.

Open **Main.storyboard** and select the menu view:

Open the Size Inspector tab, and double click on the Constraint that says **Height Equals: 60**. This will open the familiar view of the constraint's equation:

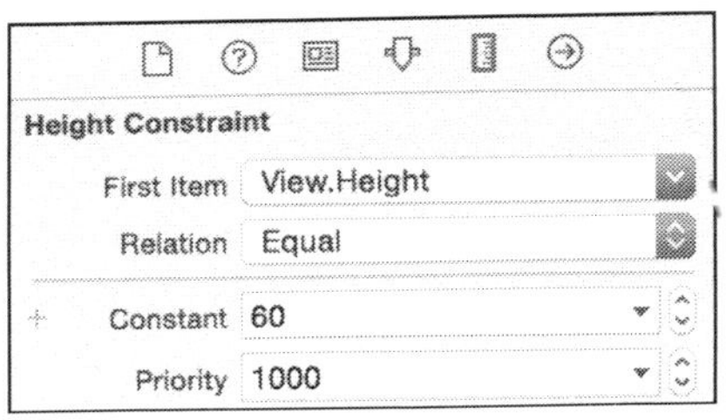

Switch to the last tab on the right – the **Connections Inspector**:

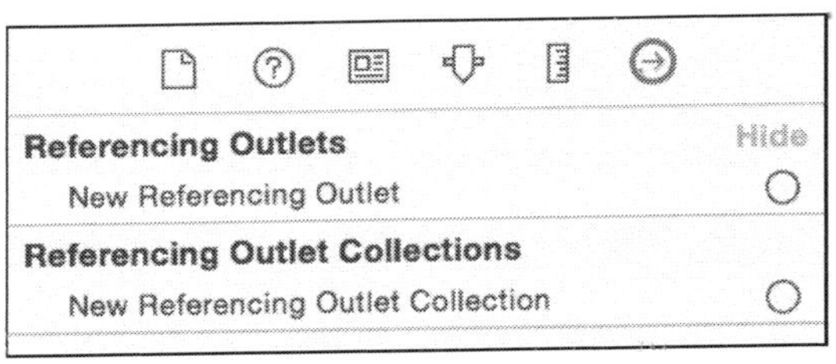

From here you can connect the constraint to its outlet in `ViewController`.

Drag from the small circle next to **New Referencing Outlet** to the view controller object:

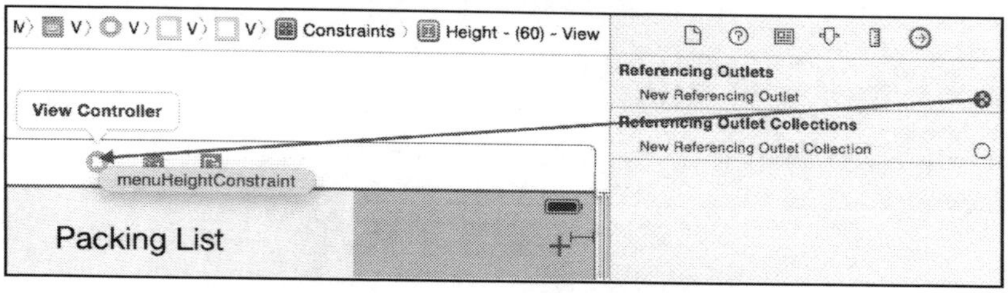

From the popup menu select the only available option: **menuHeightConstraint**. You've now created your outlet, as shown in the image below:

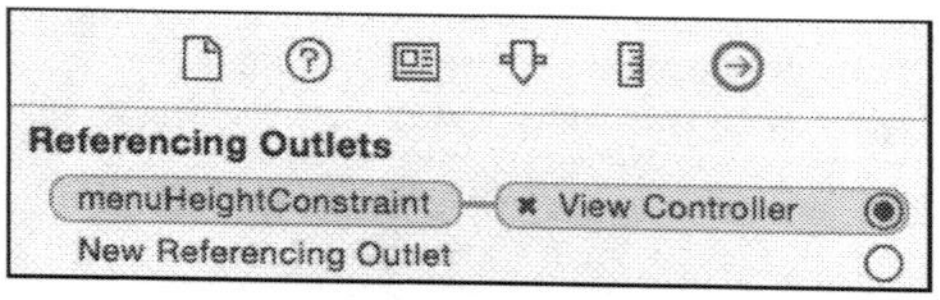

Open **ViewController.swift** and add the following three lines to `actionToggleMenu()`:

```
isMenuOpen = !isMenuOpen
menuHeightConstraint.constant = isMenuOpen ? 200.0 : 60.0
titleLabel.text = isMenuOpen ? "Select Item" : "Packing List"
```

In the code above, you first toggle the Boolean variable `isMenuOpen`, which tracks whether the menu is currently expanded or collapsed.

Next, you modify the constraint's `constant` property to either `200.0`pt or `60.0`pt – depending on the state of `isMenuOpen` – to make the menu expand or collapse as required.

In the final line of code you toggle the menu title between **Packing List** and **Select Item** as appropriate.

Build and run your project; tap the **+** button a few times and the menu should expand and contract as you had planned:

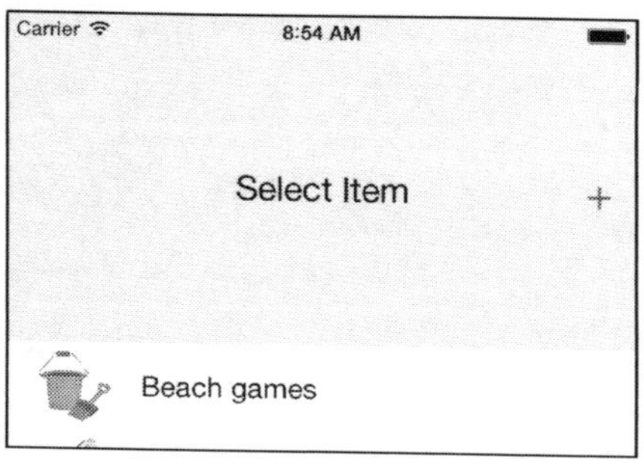

To animate the layout changes, you'll need your old friend `animateWithDuration(_:animations:)` or any of the similar APIs.

Animating layout changes

Add the following code to the bottom of `actionToggleMenu`:

```
UIView.animateWithDuration(1.0, delay: 0.0,
  usingSpringWithDamping: 0.4, initialSpringVelocity: 10.0,
  options: .CurveEaseIn, animations: {
    self.view.layoutIfNeeded()
}, completion: nil)
```

In the code above, you create a spring animation (just as you learned about in Chapter 2, "Springs") and force an update of the layout from within the `animations` closure. This is all it takes to animate your constraint modifications.

Still a little fuzzy on what's happening above? Here's a bit more background on how the animation works.

When you modify pertinent view properties inside an animation closure, they'll be animated as you would expect, and Auto Layout still sets the `bounds` and `center` of your views once it finishes its calculations.

In this case, you've already updated the constraint value but iOS hasn't had a chance to actually update the layout yet. By calling `layoutIfNeeded()` from within the animation closure, you set the center and bounds of *every* view involved in the layout. That's it – there's no magic happening in the background! :]

If you *hadn't* called `layoutIfNeeded()`, UIKit would have performed a layout anyway since you changed a constraint, which marked the layout as **dirty**.

Build and run your project again; tap the + button and you'll see the menu expand and contract with a bouncy animation.

You can even see that the menu title temporarily overlays the system menu on its way back up:

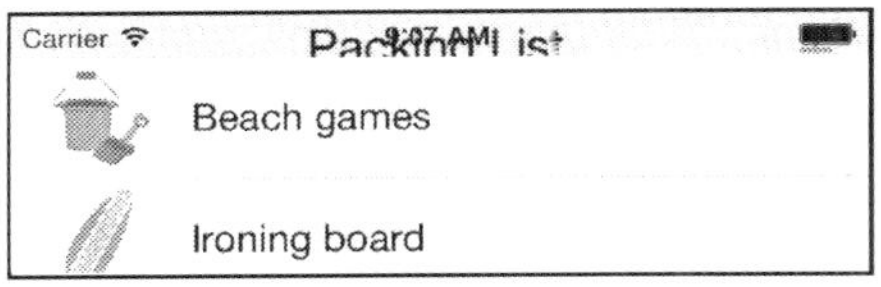

Of course, once the animation settles down it all looks good again.

Did you notice that the table view *also* shrank and grew along with the menu? Instead of covering up the table, the menu actually *pushed* the table view away as it expanded.

This is because of the existing constraint you added in the previous chapter that attaches the top of the table to the bottom of the menu. When the menu grows, the table shrinks to satisfy the constraint.

Two animations for the price of one – FTW!

To spice things up a bit, you'll now mix constraint animations with some non-constraint animations to see what new effects you can create.

Your next task is to rotate the **+** button by 45 degrees when the menu expands so it resembles an **x** – i.e. a close button.

Rotating view animations

Since you already know how to rotate views by adjusting their `transform`, add the following code to the final `animations` closure:

```
let angle = self.isMenuOpen ? CGFloat(M_PI_4) : 0.0
self.buttonMenu.transform = CGAffineTransformMakeRotation(angle)
```

When the menu expands, you set the angle of the rotation to 45 degrees (or `π/4` radians); when it contracts, you simply set the rotation back to `0`. Then you update the `transform` on the button to set the view in motion.

Build and run your project; tap the **+** button to see how the rotation animation looks alongside the call to `layoutIfNeeded()`:

The animation looks gorgeous; you can temporarily set the animation duration to 5-6 seconds to see exactly how the + sign rotates to become an **x**. You can also see the button bounce around its center thanks to the spring animation that drives both the constraint and rotation animations.

Inspecting and animating constraints

Working with outlets in a visual fashion is a relatively easy way to connect up your outlets, but sometimes you can't use Interface Builder to connect all bits of your UI to your outlets. You might add constraints from code, or maybe you just don't want to control-drag and create a massive number of outlets!

In these cases you need to inspect the existing constraints at runtime and modify in code the ones you want to animate.

Luckily, the `UIView` class has a property called `constraints`, which gives you a list of all constraints that affect the given view. How convenient is that? :]

Add the following code to the top of `actionToggleMenu()`:

```
for con in titleLabel.superview!.constraints {
  print(" -> \(con.description)\n")
}
```

This one-liner loops over all constraints affecting the menu bar view and prints them one by one to Xcode's output console.

Build and run your project; tap the + button to see all constraints neatly listed like so:

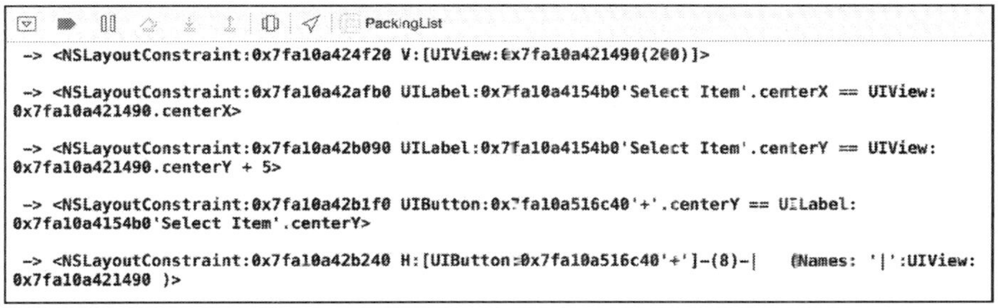

It looks a bit messy, but read through the output carefully and you'll be able to figure out what each constraint does. Take the following constraint as an example:

```
UIView:...centerX == UILabel:...'Select Item'.centerX
```

It's clear that this is a constraint between a `UIView` and a `UILabel;` the description also includes the current text of the label. `centerX` is also mentioned a few times...aha! This must be the constraint that horizontally centers the title within the menu bar; it's time to animate this bad boy.

Animating UILabel constraints

Find the following line near the top of `actionToggleMenu(_:)`:

```
isMenuOpen = !isMenuOpen
```

Then add the following code *below* that line:

```
for constraint in titleLabel.superview!.constraints {
  if constraint.firstItem as? NSObject == titleLabel &&
   constraint.firstAttribute == .CenterX {
    constraint.constant = isMenuOpen ? -100.0 : 0.0
    continue
  }
}
```

Here you loop over the list of constraints affecting the menu bar view, but this time you are looking for a certain constraint to adjust.

Do you recall the equation for the horizontal center constraint? It looked something like the following:

```
Superview.CenterX = 1.0 * UILabel.CenterX + 0.0
```

The `NSLayoutConstraint` properties map to the above equation in a very straightforward manner:

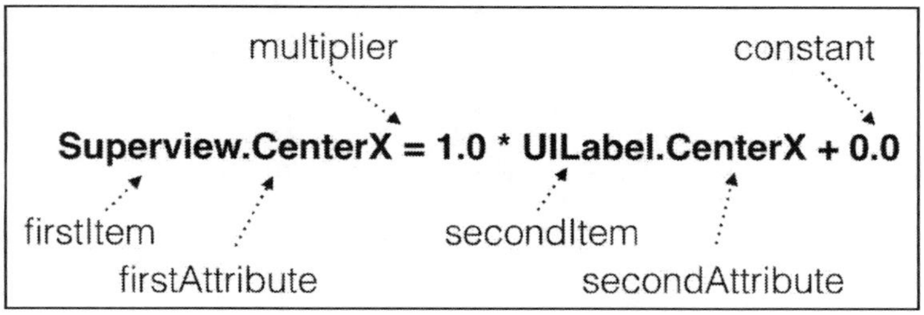

The `if` condition makes more sense now when you look back at the last piece of code you added: for each constraint, you check if the `secondItem` is the title label and if the constraint aligns with the title's `CenterX`.

When you find the correct constraint, you adjust its `constant` to `100`pt to push the title to the left when the menu opens.

> **Note**: There's slightly easier way to dynamically find an existing constraint and work with it – you'll look into it next.

Build and run your project; tap the + button to see how your new constraint logic works:

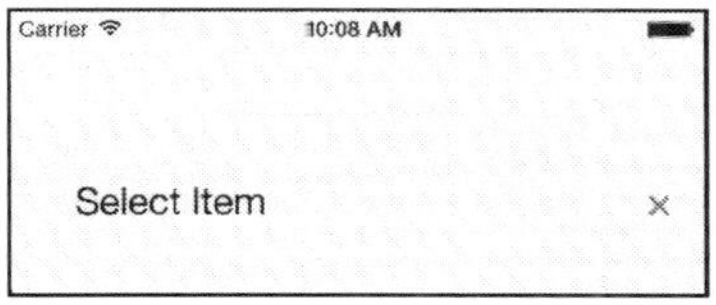

Remember you're calling `layoutIfNeeded()` from within a spring animation API, so the title animation bounces a bit.

> **Note**: If by any chance your animation doesn't kick in, check out the Center Horizontally in Superview constraint on the label; make sure the label is the first item and the menu bar view is the second.

Your UI is starting to look really cool – but you know you can take this even further. The next section shows you how to *replace* constraints to create some neat animations.

Animating by replacing constraints

At this point in the chapter you've only modified the `constant` property of your constraints. Ironically, the `constant` property is the only *mutable* property in the `NSLayoutConstraint` class! :]

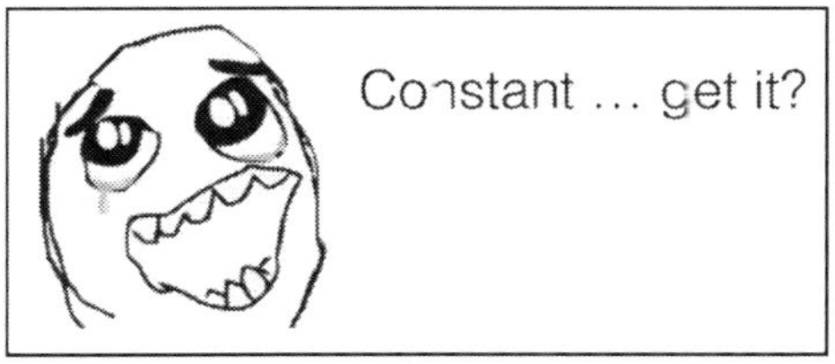

If you want to modify the `multiplier`, or change a constraint in any other way, you'll need to remove the constraint then add a new one in its place.

To learn how to do that, you'll animate the vertical alignment of the menu title to move it up a bit as the menu opens. This should leave enough empty space at the bottom of the menu to show some more content, which you'll add later in this chapter.

This time around you are going to use a different technique to make sure you've got the correct constraint.

In Interface Builder you can assign an identifier to each constraint – and that can help you easily get hold of it at run time.

Open **Main.storyboard** and find the **Align Center Y** constraint of the title label:

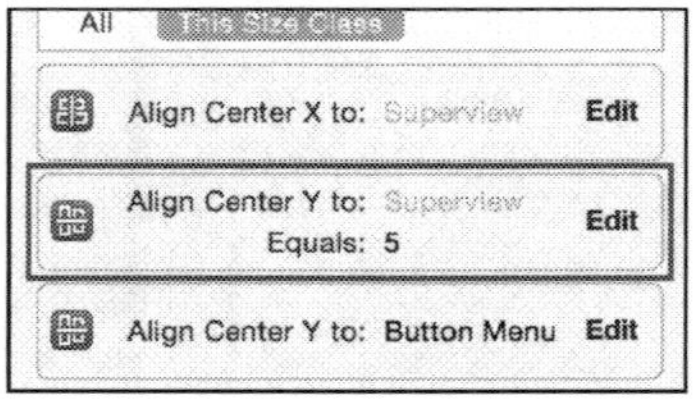

Double click the constraint and in the **Identifier** text box enter **TitleCenterY**:

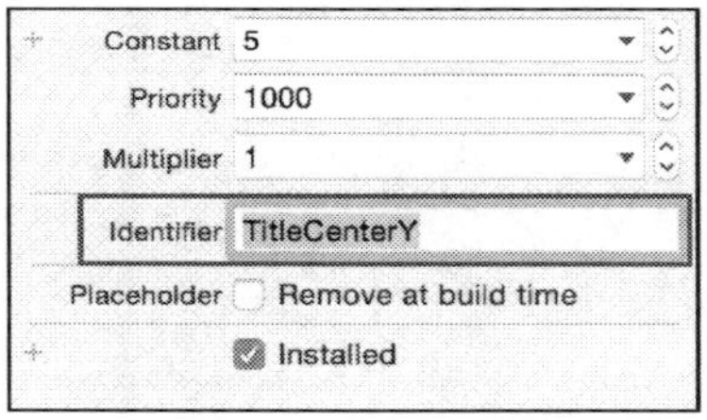

Back in **ViewController.swift** find the following spot in the code within `actionToggleMenu`, at the end of the `for` loop:

```
for constraint in titleLabel.superview!.constraints {
  if constraint.firstItem as! NSObject == titleLabel && constraint.firstAt
    constraint.constant = isMenuOpen ? -100.0 : 0.0
    continue
  }
  <-------------------- add code here
}
```

Insert the following code at the point indicated above:

```
if constraint.identifier == "TitleCenterY" {
  constraint.active = false

  //add new constraint

  continue
}
```

You check if the identifier of the constraint is the same as the one you want to replace and if so, you remove the constraint. You do that by setting `active` to `false` – this causes the view hierarchy to remove the constraint. If you don't also have a reference to it, the constraint object will be deleted from memory.

Build and run your project; tap + and observe what happens:

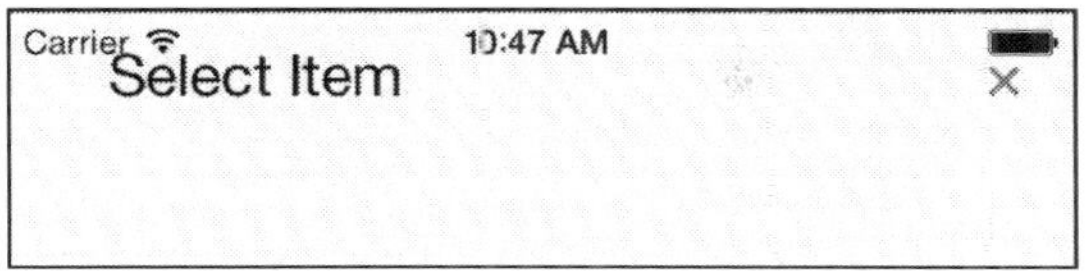

Since there's no longer a constraint to keep the view aligned, the title simply bounces to the top of its superview. The + button obediently tags along because its own `CenterY` is attached to the title's `CenterY`.

Amusing as the effect is, you'll need to add a new constraint and fix the layout.

Adding constraints programmatically

When the menu is retracted you want the title vertically centered within the menu view like so:

Or to express the constraint via its equation:

```
Title.CenterY = Menu.CenterY * 1.0 + 0.0
```

But when the menu expands you'd like to move the title a bit upwards to make space for the list of packing items later on:

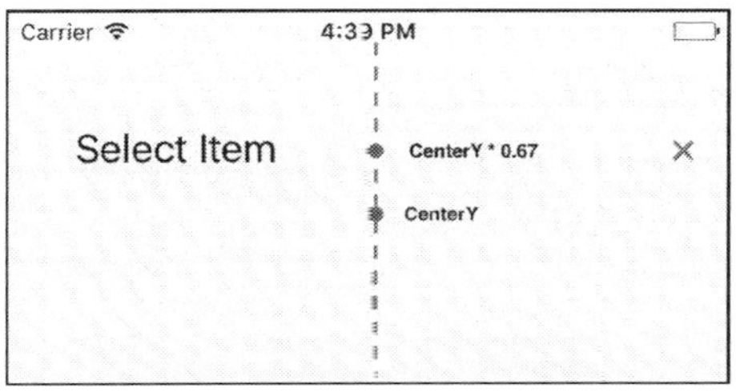

Here's the constraint's equation spelled out in detail:

```
Title.CenterY = Menu.CenterY * 0.67 + 0.0
```

Find the placeholder comment `//add new constraint` in the code you just added, and replace it with the following:

```
let newConstraint = NSLayoutConstraint(
  item: titleLabel,
  attribute: .CenterY,
  relatedBy: .Equal,
  toItem: titleLabel.superview!,
  attribute: .CenterY,
  multiplier: isMenuOpen ? 0.67 : 1.0,
  constant: 5.0)
newConstraint.identifier = "TitleCenterY"
newConstraint.active = true
```

`NSLayoutConstraint's` initializer takes a cartload of parameters but luckily they map exactly to all parts of the constraint's equation. The parameters are as follows:

- `item:` The first item in the equation, in this case the title label.
- `attribute:` The attribute of the first item of the new constraint.
- `relatedBy:` A constraint can represent either a mathematical equality or an inequality. In this book you'll only use equality expressions, so here you use `.Equal` to represent this relationship.
- `toItem:` The second item in the constraint equation; in this case, it's your title's superview.
- `attribute:` The attribute of the second item of the new constraint.
- `multiplier:` The equation multiplier as discussed earlier.
- `constant:` The equation constant.

As an additional step you give the constraint the identifier **TitleCenterY**. You will use that identifier the next time the user toggles the menu to find and replace the constraint you just created.

Finally you need to set the `active` property on the constraint to `true` and that tells Auto Layout to apply it to the current layout.

> **Note:** If you've used Auto Layout from code before you might be accustomed to a method called `addConstraint` on `UIView` to add your constraints.
>
> In iOS 8 and newer, the preferred approach now is to add constraints by setting their `active` property or calling

NSLayoutConstraint.activateConstraints(_:) with an array to activate many constraints at once.

Build and run your project; open the menu and the title should move up to a spot just above the vertical center of the menu bar as shown below:

Adding menu content

Your next job is to show a list of items in the menu; these are all possible items you can add to your packing list. The `HorizontalItemList` class that came with your starter project will assist you in displaying that list of items.

> **Note**: This chapter won't cover `HorizontalItemList` in detail; its implementation isn't relevant to creating animations. However, you're still welcome to peek into **HorizontalItemList.swift** if you want to see how it works!

Still in **ViewController.swift**, scroll to the bottom of `actionToggleMenu` and add the following code:

```
if isMenuOpen {
  slider = HorizontalItemList(inView: view)
  slider.didSelectItem = {index in
    print("add \(index)")
    self.items.append(index)
    self.tableView.reloadData()
    self.actionToggleMenu(self)
  }
  self.titleLabel.superview!.addSubview(slider)
} else {
  slider.removeFromSuperview()
}
```

If the menu is about to open, you create a new instance of `HorizontalItemList` in `slider` to hold your new items, assign a closure expression to `didSelectItem` and then finally add `slider` to the menu bar.

`didSelectItem` runs when the user taps an image in the list; in this event, you add the image index to the list of selected items and reload the table view. In the `else` branch – when the menu is about to close – you simply remove the image list from its parent view.

Build and run your project; add a few items to see what the list of images looks like:

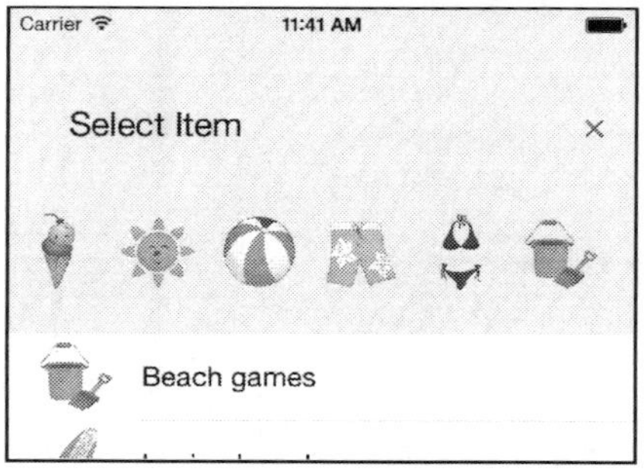

You're nearly done; the final section of this chapter will walk you through dynamically creating and animating views in code.

Animating dynamically created views

Your ultimate task, which will use everything you've learned up to this point and close out the chapter nicely, will be to create a new view, add some constraints to the view and animate it on the screen.

`showItem(_:)` in `ViewController` is called when you tap a table row. Your task is to create an image view with the tapped image index and display it at the bottom of the screen as shown below:

Add the following code to `showItem(_:)` to create an image view out of the selected image:

```
let imageView  = UIImageView(image:
  UIImage(named: "summericons_100px_0\(index).png"))
imageView.backgroundColor = UIColor(red: 0.0, green: 0.0,
  blue: 0.0, alpha: 0.5)
imageView.layer.cornerRadius = 5.0
imageView.layer.masksToBounds = true
imageView.translatesAutoresizingMaskIntoConstraints = false
view.addSubview(imageView)
```

In the code above, you load the selected image and create an image view from it. You give it a semi-transparent black background and round the corners slightly. Notice that you *don't* set the position of the image view in its parent view.

Next you'll create the constraints for the image view, one by one. Add the following code directly below the code you just added:

```
let conX = imageView.centerXAnchor.constraintEqualToAnchor(
  view.centerXAnchor)
```

This method uses the new `NSLayoutAnchor` class, which makes creating common constraints really easy. Here, you're creating a constraint between the Center X anchors of the image view and the view controller's view.

Next, add the code below to give the image view a `Bottom` constraint:

```
let conBottom = imageView.bottomAnchor.constraintEqualToAnchor(
  view.bottomAnchor, constant: imageView.frame.height)
```

This constraint sets the `Bottom` of the image view to match the `Bottom` of the view controller's view, plus the image height; this positions the image just off the bottom edge of the screen, which will serve as the starting point of the animation.

Next you are going to fix up the image width. Add the following code:

```
let conWidth = imageView.widthAnchor.constraintEqualToAnchor(
  view.widthAnchor,
  multiplier: 0.33,
  constant: -50.0)
```

This sets the image width to `1/3` of the screen width less `50`pt. The target size is `1/3` of the screen; you'll animate away the `50`pt difference to make the image "grow" into place later.

Finally, you just need to set the height of the image. Since the images are square you can just set the height as equal to the image width.

Add one final bit of code for the last constraint, then activate them all in a group:

```
let conHeight = imageView.heightAnchor.constraintEqualToAnchor(
  imageView.widthAnchor)
NSLayoutConstraint.activateConstraints([conX, conBottom, conWidth,
conHeight])
```

This last constraint is a little different from the rest, as it's the first time you've created a relationship between two properties of the same view. Don't worry – this will still work out just fine. :]

Build and run your project; tap a table row and you'll see your new image view appear like so:

This is, of course, just the starting position of your animation. Your job now is to make the image pop up from the bottom.

Adding additional dynamic animations

Add the following code to `showItem(_:)`:

```
UIView.animateWithDuration(0.8, delay: 0.0,
 usingSpringWithDamping: 0.4, initialSpringVelocity: 0.0,
 options: [], animations: {
  conBottom.constant = -imageView.frame.size.height/2
  conWidth.constant = 0.0
  self.view.layoutIfNeeded()
}, completion: nil)
```

Changing `conY`'s `constant` moves the image up and the adjustment to `conWidth` grows the image width by `50pt` to make the image return to its original size. You don't need to set the height as it's automatically constrained to the image width.

Finally you call `layoutIfNeeded()`, which kicks off the animations. Build and run your project; tap a few table rows to see your image animate:

Hang on! The image view starts from the top left of the screen then flies into the middle! What happened?

Think about it for a moment: you added a view, set some constraints, then altered those constraints and animated a layout change. However, the view never got the chance to perform its initial layout, so your image started from its default position at `(0, 0)` in the top left. Ah – that's why it's flying in like that.

To fix this, you need to make sure your initial layout happens before the animation starts. Add the following code *before* the animation call:

```
view.layoutIfNeeded()
```

This will immediately set your initial layout before anything else happens. All constraint changes you make between the call to `layoutIfNeeded()` and the next one will be part of your animation.

Build and run your project now and the animations should work as intended.

It's a little annoying that the images keep piling up on top of each other; you'll fix this in the challenge at the end of this chapter.

Don't forget to try the project in different simulators and orientations; your constraint animations should look good in all of them:

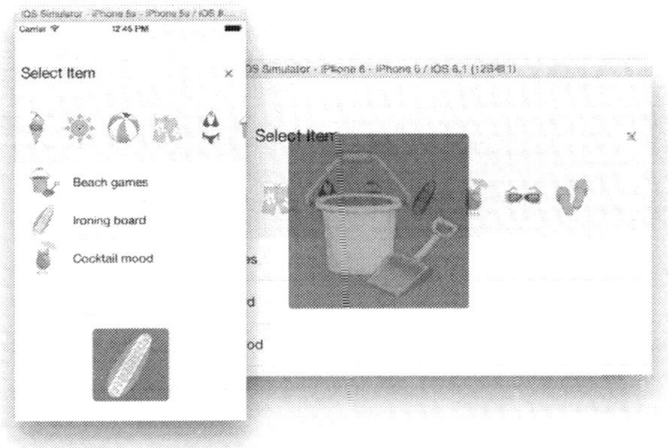

Challenges

Challenge 1: Animate the image out of the screen

Okay – now you get to fix those pesky image views that stay stuck on the screen.

In `showItem(_:)`, keep the image visible for `1` second and then animate it back out of the screen.

Use the animation method that lets you set a delay for the animation, animate the image back out of the screen, and finally remove the image view from the view hierarchy in the animation completion closure.

That's all you need to know to complete the challenge. Good luck!

You now have a good understanding of how to create view animations in Auto Layout projects. Although not all projects in this book make use of Auto Layout, try to use it when you can to keep your skillset fresh!

Section III: Layer Animations

Now that you are proficient in creating view animations, it's time to dig a bit more deeply and look into the Core Animation APIs on a lower, more powerful level.

In this section of the book, you'll learn about animating layers instead of views and how to make use of special layers.

Views vs. layers

A layer is a simple model class that exposes a number of properties to represents some image-based content. Every UIView is backed by a layer, so you can think of layers as the lower-level behind the scenes class behind your content.

A layer is different from a view (with respect to animations) for the following reasons:

- A layer is a model object – it exposes data properties and implements no logic. It has no complex Auto Layout dependencies nor does it handle user interactions.
- It has pre-defined visible traits – these traits are a number of data properties that affect how the contents is rendered on screen, such as border line, border color, position and shadow.
- Finally, Core Animation optimizes the caching of layer contents and fast drawing directly on the GPU.

To compare views and layers side by side:

Views	Layers
Complex view hierarchy layouts, Auto Layout, etc.	Simpler hierarchy, faster to resolve layout, faster to draw.
User interactions.	No responder chain overhead.
Often have custom logic or custom drawing code that executes on the main thread on the CPU.	No custom logic by default. Often cached and drawn directly on the GPU.
Very flexible, powerful, lots of classes to subclass.	Not as flexible, fewer classes to subclass.

If you need to choose between views and layers here is my tip: *choose view animations any time you can to do the job*; you will know when you need more performance or flexibility and have to switch to layer animations instead.

Don't stress yourself about it though, because you can mix and match view and layer animations freely.

By the end of this section, you will know how – and when! – to animate your views, and when it's appropriate to use layers.

Section overview

In the first five chapters, you'll re-create and improve upon some of the view animations you played with earlier in this book in your Bahama Air projects:

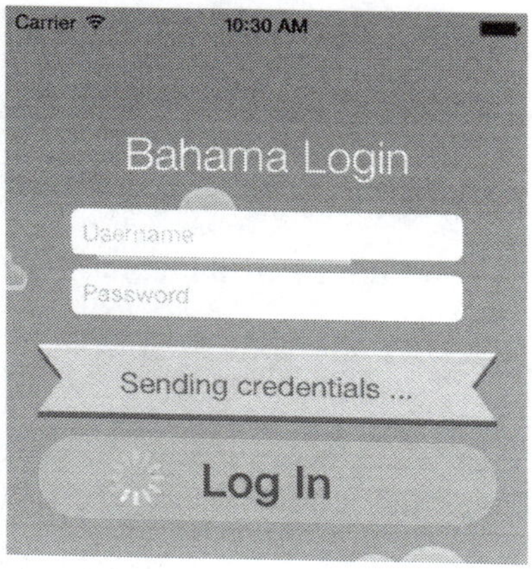

- **Chapter 8, Getting Started with Layer Animations** – You'll start with the simplest layer animations, but also learn about debugging animations gone wrong.
- **Chapter 9, Animation keys and delegates** – Here you gain more control over the currently running animations and use delegate methods to react to animation events.
- **Chapter 10, Groups and advanced timing** – In this chapter you combine a number of simple animations and run them together as a group.
- **Chapter 11, Layer Springs** – In this chapter you learn how to use `CASpringAnimation` to create powerful and flexible spring layer animations.
- **Chapter 12, Keyframe animations and struct properties** – Here you'll learn about layer keyframe animations, which are powerful and slightly different than view keyframe animations. There's some special handling around animating struct properties, which you'll also learn about.

Next, you'll move on to playing with specialized layers:

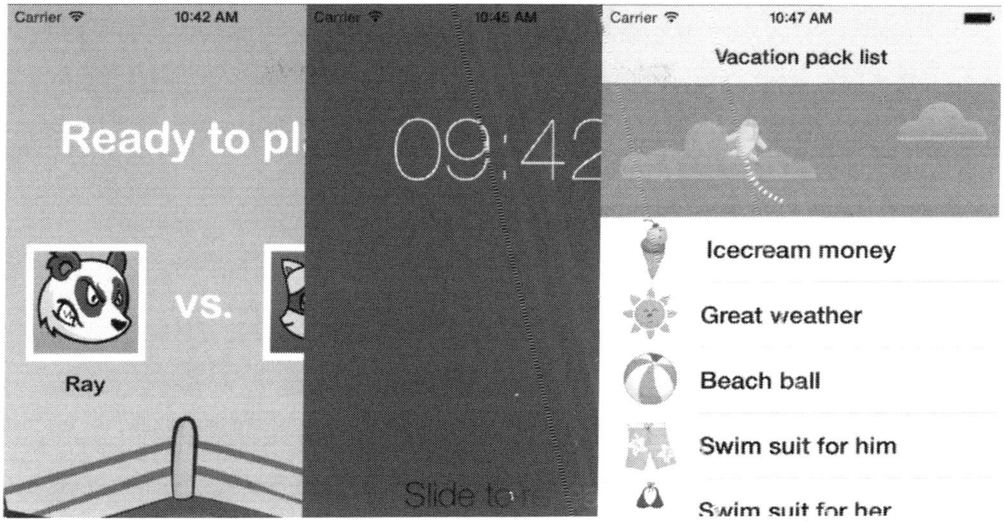

- **Chapter 13, Shapes and masks** – Draw shapes on the screen via `CAShapeLayer` and animate its special `path` property.
- **Chapter 14, Gradient animations** – Learn how to use `CAGradientLayer` to help you draw and animate gradients.
- **Chapter 15, Stroke and path animations** – Here you will draw shapes interactively and work with some powerful features of keyframe animations.
- **Chapter 16, Replicating animations** – you'll learn how to create multiple copies of your layer content and then animate them in sync.

You're in for an amazing ride – *buckle up*! :]

Chapter 8: Getting Started with Layer Animations

Layer animations work much like view animations; you simply animate a property between a start and an end value over a defined period of time and let Core Animation take care of the rendering in between.

However, layers have a bigger number of animatable properties than views; this gives you a lot of choice and flexibility when it comes to designing your effects – and many specialized `CALayer` subclasses add other properties that you can use in your animations.

This chapter will introduce you to the basics of `CALayer` and Core Animation. You'll get a feel for working with animations in layers; you'll learn how to move layers around, fade them in and out, and create animations comparable to the ones you created using UIKit.

Animatable properties

Some of the animatable properties in `CALayer` correspond directly to the view properties you worked with in previous chapters, such as `frame`, `position` and `opacity`. You'll see both the familiar and the new animatable properties used in layer animation in this chapter.

You'll re-create some of the earlier view animations but with layers, so you can draw the parallels and see for yourself where the similarities end and the new possibilities open up.

Position and size

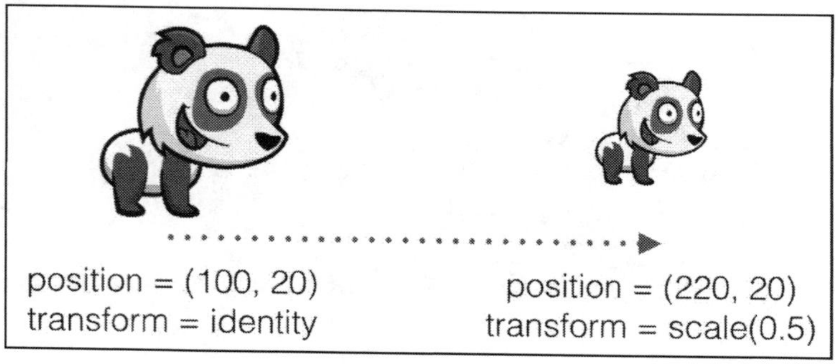

Animating the position, size or transform of a layer equally affects any view contained within that layer, just as if you had directly animated the view itself.

- `bounds`: modify this to animate the bounding frame of the layer.
- `position`: modify this to animate the position of the layer within its parent layer. You can animate `position.x` or `position.y` separately if you want to control movement on only one axis.
- `transform`: modify this to move, scale, and rotate the layer. You can even animate layers in 3D space, which you can't do with views alone. You'll learn about 3D layer transforms in Section IV, "3D Animations".

Border

You can easily animate a layer's border to change its color, width and corner radius.

- `borderColor`: modify this to change the border tint.
- `borderWidth`: modify this to grow or shrink the width of the border.
- `cornerRadius`: modify this to change the radius of the layer's rounded corners.

Shadow

You can animate all aspects of the layer's shadow:

- `shadowOffset`: modify this to make the shadow appear closer to or further away from the layer.
- `shadowOpacity`: modify this to make the shadow fade in or out.
- `shadowPath`: modify this to change the shape of the layer's shadow. You can make different 3D effects to make your layer look like it's floating with different shadow shapes and positions.
- `shadowRadius`: modify this to control the blur of the shadow; this is especially useful when simulating movement of the view towards or away from the surface where the shadow is cast.

Contents

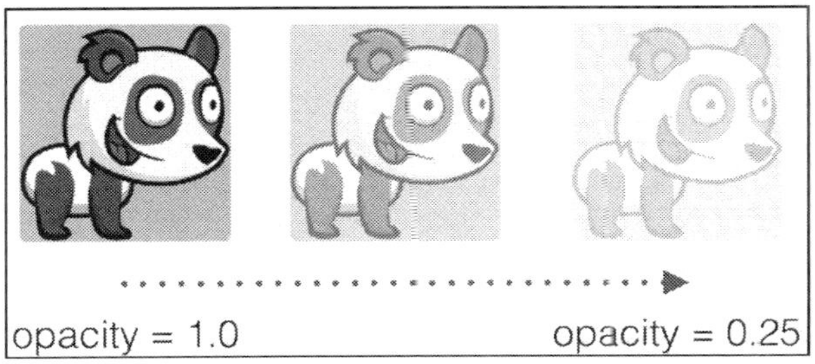

Finally, there are a few properties that control how the layer's contents are rendered:

- `contents`: modify this to assign raw TIFF or PNG data as the layer contents.
- `mask`: modify this to establish the shape or image you'll use to mask the visible contents of the layer; you'll use this property to create some very cool effects in Chapter 13, "Shapes and masks".
- `opacity` – animate the transparency of the layer contents.

Keep in mind that this is only a *partial* list of properties you can animate; subclasses of `CALayer` usually have other properties that you can animate as well.

The properties listed above are enough to get you started; it's time to get to work on your first animation with layer properties.

Your first layer animation

You'll begin with the completed Bahama Air login screen project from the end of Chapter 3, "Transitions". As always, you can build on your previous work or open the starter project included with this chapter.

Build and run your project to see the familiar sight of the Bahama Air login screen:

Your job is to remove the existing view animations and replace them one-by-one with layer-based animations.

Open **ViewController.swift** and find `viewWillAppear()`.

Remove the line below that moves the heading out of the screen bounds:

```
heading.center.x -= view.bounds.width
```

There's no need to perform this action anymore since you can specify *both* the start and end values in your layer animation.

Next, scroll down to `viewDidAppear()` and remove the animation call that moves `heading` as shown below:

```
UIView.animateWithDuration(0.5, animations: {
  self.heading.center.x += self.view.bounds.width
})
```

Build and run your project; watch the animation screen and check that the form title is no longer animated:

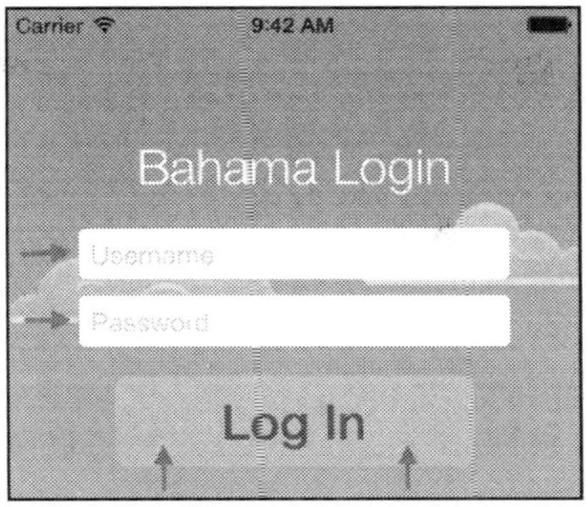

Now that you've stripped out the old view animation code, it's time to add some layer animations! Find `viewDidAppear()` and add the following code at the top of the method, underneath the call to `super`:

```
let flyRight = CABasicAnimation(keyPath: "position.x")
flyRight.fromValue = -view.bounds.size.width/2
flyRight.toValue = view.bounds.size.width/2
flyRight.duration = 0.5
```

Animation objects in Core Animation are simply data models; you create an instance of the model and set its data properties accordingly.

An instance of `CABasicAnimation` describes a *potential* layer animation: one that you might choose to run now, at a later time, or not at all.

Since the animation isn't bound to a specific layer, you can re-use the animation on other layers and each layer will run a copy of the animation independently.

In an animation model you can specify the property to animate as the `keypath` argument; that's convenient, as you'll always be animating *something* in the layer.

Here, you're animating only the `x` component of `position`. Core Animation conveniently exposes the individual members of `position`, `bounds`, and `transform` so you can animate them each separately.

Next, you set the `fromValue` and `toValue` for the property you've specified in the keypath. In this case, you want it to start off screen to the left and end up in the center of the screen.

Finally, the concept of the animation duration hasn't changed; here you set the duration to `0.5` seconds.

Now that your animation is all set up, you can add it to a layer in your app and see how it looks. Add the following line below the code you just added to add your animation to your title layer:

```
heading.layer.addAnimation(flyRight, forKey: nil)
```

`addAnimation(_:forKey:)` makes a copy of the animation object and tells Core Animation to run it on the layer. The `key` argument is for your use only; it lets you identify the animation later on if you need to change or stop the animation.

Build and run your project; you'll see the form title move to the center of the screen as shown below:

As expected, the layer – and its contained view – animate smoothly into position. This shows you how closely a view and its backing layer are bound.

> **Note:** Animating structs such as `CGRect` or `CATransform3D` isn't as straightforward as it is with object values, like you did above. You'll see how to animate structs in Chapter 12, "Keyframe Animations and Struct Properties".

Now that you have the basics nailed down, things are only going to get more interesting! :]

More elaborate layer animations

You've handled the title layer on your login screen; your next task is to take care of the username field.

Scroll to `viewWillAppear()` and remove the following line:

```
username.center.x -= view.bounds.width
```

Then remove the following view animation from the `username` field in `viewDidAppear()`:

```
UIView.animateWithDuration(0.5, delay: 0.3,
usingSpringWithDamping: 0.6, initialSpringVelocity: 0, options:
.CurveEaseOut, animations: {
  self.username.center.x += self.view.bounds.width
}, completion: nil)
```

Before you rush through and blindly copy and paste the code to create a `CABasicAnimation` for the username field, consider the following two facts:

1. A `CABasicAnimation` object is just a data model, which *is **not** bound* to any particular layer.
2. `addAnimation(_:forKey:)` *makes a* **copy** of the animation object.

It turns out that you can simply take the animation from your heading layer, adjust the animation a bit if needed and reuse it to animate your `username` field onto the screen.

Add the following code in the same spot where you deleted the code above in `viewDidAppear()`:

```
username.layer.addAnimation(flyRight, forKey: nil)
```

Build and run your project to see the resulting effect of re-using your layer animation:

Well, the animation runs, but the title and username field slide onto the screen like those oh-so-unpopular synchronized kill-bots. You'll need to recreate the timing offset you had in the original animation.

Add the following line just **before** the line where you add the `flyRight` animation to your `username` layer:

```
flyRight.beginTime = CACurrentMediaTime() + 0.3
```

The `beginTime` property of your animation sets the absolute time the animation should start; in this case you get the current time with `CACurrentMediaTime()` and add to it the desired delay in seconds.

Build and run your app again to see how things look; it appears in the center of the screen, as it was designed in Interface Builder, and starts animating `0.3` seconds later. What gives?

It's time to learn about another layer animation property called `fillMode`; below are a few examples of how this property works.

Using fillMode

The `fillMode` property lets you control the behavior of your animation at the beginning and end of its sequence.

The constant `kCAFillModeRemoved` is the default value of `fillMode`. This starts the animation at the defined `beginTime` – or instantly, if you haven't set a `beginTime` – and removes layer change from the screen when the animation completes:

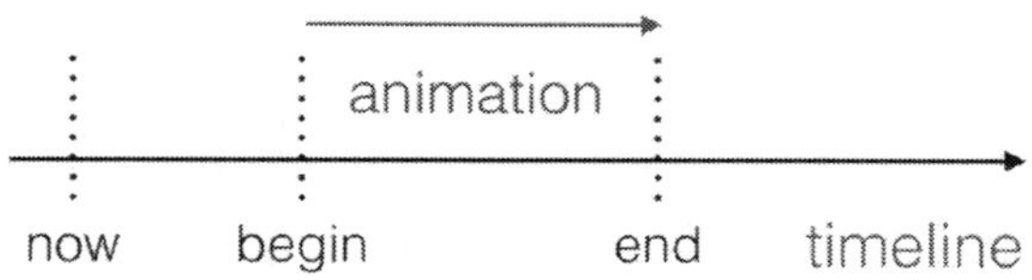

This is the approach you've used so far in this chapter. There are three other options in addition to `kCAFillModeRemoved` that you can use in your animations:

kCAFillModeBackwards

`kCAFillModeBackwards` displays the first frame of your animation instantly on the screen, regardless of the actual start time of the animation, and starts the animation at a later time:

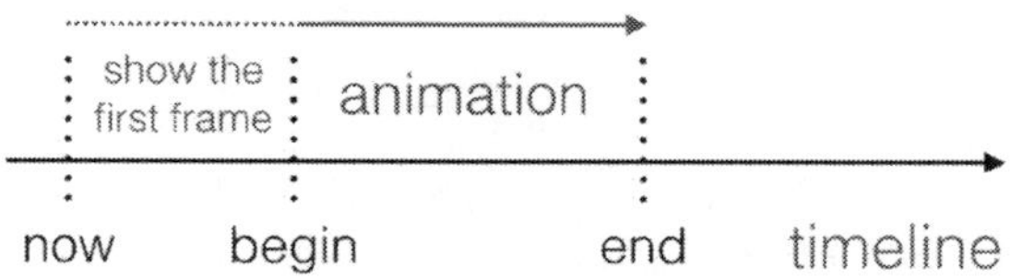

kCAFillModeForwards

`kCAFillModeForwards` plays the animation as usual, but retains the final frame of the animation on the screen until you remove the animation:

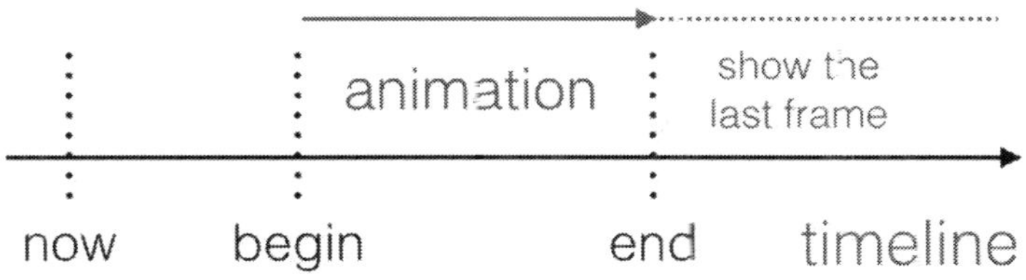

In addition to setting `kCAFillModeForwards`, you'll need to make some other changes to the layer to get the last frame to "stick" – you'll learn about this a little later in the chapter.

kCAFillModeBoth

`kCAFillModeBoth` is a combination of `kCAFillModeForwards` and `kCAFillModeBackwards`; as you'd expect, this makes the first frame of the animation appear on the screen immediately and retains the final frame on the screen when the animation is finished:

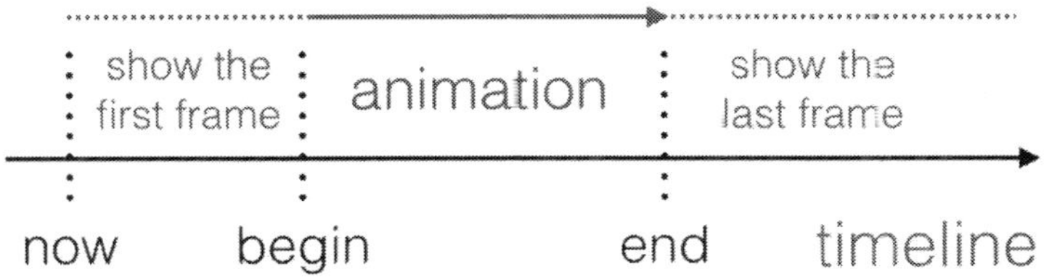

To fix the issue you discovered earlier, you'll use `kCAFillModeBoth`.

Add the following line of code to where you set up `flyRight` (`fromValue`, `toValue`, `duration`, etc.) and before you add it to a layer:

```
flyRight.fillMode = kCAFillModeBoth
```

Build and run your project; you'll see that the `username` field doesn't appear at first and the animation only starts after a `0.3` second delay. Also, the fields remain in position when the animation completes.

You can now animate your `password` field in a similar fashion. Remove the following line from `viewWillAppear()` :

```
password.center.x -= view.bounds.width
```

Then find and remove the following code in `viewDidAppear()`:

```
UIView.animateWithDuration(0.5, delay: 0.4, options:
.CurveEaseOut, animations: {
  self.password.center.x += self.view.bounds.width
}, completion: nil)
```

...and replace it with the following code:

```
flyRight.beginTime = CACurrentMediaTime() + 0.4
password.layer.addAnimation(flyRight, forKey: nil)
```

Build and run your project; you'll see all three layers flying in, with the password field arriving just a tenth of a second behind the username field:

So far, your animations have happened to end at the exact position where the form elements were originally positioned in Interface Builder. However, many times this won't be the case. In the next section of this chapter, you'll discover how to handle the situation where layers end at a different position – and you'll learn how to debug your animations along the way!

Debugging basic animations

Head into `viewWillAppear()` and add the following code to the end of the method (just for testing purposes in this section):

```
username.layer.position.x -= view.bounds.width
password.layer.position.x -= view.bounds.width
```

Now the `username` and `password` layers are initially located outside of the screen bounds. That means you can remove the following line from `viewDidAppear()` that sets `fromValue`:

```
~~flyRight.fromValue = -view.bounds.size.width/2~~
```

You might think that this new code wouldn't affect anything, but build and run your project to see what happens:

Hey – what's going on? All the form elements animate as they did before, but the `username` and `password` fields disappear at the end of the animation without a trace!

You'll need to debug the app in order to find out what's happening with your UI.

Add the following code to the end of `viewWillAppear()`:

```
delay(seconds: 5.0, completion: {
  print("where are the fields?")
})
```

`delay(seconds:completion:)` is a little function included in the starter project; it simply executes the closure expression after a given delay.

Next, add a breakpoint to that println statement so that you'll be dropped into the debugger 5 seconds after the view appears.

To add a breakpoint to your code, just click on the gutter of your editing pane and a blue indicator will show up on that line to represent your breakpoint:

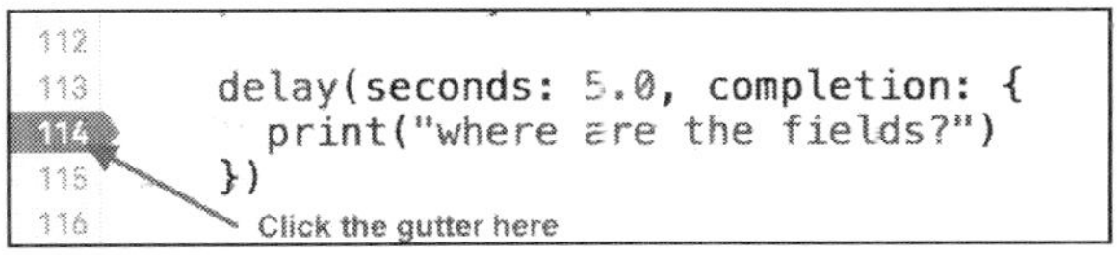

The line numbers you see in your project might differ from the ones in the screenshot above. Just be sure to set the breakpoint on the line that prints the message.

Now run the project and wait. When execution reaches the line with the breakpoint, the Xcode window will jump in front of the iPhone Simulator and show you the position where you set the breakpoint:

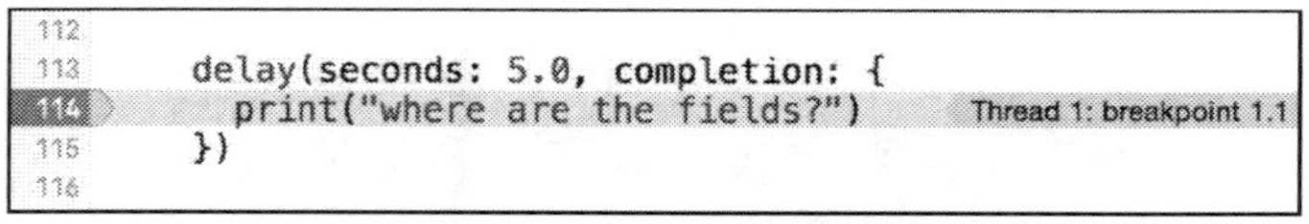

You are not interested in the code *per se*; instead, you need to debug the UI of your application and find out what happened to the missing text fields.

Find the Debug Navigator on the left hand side of the Xcode window; it will show you the current app memory footprint and CPU usage. If you don't see the Debug Navigator, ensure the 6th tab on the right is selected as shown below:

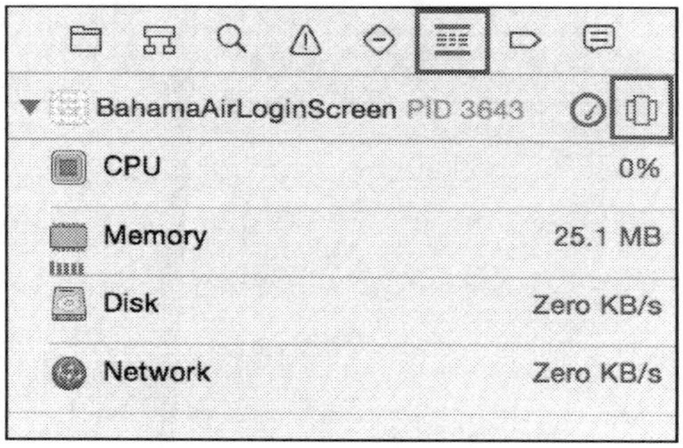

Next, click the second button to the right as indicated in the above; the button icon might differ for you, but it will still appear in the same position. You'll see a list of debugging modes available to you:

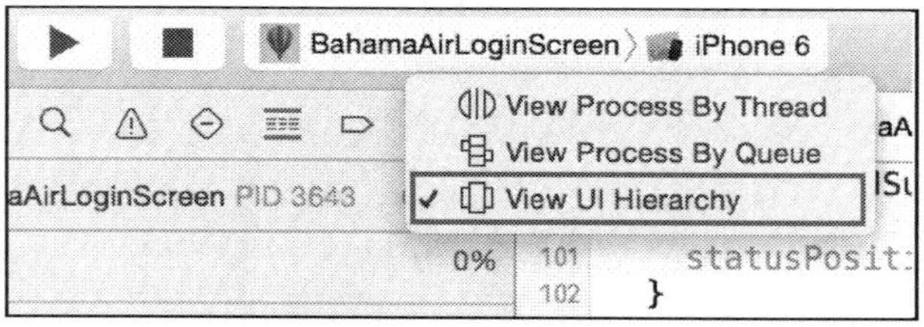

Click **View UI Hierarchy** to open the UI debugger:

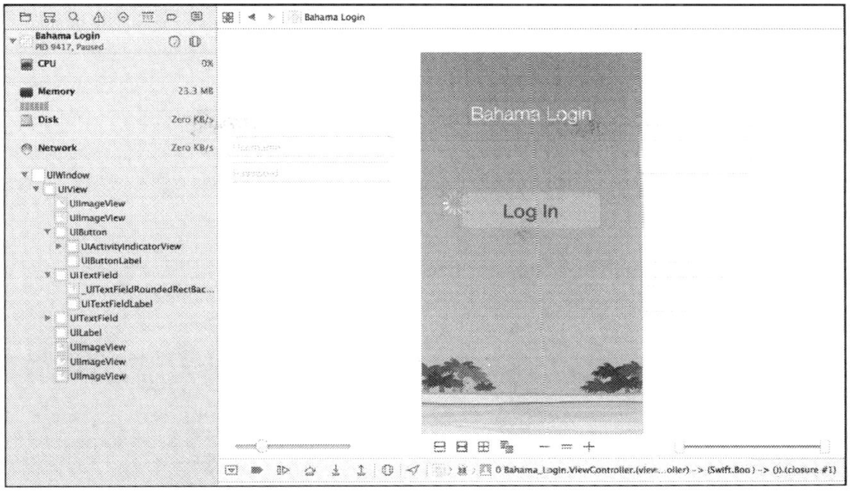

You'll see the UI hierarchy on the left hand side of the UI debugger, with the current runtime layout displayed in the center of the screen, including any hidden or transparent views as well as views outside the screen bounds.

For example you can see the spinner view inside the login button, which is at the time the breakpoint fired hidden but you can still see it in the debug view.

Let's look for the text fields now...

Aha – there are those pesky fields; they're outside of the visible screen area. Select a field to inspect its live properties in the Object Inspector (and further field properties in the Size Inspector in the next tab):

Your code change caused the fields to jump back to their initial position once the animation completed. But...why?

The answer to that lies in the next section, where you'll learn about the difference between your real UI elements and the animations on screen. You can click on the blue breakpoint to disable it so you can keep on running the project without breaks.

Animations vs. real content

When you animate a text field, you're not actually seeing the field itself animated; instead, you're seeing a cached version of it known as the **presentation layer.** The presentation layer is removed from the screen once the animation completes and the original layer shows itself again.

To start, remember you're setting the text field to be positioned off screen in `viewWillAppear`:

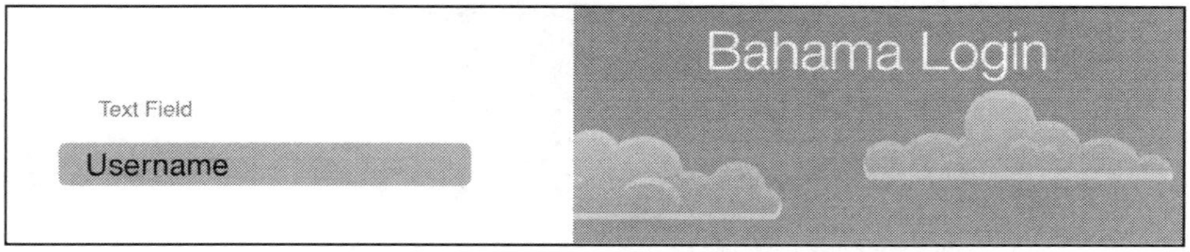

When the animation starts, a pre-rendered animation object replaces the field and the original text field is temporarily hidden:

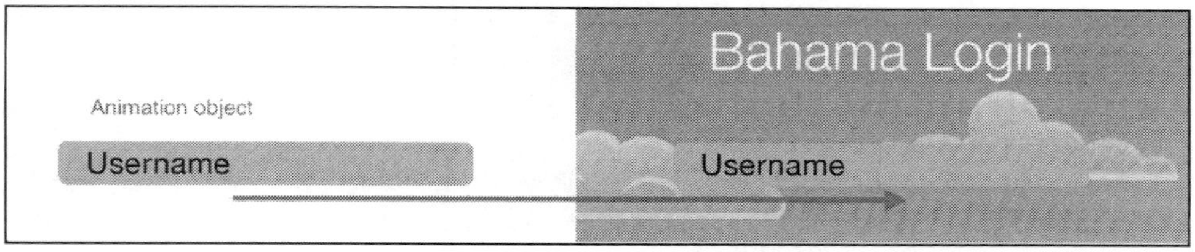

You can't tap the animated field, enter any text or engage any other specific text field functionality, because it's *not* the real text field, just a "phantom" visible representation.

As soon as the animation completes, it disappears from the screen and the original text field is un-hidden. The text field is right where you left it: off screen to the left!

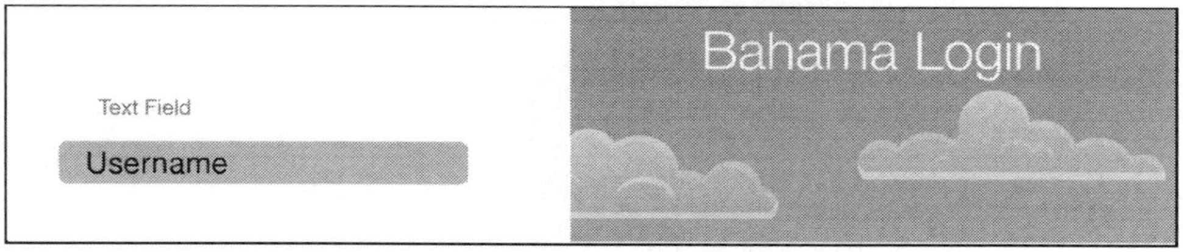

To solve this conundrum, you'll need to use another `CABasicAnimation` property: `removedOnCompletion`.

Setting `fillMode` to `kCAFillModeBoth` instructs your animation to remain on screen after it completes and also show the animation's first frame before its start. To complete the effect, you'll need to set `removedOnCompletion` accordingly; the combination of the two will leave the animation visible on the screen.

Add the following line to `viewDidAppear()`, just after you set the `fillMode`:

```
flyRight.removedOnCompletion = false
```

`removedOnCompletion` is `true` by default, so the animation disappears as soon as it completes. Setting it to `false` and combining it with the proper `fillMode` keeps the animation on the screen – and visible as well.

Build and run your project now; you should see that all elements remain on the screen as expected once the animation completes:

Success! Now tap on the username field to enter your username...oh, wait. Remember the earlier note about the difference between the actual text field and the presentation layer? You can't do anything with this pre-rendered image of a text field!

To complete the desired effect, you'll need to remove the animation and show the real text field in its place.

Updating the layer model

Once you remove a layer animation from the screen, the layer falls back to its current values for position and other properties. This means that you'll usually need to update the properties of your layer to reflect the final values of your animation.

Remove the line below from your project:

```
flyRight.removedOnCompletion = false
```

Although you know how `removedOnCompletion` works when set to `false`, you should try to avoid it whenever possible. Leaving animations on the screen is a drag on performance, so you'll let them be removed automatically and just update the original layer's position instead.

Next, find the line of code that adds the animation to username in `viewDidAppear()` and add the following line after it:

```
username.layer.position.x = view.bounds.size.width/2
```

Add the code for the `password` field – find the line that adds the animation to `password` and add the following line after it:

```
password.layer.position.x = view.bounds.size.width/2
```

This will set the actual layers to be positioned in the middle of the screen where they belong.

Build and run your project; but wait – the fields have stopped animating altogether! What's going on?

You removed the line that sets `fromValue` some time ago, but the code above updates the main layer's position; this causes the animation to start from the center of the screen.

To fix this, add the following line just after you initialize `flyRight` and set its `toValue`:

```
flyRight.fromValue = -view.bounds.size.width/2
```

Build and run your project again, and this time you'll see the fields animate as expected.

> **Note**: If the keyboard doesn't appear when you tap on a text field in the Simulator, you can activate it manually by navigating the menu to Hardware\Keyboard\Toggle Software Keyboard.

When possible, design your layers in Interface Builder with their final values, and use `fromValue` for the starting and in-between values. This reduces the complexity of keeping your model and presentation layers in sync.

Best practice

Whoa – this was a long chapter! You tried out a ton of different layer animation techniques – and that's just the start!

At this point you might be feeling a bit overwhelmed and asking yourself "Should I use `fillMode`? Should I be removing my animations? And how do I update my layer to have smooth animation completion?"

As a rule of thumb – remove your animations and consider never using `fillMode`, except if the effect you want to achieve is not possible otherwise. `fillMode` makes your UI elements lose their interactivity and also makes the screen not reflect the actual values in your layer object.

In some rare cases when you animate non-interactive visual elements `fillMode` will save your bacon – more about this in Chapter 16, "Replicating animations."

As for updating your layer properties – consider always doing it right after you add the animation to your layer. Sometimes you might get the odd flash between the initial and final animation values – in this case, try updating your layer property to the final animation value even before adding the animation.

Challenges

You covered a lot of ground in this chapter; if you want to really test that you've retained all of the concepts covered in each section feel free to take on the challenges below.

Refer back to the various sections if you need some assistance, but if you've followed along with the exercises in this chapter, you're more than capable of working through each of the three challenges in this chapter! :]

Challenge 1: Fade in the clouds with layer animations

In this challenge, you'll replace the UIKit cloud animations from Chapter 1, "Getting Started with View Animations" with layer animations instead.

If you need a recipe to follow, the steps below should give you a good starting point:

1. Remove the four UIKit animations that fade in `cloud1`, `cloud2`, `cloud3`, and `cloud4` from `viewDidAppear()`.
2. Remove the four lines from `viewWillAppear()` that set the clouds' `alpha` property to `0.0`.
3. At the bottom of `viewWillAppear()`, create a `CABasicAnimation` with `opacity` as the keypath.
4. Set `fromValue` to `0.0`, `toValue` to `1.0`, and `duration` to `0.5`. You'll need to set `fillMode` to `kCAFillModeBackwards` to hide the clouds when the app starts.
5. Set the `animation`'s `beginTime` to `CACurrentMediaTime() + 0.5` and add the animation to `cloud1`.
6. Set the `animation`'s `beginTime` to `CACurrentMediaTime() + 0.7` and add the animation to `cloud2`.
7. Set the `animation`'s `beginTime` to `CACurrentMediaTime() + 0.9` and add the animation to `cloud3`.
8. Set the `animation`'s `beginTime` to `CACurrentMediaTime() + 1.1` and add the animation to `cloud4`.

The end result should recreate the initial cloud transition with layer animations as shown below:

Challenge 2: Animating colors

In this challenge you'll re-create the login button tint animation.

First, remove your old UIKit code as shown below:

```
self.loginButton.backgroundColor = UIColor(red: 0.85, green: 0.83,
blue: 0.45, alpha: 1.0)
```

Then scroll down to `resetForm()` and remove the following line:

```
self.loginButton.backgroundColor = UIColor(red: 0.63, green: 0.84,
blue: 0.35, alpha: 1.0)
```

Create a new top-level function in **ViewController.swift** (e.g. a top-level function will be located outside of the class body – add it below the `delay` function):

```
func tintBackgroundColor(#layer: CALayer, toColor: UIColor)
```

In this new method, create a basic animation and run it on the `layer` parameter, keeping in mind these key requirements:

- Animate the `backgroundColor` property.
- Set `fromValue` to the current background color: `layer.backgroundColor`.
- Set `toValue` to `toColor.CGColor`; Core Animation uses `CGColor` values for colors.
- Set the animation `duration` for `1.0` second.
- Add the animation to `layer`.
- Don't forget to set the `backgroundColor` property on the layer itself so it retains the final animation color.

Now that `tintBackgroundColor` is complete, you can use it on your login button. To do that add, the following code to the very bottom of `login()`:

```
let tintColor = UIColor(red: 0.85, green: 0.83, blue: 0.45, alpha:
1.0)
tintBackgroundColor(layer: loginButton.layer,
 toColor: tintColor)
```

Build and run your project; you'll see the button change its tint as soon as you tap it:

Now find the call to `animateWithDuration()` within `resetForm()` and replace `completion: nil` with the following code:

```
completion: {_ in
  let tintColor = UIColor(red: 0.63, green: 0.84, blue: 0.35,
alpha: 1.0)
  self.tintBackgroundColor(layer: self.loginButton.layer,
    toColor: tintColor)
}
```

This will tint the button back to green when the animation is complete.

As an added bonus, since your new function `tintBackgroundColor` is a top-level function, you can re-use it anywhere you like in your project!

Challenge 3: Animating corner radius

In this challenge you won't recreate one of your existing view animations; instead, you'll animate the layer specific property `cornerRadius`.

Just like you did in Challenge 2 above, create the following new top-level function in **ViewController.swift**:

```
func roundCorners(#layer: CALayer, #toRadius: CGFloat)
```

This method will take a `layer` parameter and run a basic animation on it that animates the corner radius from its current value to the supplied `toRadius`.

Simply repeat the routine from Challenge 2, but follow these requirements instead:

- Animate the `cornerRadius` property.
- Set `toValue` to `toRadius`.
- Set the animation `duration` to `0.33` seconds.
- Add the animation to `layer`.
- Don't forget to set the `cornerRadius` on the layer.

Once you've completed `roundCorners()`, add the following line to the bottom of `login()`:

```
roundCorners(layer: loginButton.layer, toRadius: 25.0)
```

This should round the button when you tap it. To reverse the effect when the authentication process is done, add the following code to `resetForm()` after the call to `tintBackgroundColor`:

```
roundCorners(layer: self.loginButton.layer, toRadius: 10.0)
```

Build and run your project; you'll see the button appear with its initial color and corner radius:

Now tap the button to see it change in shape and color:

Once all animations complete, the button will return to its initial color and corner radius.

That's it for this chapter; by now you have a solid understanding of how to create basic layer animations, which is the perfect starting point to tackle the animation keys and delegate methods in the next chapter!

Chapter 9: Animation Keys and Delegates

One of the tricky parts about UIKit animations and the corresponding closure syntax is that once you create and run a view animation you can't pause it, stop it, or access it in any way.

With Core Animation, however, you can easily inspect animations that are running on a layer and stop them if you need to.

Furthermore, you can even set a delegate object on your animations and react to animation events. In contrast to the completion block you've seen in UIView animations, you can receive delegate callbacks for when an animation begins and ends (or is interrupted).

In this chapter you'll continue to work with the Bahama Air login project and use animation delegates to make your animations more interactive.

Introducing animation delegates

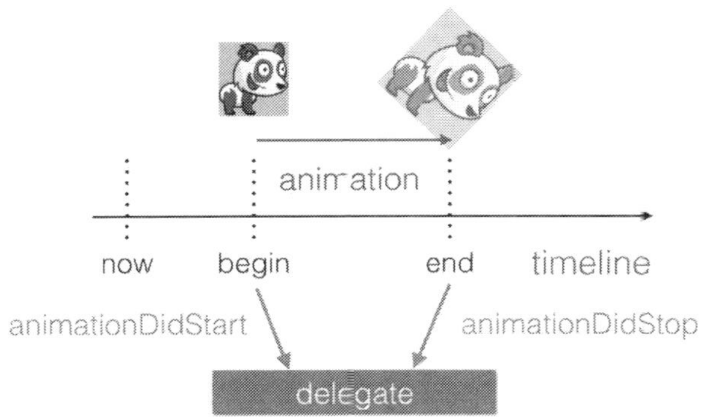

`CAAnimation` and its subclass `CABasicAnimation` implement the delegate pattern and let you respond to animation events.

`CAAnimation` doesn't have a specific protocol that its delegates must implement; rather, every instance of `NSObject` already implements the following two animation delegate methods that you can override as needed:

```
func animationDidStart(anim: CAAnimation)
func animationDidStop(anim: CAAnimation, finished flag: Bool)
```

This isn't the usual way of handling delegation in UIKit or Cocoa, but in this case this is just the way things work. Check the headers of the `CoreAnimation` module and you'll see that it defines the two above delegate methods in an extension to `NSObject`.

You can either open the starter project for this chapter, or carry on with your own project if you've completed the previous chapter and its challenges.

Your first task is to make each form element pulse once when it reaches its final position on the screen using `animationDidStop()`.

Open **ViewController.swift** and add the following code to `viewDidAppear()`, just before the line where you add the animation to your `heading` layer:

```
flyRight.delegate = self
```

Then add the delegate method to the class:

```
override func animationDidStop(anim: CAAnimation, finished flag:
Bool) {
  print("animation did finish")
}
```

This simply prints out a line to the console to show that you are, in fact, calling your delegate method.

Build and run your project; you should see the following output in the Xcode console:

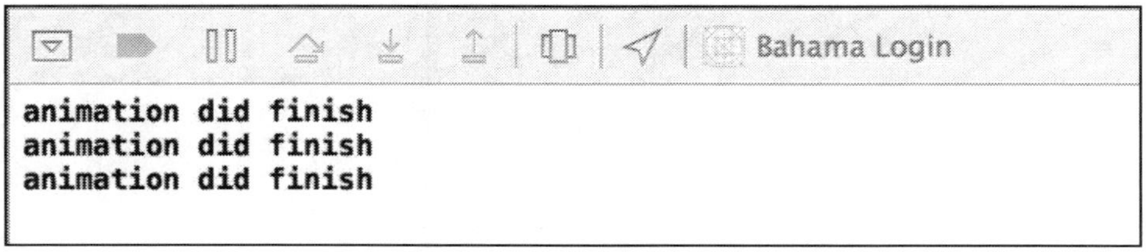

Okay, so your delegates are being called – but how do you discern *which* animation stopped in the code above? Remember, you added the same animation to three different layers! The following section shows you how to manage this with key-value pairs.

Key-value coding compliance

The CAAnimation class and its subclasses are key-value coding compliant, which means you can treat them like dictionaries and add new properties to them at run time.

You'll use this mechanism to assign a name to the flyRight animation so that you can identify it out of the pack of other active animations.

Scroll back to viewDidAppear() and add the following code just after the line where you set flyright's delegate:

```
flyRight.setValue("form", forKey: "name")
flyRight.setValue(heading.layer, forKey: "layer")
```

In the code above, you create the key name on the flyRight animation and set it to form. Now you can check for this name key from your delegate callbacks to identify the animation as belonging to one of your form controls.

You also assign heading.layer to the layer key so you have a reference back to the layer the animation belongs to.

You can leave the name unchanged, but you should update the layer key each time you add the animation to a layer.

Find the line where you add the animation to the username layer, and add the following just before it:

```
flyRight.setValue(username.layer, forKey: "layer")
```

Similarly, find the line where you add the animation to the password layer, and add the following just before it:

```
flyRight.setValue(password.layer, forKey: "layer")
```

Now each copy of flyRight carries a reference to the layer on which it runs.

Switching on key values

Now that you have the keys set on your animation, you can check for them in the animation delegate methods.

Add the following code to the bottom of animationDidStop:

```
if let name = anim.valueForKey("name") as? String {
  if name == "form" {
    //form field found
  }
}
```

In the code above you use valueForKey() to get the value of name from the animation and attempt to cast the value to String. This returns an optional value as the running animation might or might not have a key called name, which might or might not contain a string value! :]

The optional binding statement takes care of these checks for you. If you can unwrap the value, then you have a value you can test for. If not, then your code carries on.

Now you have a spot to run some code when the form animation completes. Replace the comments //form field found with the following:

```
let layer = anim.valueForKey("layer") as? CALayer
anim.setValue(nil, forKey: "layer")

let pulse = CABasicAnimation(keyPath: "transform.scale")
pulse.fromValue = 1.25
pulse.toValue = 1.0
pulse.duration = 0.25
layer?.addAnimation(pulse, forKey: nil)
```

Note that valueForKey() always returns an AnyObject?; therefore you must cast the result to your desired type. Don't forget that the cast operation can fail, so you must use optionals in the example above to handle error conditions, such as when the name key exists but the layer key does not.

Once that's done, you set the value of layer to nil to remove the reference to the original layer.

Finally, you create an animation that bumps the scale of the layer by a tiny bit (a factor of 1.25), then animates the layer back to its original size (a factor of 1.0).

Note that you're using optional chaining here with layer? – that means the addAnimation call will be skipped if there isn't a layer stored in the animation. And since you set the layer to nil earlier, this pulse animation will only happen the first time the form field flies in from the right.

Build and run your project; you should see that any time a flyRight animation completes, the element will pulse once before it comes to rest:

This gives the animations a nice edge and draws the user's attention to these controls.

That takes care of animations that have already stopped; but how can you work with animations that are *still running*? That's where **animation keys** come in.

Animation Keys

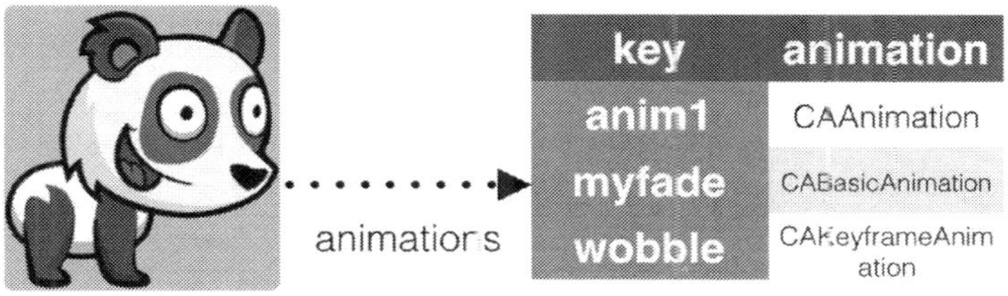

You've probably noticed that `addAnimation(_:key:)` has two parameters; so far, you've only been using the first to pass in the animation object itself.

The `key` parameter is a string identifier that lets you access and control the animation after it's been started.

In this part you'll create another layer animation, learn how to run more than one animation at a time, and discover how to use animation keys to control running animations.

You're going to add a new animated label to your form that gives some basic instructions to the user, as shown below:

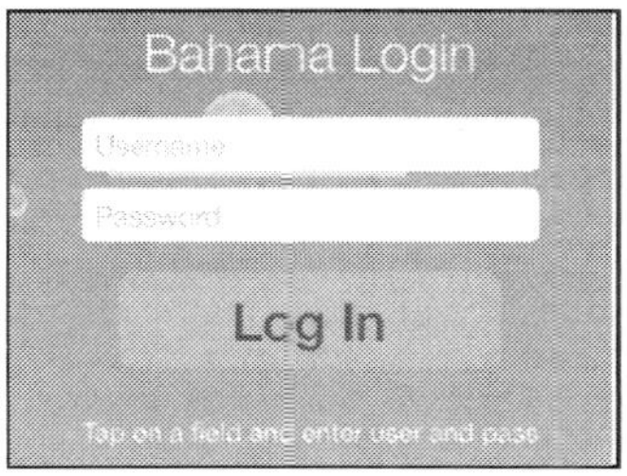

Your new label will animate slowly from right to left. As soon as the user starts to enter their username or password, this label will stop moving and jump directly to its final position; there's no need to continue the animation once the user knows what to do.

First you'll need to add some code that sets up the label to animate. Add the following property to the end of the property declarations at the top of `ViewController`:

```
let info = UILabel()
```

This is the property for your new label; you initialize it right away so you don't need to declare it as an optional type.

Next, add the following code to the bottom of `viewDidLoad` to set up the various properties of your label:

```
info.frame = CGRect(x: 0.0, y: loginButton.center.y + 60.0,
  width: view.frame.size.width, height: 30)
info.backgroundColor = UIColor.clearColor()
info.font = UIFont(name: "HelveticaNeue", size: 12.0)
info.textAlignment = .Center
info.textColor = UIColor.whiteColor()
info.text = "Tap on a field and enter username and password"
view.insertSubview(info, belowSubview: loginButton)
```

This adds the label just underneath the login button. When the user taps the login button, it will move down and cover the instructions, since the user won't need them anymore.

Now you need to slide the instructions in from the right when the app first opens. Find `viewDidAppear()` and add the following code to the end of that method:

```
let flyLeft = CABasicAnimation(keyPath: "position.x")
flyLeft.fromValue = info.layer.position.x +
  view.frame.size.width
flyLeft.toValue = info.layer.position.x
```

```
flyLeft.duration = 5.0
info.layer.addAnimation(flyLeft, forKey: "infoappear")
```

This animates your label much like your form fields, only your label will slide in from the right side of the screen and fly to the left. Note that you set the animation's key to `infoappear`; you'll use this value to find and then stop the animation when the user starts to enter text in either the username or password field.

Adding a second layer animation

You'll now add a second animation to the label that will fade in the instructions while the label slides in.

Add the following code to the end of `viewDidAppear`:

```
let fadeLabelIn = CABasicAnimation(keyPath: "opacity")
fadeLabelIn.fromValue = 0.2
fadeLabelIn.toValue = 1.0
fadeLabelIn.duration = 4.5
info.layer.addAnimation(fadeLabelIn, forKey: "fadein")
```

The code above fades in the label from a barely visible opacity of `0.2` to a fully visible opacity of `1.0`. The above animation runs on a different property – `opacity` – than the previous animation you added – `position` – and has an entirely different duration. This shows you it's possible to run multiple animations independently of each other on the same layer.

> **Note**: If you need to synchronize animations on a layer, then you'll need to use **animation groups** to achieve this; this technique is covered in the next chapter.

Run the project to see the combined animations in action:

So far, so good. Now comes the tricky part – cancelling the animation if the user starts to enter their username or password.

Identifying running animations

You'll need to know when the user taps on either the username or password field. Add the following to the very bottom of **ViewController.swift**, outside the class definition:

```
extension ViewController: UITextFieldDelegate {
  func textFieldDidBeginEditing(textField: UITextField) {
    print(info.layer.animationKeys())
  }
}
```

This will add a class extension to say `ViewController` conforms to the `UITextFieldDelegate` protocol. Separating protocols into their own extensions like this helps keep the file organized.

The one method you need to implement, `textFieldDidBeginEditing`, will be called when the user starts editing a text field. For now, you'll just print out a list of all the active animations running on the label.

Next, add the following code to the bottom of `viewDidAppear`:

```
username.delegate = self
password.delegate = self
```

This will make the class a delegate of both text fields.

Build and run your project; tap either the username or password field before the label animation completes and you should see the following output in your Xcode console:

Success! Once you know which animations are running, you can do several things with them:

1. Call `removeAllAnimations()` on the layer to stop all running animations or `removeAnimationForKey(_:)` to remove just one.

2. Enumerate over the list of animations returned by `animationKeys()`. The animation objects are immutable, so you can't modify the animation while they're in progress.

3. Fetch an animation by key using `animationForKey(_:)`. As before, the returned animation object will be immutable.

To finish your "stop animation" effect, you'll cancel the animation that moves the label, but leave the fade animation running as it would look weird for the opacity of the label to jump directly to `1.0`.

Add the following code to `textFieldDidBeginEditing`:

```
info.layer.removeAnimationForKey("infoappear")
```

This removes the slide-in animation and causes the `info` label to jump straight to the center of the screen – without affecting the fade-in animation.

Build and run your project one final time; tap either of the text fields and you'll see the instructions jump straight to the center of the screen and continue to fade in:

That's a wrap! You've learned about delegate methods, accessing animations by keys, and created your first composite layer animation as an added bonus! :]

Why not test your knowledge with the following challenge?

Challenge

In this challenge you'll strengthen your knowledge of animation delegates and key-value coding of animation objects by replacing the existing cloud animation with layer animations.

Replace the `animateCloud(cloud: UIImageView)` method with the following:

```
func animateCloud(layer: CALayer) {
  //1
  let cloudSpeed = 60.0 / Double(view.layer.frame.size.width)
  let duration: NSTimeInterval =
Double(view.layer.frame.size.width - layer.frame.origin.x) *
cloudSpeed

  //2
  let cloudMove = CABasicAnimation(keyPath: "position.x")
  cloudMove.duration = duration
  cloudMove.toValue = self.view.bounds.size.width +
layer.bounds.width/2
  cloudMove.delegate = self
  cloudMove.setValue("cloud", forKey: "name")
  cloudMove.setValue(layer, forKey: "layer")

  layer.addAnimation(cloudMove, forKey: nil)
}
```

This method has a similar implementation to the one that animates the clouds using UIKit. In fact, the first few lines of part `//1` above are almost identical to the UIKit implementation.

In the second part of the above method you create an instance of `CABasicAnimation` for the layer movement and set a name and layer on the animation.

Next, replace the calls in `viewDidAppear()` to `animateCloud()` with the following:

```
animateCloud(cloud1.layer)
animateCloud(cloud2.layer)
animateCloud(cloud3.layer)
animateCloud(cloud4.layer)
```

Your task now is to complete the animation by implementing the delegate code to reset each of the clouds.

You already know how to do this through `animationDidStop(_: finished:)`. Just follow these key points:

- Check if the animation name is "cloud".

- If so – fetch the animation's layer from the "layer" key.
- Set the layer's `position.x` to `-layer.bounds.width/2`.
- Wait for half a second (use the `delay()` function) and call `self.animateCloud()`, passing in the current layer.

Build and run your project; check that the clouds reappear once they've left the screen:

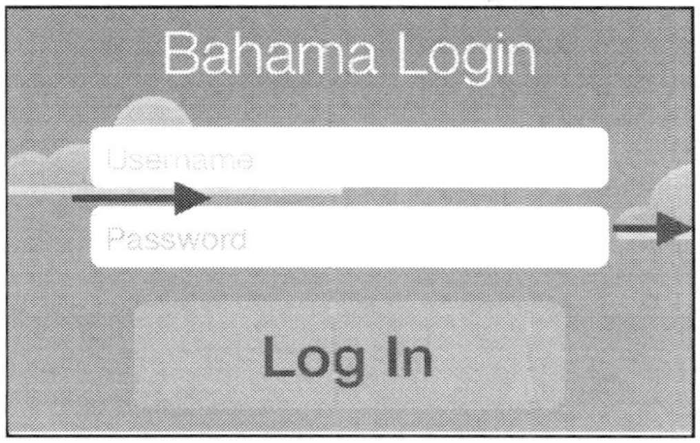

Congratulations – you've learned the basic layer animation techniques and are ready to move on to creating more complex animations. You'll learn about animation groups next in Chapter 10, "Groups and advanced timing".

Chapter 10: Groups and Advanced Timing

In the previous chapter you learned how to add multiple, independent animations to a single layer. But what if you want your animations to work synchronously and stay in step with each other? It's no fun having to fiddle with the math and timings of all the animations separately. That's where **animation groups** come in.

This chapter shows you how to group animations using `CAAnimationGroup`, which lets you add several animations to a group and adjust properties such as `duration`, `delegate`, and `timingFunction` all at once.

Grouping animations results in simplified code, and ensures that all your animations will synchronize as one, solid unit.

CAAnimationGroup

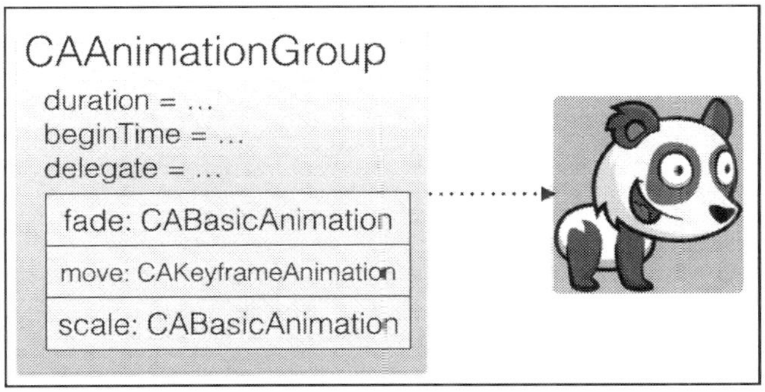

To start off, you'll extend your Bahama Air login screen using animation groups to add some new animation to the login button.

Open the starter project for this chapter, or carry on with your project from the previous chapter and challenge.

Open **ViewController.swift** and remove the following code from `viewWillAppear()`:

```
loginButton.center.y += 30.0
loginButton.alpha = 0.0
```

Then remove the following code from `viewDidAppear()`:

```
UIView.animateWithDuration(0.5, delay: 0.5,
usingSpringWithDamping: 0.5, initialSpringVelocity: 0, options:
nil, animations: {
  self.loginButton.center.y -= 30.0
  self.loginButton.alpha = 1.0
}, completion: nil)
```

...and in its place add the following code:

```
let groupAnimation = CAAnimationGroup()
groupAnimation.beginTime = CACurrentMediaTime() + 0.5
groupAnimation.duration = 0.5
groupAnimation.fillMode = kCAFillModeBackwards
```

This code creates a new animation group for your use. `CAAnimationGroup` inherits from `CAAnimation`, so you can work with the same properties you already know and love such as `beginTime`, `duration`, `fillMode`, `delegate`, and `removedOnCompletion`.

You'll add one final animation to the login button to scale, rotate, and fade it in with the end effect that the button falls neatly into place on the screen.

Add the first animation by adding the following code directly below the group animation code you just added:

```
let scaleDown = CABasicAnimation(keyPath: "transform.scale")
scaleDown.fromValue = 3.5
scaleDown.toValue = 1.0
```

In the code above you start with a very large version of the button and, over the course of the animation, shrink it to its normal size.

Here you specify only the `fromValue` and `toValue`, but you don't say what the `duration` of the animation should be nor do you set the `fillMode` of the animation. Where will those values come from?

You might have already guessed that since these values will be the same for all animations in the group, you'll set them on the group as a whole instead of on each animation separately.

Now add code for the next animation below the code you just added:

```
let rotate = CABasicAnimation(keyPath: "transform.rotation")
rotate.fromValue = CGFloat(M_PI_4)
rotate.toValue = 0.0
```

This animation is similar to the previous one, but it animates the `rotation` component of the layer transform instead of the `scale` component. The animation starts with the layer rotated at a 45-degree angle and moves it to its normal orientation of zero degrees.

All that's left to add is the fade-in animation. Add the following code again below the lines you just added:

```
let fade = CABasicAnimation(keyPath: "opacity")
fade.fromValue = 0.0
fade.toValue = 1.0
```

This is the basic fade-in animation you've seen multiple times in this book.

Now add the code below to combine all animations and add them to the button:

```
groupAnimation.animations = [scaleDown, rotate, fade]
loginButton.layer.addAnimation(groupAnimation, forKey: nil)
```

To group animations, you simply add them to an array and assign that array as the value of the `animations` property of the group, just as you would with an ordinary `CABasicAnimation`.

> **Note**: Since `animations` is an immutable array, you can't add the animations one by one; you need to create them all first and then assign them in the array all at once.

Build and run your project to see the end result:

The button flies in and rotates as expected, but the animation looks stiff; in real life, objects tend to accelerate as they fall through space.

Fortunately it's easy to add some realism to your animation; this is a great opportunity to learn about using easing with Core Animation.

Animation easing

You've already seen easing in action in the first chapters of this book that dealt with UIKit animations. Easing in layer animations is conceptually the same thing; only the syntax is different.

`CAMediaTimingFunction` has a few pre-defined easing functions, which you can use by name:

- `kCAMediaTimingFunctionLinear` runs the animation with an equal pace throughout its whole duration.
- `kCAMediaTimingFunctionEaseIn` alters the animation so it starts slower and finishes at a faster pace.

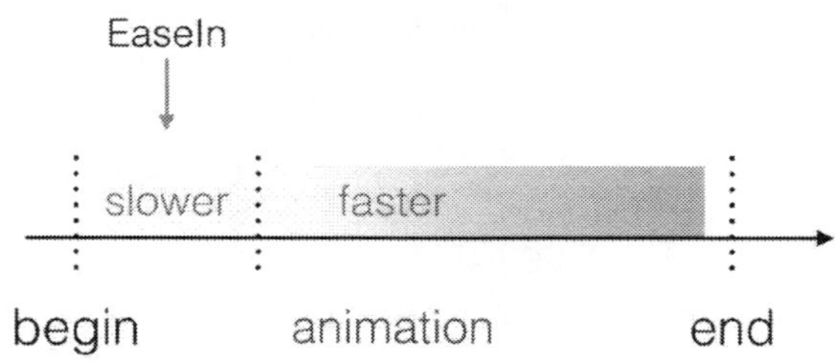

- `kCAMediaTimingFunctionEaseOut` produces the opposite effect of `kCAMediaTimingFunctionEaseIn`; the animations starts out faster and slows down as it finishes.

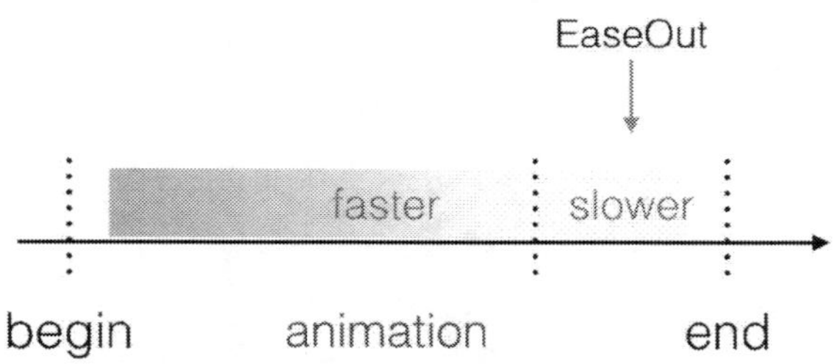

- `kCAMediaTimingFunctionEaseInEaseOut` slows the animation in the beginning and at the end, but increases the pace during the middle section.

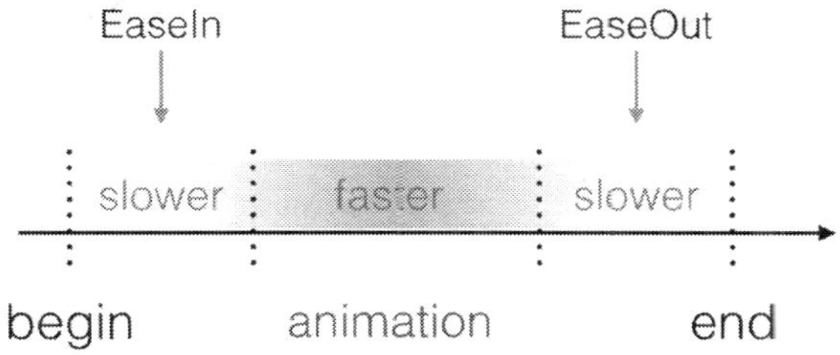

If you think about how objects accelerate as they fall through space, you'll see that you should use an ease-in animation that speeds up towards the end.

Find the piece of code in `viewDidAppear()` where you initialize `groupAnimation` and add the following line after that:

```
groupAnimation.timingFunction = CAMediaTimingFunction(
  name: kCAMediaTimingFunctionEaseIn)
```

This will set the animation easing on your animation group as a whole.

Build and run your project; the change is subtle, but the animation looks more realistic and snappier:

Note: Although it's beyond the scope of this chapter, you can build your own custom easing function.

Read up on the convenience initializer `CAMediaTimingFunction(controlPoints:(float)c1x :(float)c1y :(float)c2x :(float)c2y)` in the Apple documentation or elsewhere on the web; this lets you define your easing function based on the control points of a cubic Bézier curve.

More timing options

The final section of this chapter explores four more animation properties that let you control the timing of your animation.

Repeating animations

`repeatCount` lets you repeat your animation a specified number of times.

To show how this works, you'll make the instructions fly onto the screen repeatedly instead of just once. Find the code in `viewDidAppear()` where you set the properties of the `flyLeft` animation such as duration, and set the number of animation repeats to `4`:

```
flyLeft.repeatCount = 4
```

Build and run your project; you'll see the instructions fly in a total of four times, after which the label remains centered under the login button.

If you want to set the total repeat time in seconds, instead of setting the number of repeats, use the `repeatDuration` property instead of `repeatCount`.

However, the fact that the label flies off the screen each time it repeats looks a little weird. How could you create a fluid, reversing animation to make the label fly off the screen in the exact manner in which it entered?

It's far easier than you might think. Add the following code just after you set the `repeatCount`:

```
flyLeft.autoreverses = true
```

This will run your animation in reverse each time it completes, then run it in forward motion again.

Build and run your project; you'll see the label fly in, then out, then in again, and so forth:

That was easy and cool-looking, but there's still a little imperfection in your animation. The instructions animate four times, but the label then jumps straight to the center of the screen.

This is because a single animation cycle moves the label to the screen center and then out again. So when you run the animation four times, the final cycle ends with the label off the screen. This is why the label appears to jump to the center of the screen. You can't run *half* an animation cycle – or can you? :]

Change the `repeatCount` from `4` to to `2.5` as shown below:

```
flyLeft.repeatCount = 2.5
```

Build and run your project now; you should see the animation finishes smoothly at the precise location you intended:

Changing the animation speed

Although they look nice, some of these animations feel a bit slow. You can control the speed of the animation independently of the duration by setting the `speed` property.

Still in the properties for `flyLeft`, add the following code after the line that sets the `autoreverses` property:

```
flyLeft.speed = 2.0
```

Even though the animation group duration is set to 5 seconds, the animation will complete in just 2.5 seconds since it runs at **double** the speed.

You can set the speed of an animation on its own, but you can also set the speed of a layer as well. The layer conforms to the same timing protocol as an animation: you simply set the `speed` of the layer to affect all animations you run on that layer.

Add the following code after the `flyLeft.speed` line you just added:

```
info.layer.speed = 2.0
```

Build and run your project; the `flyLeft` animation runs at double speed as before – but wait! The animation that moves the `info` label runs at *quadruple speed*! What's going on?

Lesson learned: speeds multiply hierarchically. First you set a speed of `2.0` on the `info` layer, and *then* you set the speed of `flyLeft` to `2.0` as well! You end up with the info layer running at `2.0 x 2.0 = 4.0` times the normal speed.

Just for fun, you can make everything on the screen run super fast by adjusting the `speed` property of the top-level view controller's `layer`. Add the following line underneath the line you just added:

```
view.layer.speed = 2.0
```

Build and run your project; you'll see that the form title, the text fields and even the clouds in the sky are double-stepping their way around the screen.

Due to the multiplication factor of animations, the fade animation on the `info` label runs at 4x speed, and the animation moving the info label across the screen runs at 8x speed! Wheeeee! :]

Now that you've had some fun with your project, delete all the repeating and speed adjustments as shown below:

```
flyLeft.repeatCount = 2.5
flyLeft.autoreverses = true
flyLeft.speed = 2.0
info.layer.speed = 2.0
view.layer.speed = 2.0
```

Playing with animation speeds, reversing and repeating was fun, but your user will likely not appreciate UI elements zipping around the screen like that! :]

But if you do need to adjust animation speeds locally, you can now do so on the animation level as well as for an entire layer.

Challenges

You learned quite a lot of new stuff in this chapter; so instead of having to solve a challenge on your own I'm giving you a free pass and walking you through a few more examples of what you learned above.

The challenge below is optional, but by working through it you'll get some more experience with animation groups – which is never a bad thing! :]

Challenge 1: Group animations for all form elements

In this challenge, you'll create a group of animations and run it on your form elements. Since this code will replace the existing form animations, the first thing you need to do is remove some existing code.

First remove the following code from `viewWillAppear()`:

```
username.layer.position.x -= view.bounds.width
password.layer.position.x -= view.bounds.width
```

Then delete the code block in `viewDidAppear(animated:)` that starts and ends with the two lines below:

```
let flyRight = CABasicAnimation(keyPath: "position.x")
...
...
...
password.layer.position.x = view.bounds.size.width/2
```

There's nothing wrong with all that code; it's simply easier to delete it and start afresh.

To start, create the following animation group in `viewDidAppear`, in the same spot where you just deleted the block of code:

```
let formGroup = CAAnimationGroup()
formGroup.duration = 0.5
formGroup.fillMode = kCAFillModeBackwards
```

This creates your group and sets its duration and fill mode.

Next – define the first animation like so:

```
let flyRight = CABasicAnimation(keyPath: "position.x")
flyRight.fromValue = -view.bounds.size.width/2
flyRight.toValue = view.bounds.size.width/2
```

This animation is identical to the `flyRight` animation you used before; the only difference is that the new animation inherits its duration from the group.

Add the definition for the second animation next:

```
let fadeFieldIn = CABasicAnimation(keyPath: "opacity")
fadeFieldIn.fromValue = 0.25
fadeFieldIn.toValue = 1.0
```

This new animation fades in the elements as they fly into the screen.

To run the animations on the title label, add the following code:

```
formGroup.animations = [flyRight, fadeFieldIn]
heading.layer.addAnimation(formGroup, forKey: nil)
```

Here you set the group's `animations` and run the animation on the `heading` layer. If you build and run your project right now, you'll notice that the form title fades in as it moves to its final position:

Keep up the momentum and finish up the challenge by animating the `username` and `password` fields in a similar manner.

Since you want your animation delegate method to kick in when the group animation completes, you'll need to set the delegate and keys on `formGroup` rather than on the individual animations.

Add the following code after the point where you add the `formGroup` animation to the `heading`'s layer:

```
formGroup.delegate = self
formGroup.setValue("form", forKey: "name")
formGroup.setValue(username.layer, forKey: "layer")
```

Add the following final piece of code to adjust the animation delays and run the animation group on the respective text fields:

```
formGroup.beginTime = CACurrentMediaTime() + 0.3
username.layer.addAnimation(formGroup, forKey: nil)

formGroup.setValue(password.layer, forKey: "layer")
formGroup.beginTime = CACurrentMediaTime() + 0.4
password.layer.addAnimation(formGroup, forKey: nil)
```

Build and run the project once more for a smooth and flawless animation:

When all the animations finish you'll still have the original, beautiful end state of your form fields on the screen:

Working through this challenge gave you some more valuable experience in working with groups and delegates; at this point you're ready to move on to the next chapter and add some bounciness to your layer animations.

Chapter 11: Layer Springs

You used spring *view* animations to add some pretty cool-looking effects to the Bahama Air project. Now it's time to learn how to create spring animations for layers! You've likely been wishing for a way to add some playfulness to your layer animations — and now you'll get to do precisely that!

Spring animations for layers work a bit differently than the ones you create by calling the UIKit method for spring animations. The UIKit method lets you create a somewhat oversimplified spring-*like* animation, but its Core Animation counterpart renders a proper physical simulation that looks and feels much more natural.

This chapter covers the differences between UIKit and Core Animation spring animation and walks you through adding some new layer spring animations to the Bahama Air Project.

First though, you're going to bounce through a bit of theory! :]

Damped harmonic oscillators

Damped Harmonic What?

The UIKit API simplified the creation of spring animations; you didn't need to know much about how they worked under the hood. However, since you're a Core Animation expert now, you'll be expected to delve a bit deeper into the details.

Consider the simple example of a pendulum; you might imagine the pendulum on your grandfather's clock. It's too tall for the shelf, so has stood 90 years on the floor.

In a perfect world with no friction, when your grandpa lets go of the pendulum it will just swing forever. Tick, tock, tick, tock, tick, tock…:

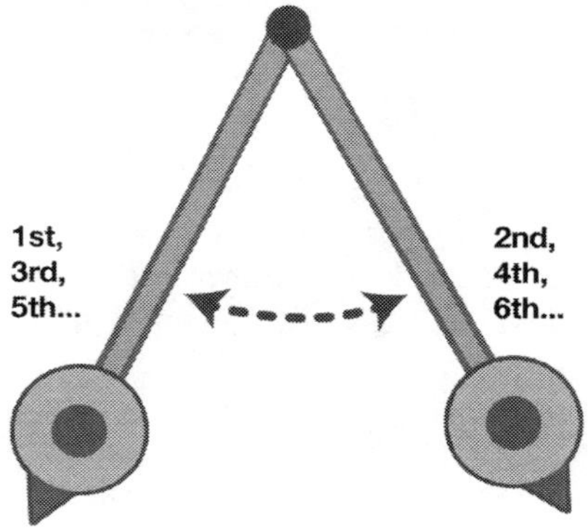

If grandpa were to attach a frictionless pen to the pendulum and slowly slide a sheet of paper underneath, he'd see a graph similar to the following:

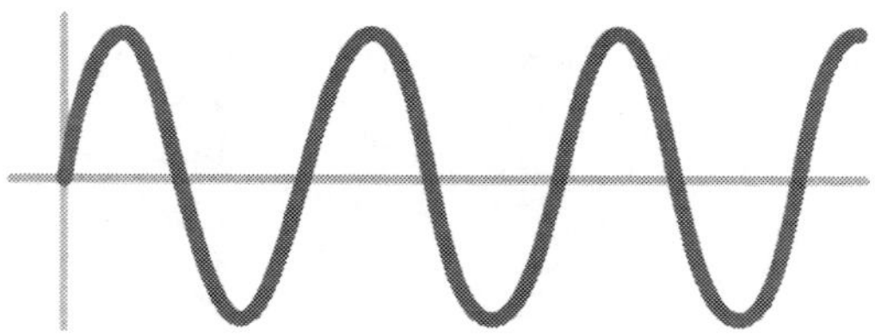

This is an example of a **harmonic oscillator**: the pendulum moves back and forth (or *oscillates*) by equal amounts about its equilibrium point (the point where the pendulum sits when it's at rest). Without friction, the pendulum would keep swinging forever.

In the real world, however, the system loses energy due to friction and ultimately settles at its equilibrium point:

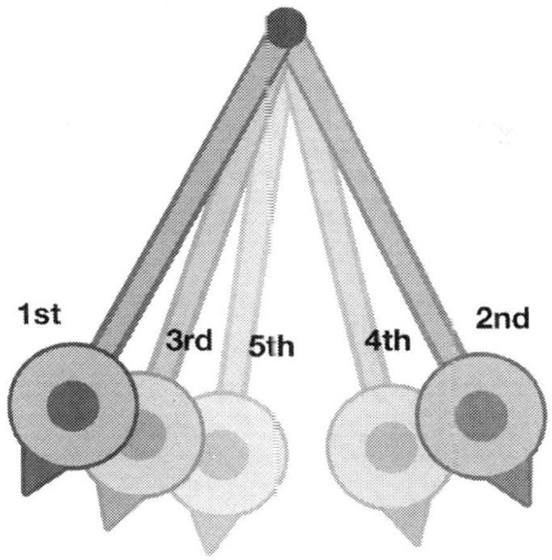

If grandpa slid a piece of paper underneath the pendulum now the graph would look much like this:

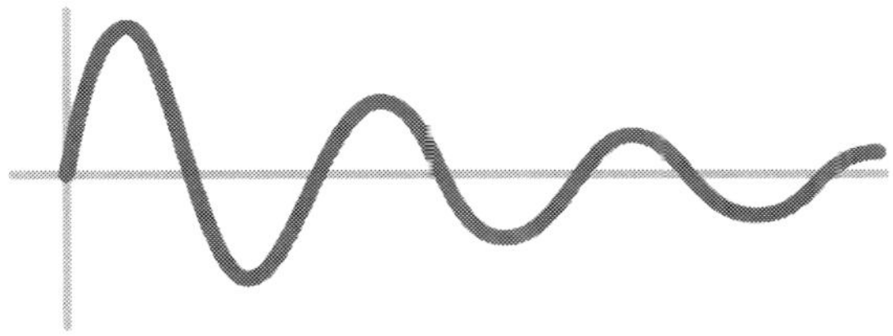

This is a **damped** harmonic oscillator – there are forces acting against (or *damping)* the oscillation, so it slows down by a little bit each time until it comes to rest.

That wasn't so bad!

The length of time it takes the pendulum to settle down, and ultimately the way the graph of the oscillator looks, depends on the following parameters of the oscillating system:

- Any **damping:** this is due to air friction, mechanical friction and other external slowing forces acting on the system.
- The **mass:** the heavier the pendulum, the greater the length of time it will swing.
- The **stiffness:** the stiffer the "spring" of the oscillator, which in this case is Earth's gravity, the harder the pendulum will swing at first, and the faster the system will settle down. Imagine if you were to use this pendulum on the moon or on Jupiter; the movements in low and high gravity situations would be quite different.
- The **initial velocity:** did your grandpa simply let the pendulum go, or did he give the pendulum a push?

"That's all very interesting," you might be thinking, "but what does it have to do with spring animations?"

A great question, with a great answer! Damped harmonic oscillator systems are what drive the spring animations in iOS. The next section talks about this in more detail.

UIKit vs. Core Animation springs

You've likely noticed that a damped harmonic oscillator involves many more variables than does a simple UIKit spring animation.

When you use `UIView.animateWithDuration(_:delay:usingSpringWithDamping:initialSpringVelocity:options:animations:completion:)` the only spring-relevant parameters are the damping and the initial velocity.

UIKit adjusts all the other variables in a dynamic manner to make the system settle down in the given **duration**.

That's why the UIKit spring animations sometimes feel a bit – well, *forced*. UIKit animations are just a bit too jumpy, and to a trained eye, a tad unnatural.

Luckily, Core Animation lets you create proper spring animations for your layer properties via the **CASpringAnimation** class.

`CASpringAnimation` creates the spring animations for UIKit behind the scenes, but when you call it directly you can set the various variables of the system and let the animation settle down by itself.

The drawback to this approach is that you can't tell the animation what its duration *should be*; that's determined by the system itself, given the variables you provide.

Since you know how damped harmonic oscillators work, it's no surprise that `CASpringAnimation` exposes the following properties:

- `damping` – the damping applied to the system
- `mass` – the mass of the weight in the system
- `stiffness` – the stiffness of the spring attached to the weight
- `initialVelocity` – the initial *push* applied to the weight.

If at any time you're wondering which variables you need to adjust to get your animation working the way you want, simply think back to the grandfather clock example and that should get you straightened around.

That's enough prep for now – it's time to open up Xcode and lay down some spring animation code.

Creating your first layer spring animation

Open the starter project for this chapter, or alternatively if you worked through the project from the previous chapter you can pick up where you left off.

Run the project and watch for the scaling animation applied to the text fields when they reach their final destination:

This little scaling animation lets the user know the field is active and ready to be used. However, the animation ends somewhat abruptly. You can make it look much nicer by replacing the existing animation with a proper spring animation.

Open **ViewController.swift** and find `animationDidStop(_:finished:)`. The piece of code that creates the scale animation is as follows:

```
let pulse = CABasicAnimation(keyPath: "transform.scale")
pulse.fromValue = 1.25
pulse.toValue = 1.0
pulse.duration = 0.25
layer?.addAnimation(pulse, forKey: nil)
```

Since `CASpringAnimation` descends from `CABasicAnimation`, you only need to replace the class name and set the spring damping.

To do that, find the following line:

```
let pulse = CABasicAnimation(keyPath: "transform.scale")
```

...and replace it with the following:

```
let pulse = CASpringAnimation(keyPath: "transform.scale")
pulse.damping = 2.0
```

Run your project and enjoy your new spring animation!

Hold on — something's wrong with that animation. Run the project few more times and watch the animation closely; you'll notice the animation cuts off and jumps to its final frame at about `0.25` seconds in.

This is a case of your code doing precisely what you told it to do:

- You create a spring animation using a custom `damping` value and the defaults for all other system variables
- But you *also* tell it to run for `0.25` seconds by setting its `duration` property.

The spring system can't settle within `0.25` seconds; the variables you provided mean the animation should run for a few seconds before it settles down.

Here's a visual demonstration of how you cut off the spring animation:

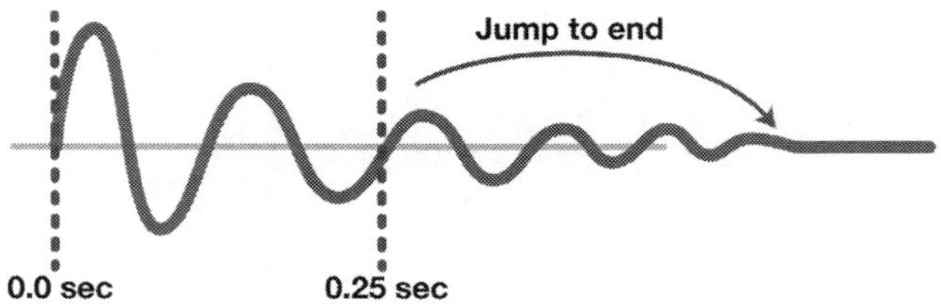

Fortunately, this is an easy fix. Once you set all system variables such as `stiffness` and `damping`, ask your `CASpringAnimation` how much time it will take to settle down and set that as the duration of the animation.

Replace `pulse.duration = 0.25` with the following:

```
pulse.duration = pulse.settlingDuration
```

`settlingDuration` estimates the time required for the system to settle; you can use that value to let Core Animation know how long the animation should remain on the screen.

Run your project again to enjoy smooth wobbly-bobbly animations:

It looks better, but *boy* does it run a long time. With the given parameters, the animation will take `1.93` seconds to settle down – that's way too long for an effect that's only meant to close off the preceding transition animation.

Think back to the pendulum example from the chapter's introduction: do you need *more* or *less* damping to decrease the animation's duration?

You're right — a greater damping value means the pendulum will settle faster. Change your animation's damping to `7.5` for a more subtle effect:

```
pulse.damping = 7.5
```

Run the project again; this time, the scaling effect is smooth as silk.

Spring animation properties

That takes care of your first spring animation; all you had to do was adjust the damping and everything worked itself out.

But what about `stiffness`, `initialVelocity`, and `mass`?

`CASpringAnimation` comes with pre-defined values for all its springy properties:

Property	Default Value
`damping`	`10.0`
`mass`	`1.0`
`stiffness`	`100.0`
`initialVelocity`	`0.0`

In this section you'll add input validation to the text fields and make the fields jump if the user enters too few characters. You'll use all four properties of `CASpringAnimation` to produce the precise effect you want.

Scroll to the very bottom of **ViewController.swift** and find the class extension that makes `ViewController` conform to the `UITextFieldDelegate` protocol.

Add to the `extension` body the following callback method:

```
func textFieldDidEndEditing(textField: UITextField) {
  if textField.text?.characters.count < 5 {
    // add animations here
  }
}
```

The callback `textFieldDidEndEditing()` receives as a parameter the text field that just lost focus. In the code above you check whether the text value of that field is shorter than 5 characters; if so, you play an animation to attract the user's attention to that field.

Add the following code below the comment `// add animations here`:

```
let jump = CASpringAnimation(keyPath: "position.y")

jump.fromValue = textField.layer.position.y + 1.0
jump.toValue = textField.layer.position.y
jump.duration = jump.settlingDuration
textField.layer.addAnimation(jump, forKey: nil)
```

Run your project; click (or tap if on a device) inside the username text field, then immediately click (or tap) inside the password field.

This triggers `textFieldDidEndEditing()`, and since you didn't enter any text, the validation failure animation plays.

At present, the animation simply moves the field one point down and animates it one up back to its original location. That's not much fun — but you can easily fix that with your animation ninja skills!

Initial Velocity

This property lets you specify the starting speed of the animation. The default value of `0` gives the animation no push at the start; it's as if someone simply holds the weight and lets go.

A positive value gives the animation a push in the direction of the equilibrium point, while a negative value starts the animation moving away from the equilibrium point.

Your jump animation should be quite visible, so give it a good push of `100.0` at the start. Add the following line just after the point where you initialize the animation object:

```
jump.initialVelocity = 100.0
```

Check out your spring animation again:

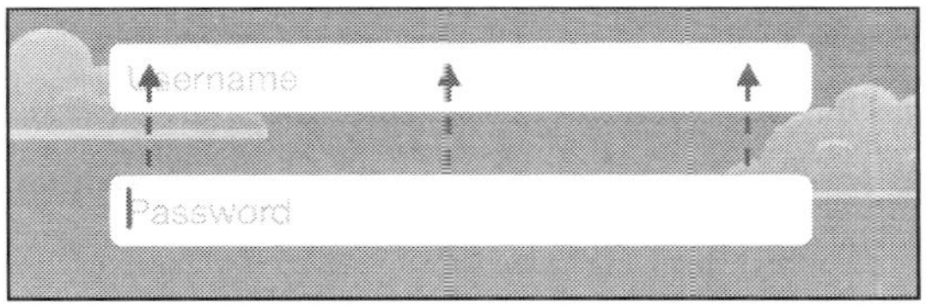

Even with a position delta of just `1` point, the field jumps much higher due to the extra push at the start. The field then oscillates a bit before settling down.

Mass

It looks better, but the jump animation settles a *bit* too fast. Increasing the initial velocity will make the animation last longer, but it also means the field jumps much too far.

What if you increase the *mass* of the attached weight instead, for an animation that lasts longer? Sounds good!

The default mass value is `1.0` (in your mind, you can choose pounds, kilograms, or any other measurement unit you fancy) and you can use any positive value that helps you achieve the desired effect.

For your current animation increase the mass to **10.0** like so (the new code is underlined below):

```
let jump = CASpringAnimation(keyPath: "position.y")
jump.initialVelocity = 100.0
jump.mass = 10.0
```

Run your project; the change above increases the duration of your animation — but the extra mass means the text field jumps a little higher than planned.

No worries – you are still on the right path. Just couple more adjustments and you'll have this effect licked!

> **Note**: Adjusting the spring variables might not feel intuitive at the moment, but as you experiment further with these values you'll start to understand how to best achieve your desired effect.

Stiffness

The spring animation overshoots the target due to its high initial velocity and its extra mass. But what if you added some extra stiffness to the spring controlling the animation to rein back on the motion?

`stiffness` can take any positive value that you fancy: **0** creates a a very soft spring (bouncy bouncy), **100** is the default value (bouncy), and every increment above **100** makes the spring stiffer and stiffer (less bouncy bouncy).

In your animation, increase the `stiffness` to **1500** to restrain the jump to a sensible size; the new line of code is underlined below:

```
let jump = CASpringAnimation(keyPath: "position.y")
jump.initialVelocity = 100.0
jump.mass = 10.0
jump.stiffness = 1500.0
```

Run your project; the animation now jumps just the right distance and feels *tight*; this should definitely grab the attention of the user.

Damping

The animation looks great, but it does seem to go on a bit too long. You'll increase the system damping to make the animation settle faster.

The damping coefficient applied to the system can be any positive value; zero will make your animation oscillate forever.

Increase the damping of your animation to `50.0`:

```
let jump = CASpringAnimation(keyPath: "position.y")
jump.initialVelocity = 100.0
jump.mass = 10.0
jump.stiffness = 1500.0
jump.damping = 50.0
```

Run the project now and enjoy a fine, subtle animation that attracts the user's attention without annoying them:

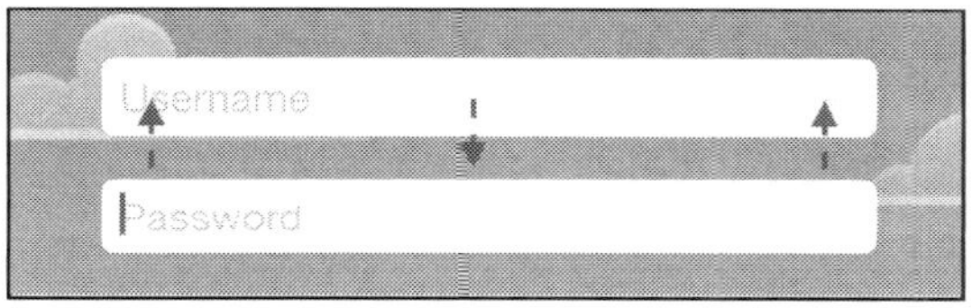

Specific layer properties

So far in this chapter you've created layer spring animations for the `transform` and `position` properties. Techincally, you could have created a comparable bouncy effect using the UIKit spring APIs, although at the expense of smoothness and quality.

To wrap up with `CASpringAnimation`, you'll create a spring animation on a layer property that you *can't* create with view animations alone.

The validation animation is maybe a bit too subtle and smooth right now...

You'll add a not-so-subtle flashing red border around the text field that contains invalid input.

In `textFieldDidEndEditing()`, inside the `if` statement and just after you add the jump animation to the text field, add the following code to set a border on your text field:

```
textField.layer.borderWidth = 3.0
textField.layer.borderColor = UIColor.clearColor().CGColor
```

This code adds a transparent border around your text field; next, you'll animate that border color.

Add the following code just below the line that sets a transparent color on the border:

```
let flash = CASpringAnimation(keyPath: "borderColor")
flash.damping = 7.0
flash.stiffness = 200.0
flash.fromValue = UIColor(red: 0.96, green: 0.27, blue: 0.0,
  alpha: 1.0).CGColor
flash.toValue = UIColor.clearColor().CGColor
flash.duration = flash.settlingDuration
textField.layer.addAnimation(flash, forKey: nil)
```

Here you create a spring animation with `damping` and `stiffness` values that flash the border in sync with the text field jumping.

A simple `CABasicAnimation` would have animated the border color from red to transparent. But because you've chosen a spring animation, the border color starts from red and oscillates a bit around the final transparent color.

Run the app to appreciate the end effect; the field border flashes a few times before it settles down and disappears:

And that ends your crash course on layer spring animations!

Challenges

Challenge 1: Convert corner radius and background animations to springs

You have a pretty solid understanding of layer spring animations by now, so I'll leave you to figure out the solution to this challenge on your own.

Your task is to revisit the code in both `tintBackgroundColor(layer:, toColor:)` and `roundCorners(layer:, toRadius:)`, replace the existing code with spring animations and configure the animations so that you can clearly see the rounded corners bounce without overdoing it.

Working through this challenge on your own will give you some time to experiment with the properties of `CASpringAnimation` and give you a feeling for what values work well.

When you've finished, you'll be ready to move on to the next chapter and tackle layer keyframe animations.

Chapter 12: Keyframe Animations & Struct Properties

Keyframe animations on layers are a bit different than view keyframe animations. View keyframe animations are a simple way to combine independent simple animations together; they can animate different views and properties, and the animations can overlap or have gaps in between.

In contrast, `CAKeyframeAnimation` lets you animate a single property on a given layer. You can define different key points of the animation, but you can't have any gaps or overlaps in your animation. Even though that sounds restrictive at first, you can create some very compelling effects with `CAKeyframeAnimation`.

In this chapter, you'll create a number of layer keyframe animations, from the very basic, to more advanced animations that simulate real-world collisions. In Chapter 15, "Stroke and path animations", you'll learn how to take layer animations even further and animate your layers along a given path.

For now, you'll walk before you run and create a funky wobbly effect for your first layer keyframe animation.

Introducing keyframe animations

Think for a moment how a basic animation works. Using `fromValue` and `toValue`, Core Animation progressively modifies a particular layer property between those values over a specified `duration`.

For instance, when you rotate a layer between 45° and -45° (or `π/4` and `7π/4` for you math types out there :]) you only need to specify those two values and the layer renders all intermediate values to complete the animation:

CAKeyframeAnimation uses an array named values, instead of fromValue and toValue. The elements of values are the measured milestones of your animation. You'll also need to supply the time that the animation should reach each value's key point.

Take a look at the following simple layer keyframe animation example:

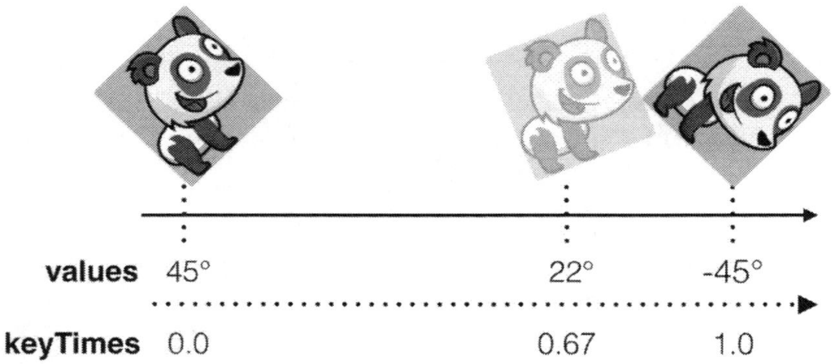

In the above animation, the layer rotates from 45° to -45°, but this time it has two separate stages: first, it rotates from 45° to 22° during the first two-thirds of the animation duration, and then it rotates all the way to -45° in the time remaining.

In essence, animating layers with keyframes requires you to provide key values for the property you're animating, along with a corresponding number of number of relative key times that progress between 0.0 and 1.0.

Creating a layer keyframe animation

Open the starter project for this chapter, or alternatively if you worked through the project from the previous chapter you can pick up where you left off.

Open **ViewController.swift** and find `resetForm()`; this method executes when you finish animating the different login status messages from "Connecting" to "Authorizing" and so on. You'll animate the form title slightly on the faux failed authentication attempt to tell the user that that an error has occurred.

Add the following code to the beginning of `resetForm()`:

```
let wobble = CAKeyframeAnimation(keyPath: "transform.rotation")
wobble.duration = 0.25
wobble.repeatCount = 4
wobble.values = [0.0, -M_PI_4/4, 0.0, M_PI_4/4, 0.0]
wobble.keyTimes = [0.0, 0.25, 0.5, 0.75, 1.0]
heading.layer.addAnimation(wobble, forKey: nil)
```

Here you create a new `CAKeyframeAnimation` in the same way you usually do for a `CABasicAnimation`: you specify a `keyPath`, set the animation's total duration and indicate how many times you want it to repeat.

Then you set up your animation values in the `values` array: you rotate the layer from `0°` to `-45°` (equal to `π/4`), back to `0°`, all the way to `45°` and finally back to `0°`. The animation starts and ends on the same value, which makes repeating it an easy task.

Finally, you set the key times for the values of the animation, making sure to set the start and end times to `0.0` and `1.0` respectively to avoid any jumps in your animation.

Build and run your project; tap on the login button, wait until the end of the sequence and you'll see the title wobble to alert the user that their login attempt failed:

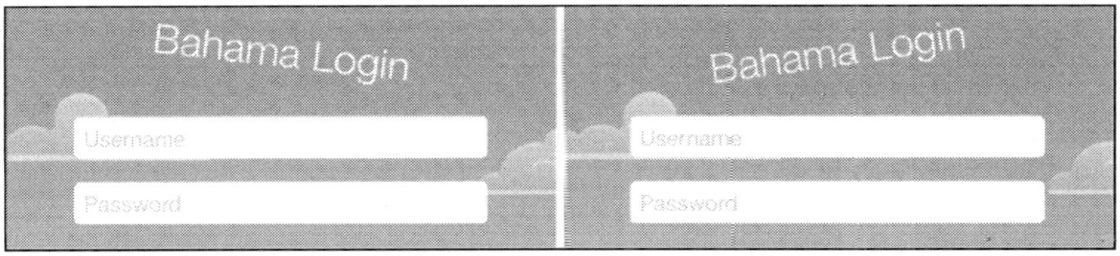

Keen-eyed readers have probably noticed that I haven't yet covered animations on `struct` properties. Most of the time you can get away with animating a single component of a `struct`, such as the `x` component of a `CGPoint`, or the `rotation` component of a `CATransformation3D`, but there's more to animating `struct` values than you might think at first.

Animating struct values

Struct instances are first-class citizens in Swift. In fact, there's very little difference between working with them and working with class instances in terms of syntax.

However, Core Animation is an Objective-C framework built on C, which means that structs are handled *very* differently. Objective-C APIs like to deal with objects, so structs need some special handling.

This is why it's relatively easy to animate a layer property such as a color or a number, but it's not quite as easy to animate a struct property such as a `CGPoint`.

There are many animatable properties of `CALayer` that hold struct values, including `position` of type `CGPoint`, `transform` of type `CATransform3D`, and `bounds` of type `CGRect`. To help manage this, Cocoa includes the `NSValue` class, which "boxes in" or "wraps" a struct value as an object, namely, `NSValue`.

`NSValue` comes with a number of convenience initializers you can use for each struct you need to box, including the following:

```
init(CGPoint point: CGPoint)
init(CGSize size: CGSize)
init(CGRect rect: CGRect)
init(CATransform3D t: CATransform3D)
```

How would you use these initializers to box your values? Here's what a sample `position` animation using `CGPoint` would look like:

```
let move = CABasicAnimation(keyPath: "position")
move.duration = 1.0
move.fromValue = NSValue(CGPoint: CGPoint(x: 100.0, y: 100.0))
move.toValue = NSValue(CGPoint: CGPoint(x: 200.0, y: 200.0))
```

If you try to assign a `CGPoint` directly to `fromValue` or `toValue` you'll get an error, which will remind you to use `NSValue` instead. Instead, you're boxing the `CGPoint` in an `NSValue` before assigning it to `fromValue` and `toValue`.

The same thing happens with keyframe animations: if you try to assign an array of `CGPoint` instances as the values of your animations, you'll receive an error since you have to use an array of boxed `CGPoint` NSValues instead.

The final section of this chapter will walk you through boxing your struct properties as you add the final layer keyframe animation involving, of all things, a hot-air balloon! :]

Intermediate keyframe animations

First you need to add the balloon image on screen. Open **ViewController.swift,** then add the following code to the bottom of `login()`:

```
let balloon = CALayer()
balloon.contents = UIImage(named: "balloon")!.CGImage
balloon.frame = CGRect(x: -50.0, y: 0.0,
 width: 50.0, height: 65.0)
view.layer.insertSublayer(balloon, below: username.layer)
```

In the code above, you create a new layer with the balloon image as its contents. If you need to show an image on screen but don't need all the benefits of using a view—auto layout constraints, attaching gesture recognizers and so forth—you can simply use a `CALayer` like in the code example above.

You position the layer near the top left corner, just outside of the visible area of the screen. Finally, you insert the layer below the `username` field so the balloon appears behind all the other elements in your form.

Now you can create the animation in few familiar steps. Add the following code underneath the previous code:

```
let flight = CAKeyframeAnimation(keyPath: "position")
flight.duration = 12.0
```

Here you create a keyframe animation and set its `duration` to `12.0`, the approximate duration of the faux authentication process.

Next, add the following key value points and times:

```
flight.values = [
  CGPoint(x: -50.0, y: 0.0),
```

```
    CGPoint(x: view.frame.width + 50.0, y: 160.0),
    CGPoint(x: -50.0, y: loginButton.center.y)
  ].map { NSValue(CGPoint: $0) }
  flight.keyTimes = [0.0, 0.5, 1.0]
```

Note how you use `map` to neatly convert an array of points into an array of points boxed as `NSValues`. Ain't Swift great? :]

This animates the balloon along the path that connects the three points you assigned to `values`, like so:

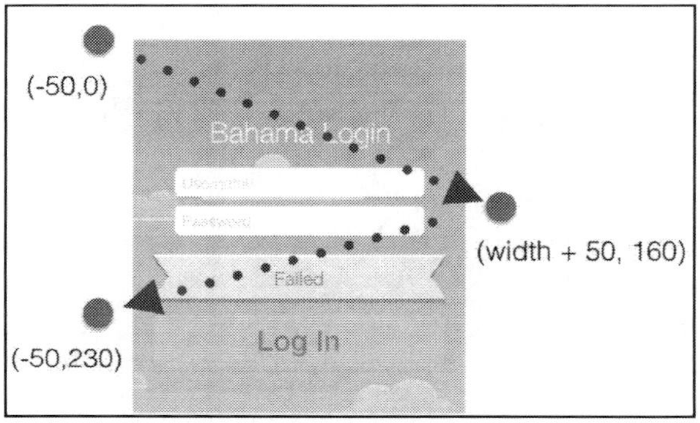

Add the final few following lines to run the animation and to set the final position of the balloon layer:

```
  balloon.addAnimation(flight, forKey: nil)
  balloon.position = CGPoint(x: -50.0, y: loginButton.center.y)
```

Build and run your project; watch as the balloon flies across the screen as soon as you tap the **Log In** button:

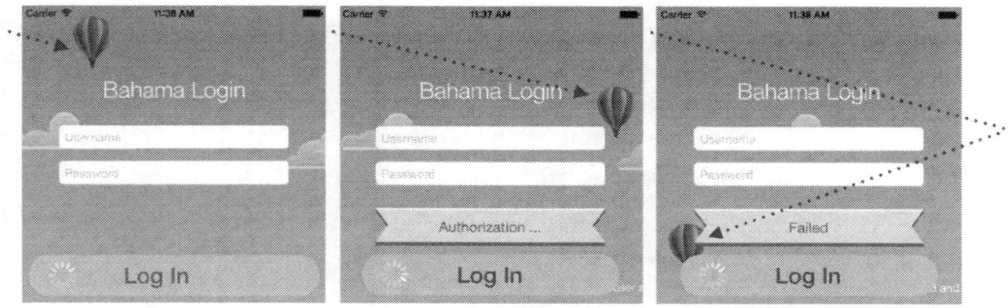

You can use the same technique to animate other struct properties such as `bounds`, `position`, and `transform`.

If you want to animate the balloon over a more complex set of points, such as a smooth curved path, stay tuned for Chapter 15, "Stroke and path animations" where you'll learn how to animate a layer over an arbitrary path using a special case of keyframe animation.

You've covered all of the chapters in this book that deal with basic layer animations; the next four chapters will introduce you to some of the cool animations you can create using specialized layers.

Chapter 13: Shapes and Masks

This chapter marks a bit of a shift in this section of the book: not only are you going to start working with a different sample project, but you'll work with multi-layer effects, create layer animations that appear to interact physically with each other and morph between shapes as the animation runs.

If that sounds like a lot to take in, just think back to the great-looking animations you created in previous chapters with a relatively small bit of code.

The shapes in this chapter will be handled by `CAShapeLayer`, which is a `CALayer` subclass that lets you draw various shapes on the screen, from the very simple to the very complex:

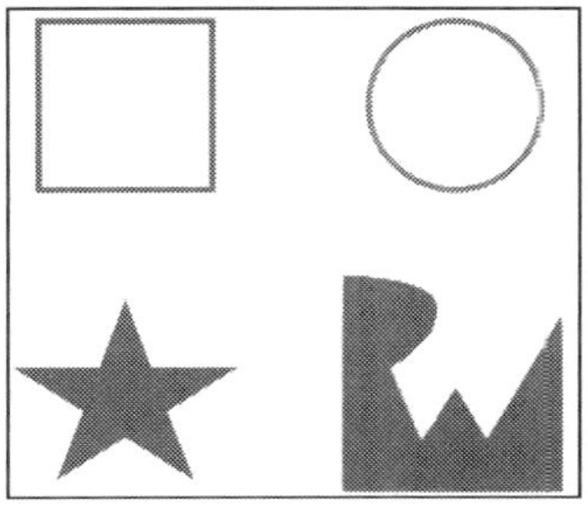

Instead of taking some sort of drawing instructions `CALayer` draws on screen a `CGPath` you give to it. This comes in handy since Core Graphics already defines a very extensive API of drawing instructions for building `CGPath` shapes.

If using the C API of Core Graphics is too low level for your taste you can always use the `UIBezierPath` class to define a shape and then use its `CGPath` property to get its Core Graphics representation. You will give that a try later in this very chapter.

After you create your desired shape you can set such properties on it as the stroke color, fill color and stroke dash pattern. Of course, by now you're likely asking "...but can I *animate* these properties?" Yes, you can:

- `path` – morph the layer's shape into a different shape.
- `fillColor` – change the fill tint of shape to a different color.
- `lineDashPhase` – create a marquee or "marching ants" effect around your shape.
- `lineWidth` – grow or shrink the size of the stroke line of your shape.

There are two more animatable properties that you can use when drawing shapes; you'll learn about these in Chapter 15, "Stroke and path animations."

The project for this chapter simulates the starting screen of a combat game that is searching for an online opponent. You'll simulate some online communication and add some animations to show the communication state.

By the end of this chapter the project will look much like the screen below:

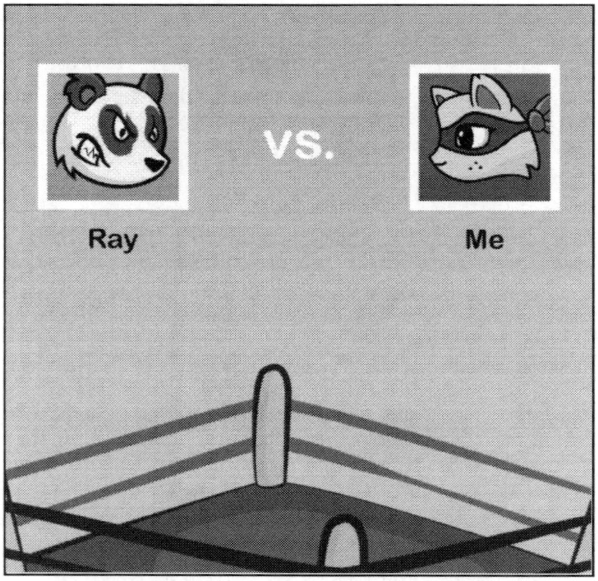

This chapter is designed to show you how to animate the new properties discussed above in the context of a common project you'd work on in real life. This will require a *bit* of extra work, but I know you'll enjoy the ride! :]

Finishing up the avatar view

Open the starter project for this chapter, select **Main.storyboard** and take a look at the user interface you'll be working with in this chapter:

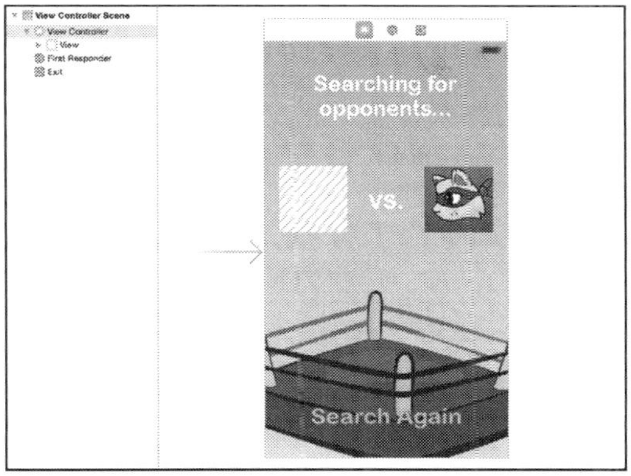

The project setup is fairly straightforward: a single view controller to display a nice background image, some labels, a "Search Again" button, and two avatar images, one of which will be empty until the app "finds" an opponent.

The two avatars are each an instance of the class `AvatarView`. In this section of the chapter, you'll quickly finish writing the class code while you learn how it works.

Open **AvatarView.swift** and have a look at `didMoveToWindow()`, where you'll build up the following elements of the avatar view:

- `photoLayer` – the avatar's image layer.
- `circleLayer` – a shape layer for drawing a circle.
- `maskLayer` – another shape layer for drawing a mask.
- `label` - a label to show the player's name.

You'll layer these on top of each other to build the composite avatar view as follows:

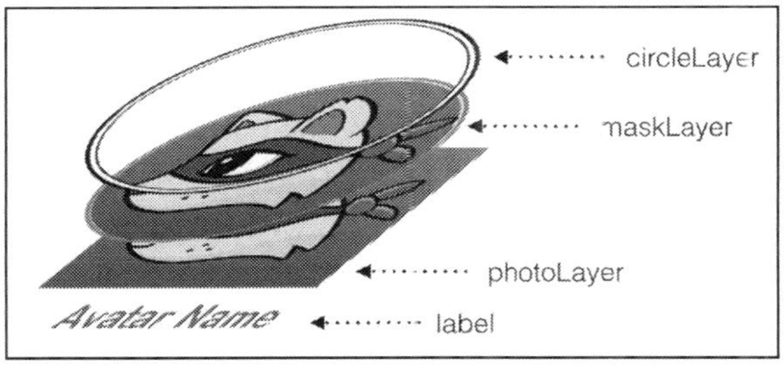

The above components already exist in the project, but haven't been added to the view – that's your first task. Add the following code to `didMoveToWindow()`:

```
photoLayer.mask = maskLayer
```

This simply masks the square image above with the circle-shaped mask in `maskLayer`.

Build and run your project to see how things look or you can also see the change right in the storyboard thanks to `@IBDesignable`:

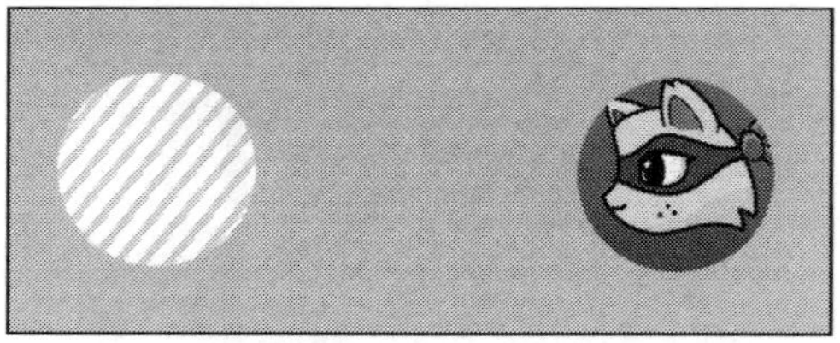

Now add the border layer to the avatar view's layer in `didMoveToWindow`,:

```
layer.addSublayer(circleLayer)
```

This adds the circular-shaped layer to the avatar, which frames it in nicely:

Both the mask layer and the frame layer are instances of `CAShapeLayer`; you'll make use of this fact when you animate them in the next section.

There's one more piece to add – the player name label. Add the following code to `didMoveToWindow()`:

```
addSubview(label)
```

This wraps up the avatar view like so:

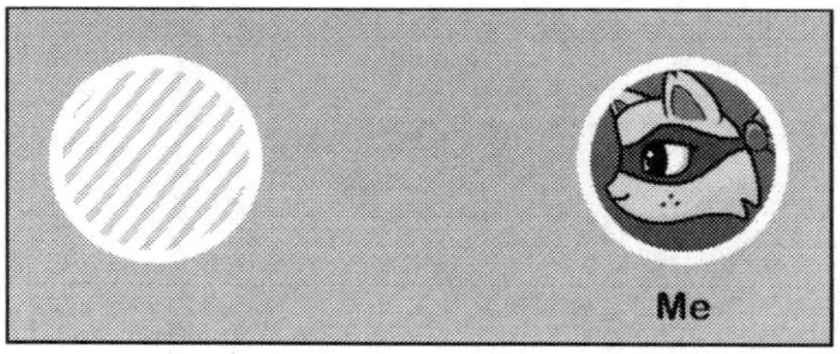

Now you're ready to add some animations!

> **Note:** You may have noticed that the view doesn't look quite right in the storyboard. This is because a lot of the effects you've added extend outside the frame of the view and get clipped. Not to worry though: at actual runtime, the views will look correct.

Creating the bounce-off animation

The first animation you'll create will make it appear as if the two avatars are bouncing off each other while your project "searches" for an opponent.

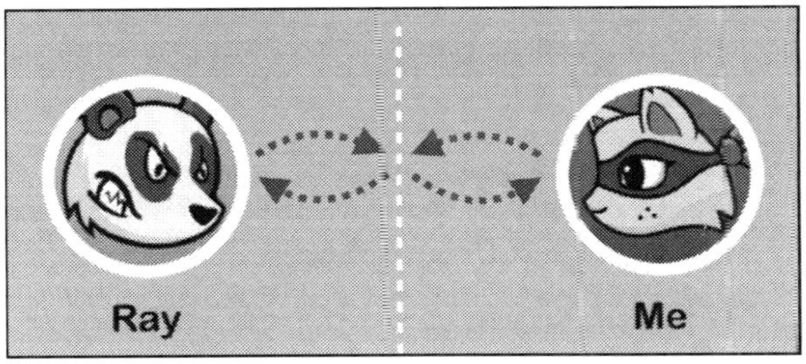

Open **ViewController.swift** and add the following line to `viewDidAppear()`:

```
searchForOpponent()
```

This method kicks off your searching-for-opponent animation.

Add the code below to `ViewController` to create the first iteration of this method:

```
func searchForOpponent() {
  let avatarSize = myAvatar.frame.size
  let bounceXOffset: CGFloat = avatarSize.width/1.9
  let morphSize = CGSize(
    width: avatarSize.width * 0.85,
    height: avatarSize.height * 1.1)
}
```

A bit of math is involved in this animation – but not too much! :]

First, you calculate the horizontal distance the avatars should move when they bounce towards each other and save that value in `bounceXOffset`. You'll use the morph size later to add an extra effect when the two avatars collide.

Now that you know the x-offset, you can calculate the locations to which the avatars should move.

Add the following code to `searchForOpponent()`:

```
let rightBouncePoint = CGPoint(
  x: view.frame.size.width/2.0 + bounceXOffset,
  y: myAvatar.center.y)
let leftBouncePoint = CGPoint(
  x: view.frame.size.width/2.0 - bounceXOffset,
  y: myAvatar.center.y)
```

When the avatars reach the right and left bounce points, respectively, they will just barely touch each other, at which point you'll animate them away from each other again.

Finally add the following code to `searchForOpponent()`:

```
myAvatar.bounceOffPoint(rightBouncePoint, morphSize: morphSize)
opponentAvatar.bounceOffPoint(leftBouncePoint, morphSize:
morphSize)
```

`bounceOffPoint()` doesn't yet exist; you'll add it in just a moment. It takes two parameters: the point to where the avatar should move and the size to which it should morph. That's all you need to create your animation.

Open **AvatarView.swift** and add the bounce method below:

```
func bounceOffPoint(bouncePoint: CGPoint, morphSize: CGSize) {
  let originalCenter = center

  UIView.animateWithDuration(animationDuration, delay: 0.0,
usingSpringWithDamping: 0.8, initialSpringVelocity: 0.0, options:
[], animations: {
    self.center = bouncePoint
  }, completion: {_ in
    //complete bounce to
  })
}
```

In the above method you first store the `center` coordinate of the avatar view; you'll need this later to animate the view back to its original location. Next, you use a spring animation to move the avatar view to the `bouncePoint` coordinate.

Now you need something to animate the avatar to its starting location. Add the following code to the end of `bounceOffPoint`:

```
UIView.animateWithDuration(animationDuration, delay:
animationDuration, usingSpringWithDamping: 0.7,
initialSpringVelocity: 1.0, options: [], animations: {
```

```
    self.center = originalCenter
  }, completion: {_ in
    delay(seconds: 0.1) {
      self.bounceOffPoint(bouncePoint, morphSize: morphSize)
    }
  })
```

The above code uses another spring animation to move the avatar back to its original location. After a slight delay, you re-start the animation again from the `completion` closure.

Build and run your project to see how the bounce animation looks.

Note that when the avatars views touch they stay together for a short period, as if there's tension building between them. This short period is where you'll add the "squishing" effect using shape morphing techniques.

Morphing shapes

When the two avatars collide, they should squish a little in this perfectly-elastic collision. The view controller will pass in a morph size that makes the avatar image slightly taller and narrower for this effect:

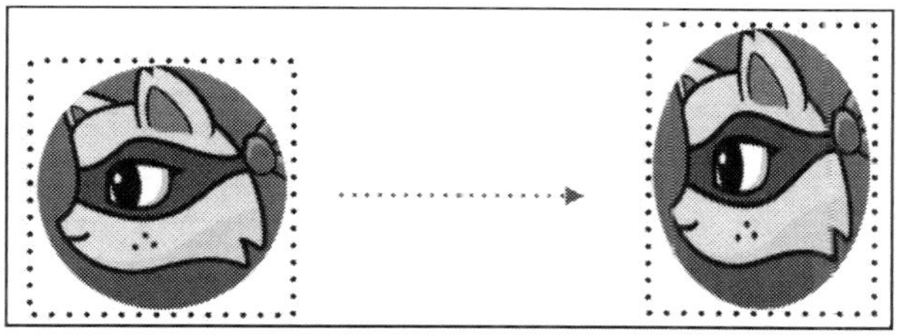

This will make it look like the avatars are pressing against each other when they meet in the middle of the screen.

The first thing to take care of is the frame to use for the morphing effect. And just to complicate things a little, the frame will be different for each avatar, depending on whether it animates from the left or the right.

Add the following code to the bottom of `bounceOffPoint()`:

```
let morphedFrame = (originalCenter.x > bouncePoint.x) ?

  CGRect(x: 0.0, y: bounds.height - morphSize.height,
    width: morphSize.width, height: morphSize.height):

  CGRect(x: bounds.width - morphSize.width,
    y: bounds.height - morphSize.height,
    width: morphSize.width, height: morphSize.height)
```

If the avatar animates from left to right, then the final position of the morphed avatar will touch the right edge of the original frame. It's the exact opposite for the avatar animating from right to left, as it will end up on the left edge of the original frame.

This means the avatar images end up touching slightly in the center of the screen, like so:

Finally you can add the shape-shifting animation code to the bottom of `bounceOffPoint()`:

```
let morphAnimation = CABasicAnimation(keyPath: "path")
morphAnimation.duration = animationDuration
morphAnimation.toValue = UIBezierPath(
  ovalInRect: morphedFrame).CGPath
morphAnimation.timingFunction = CAMediaTimingFunction(
  name: kCAMediaTimingFunctionEaseOut)
```

Here, you create a `CABasicAnimation` and set its `keyPath` as the `path` property. As with any other property layer animation, you only need to set the end value and Core Animation will render the intermediate states for you.

You then set the duration and use the class `UIBezierPath` to create an oval path for the effect. `UIBezierPath` is quite handy as it features a number of convenience `init` methods, including the one you used above which takes a `CGRect` and creates an oval path that fits into the `CGRect`.

Finally, you set the animation to ease-out which helps build the tension before the avatars bounce off.

That was a long haul, but all that's left is to add the animation to the avatar before you can see your crazy shape shifting in action!

Add the following line of code to the bottom of `bounceOffPoint()`:

```
circleLayer.addAnimation(morphAnimation, forKey: nil)
```

Build and run your project to see the end result:

The avatar frames squish neatly against each other and then bounce off, like two angry battling amebae floating in the pre-historic sea!

The effect isn't quite complete, as only the frames morph, leaving the images underneath unchanged. Recall that you set the mask of the avatar image to be a `CAShapeLayer` – that's the same class as the avatar frame. So *theoretically* you could re-use the animation object on your frame for your mask.

Will theory work in practice? Give it a try, and add the following line to the bottom of `bounceOffPoint()`:

```
maskLayer.addAnimation(morphAnimation, forKey: nil)
```

Build and run your project again; this time you should see both the frame and mask morph in perfect sync:

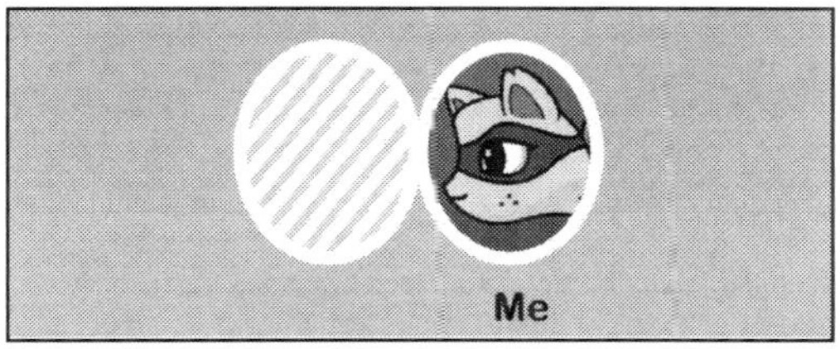

Awesome – you've just created a really nice-looking animation with only a bit of math and a few well-designed chunks of code! In the space of this chapter, you've learned how to create and animate shapes and how to use and animate shape layers as masks.

Challenges

The challenges in this chapter are optional; but I encourage you to work through them to practice your skills and add some real polish to your project. However if you're eager to start with gradient animations then you can head straight on to the next chapter.

Challenge 1: Finish the communication state animations

For this challenge, you get a bit of a breather as you can simply follow along with the instructions below. Your task in this challenge is to add some status messages to show to the user as your faux "searching for an opponent" task progresses.

Open **ViewController.swift** and add the following code to the bottom of `searchForOpponent()`:

```
delay(seconds: 4.0, foundOpponent)
```

The app will continue to "search" for four seconds before calling `foundOpponent()`, which will indicate to the player that the app has found an opponent.

Add the following method to the `ViewController` class:

```
func foundOpponent() {
  status.text = "Connecting..."

  opponentAvatar.image = UIImage(named: "avatar-2")
  opponentAvatar.name = "Ray"
}
```

Build and run your project and after about four seconds, you'll see the opponent's avatar appear:

Now that the app has found an opponent, it will start "connecting" the two players. All of this, of course, is just a simulation so you get to build a nice animation.

Add the following code to the bottom of `foundOpponent()`:

```
delay(seconds: 4.0, connectedToOpponent)
```

This inserts another four-second delay after the app displays the opponent's avatar, after which you'll call the "connected state" method in the next code block.

Add the following new method to the class:

```
func connectedToOpponent() {
  myAvatar.shouldTransitionToFinishedState = true
  opponentAvatar.shouldTransitionToFinishedState = true
}
```

The above method sets `shouldTransitionToFinishedState` to `true` on both avatar views. This triggers a new animation that you will create in the next challenge, so for now nothing will happen.

Finally, you need to adjust the UI for the final state. Add the following code to the bottom of `connectedToOpponent()`:

```
delay(seconds: 1.0, completed)
```

This code gives the animation a second to wrap up and then calls the final step in the sequence: `completed()`.

Add the final method below to the `ViewController` class:

```
func completed() {
  status.text = "Ready to play"
  UIView.animateWithDuration(0.2) {
    self.vs.alpha = 1.0
    self.searchAgain.alpha = 1.0
  }
}
```

`completed()` sets the status message at the top of the screen to "Ready to play", then fades in the "vs." label and the "Search Again" button to restart the animation sequence. The button is already connected to `actionSearchAgain()` so you can tap it to restart the animations.

Build and run to see the entire sequence of animations:

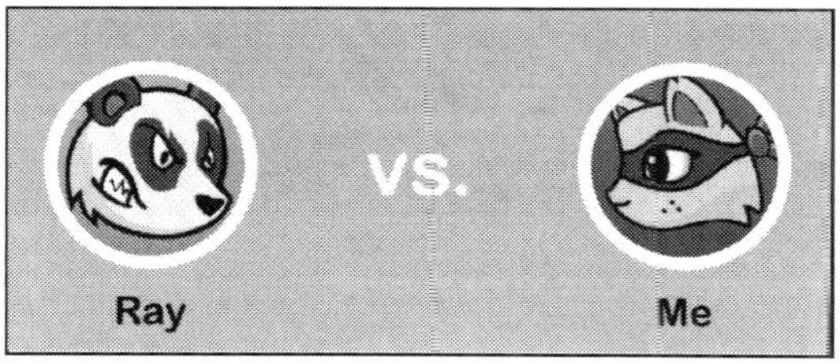

Challenge 2: Morph the avatars to squares

At this point the avatars just keep bouncing forever. However once the game is connected to an opponent you'd like to stop the animation and reflect the state change in the UI.

In this challenge you are going to make use of the `shouldTransitionToFinishedState` property of the avatar class; when it's set to `true` you'll break the bounce animation and morph the avatars into a square shape.

Open **AvatarView.swift** and add a new variable called `isSquare` and set its initial value to `false`. Scroll to `bounceOffPoint()` and find the animation completion block where there's a recursive call to `bounceOffPoint()`.

You'll need to wrap that call in a conditional so it only runs when `isSquare` is still `false`.

Next you'll run an extra animation while the avatars bounce off each other one last time. Find the `//complete bounce to` comment and replace it with the following:

```
if self.shouldTransitionToFinishedState {
    self.animateToSquare()
}
```

Finally, add the `animateToSquare()` method to `AvatarView` and write the code to do the following:

1. Set `isSquare` to `true`.
2. Create a Bezier path with `UIBezierPath(rect:)` by using the avatar's `bounds` rectangle, and store the `CGPath` of this bezier path in a constant called `squarePath`.
3. Create a new layer animation with a keypath of `path` and set its `duration` to `0.25` seconds.
4. Set the `fromValue` of the animation to the `circleLayer.path` and the `toValue` to `squarePath`. This defines a morph animation from a circle to a square shape.
5. Add the animation to the `circleLayer` and then set its `path` property to the `squarePath`.
6. Similarly, add the animation to the mask layer as well and set its `path` property to `squarePath`.

Build and run your project; the final bounce will look much fancier. While the avatars touch for the last time they'll still look like this:

Then as they bounce back to their starting point, they'll morph into squares for a superb *wow* effect:

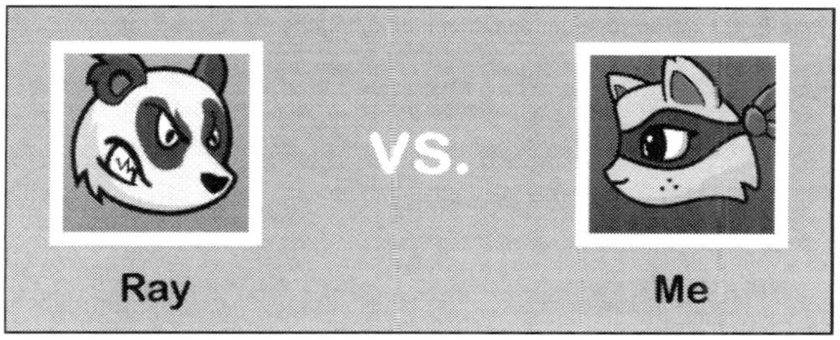

By now you know the basic animation techniques to work with shape layers and masks. You've likely already thought up many ways to apply shape animations in your own applications.

You continue to work with shapes and `CAShapeLayer` animations in Chapter 15, "Stroke and path animations". The next chapter, Chapter 14, "Gradient animations" shows you how to add some really neat effects to your animations using animated gradients.

Chapter 14: Gradient Animations

A lot of the look and feel of iOS comes from very subtle animations in the UI. One of the nicest is a simple little animation that you see multiple times per day: the "slide to unlock" label on the lock screen. In this chapter you'll learn how to mimic this effect with a moving gradient and how to animate the colors and layout of those gradients:

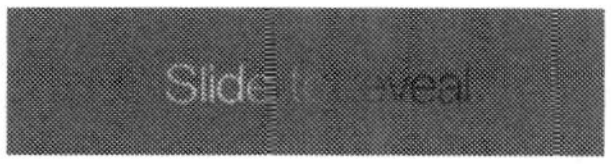

You'll animate the gradient for a "Slide to reveal" label and then reveal a cool mystery effect when the user swipes over the label. You'll have to work through this chapter, however, to see what this cool effect is! :] As an extra bonus, you'll learn how to create a layer mask out of a piece of text and use it to mask a gradient.

Drawing your first gradient

Open the starter project for this chapter and select **Main.storyboard** to see how the UI looks at present:

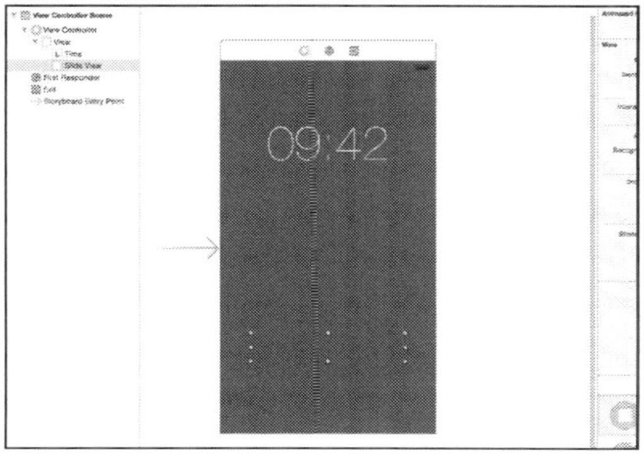

There's a static label on top that mimics the iPhone clock on the lock screen and another view near the bottom.

The bottom view, which displays no content yet, is an instance of `AnimatedMaskLabel` that's included with the starter project. You'll work with this class throughout this chapter to add gradient animations.

Build and run your project; you'll see just the faux clock appear at the top of the screen:

You'll first draw the base gradient of `AnimatedMaskLabel`. Add the following code to **AnimatedMaskLabel.swift** inside the `gradientLayer` property code after the `//Configure the gradient here` comment:

```
gradientLayer.startPoint = CGPoint(x: 0.0, y: 0.5)
gradientLayer.endPoint = CGPoint(x: 1.0, y: 0.5)
```

This defines the orientation of the gradient and its start and end points as illustrated below:

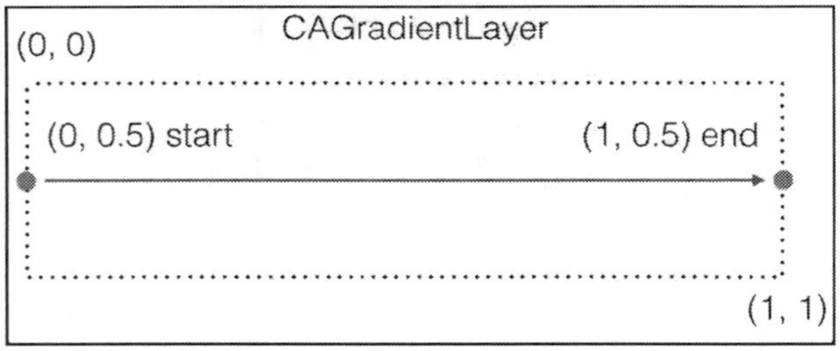

Now add the following code to define the colors that build up the gradient after the code you just added:

```
let colors = [
  UIColor.blackColor().CGColor,
  UIColor.whiteColor().CGColor,
  UIColor.blackColor().CGColor
]
gradientLayer.colors = colors
```

The gradient above starts with a black color, blends to white, and finally blends back to black.

You can also specify where exactly in the gradient's frame these colors should appear. Add the following code below:

```
let locations = [
  0.25,
  0.5,
  0.75
]
gradientLayer.locations = locations
```

This sets up the gradient color milestones as follows:

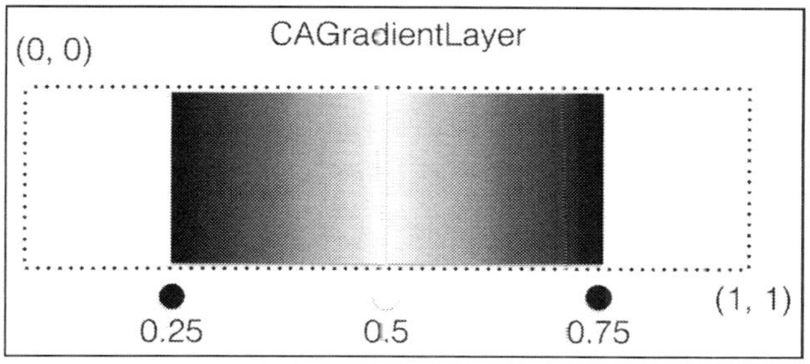

You can have as many key points and color milestones as you like, but the text gradient animation in this chapter only needs the simple black-white-black gradient shown above.

Add the following code to `layoutSubviews()` to give the gradient a frame:

```
gradientLayer.frame = bounds
```

All that you need to do now is add the gradient to the view's layer to see it in action. Add the line of code below to the end of `didMoveToWindow()`:

```
layer.addSublayer(gradientLayer)
```

Build and run your project; you should see the app display the exact gradient you're looking for:

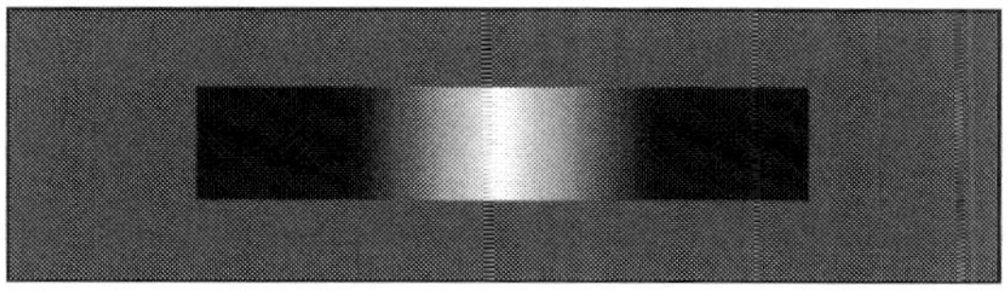

That's a great start! Now you need to figure out how to animate this gradient.

Animating gradients

`CAGradientLayer` offers you four animatable properties along with the ones inherited from `CALayer`:

- `colors`: animate the gradient's colors to give it a tint.
- `locations`: animate the color milestone locations to make the colors move around inside the gradient.
- `startPoint` and `endPoint`: animate the extents of the layout of the gradient.

In this section you'll animate `locations` to make the gradient "move".

Add the following code to the end of `didMoveToWindow()`:

```
let gradientAnimation = CABasicAnimation(keyPath: "locations")
gradientAnimation.fromValue = [0.0, 0.0, 0.25]
gradientAnimation.toValue = [0.75, 1.0, 1.0]
gradientAnimation.duration = 3.0
gradientAnimation.repeatCount = Float.infinity
```

In the above layer animation you begin by pushing the three color milestones to the left edge of the gradient's frame and end the animation with all three pushed towards the right edge:

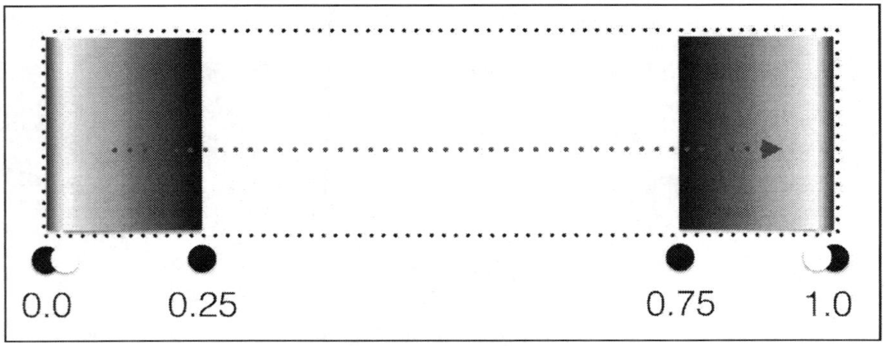

The animation lasts 3 seconds and will repeat forever since you set `repeatCount` to `Infinity`.

Finally, add the following line to the end of `didMoveToWindow()`:

```
gradientLayer.addAnimation(gradientAnimation, forKey: nil)
```

This will add the animation to the gradient layer. Build and run your project and you'll see the animation take shape:

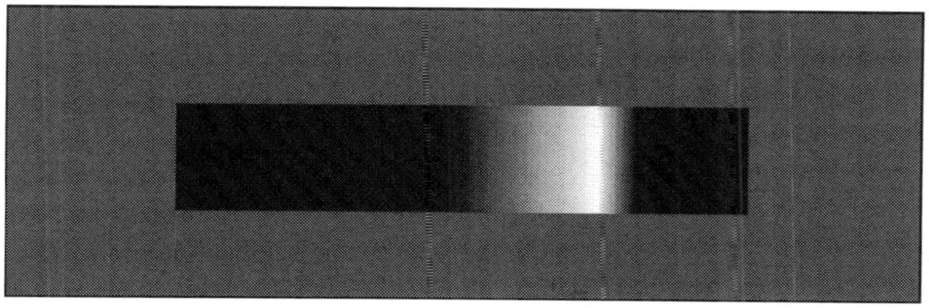

This looks pretty nice, but the gradient is quite harsh, especially near the middle. No problem: just enlarge the gradient bounds and you'll get a much gentler gradient.

Find the line `gradientLayer.frame = bounds` in `layoutSubviews()` and replace it with the following code that sets a much larger frame for the gradient layer:

```
gradientLayer.frame = CGRect(
  x: -bounds.size.width,
  y: bounds.origin.y,
  width: 3 * bounds.size.width,
  height: bounds.size.height)
```

This sets the gradient frame to three times the width of the visible area. The animation enters the view, passes right through it, and exits out the right hand side:

Build and run your project to see what your changes look like:

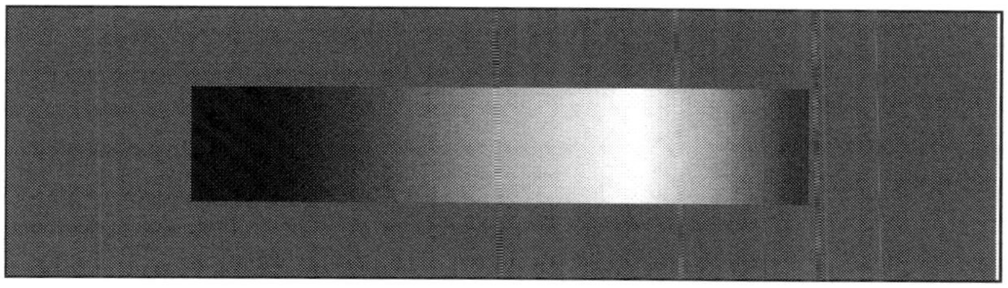

That looks more like the smooth gradient you're going for. Now that you have the gradient, you'll need to create the text layers to use as a mask.

Creating a text mask

In this section you'll render the string stored in the `text` property of `AnimatedMaskLabel` and use that to mask the gradient layer.

Create a new constant property inside the `AnimatedMaskLabel` class to hold the text attributes as follows:

```
let textAttributes: [String: AnyObject] = {
  let style = NSMutableParagraphStyle()
  style.alignment = .Center

  return [
    NSFontAttributeName:UIFont(name: "HelveticaNeue-Thin",
      size: 28.0)!,
    NSParagraphStyleAttributeName: style
  ]
}()
```

Next you need to create a temporary graphic context in order to render the text as an image. A natural place to do this is in the property observer for the `text` property. Add the following code after the `setNeedsDisplay()` call:

```
UIGraphicsBeginImageContextWithOptions(frame.size, false, 0)
```

Here you create an empty graphics context with the same size as the view; now you just need to draw the text in this context.

Add the following code to draw the text and fetch the results as a `UIImage`:

```
text.drawInRect(bounds, withAttributes: textAttributes)
let image = UIGraphicsGetImageFromCurrentImageContext()
UIGraphicsEndImageContext()
```

`drawInRect(_:withAttributes:)` does the drawing, while `UIGraphicsGetImageFromCurrentImageContext()` fetches everything you drew and gives it back to you as an instance of `UIImage`.

Now you can use that image to create a mask on your gradient layer. To do that, first create a layer out of the image as follows:

```
let maskLayer = CALayer()
maskLayer.backgroundColor = UIColor.clearColor().CGColor
maskLayer.frame = CGRectOffset(bounds, bounds.size.width, 0)
maskLayer.contents = image.CGImage
```

You create maskLayer as an empty layer simply by using the default initializer of CALayer. You then set a fully transparent layer background since you're going to use the layer as a mask. Then you offset the layer frame by the width of the view; this way, the mask will show up in the center of the gradient. This is necessary as your "stretched" gradient is currently three times as wide as the visible view. Finally, you assign the image object directly to the contents property of the layer.

Add one more line to set the new layer as a mask for the gradient:

```
gradientLayer.mask = maskLayer
```

Build and run your project to see the fully developed animation in action:

Hey – that looks really slick! But you haven't yet discovered what's revealed when the user swipes across the label – and are you limited to a monochrome palette for your gradient? All will be revealed – as you work through the challenges below! :]

Challenges

I know the suspense is killing you; these two challenges will add a slide gesture recognizer to the label and add one additional color effect to the gradient animation.

Challenge 1: Slide to reveal gesture recognizer

Open **ViewController.swift** and add the following code to viewDidLoad():

```
let swipe = UISwipeGestureRecognizer(target: self,
  action: "didSlide")
swipe.direction = .Right
slideView.addGestureRecognizer(swipe)
```

This creates a slide-to-right gesture recognizer and attaches it to slideView. The recognizer will call didSlide() on ViewController.

didSlide() is already implemented for you, so all you need to do now is fire up the application and slide your finger over the animating label to reveal what lies beneath.

Challenge 2: Psychedelic gradient animations

In the final challenge of this chapter you'll experiment with adding more colors to the gradient and observe the effects.

If you'd like something to guide your exploration, try using the following list of colors for your gradient:

- `UIColor.yellowColor()`
- `UIColor.greenColor()`
- `UIColor.orangeColor()`
- `UIColor.cyanColor()`
- `UIColor.redColor()`
- `UIColor.yellowColor()`

You'll need to adjust the `locations` values as well to keep all of your colors in order. Start your animation with the following `locations: 0.0, 0.0, 0.0, 0.0, 0.0` and `0.25`. Then animate the locations to: `0.65, 0.8, 0.85, 0.9, 0.95` and `1.0`.

Build and run your project; play around with the animation and the various parameters until you have it tuned it to your own design preferences:

This brings the chapter to a close; you've seen how easy it is to animate gradients as well as how to implement some advanced layer masking tricks with text layers.

The next chapter covers stroke animations for shapes, which is the final topic you'll cover in this section of the book on layer animations; you'll learn how to draw shapes interactively, and as a bonus, you'll cover advanced keyframe animations.

Chapter 15: Stroke and Path Animations

This chapter wraps up the layer animations section of this book; you'll learn about stroke and path animations as you add a cool pull-to-refresh animation to your existing Pack List project that entertains the user while the app pretends to fetch new data from the Internet:

Along the way, you'll learn how to animate the drawing of shapes, and as a bonus, you'll look at a special kind of keyframe animation that you can use to move an object along any arbitrary path.

Creating interactive stroke animations

Open the starter project for this chapter, then build and run it to see how the UI looks:

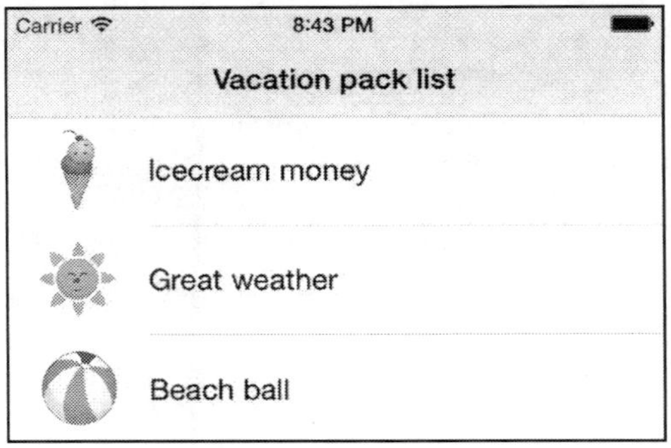

There's existing code in **ViewController.swift** to populate the table for you with a number of vacation items. Pull down the table and you'll see a refresh view appear at the top of the screen:

The refresh view stays visible for four seconds, then retracts. Your job here is to add an amusing animation to entertain users while they wait.

The refresh view already contains all the code for the pulling and releasing actions; you just need to worry about adding the animations.

> **Note**: The pull down to refresh code is based on one of our video tutorials. If you would like to know more about how it works check out parts 15 through 17 of the *Swift Scroll View School* at the following link: http://www.raywenderlich.com/video-tutorials.

The first step in building your animation is to create a circle shape. Open **RefreshView.swift** and add the following code to `init(frame:scrollView:)`:

```
ovalShapeLayer.strokeColor = UIColor.whiteColor().CGColor
ovalShapeLayer.fillColor = UIColor.clearColor().CGColor
ovalShapeLayer.lineWidth = 4.0
ovalShapeLayer.lineDashPattern = [2, 3]
let refreshRadius = frame.size.height/2 * 0.8
ovalShapeLayer.path = UIBezierPath(ovalInRect: CGRect(
  x: frame.size.width/2 - refreshRadius,
  y: frame.size.height/2 - refreshRadius,
  width: 2 * refreshRadius,
  height: 2 * refreshRadius)
).CGPath

layer.addSublayer(ovalShapeLayer)
```

`ovalShapeLayer` is a class property of type `CAShapeLayer`. You're already quite familiar with shape layers; here you simply set the stroke and fill colors and set the circle diameter to be `80%` of the view height, which ensures a comfortable margin around the shape.

There's one property in the code above that you haven't encountered yet: `lineDashPattern`. This property lets you set a dash pattern for the shape stroke; you simply you provide an array with the length of the dash and the length of the gap in pixels.

Build and run your project to see how the circle looks:

That looks really nice – and it was easy to create. This will serve you well as a circular progress bar.

`RefreshView` calls `redrawFromProgress()` whenever the user scrolls; this makes it a convenient place to update the visuals of the progress bar.

Add the following code to `redrawFromProgress()`:

```
ovalShapeLayer.strokeEnd = progress
```

As `progress` increases from `0.0` to `1.0`, the stroke end of the shape moves forward towards the starting point of the stroke.

This is how the shape looks when `progress` is `0.25`:

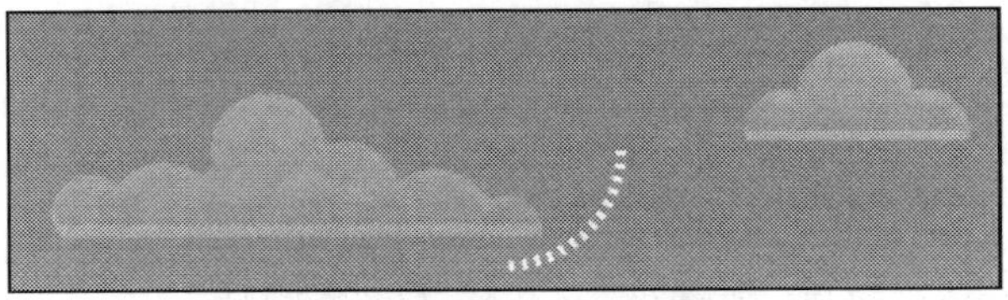

Here it is halfway around, at `0.5`:

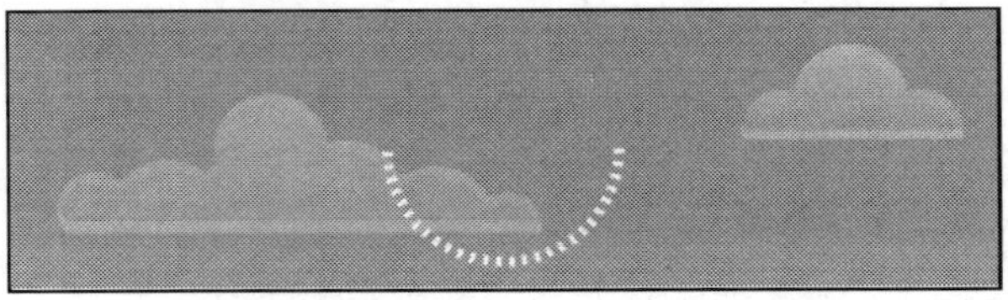

Build and run your project; drag the table view up and down to see the stroke length change.

Now you'll add a cool-looking airplane to the refresh control.

Scroll back to `init(frame:scrollView:)` and add the following code to the bottom of the method:

```
let airplaneImage = UIImage(named: "airplane.png")!
airplaneLayer.contents = airplaneImage.CGImage
airplaneLayer.bounds = CGRect(x: 0.0, y: 0.0, width:
airplaneImage.size.width, height: airplaneImage.size.height)
airplaneLayer.position = CGPoint(x: frame.size.width/2 +
frame.size.height/2 * 0.8, y: frame.size.height/2)

layer.addSublayer(airplaneLayer)
```

The code should look familiar – you've already done this few times in previous chapters. You simply load *airplane.png* and assign it as the contents of a layer on the screen, then position the airplane layer at the location where the circle starts drawing.

Build and run your project to see the airplane appear when you pull the table view down:

The plane should fade in as the user pulls the table down.

Add the following code to `init(frame:scrollView:)`:

```
airplaneLayer.opacity = 0.0
```

This makes the airplane completely transparent to start.

Now add the following code to `redrawFromProgress()` to progressively change the `opacity` of the airplane layer as the user pulls down:

```
airplaneLayer.opacity = Float(progress)
```

`opacity` is of type `Float` so you need to convert `progress` from a `CGFloat`.

Build and run your project; pull down the table and you should see the airplane appear gradually:

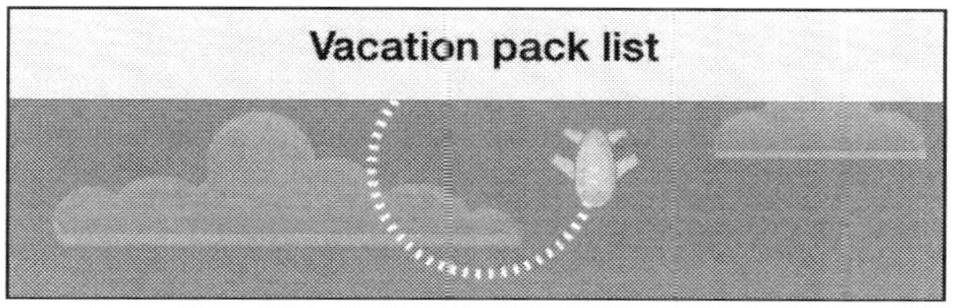

This wraps up the interactive animation part of this chapter. The next section walks you through animating a progress indicator to keep the users engaged while they wait for the faux refreshed data.

Animating both stroke ends

In this section, you'll animate *both* the `strokeStart` and `strokeEnd` properties to make the shape "run around".

You'll start the animation when the app starts to fetch the faux data. Add the following code to the end of `beginRefreshing()`:

```
let strokeStartAnimation = CABasicAnimation(
 keyPath: "strokeStart")
strokeStartAnimation.fromValue = -0.5
strokeStartAnimation.toValue = 1.0

let strokeEndAnimation = CABasicAnimation(keyPath: "strokeEnd")
strokeEndAnimation.fromValue = 0.0
strokeEndAnimation.toValue = 1.0
```

This code creates two animations: the first one animates `strokeStart` from `-0.5` to `1.0`. This is a simple and cheap animation trick; while the value animates from `-0.5` to `0.0` nothing happens, as all negative values for these properties simply mean no part of the shape is visible.

This gives the second animation – the one on `strokeEnd` – a bit of a head start. This draws a small bit of the shape on the screen, until `strokeStart` catches up with `strokeEnd` at the end of the animation.

Add the following code the end of `beginRefreshing()` to run the two animations simultaneously:

```
let strokeAnimationGroup = CAAnimationGroup()
strokeAnimationGroup.duration = 1.5
strokeAnimationGroup.repeatDuration = 5.0
strokeAnimationGroup.animations = [strokeStartAnimation,
strokeEndAnimation]
ovalShapeLayer.addAnimation(strokeAnimationGroup, forKey: nil)
```

In the code above, you create an animation group and repeat the animation five times; this should be long enough to keep the animation running while the refresh view is visible. Then you add both animations to the group and add the group to the progress bar.

Build and run your project; pull and release the table to see your animation in action:

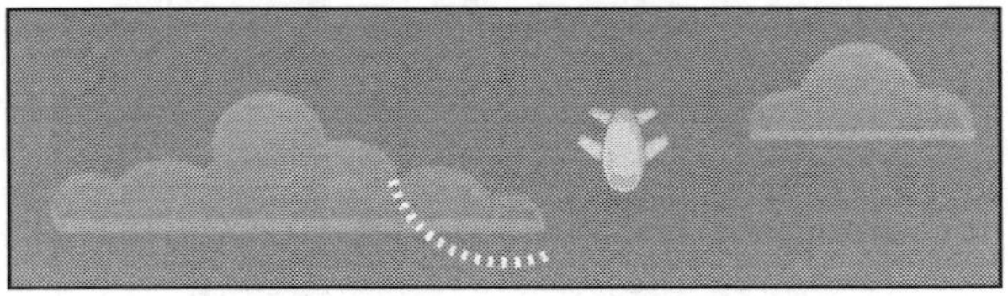

You've just created your own custom spinner! :] Although it looks pretty neat, you can make it even cooler with just a little effort – and some help from layer path animations!

Creating path keyframe animations

You saw how to animate a layer using a keyframe animation and the `values` property in Chapter 12, "Keyframe animations and struct properties"; to animate a layer along a path you do much the same thing but you assign a `CGPath` to the animation's `path` property instead.

Core Animation will then calculate the intermediate positions of the layer along the `CGPath` and animate it nicely over the animation's duration.

Add the following code to beginRefreshing():

```
let flightAnimation = CAKeyframeAnimation(keyPath: "position")
flightAnimation.path = ovalShapeLayer.path
flightAnimation.calculationMode = kCAAnimationPaced
```

Here you create a new CAKeyframeAnimation and, much like before, set the animated property to position. But this time you assign a value to path; in this case you can re-use the circular path of ovalShapeLayer.

Finally you set the animation calculationMode to a paced mode – this will make sure that the layer animates smoothly along the path.

calculationMode is yet another way you can control the timing of your animation. When you set that property to kCAAnimationPaced Core Animation animates your layer with a constant pace ignoring any key times you've set. This is very useful for producing smooth animations across an arbitrary path.

Another possible value to use is kCAAnimationDiscrete – this calculation mode makes Core Animation jump from key value to key value without any interpolation. Yes you got it right – Core Animation has a special mode to produce animations that don't animate anything :]

Enough calculation mode fun – back to the task at hand.

Now you need to create a group out of this animation and run it on the airplane layer; you need the group later on as you'll add a second animation to complement the first.

Add the following code to beginRefreshing():

```
let flightAnimationGroup = CAAnimationGroup()
flightAnimationGroup.duration = 1.5
flightAnimationGroup.repeatDuration = 5.0
flightAnimationGroup.animations = [flightAnimation]
airplaneLayer.addAnimation(flightAnimationGroup, forKey: nil)
```

In the code above, you create the group and give it the same duration and repeat count as the progress bar stroke animation. You then add flightAnimation as the only item in the group and add the group to the airplane layer.

Run the animation and check out the pilot's skills:

You've never seen an airshow like this one: the airplane performs loops in the sky and stays perfectly vertical! :] As amusing as this is, you should probably make the plane fly more naturally.

> **Note**: `CAKeyframeAnimation` has a special property called `rotationMode`, which when set to `kCAAnimationRotateAuto` will automatically orient your layer in the direction it's moving. However, you'll create this effect manually in this chapter, as it's an easy task for simple, circular paths.

Insert the following new animation code **above** the line where you create `flightAnimationGroup`:

```
let airplaneOrientationAnimation = CABasicAnimation(
 keyPath: "transform.rotation")
airplaneOrientationAnimation.fromValue = 0
airplaneOrientationAnimation.toValue = 2 * M_PI
```

`airplaneOrientationAnimation` rotates the layer a full `360` degrees – from `0` to 2π – via its `transform`. In other words, the airplane image will rotate in a full circle around its center, and since you move the airplane layer along the circular path at the same time, the flight will end up looking natural.

Now you just need to add `airplaneOrientationAnimation` to the animation group.

Add the new animation to the array as shown below:

```
flightAnimationGroup.animations = [flightAnimation,
airplaneOrientationAnimation]
```

Build and run your project and enjoy your completed pull-down-to-refresh control:

If you'd like to experiment with air acrobatics, you can try setting the rotation animation to go from `0` to 4π – good fun!

Keep in mind that you're not limited to simple paths such as squares or circles. You can feed just about any `CGPath` to your keyframe animation and send your layer along some extremely complicated paths.

If you're going to create more complex path animations and want to stay sane, you'd do well to keep in mind the note about `rotationMode` earlier in this chapter.

Section conclusion

This wraps up the basic layer animations section. You've been through a lot – and learned a ton of things along the way!

In this section of the book you covered:

- Basic movement, fading, rotation, and scaling animations
- Groups and keyframe animations
- Shapes, masks, and gradient animations
- Stroke and path animations

The next chapter will guide you through a totally new field of expertise – making some animation clones of your own!

Chapter 16: Replicating Animations

In this chapter you're going to try something completely new – using a container layer that lets you **replicate** animations.

Let me introduce you to my favorite layer class: `CAReplicatorLayer`.

The idea behind `CAReplicatorLayer` is simple. You create some content — it could be a shape, an image or anything else you can draw with layers — and `CAReplicatorLayer` makes copies of it on the screen, like so:

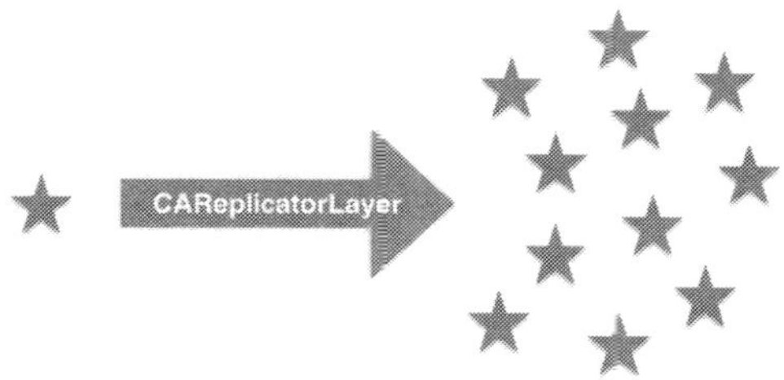

"Why would I need to clone shapes or images?" you would ask. And you would be right to ask that; it's not often you'd need the exact thing cloned a number of times.

`CAReplicatorLayer`'s superpowers come from the fact you can easily instruct it to make each clone slightly different from its ancestor.

For example, you could progressively change the tint of each copy. Your original layer could be magenta, while you progress the tint towards cyan as you create each copy:

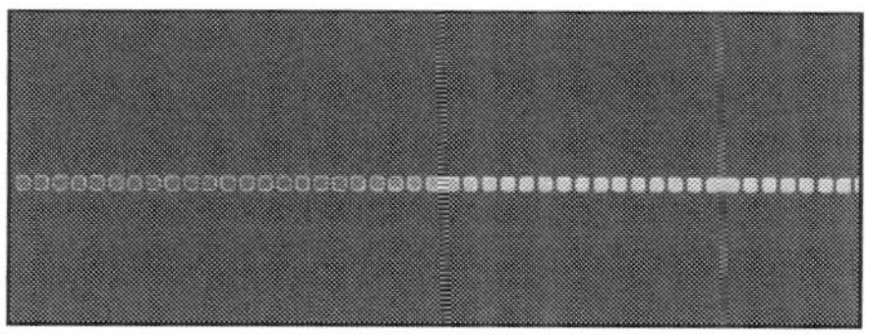

Furthermore, you can apply a transform between copies; for example, you can apply a simple rotation transform between each copy to draw them in a circle, as shown below:

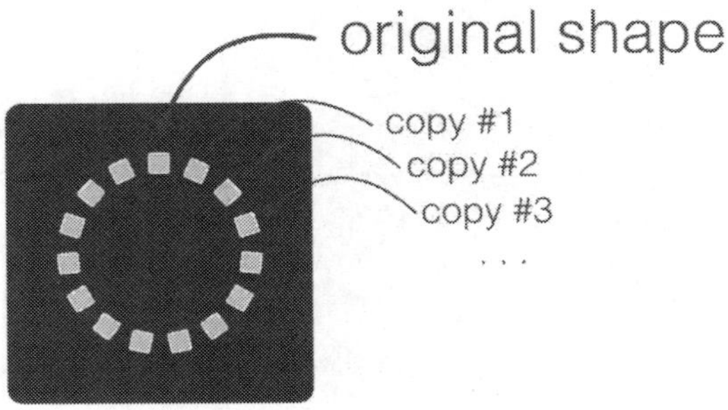

But the best feature of all is the ability to set an animation delay to follow each copy. When you set an `instanceDelay` of `0.2` seconds and add an animation to your original content, the first copy will animate with a delay of `0.2` seconds, the second copy will animate in `0.4` seconds, the third one in `0.6` seconds and so forth.

You can use this to create engaging and complex animations where you animate multiple elements in a synchronous manner.

In this chapter, you're going to work on a personal assistant app that will "listen" to your questions and answer back. As a wink to Apple's own personal assistant Siri, your project has been named Iris. :]

You're going to create two different replications. First, you'll create the visual feedback animation that plays while Iris talks, which will look much like a psychedelic sine wave:

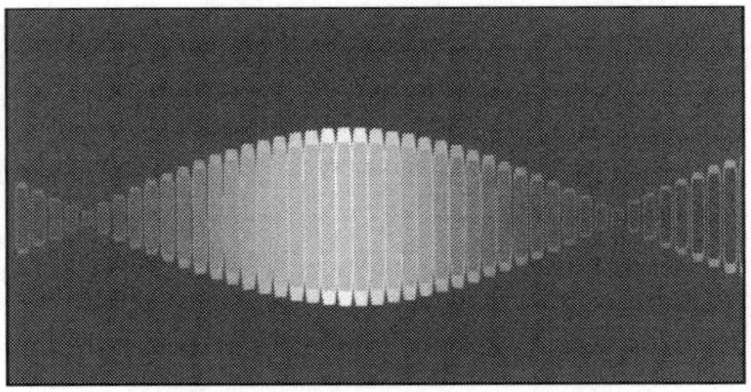

Then you'll use `CAReplicatorLayer` to create an interactive microphone-driven audio wave, which will provide visual feedback while the user speaks:

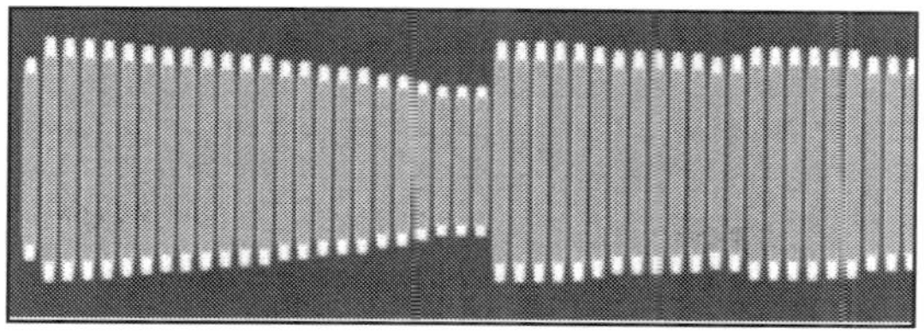

These two animations will introduce you to many features of `CAReplicatorLayer`. To cover every feature this layer offers would fill an entire book on its own! :]

But you don't need to listen to me yammer on about how much I like creating animations with `CAReplicatorLayer`; it's time to experience the magic for yourself.

Replicating like rabbits

Starter project overview

Launch the starter project for this chapter and open **Main.storyboard** – you'll notice that the project setup is quite straightforward:

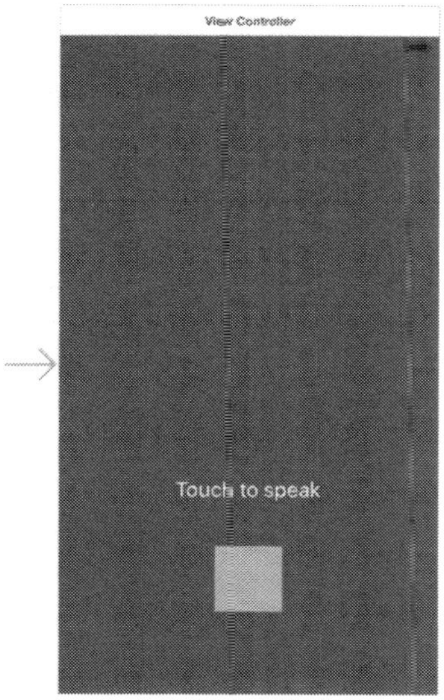

There is only a single view controller, which features a button and a label. The user asks their question while they hold down the button; when they release the button Iris will speak in response. The label will display the mic input levels and Iris' answer.

Open **ViewController.swift**; note the button events are already connected to actions. When the user touches down on the button `actionStartMonitoring()` fires; when the user lifts their finger, `actionEndMonitoring()` fires.

Right now `ViewController` doesn't do much and simply calls `startSpeaking()` from within `actionEndMonitoring()` when the user lifts their finger.

The project features two more classes that are beyond the scope of this chapter, but they'll help you develop a fun and functional app while letting you focus on the animation parts. They are as follows:

- `Assistant` – the artificial intelligence assistant. It has a list of predefined amusing answers and speaks them in response to the user's questions.
- `MicMonitor` – monitors the input levels on your iPhone's microphone and repeatedly calls a closure expression that you provide. This is where you have the chance to update the display.

Everything is ready for you to jump in and add some cool animations!

Setting up the replicator layer

Open **ViewController.swift** and add the following two properties:

```
let replicator = CAReplicatorLayer()
let dot = CALayer()
```

`dot` will be a simple shape drawn using the `CALayer` basic properties such as background and border color. `replicator` will help you get multiple `dot` copies on screen.

Next, add the following constants you'll need to create your animation:

```
let dotLength: CGFloat = 6.0
let dotOffset: CGFloat = 8.0
```

You'll use the first constant as the width and height of the `dot` layer, while the second constant holds the offset between each `dot` replication.

To finish off the setup, you'll have to add the replicator layer to the view controller's view. Add the following to `viewDidLoad()`:

```
replicator.frame = view.bounds
view.layer.addSublayer(replicator)
```

Here you make the replicator layer the same size as the view controller's view and add it as a sub-layer. If you were to run the project at this point, nothing would appear to have changed; that's because you didn't add any visible content to replicate.

The next step is to dress up the `dot` layer and add it to `replicator` in order to display the replications. Append the following to `viewDidLoad()`:

```
dot.frame = CGRect(
  x: replicator.frame.size.width - dotLength,
  y: replicator.position.y,
  width: dotLength, height: dotLength)
dot.backgroundColor = UIColor.lightGrayColor().CGColor
dot.borderColor = UIColor(white: 1.0, alpha: 1.0).CGColor
dot.borderWidth = 0.5
dot.cornerRadius = 1.5
```

You first position the `dot` layer towards the right edge of the replicator and therefore, the right edge of the screen. Then you set the layer's background color and add a border. At this point the layer will look like the following:

To see it displayed on the screen, add the following:

```
replicator.addSublayer(dot)
```

This adds `dot` to `replicator`. Run your project and you'll see it show up:

So far so good – what you see is what you would expect from adding just about any layer to any other layer.

"But where's the magic you promised us?" you're asking. Hang tight – you're almost there! :]

You're going to work with three `CAReplicatorLayer` properties that will help you access that replication magic:

- `instanceCount` – sets the number of copies you want

- `instanceTransform` – sets the transform to apply between copies
- `instanceDelay` – sets the animation delay between copies

You want the replication to fill the screen, so you'll have to divide the screen width by the offset between copies (`dotOffset`) to get the number of dots needed to fill up the width. This will give you more replications on iPhone 6 Plus and fewer on an iPhone 5.

Add the following line to **`viewDidLoad()`** to set the number of copies (including the original copy):

```
replicator.instanceCount = Int(view.frame.size.width / dotOffset)
```

On an iPhone 6 Plus `instanceCount` ends up as `51`; on an iPhone 6 `46`, and on iPhone 4 and 5 series, `40`.

Run the project again; hey, where are all the copies?

No, the photocopier isn't on the fritz again. :] All your copies of `dot` are there, but they're all on top of each other. You'll need to apply a transform to show them all.

Add the following:

```
replicator.instanceTransform = CATransform3DMakeTranslation(
  -dotOffset, 0.0, 0.0)
```

In the code above, you first set a translation transform between each replication. You then take the negative value of `dotOffset` for the translation on the X axis because you want the copies to progress from right to left.

`replicator` will consider `dot` and subtract `8.0` points from its `position` – the first copy will appear at this point. The second copy will appear at another `8.0` points to the left and so forth.

Run your project; you'll see all copies line up in the middle of the screen, each replication translated `8` points from the previous one:

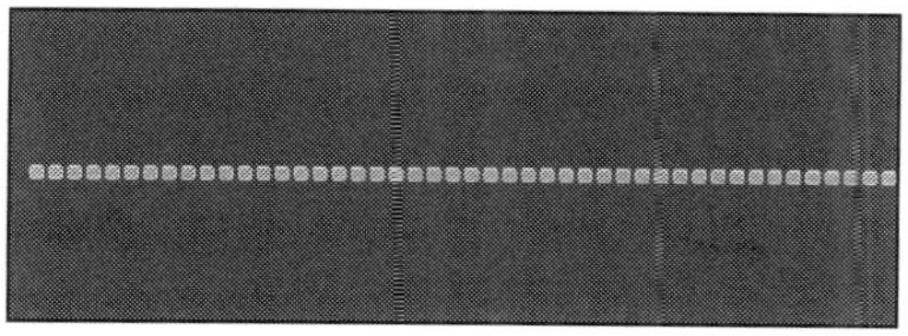

Your first replicated animation

To understand what `instanceDelay` does, you'll add a little test animation to `dot`. Add the following to the end of `viewDidLoad()`:

```
let move = CABasicAnimation(keyPath: "position.y")
move.fromValue = dot.position.y
move.toValue = dot.position.y - 50.0
move.duration = 1.0
move.repeatCount = 10
dot.addAnimation(move, forKey: nil)
```

This animation simply moves `dot` up `50.0` points and repeats that action `10` times. Run the project and you'll see all clones obediently moving across the screen like so many synchronized kill-bots.

Next you'll add a bit of delay to the animation. Insert the following line of code:

```
replicator.instanceDelay = 0.02
```

Run your project once more and observe how all copies follow the original `dot` animation, but only after an ever-increasing delay:

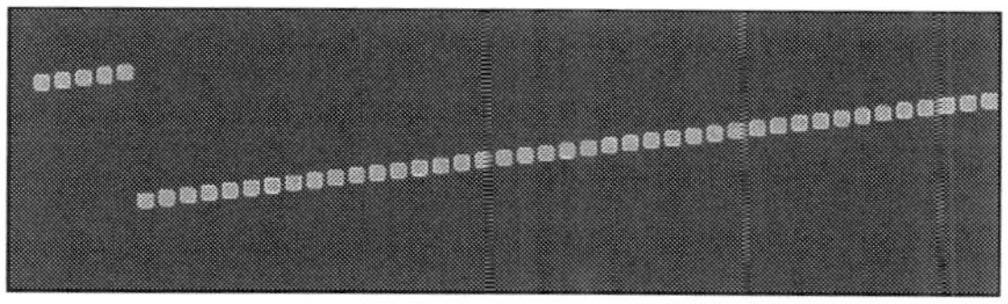

Now that you have the basics covered, it's time to move on to cooler animations.

Before you go on, delete the test animation; you're going to create much cooler ones in its place:

```
let move = CABasicAnimation(keyPath: "position.y")
move.fromValue = dot.position.y
move.toValue = dot.position.y - 50.0
move.duration = 1.0
move.repeatCount = 10
dot.addAnimation(move, forKey: nil)
```

Replicating multiple animations

CAReplicatorLayer simply replicates the content and animations you create in the manner you instruct. But it's up to you to come up with some cool animations that would look even *cooler* when replicated.

In this section, you'll work on the animation that plays while Iris speaks. To do this, you'll combine a number of simple animations with different delays to produce the final effect.

Scale animation

First you'll continuously scale the dot layer up and down to produce a wave of dots.

Find startSpeaking() and add the following scale animation:

```
let scale = CABasicAnimation(keyPath: "transform")
scale.fromValue = NSValue(CATransform3D: CATransform3DIdentity)
scale.toValue = NSValue(CATransform3D:
  CATransform3DMakeScale(1.4, 15, 1.0))
scale.duration = 0.33
scale.repeatCount = Float.infinity
scale.autoreverses = true
scale.timingFunction = CAMediaTimingFunction(name:
  kCAMediaTimingFunctionEaseOut)
dot.addAnimation(scale, forKey: "dotScale")
```

This is a simple layer animation like the many others in this section of the book. You scale the dot layer vertically 15-fold and run the animation continuously back and forth.

Run the project and tap the gray button; this calls actionStartMonitoring(), actionEndMonitoring() and finally your code in startSpeaking(). You should see your original dot layer animate and all copies follow with their respective delays:

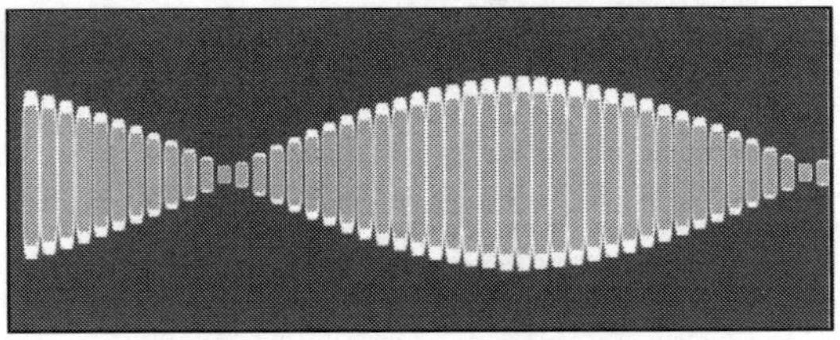

Congrats — you're off to a great start with CAReplicatorLayer!

> **Note**: For some extra-curricular fun, try changing the timing function of the animation to see what other cool waveforms you can create.

Opacity animation

Next you'll make the original `dot` layer fade in and out. This will make the wave some dimension and change the alpha as it grows and shrinks to simulate light conditions. It will look much like a spinning twisty ribbon candy.

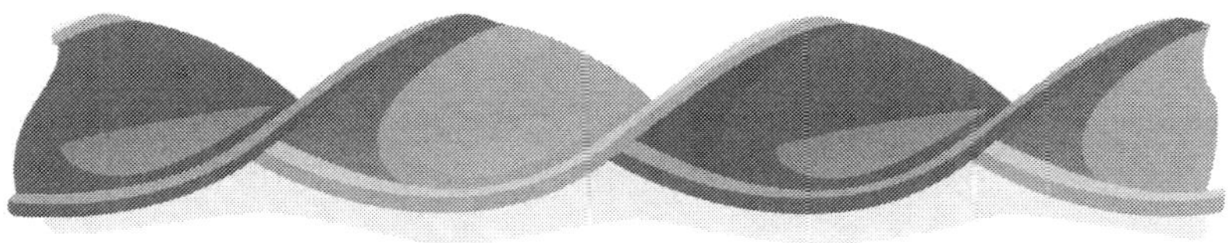

Add the following fade animation to `startSpeaking()`:

```
let fade = CABasicAnimation(keyPath: "opacity")
fade.fromValue = 1.0
fade.toValue = 0.2
fade.duration = 0.33
fade.beginTime = CACurrentMediaTime() + 0.33
fade.repeatCount = Float.infinity
fade.autoreverses = true
fade.timingFunction = CAMediaTimingFunction(name:
  kCAMediaTimingFunctionEaseOut)
dot.addAnimation(fade, forKey: "dotOpacity")
```

You fade the `dot` layer from opacity `1.0` to `0.2` over the duration of the scale animation. This time around, you start the animation with a delay of `0.33` seconds; this starts the fade-out effect when the wave it at its fullest.

Run your project and enjoy the new effect as the two animations run simultaneously:

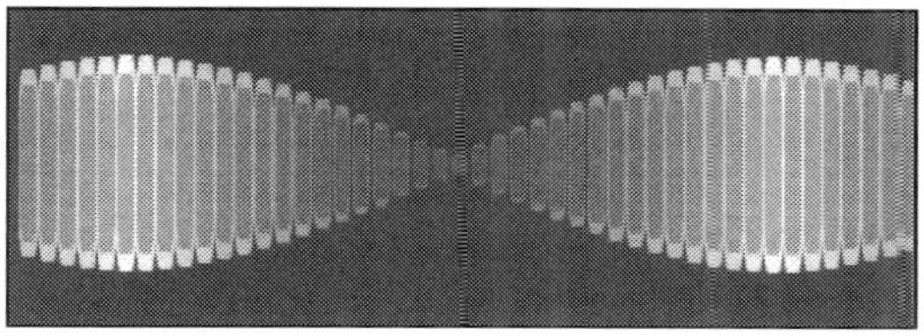

Tint animation

If you push your imagination (and squint a little) you can imagine the wave twisting around and around on your screen. That impression would be a lot more clear if you animated its tint, as if the wave had a different color on each side.

This should be an easy enough task – all you have to do is animate the background color of `dot`.

Add a third animation to `startSpeaking()`:

```
let tint = CABasicAnimation(keyPath: "backgroundColor")
tint.fromValue = UIColor.magentaColor().CGColor
tint.toValue = UIColor.cyanColor().CGColor
tint.duration = 0.66
tint.beginTime = CACurrentMediaTime() + 0.28
tint.fillMode = kCAFillModeBackwards
tint.repeatCount = Float.infinity
tint.autoreverses = true
tint.timingFunction = CAMediaTimingFunction(name:
  kCAMediaTimingFunctionEaseInEaseOut)
dot.addAnimation(tint, forKey: "dotColor")
```

This animation changes the dot's tint from magenta to cyan and back. You use a duration of `0.66` seconds; this is twice the frequency of the scaling animation and gives the impression that the color changes every time the wave "twists".

You also give the animation a delay of `0.28` seconds; this makes the color tint animation start just before the "twist" occurs in the wave. This subtle effect provides a hint of the next color just before the wave "twists" as if there's a bit of reflection going on.

Run the project to check out the new effect:

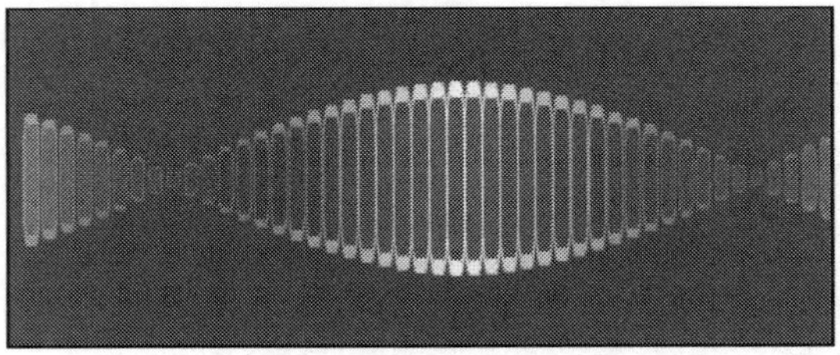

Animating CAReplicatorLayer properties

So far you've created a pretty dazzling effect by animating the content in your `replicator` layer. But since `CAReplicatorLayer` is a layer itself, you can animate a number of its own properties too.

You can animate `CAReplicatorLayer`'s basic properties like `position`, `backgroundColor` or `cornerRadius` but, you can create some interesting effects by animating some of the special properties in this layer that aren't present in other layers.

The animatable properties unique to `CAReplicatorLayer` include the following:

- `instanceDelay` – animate the amount of delay between instances
- `instanceTransform` – change the transform between replications on the fly
- `instanceColor` – change the blend color used for all instances
- `instanceRedOffset`, `instanceGreenOffset`, `instanceBlueOffset` – apply a delta to apply to each instance color component
- `instanceAlphaOffset` – change the opacity delta applied to each instance

In this section, you'll animate the instance transform to make the speech wave even *more* psychedelic!

Add one more animation to the end of `startSpeaking()`:

```
let initialRotation = CABasicAnimation(keyPath:
  "instanceTransform.rotation")
initialRotation.fromValue = 0.0
initialRotation.toValue   = 0.01
initialRotation.duration = 0.33
initialRotation.removedOnCompletion = false
initialRotation.fillMode = kCAFillModeForwards
initialRotation.timingFunction = CAMediaTimingFunction(name:
  kCAMediaTimingFunctionEaseOut)
replicator.addAnimation(initialRotation, forKey:
  "initialRotation")
```

This animation affects just the rotation component of the instance transform; that is, it preserves the translation component you set for the instances in `viewDidLoad()` and only animates the rotation.

You animate the rotation between instances from `0.0` radians to `0.01` radians. Each replication will appear slightly rotated compared to its neighbor.

Run your project; enjoy your replicating animations on a totally new level — or should I say *curve*? :]

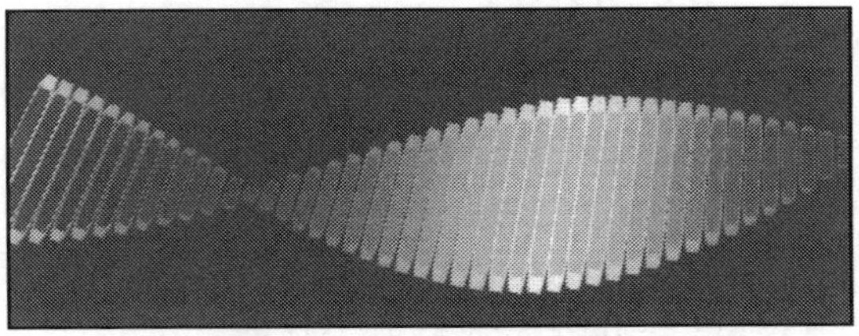

The `instanceRotation` animation above looks nice — but when I say *psychedelic*, I mean *PSYCHEDELIC*! What if you were to combine the effect of all running replication animations AND twist and spin the wave at the same time?

Add the animation below to complete the effect:

```
let rotation = CABasicAnimation(keyPath:
  "instanceTransform.rotation")
rotation.fromValue = 0.01
rotation.toValue   = -0.01
rotation.duration = 0.99
rotation.beginTime = CACurrentMediaTime() + 0.33
rotation.repeatCount = Float.infinity
rotation.autoreverses = true
rotation.timingFunction = CAMediaTimingFunction(name:
  kCAMediaTimingFunctionEaseInEaseOut)
replicator.addAnimation(rotation, forKey: "replicatorRotation")
```

Here, you run a second animation on `instanceTransform.rotation` that starts once the first animation has finished. You then animate the transform rotation from `0.01` radians (the final value of the first animation) to `-0.01` radians and back.

This gives the speech animation a final, crazy boost:

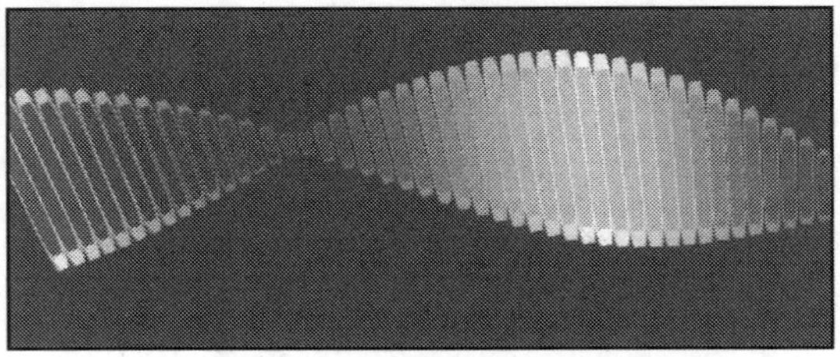

This is an outstanding (if not hypnosis-inducing) animation, and you created it by combining just a few select animations. The trick is to know which properties to animate and how to select the correct delays and durations to get the effect you're looking for.

> **Note**: Personally, I think the effect looks best if I rotate my head 45 degrees right. But be careful not to watch it too long - it could make you dizzy! :]

All that's left is to give your not-so-helpful assistant, Iris, the ability to listen and to respond.

First you'll give the power of speech to Iris. The starter project class named `Assistant` will help you do that. Add the following to the top of `startSpeaking()`:

```
meterLabel.text = assistant.randomAnswer()
assistant.speak(meterLabel.text!, completion: endSpeaking)
speakButton.hidden = true
```

You first get a random answer from the `Assistant` class and visualize it via the `meterLabel`. Then you call `speak(_:completion:)` on `assistant`; once that's done you simply call `endSpeaking()`.

> **Note**: You'll probably notice that Iris speaks way too fast in iOS 8; this is a bug that's been fixed in iOS 9.

Next you'll add the code in `endSpeaking()` that removes all running animations and gracefully returns the wave to its initial state.

Insert the following into `endSpeaking()`:

```
replicator.removeAllAnimations()
```

This removes the animations on `instanceTransform`.

Next you need to animate the `dot` layer back to its original scale. Add:

```
let scale = CABasicAnimation(keyPath: "transform")
scale.toValue = NSValue(CATransform3D: CATransform3DIdentity)
scale.duration = 0.33
scale.removedOnCompletion = false
scale.fillMode = kCAFillModeForwards
dot.addAnimation(scale, forKey: nil)
```

For this animation you don't specify a `fromValue`; this means that Core Animation will start the animation from the current value and animate the transform to `CATransform3DIdentiy`.

This is necessary because at any given time each of the replicated instances has a different `transform`. Omitting `fromValue` animates each replication from its current scale to the animation's final value.

Finally, add the following code to remove the rest of the currently running animations from `dot` and reset the speak button state:

```
dot.removeAnimationForKey("dotColor")
dot.removeAnimationForKey("dotOpacity")
dot.backgroundColor = UIColor.lightGrayColor().CGColor

speakButton.hidden = false
```

Run the project again; this time, Iris will speak a random answer right back at you!

When Iris is done speaking, the wave will gracefully animate back to its initial state:

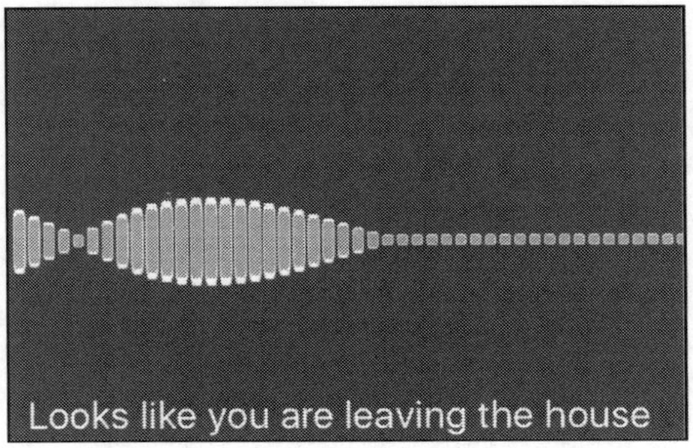

Interactive replication animations

Right now you need to press the speak button each time to see and hear Iris' answer. But you don't get to actually *ask* her anything, which, to be honest, is the really fun part.

In this final section you'll create an animation that displays the microphone input while you ask Iris your questions.

> **Note:** In case the microphone in the iOS simulator does not work for you use a physical device to test your app in this part of the chapter.

Add the following to `actionStartMonitoring()`:

```
dot.backgroundColor = UIColor.greenColor().CGColor
```

```
monitor.startMonitoringWithHandler {level in
  self.meterLabel.text = String(format: "%.2f db", level)
}
```

The above method fires when the user presses on the speak button. To indicate the app is "listening", you change the `dot` layer color to green. Then you call `startMonitoringWithHandler()` on the monitor instance.

> **Note**: The `MicMonitor` class is pretty simple – peek inside **MicMonitor.swift** if you're interested to see how it gets the microphone levels.

The closure block you provide as a parameter executes repeatedly and gets the current microphone level as a parameter.

Run the app and hold the button; speak to the device and you'll see the current mic levels displayed. If iOS prompts you for microphone access, simply tap OK on the system alert:

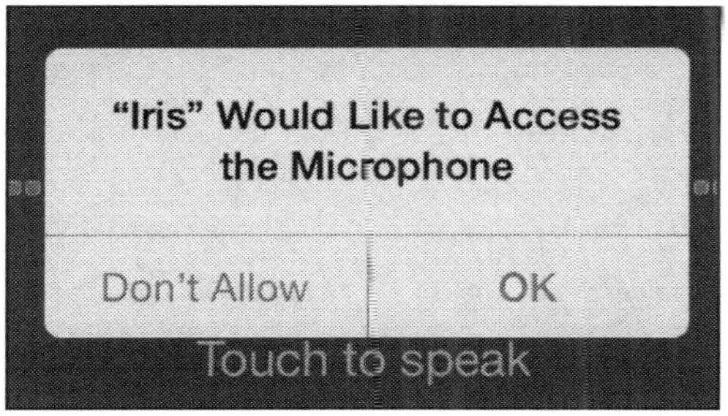

So far so good; all you need now is to use the `level` variable to animate the replicator content accordingly.

First of all, you'll need to normalize the mic level to something you can use for your animations. `level` has a value in the rage of `-160.0` db to `0.0` db, `-160.0` db being the quietest and `0.0` db meaning extremely loud sound.

Add the following underlined code to the handler block to convert the level value to something useful and store it in `scaleFactor`:

```
monitor.startMonitoringWithHandler {level in
  self.meterLabel.text = String(format: "%.2f db", level)

  let scaleFactor = max(0.2, CGFloat(level) + 50) / 2
}
```

`scaleFactor` will store values between `0.1` and `25.0` – you can use this to scale `dot` to a reasonable size to represent the microphone input levels.

Add the following instance property to the `ViewController` class:

```
var lastTransformScale: CGFloat = 0.0
```

For the scaling animation, you'll need to save the last scaled value to this property. Since you'll constantly overwrite the running scale animation, you need to keep track of the last value the layer was supposed to scale to.

Now jump back to the microphone handler closure and add to it the following code, which animates from the last transform to the new one you calculated from the current microphone levels:

```
let scale = CABasicAnimation(keyPath: "transform.scale.y")
scale.fromValue = self.lastTransformScale
scale.toValue = scaleFactor
scale.duration = 0.1
scale.removedOnCompletion = false
scale.fillMode = kCAFillModeForwards
self.dot.addAnimation(scale, forKey: nil)
```

This layer animation runs only on the y-axis of the `scale` component of the `dot` layer `transform`. You animate the scale from the last value used to the current `scaleFactor`.

Finally, still inside the handler, add the following code to save the current `scaleFactor` value for the next handler call:

```
self.lastTransformScale = scaleFactor
```

This code ought to bring the replicator layer to life. Run the project, hold the button and speak. You'll see an actual audio wave show up on screen – all handled by the replicator layer while you simply animate the original `dot` layer:

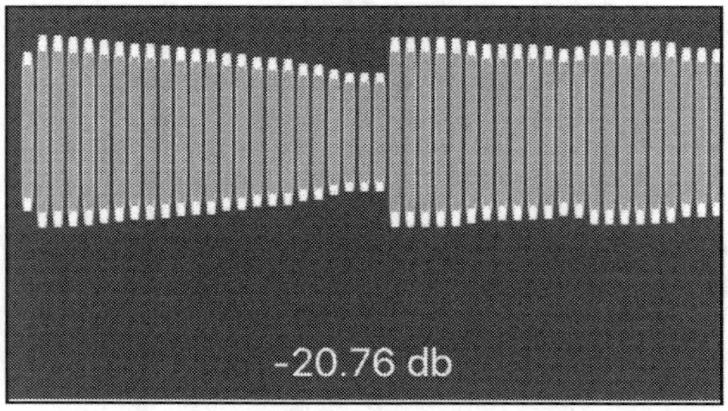

But when you let go of the speak button, the result is somewhat baffling:

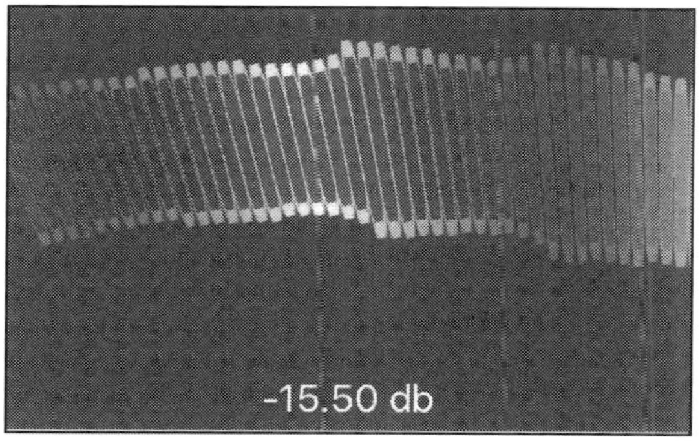

Aha - you need to reset the animations and stop monitoring the microphone. You can take care of that in `actionEndMonitoring()`.

Insert the following at the top of that method:

```
monitor.stopMonitoring()
dot.removeAllAnimations()
```

Here you disable the microphone monitor by calling `stopMonitoring()` and removing all animations running on the `dot` layer. This way the app can move on and display the Iris animation.

Give the app a try – isn't talking to Iris a lot of fun? :]

The microphone input animation ends somewhat abruptly, but you'll get to fix that in the challenges below.

That was a big chapter, but you've pulled through and are now ready to create your own `CAReplicatorLayer` animations.

Challenges

Challenge 1: Smooth the transition between microphone input and Iris animations

Your first challenge is to not just remove the two animations running on the `dot` layer by calling `dot.removeAllAnimations()`, but to animate the wave back to a state suitable for the next animation to be run.

Take this challenge in three steps:

First, delete the line where you remove the running animations on `dot` from `actionEndMonitoring()`.

Then, in its place, animate the scale of `dot` back to a value of `1.0` on the y-axis. Leave the animation on the screen to wait for the Iris animation to start — don't remove it when it's done.

Finally, add another animation that changes the `dot` tint from green to magenta. For this animation, use a `fillMode` of `kCAFillModeBackwards` – without it, the replicator layer will reset the tint to the final value retroactively.

Mind the durations of these two new animations – they should finish before the Iris animation starts.

When you've completed this challenge, the two animations should blend nicely into each other like so:

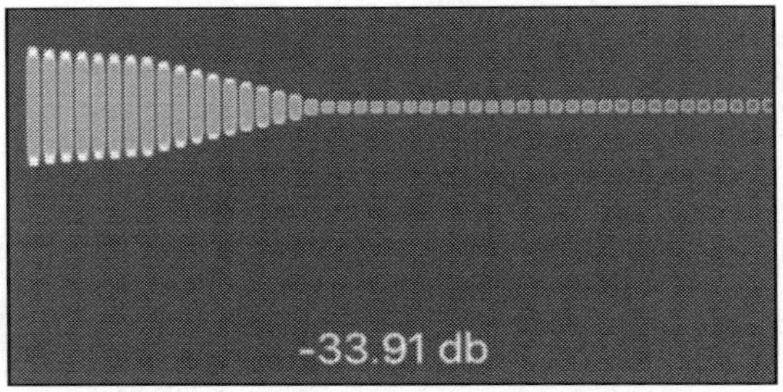

The next section adds a new dimension to your animations – literally! :] Read on to see how to add eye-catching 3D animations to your projects that really make your apps come to life.

Section IV: 3D Animations

Up to this point in the book you've only worked with animations in two dimensions, and for good reason – this is the most natural way to animate elements on a flat device screen. After all, buttons, text fields, switches, and images in the flat post-iOS 7 world don't have a third dimension; these elements exist in a plane defined by X and Y axes:

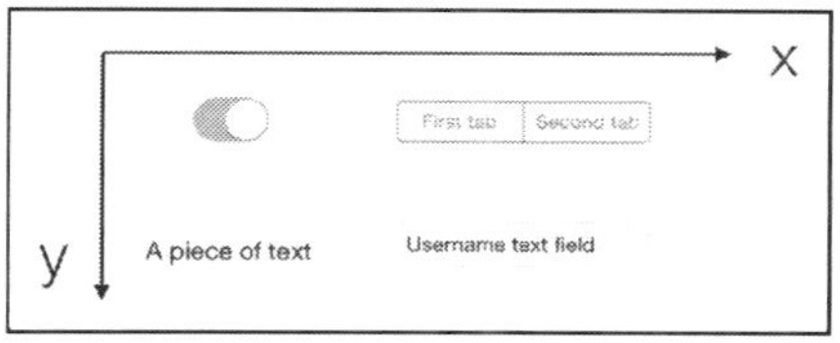

Core Animation helps you float free from this two dimensional world; although it isn't a true 3D framework, Core Animation has a lot of smarts to help you position two-dimensional objects in 3D space.

In other words, your layers and animations still take place in two dimensions, but you can rotate and position each element's 2D plane in a 3D space like so:

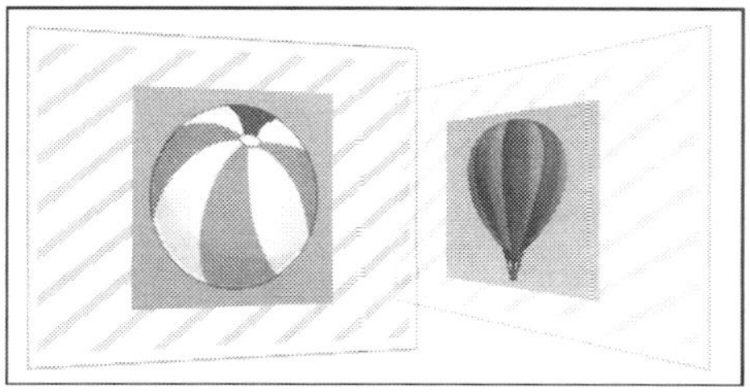

Shown above are two 2D images that are rotated in 3D space. The perspective distortion gives you an idea of how they are positioned from the renderer's point of view.

This section of the book will show you how to position and rotate layers in 3D space. You'll work with a special property of `CATransform3D`: namely, the transformation class applied to layers. `CATransform3D` is similar to `CGAffineTransform`, but in addition to letting you scale, skew and translate in the x and y directions, it also brings in the third dimension: z. The z-axis runs straight out of the device screen towards your eyes.

`CATransform3D` lets you determine where the rendering camera is located respective to the device's screen; this affects the amount of perspective distortion Core Animation applies to your views.

Consider the following few examples to better understand how perspective works. If you stand very, very close to an object, such as right in front of a skyscraper, the object will take up most of your view and you'll see a lot of perspective as the lines of the skyscraper recede into the distance.

In a similar way, setting the camera very close to the screen distorts your layer's perspective accordingly:

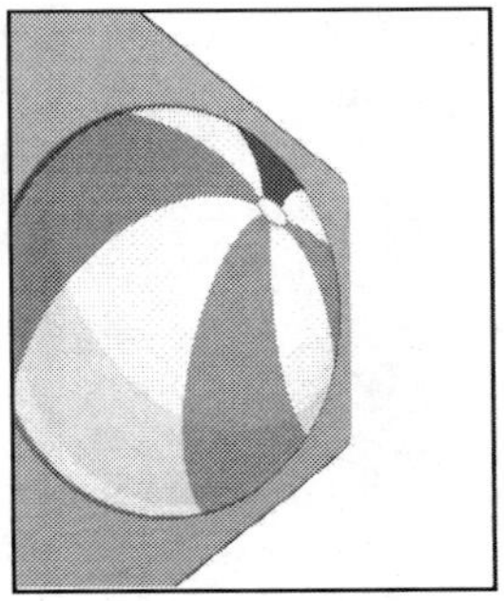

If you move the camera back from the object, there is less perspective distortion applied, just as you don't see as much perspective distortion when you view a skyscraper from a few blocks away:

Finally, if you set a great distance between the camera and the screen there won't be any noticeable perspective – just as you won't notice any perspective distortion on a skyscraper you view from across the city:

The image is still distorted, but notice how the top and bottom lines of the image frame are almost parallel. You're still looking at it at an angle, but the perspective distortion is very minor.

In the next two chapters you'll learn how to set up your layers in 3D space, how to choose the distance from the camera to your layer, and how to create animations in your 3D scene. With a bit of knowledge about perspective under your belt, the rest of this chapter should be a walk in a three-dimensional park! :]

Chapter 17: Simple 3D Animations

In this chapter you'll get to try out your newfound knowledge about camera distance and perspective as was covered in the introduction to this section.

Once you set up your layer's perspective, you can work on the layer's transform as you usually would; but now you can rotate, translate and scale your layer in three dimensions.

The project for this chapter features a folding pull-out menu as popularized in many apps, such as Taasky:

Office Buddy is an office helper app for employees to access categorized information about day-to-day company life.

The starter project already has all the code to make the menu functional, but it only works in 2D – your task is to bring the menu into the third dimension and give it life!

Creating 3D transformations

Open the starter project for this chapter and build and run it to see what the initial version of the Office Buddy app looks like:

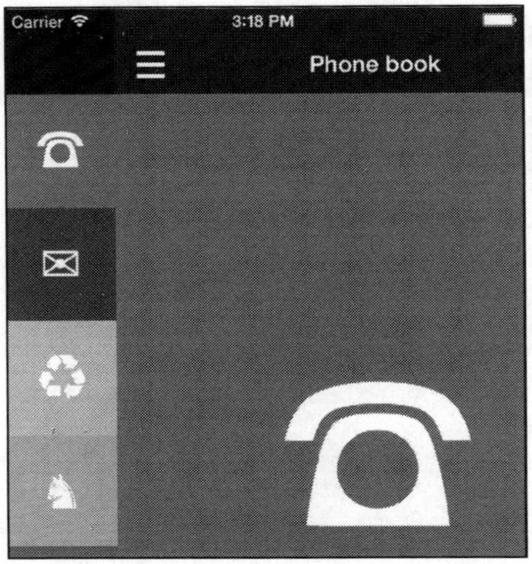

Tap the menu button to reveal the side menu; alternatively, you can swipe right to reveal the side menu.

As you can see, this app is as flat as they come. But armed with your new insight on 3D perspective, you're going to add some depth to the menu.

Open **ContainerViewController.swift**; this controller displays both the menu view controller and the content view controller on the screen. It also handles pan gestures so the user can open and close the menu.

Your first task is to build a class method that creates the corresponding 3D transform for a given percentage of "openness" of the side menu.

Add the following method declaration to **ContainerViewController.swift**:

```
func menuTransformForPercent(percent: CGFloat) -> CATransform3D {

}
```

The above method accepts a single parameter of the current progress of the menu, which was calculated by the code in `handleGesture(_:)`, and returns an instance of `CATransform3D`. You're going to assign the result of this method directly to the menu layer's `transform` property.

Add the following code to your new method:

```
var identity = CATransform3DIdentity
identity.m34 = -1.0/1000
```

This code might look a bit surprising; so far you've only used *functions* to create or modify transforms. This time, however, you're modifying one of the class' *properties*.

> **Note**: Why is this property called m34? View and layer transforms are expressed as two-dimensional math matrices. In the case of a layer transform matrix, the element in the 3rd row at the 4th column sets your z-axis perspective. You can set this element directly to apply the desired perspective transform.

So you create a new `CATransform3D` struct and you set its `m34` property to `-1.0/1000`...

Keep explaining, dude.

Okay, I'll back up a little. To enable 3D transforms on a layer you need to set `m34` to `-1.0 / [camera distance]`. Since you read through the introduction for this section, you have some understanding of how the camera distance affects the scene perspective.

But why are you using `1000` for the camera distance? The distance is expressed in points between the camera and the front of the scene – but as to what value to use, the truth is that you need to try different values and see what looks good for your particular animation.

Working with camera distance

For UI elements in an average app you can consult the following reference table for some guidelines on an appropriate camera distance:

distance	
0.1...500	Very close, lots of perspective distortion.
750...2,000	Nice perspective, content is clearly visible.
2,000 and up	Almost no perspective distortion.

For the Office Buddy app, a distance of `1000` points will give the menu a nice subtle perspective. You can see it in action once you finish working on the current method.

Add the following code to the bottom of `menuTransformForPercent()`:

```
let remainingPercent = 1.0 - percent
let angle = remainingPercent * CGFloat(-M_PI_2)
```

In the above code you calculate the current angle of the menu based on its "openness" value.

Now add the following code to the bottom of `menuTransformForPercent()`:

```
let rotationTransform = CATransform3DRotate(identity, angle,
  0.0, 1.0, 0.0)
let translationTransform =
  CATransform3DMakeTranslation(menuWidth * percent, 0, 0)
return CATransform3DConcat(rotationTransform,
  translationTransform)
```

Here you use `rotationTransform` to rotate the layer away from you around its y-axis. The menu is moving in from the left, so you also create a translation transform to move it along the x-axis, eventually to `menuWidth` at `100%`. Finally, you concatenate the two transforms and return the result.

Now you can use `menuTransformForPercent()` to update the menu transform as the user pans right or left.

Remove the following line from `setToPercent()` that modifies the menu's origin:

```
menuViewController.view.frame.origin.x = menuWidth *
CGFloat(percent) - menuWidth
```

You don't need the above line anymore because you will move the menu via its `transform`. Add the following code to `setToPercent(percent:)`:

```
menuViewController.view.layer.transform =
menuTransformForPercent(percent)
```

Build and run your project, open and close couple of times the side menu; pan right to see how the menu rotates around its y-axis:

The menu rotates in 3D, but it's rotating around its horizontal center, which separates the menu from the content view controller.

Moving the layer's anchor point

By default, the x anchor point of a rotation is set to `0.5`. You need to set the x anchor point to `1.0` to make the menu rotate around its right edge like a hinge, as shown below:

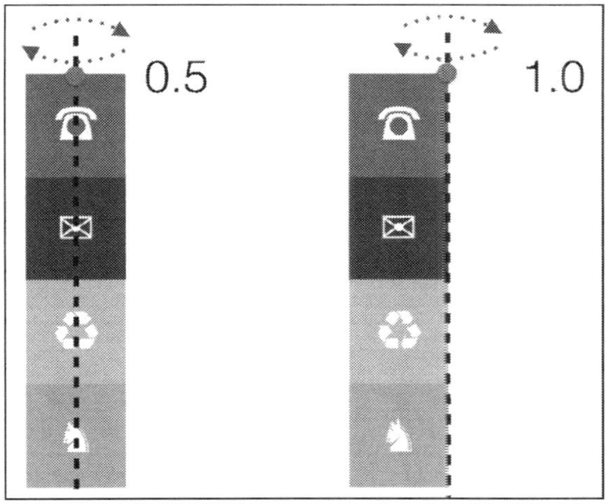

All transforms are calculated around the layer's anchor point. You also use the anchor point as your reference point when setting the `position` of the layer. This means it's best to change the layer's `anchorPoint` before you set its position on the screen.

Find the following line in `viewDidLoad()` where you set the menu frame:

```
menuViewController.view.frame = CGRect(x: -menuWidth, y: 0, width:
menuWidth, height: view.frame.height)
```

Now insert the following code just **above** that line:

```
menuViewController.view.layer.anchorPoint.x = 1.0
```

This rotates the menu around its right edge.

Build and run your project again, then pan horizontally through the view and observe how the effect has changed:

That looks much better! :]

You're almost done – there's just a few more bits to take care of.

Creating perspective through shading

Shading lends a lot of realism to 3D animations; to that end, you will rotate the menu out of the "shadow" of the left side of the content view controller.

You're not using any advanced shading techniques here; instead, you can simulate this by changing the alpha of the menu as it rotates.

Add the following code to `setToPercent()`:

```
menuViewController.view.alpha = CGFloat(max(0.2, percent))
```

In the code above, you assign the `percent` value directly to the layer's `alpha`, but you limit it to `0.2` to ensure the menu remains visible when it's edge-on to the user and doesn't disappear completely.

Since the background of this app is black, lowering the alpha of the menu view makes the black color show through the menu and simulates a shadow effect.

Build and run your project and observe the effect:

It's a small detail, but it really makes your 3D animation "pop"! :]

You might have noticed that when you tap the menu button the first time, the animation does not play in 3D – the effect only kicks in on the second and subsequent animations.

That's because you're not setting the 3D animation parameters and the layer transforms until *after* the first time you toggle the menu. This is easy to fix – as soon as the menu view controller loads, set the menu progress to `0.0` to set the proper menu layer transform.

Add the following to the bottom of `viewDidLoad()`:

```
setToPercent(0.0)
```

This will get the starting frames and layer transforms in place from the start. Build and run your project again; tap the menu button and you'll see that the animation works properly the first time through.

Rasterizing for efficiency

There's one last task to make your animation "perfect". If you stare at the menu long enough while you pan back and forth you'll notice the borders of the menu items look pixelated, as shown below:

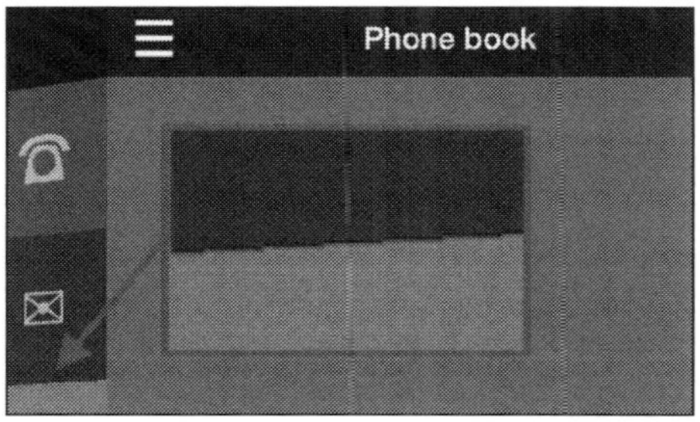

Core Animation continually redraws all contents of the menu view controller and recalculates the perspective distortion for all elements as it moves, which isn't terribly efficient – hence the jagged edges.

It's better to let Core Animation know that you won't change the menu contents during the animation so that it can render the menu once and simply rotate the rendered and cached image.

That sounds complicated at first, but you'll see it's quite easy to implement. Scroll to `handleGesture()` and find the `.Began` case block; this code executes when the user starts the pan action. This is where you'll instruct Core Animation to cache the menu.

Add the following code to the end of the `.Began` case block:

```
// Improve the look of the opening menu
menuViewController.view.layer.shouldRasterize = true
menuViewController.view.layer.rasterizationScale =
  UIScreen.mainScreen().scale
```

`shouldRasterize` instructs Core Animation to cache the layer contents as an image. You then set `rasterizationScale` to match the current screen scale and you're golden!

Build and run your project again to see how your graphics have improved:

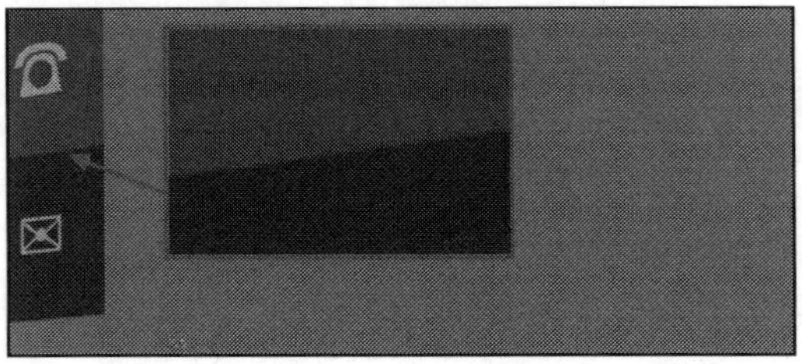

Core Animation really shines in this instance – working with 2D images is one of the things this framework really does well! :]

To avoid any unnecessary caching while using the app, you should turn off rasterization as soon as the animation is done.

Find the empty animation `completion` closure inside the `.Failed` case and add the following code:

```
self.menuViewController.view.layer.shouldRasterize = false
```

Now you're only activating rasterization during the animation. How efficient of you!

In only a few pages, you learned about camera distance, perspective, and how to set up your 3D scene and apply animations to it.

There's one more chapter in this section, which contains some more 3D fun – but before you go, take a look at this chapter's challenge first.

Challenges

Challenge 1: Create your own 3D animation

For this challenge you are going to create a 3D rotation animation for the menu button. As the user pans the button will rotate alongside the menu view controller.

Specifically, you will create a rotation around both the x- and y-axes to make the menu button flip on its diagonal like so:

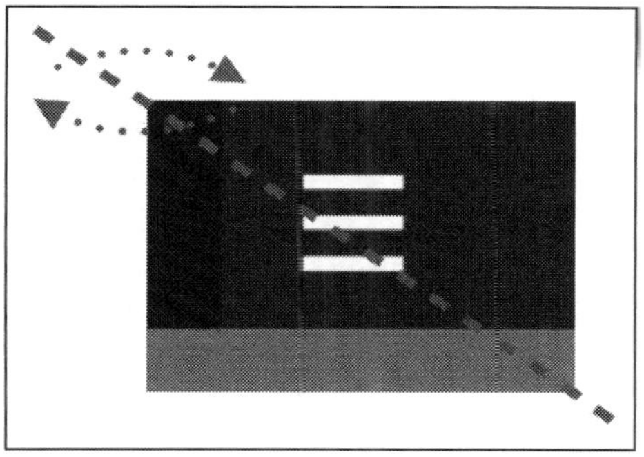

Add the following code to `setToPercent()` in **ContainerViewController.swift**:

```
let centerVC = (centerViewController as!
UINavigationController).viewControllers.first as?
CenterViewController
```

This fetches the current content view controller so you can work with it.

The menu button is accessible via the `menuButton` property of `CenterViewController`. For this challenge, adjust the 3D transform of the button's `imageView`.

If you directly rotate the button rather than use the 3D transform, it will clash with the navigation bar views underneath and might get partially obscured by the navigation bar.

In contrast, the button's own 2D space is already positioned on top of all navigation bar views before you rotate it – so if you rotate `menuButton.imageView` it rotates within the button's own plane, which is on top of the navigation bar at all times.

Another gotcha is that the first time the code runs `menuButton` will be `nil`, so you should treat it like an optional, even though it is implicitly unwrapped.

For the rotation, create a transform just like you did earlier in this chapter, but this time rotate the view around the x- and y-axes. If necessary, have a look at the documentation for `CATransform3DRotate()`.

This time you don't need to calculate the remaining percentage; to get the rotation angle, simply multiply the progress by M_PI.

When you are finished with your solution the button image should flip around while you pan through the screen like so:

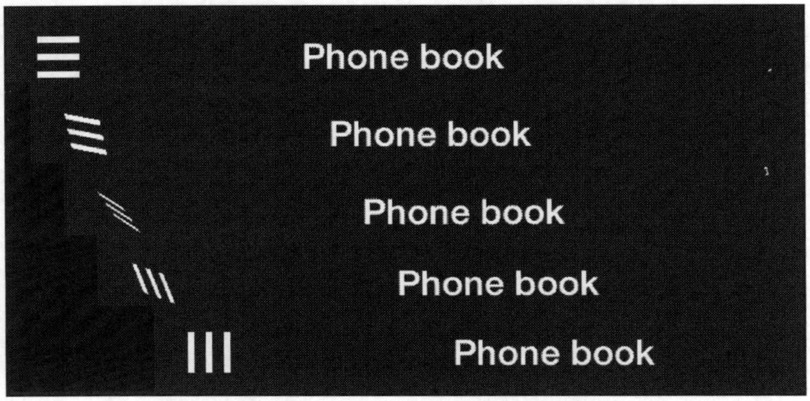

That's it! Head on in to the next chapter for more awesome animations in 3D!

Chapter 18: Intermediate 3D Animations

In the previous chapter, you learned that applying perspective to a single view isn't a complicated task; in fact, once you know the secret of `m34` and camera distance you can create all kinds of 3D animations.

This chapter builds on what you've already learned and shows you how to create convincing 3D animations with more than one view.

The starter project for this chapter is a simple hurricane image gallery. By the end of this chapter, you'll have a 3D effect to get an overall view of the images in the gallery:

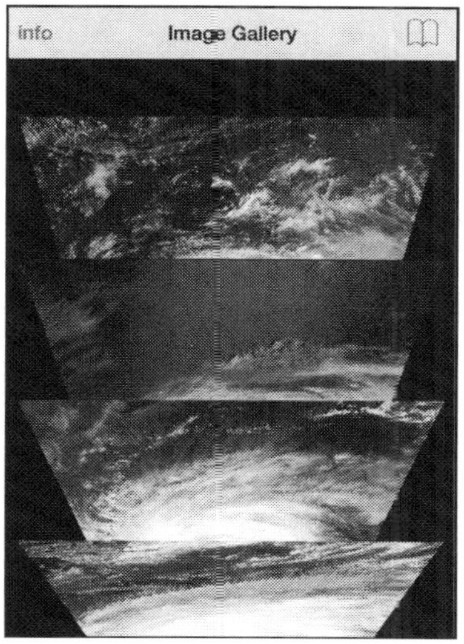

You'll be able to tap on a photo to bring it full screen, and tapping the top right button fans all the images open again – with a cool animation to take you between the two states, of course!

Ready to get started? Hang on to your hat and prepare to get blown away by this "stormy" project ! :]

Exploring the starter project

Open the starter project from the Resources folder for this chapter; build and run it to see what you have to start with:

All you have is a blank screen with two bar buttons on top: the left one shows the NASA image credits and the right one invokes the method that shows or hides the gallery as appropriate.

First, you'll need to display all images on the screen and set them up so they're ready for your "fan" animation.

Open **ViewController.swift** and inspect the class code. You'll see an array called `images` – this array contains some slightly customized image views. The `ImageViewCard` class inherits from `UIImageView` and adds a string property to hold the hurricane title and a property called `didSelect` so you can easily set a tap handler on the image.

Your first task is to add all images to the view controller's view. Add the following code to the end of `viewDidAppear()`:

```
for image in images {
  image.layer.anchorPoint.y = 0.0
  image.frame = view.bounds

  view.addSubview(image)
}
```

In the code above, you loop over all images, set each image's anchor point to `0.0` on the y-axis, and resize each image so it takes up the full screen. When that's done, you add each image to `view`.

Setting the anchor point lets the images rotate around their upper edge rather than the default of the center, as illustrated below:

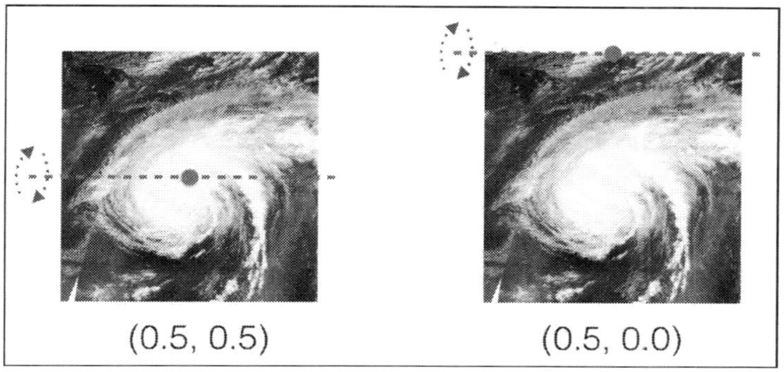

This will make it a lot easer to fan out the images in 3D space.

Build and run your project to see what you've achieved so far:

Hmm – you only see the last image you added to `view`. That's because all images have the same frame, so you only see the last image you added: Hurricane Irene.

To make it more obvious which hurricane image is being displayed, add the following line at the end of `viewDidAppear()`:

```
navigationItem.title = images.last?.title
```

This code takes the name of the last hurricane image in the collection and sets it as the navigation title of the view controller, like so.

Build and run again to familiarize yourself with Irene:

Notice that you didn't set any perspective transforms on the images; you're going to set a perspective directly on the view controller's view instead.

In the previous chapter you adjusted the `transform` property on a single view and then rotated it in 3D space. But since your current project has more individual views that you'd care to manipulate in 3D, you can set the perspective of their parent view instead to save yourself a bunch of work.

Add the following code to `viewDidAppear()`:

```
var perspective = CATransform3DIdentity
perspective.m34 = -1.0/250.0
view.layer.sublayerTransform = perspective
```

Here you use the layer property `sublayerTransform` to set the perspective of all sublayers of the view controller's layer. The sublayer transform is then combined with each individual layer's own transform.

This lets you focus on managing the rotation or translation of your subviews without having to worry about perspective. You'll see how this works in more detail in the next section.

Transforming the gallery

`toggleGallery()` is hooked up to the Browse bar button on the right and is where you'll apply your 3D transform to the four images.

Add the following variable to `toggleGallery()`:

```
var imageYOffset: CGFloat = 50.0
```

Since you don't just rotate all images in place but simply move them around to produce the "fan" animation, you use `imageYOffset` to set the offset of each image.

Next you need to iterate through all the images and run their individual animations.

Add the following code to `toggleGallery()`:

```
for subview in view.subviews {
  if let image = subview as? ImageViewCard {
    // more code here
  }
}
```

Here you loop through all subviews of the view controller's view and act only on the subviews that are instances of `ImageViewCard`.

Add the following code inside the `if` block you added above, to replace the `more code here` comment:

```
var imageTransform = CATransform3DIdentity

//1
imageTransform = CATransform3DTranslate(
  imageTransform, 0.0, imageYOffset, 0.0)
//2
imageTransform = CATransform3DScale(
  imageTransform, 0.95, 0.6, 1.0)
//3
imageTransform = CATransform3DRotate(
  imageTransform, CGFloat(M_PI_4/2), -1.0, 0.0, 0.0)
```

You start by assigning the identity transform to `imageTransform` and then add a series of adjustments to it. This is what each individual adjustment does to the image:

1. Move the image on the y-axis with `CATransform3DTranslate`; this offsets the image from its default `0.0` y-coordinate as shown below:

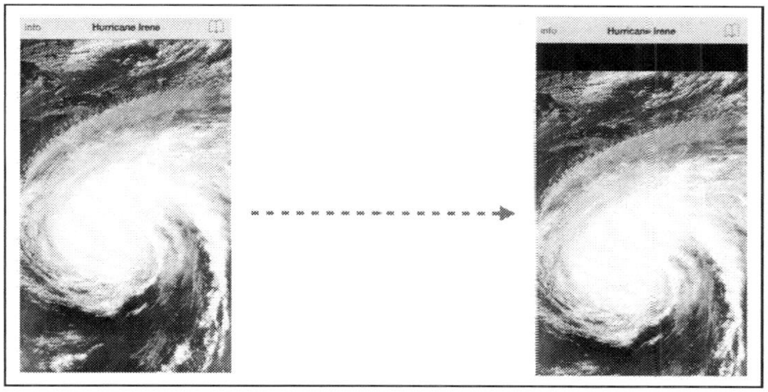

Later, you'll calculate the `imageYOffset` of each image separately; for now all images move by the same amount so you'll still see only the top one for the moment.

2. Scale the image by adjusting the scale component of the transform using `CATransform3DScale`. You shrink the image just a little on the x-axis, but you scale it down to `60%` on the y-axis to enrich the rotation 3D effect:

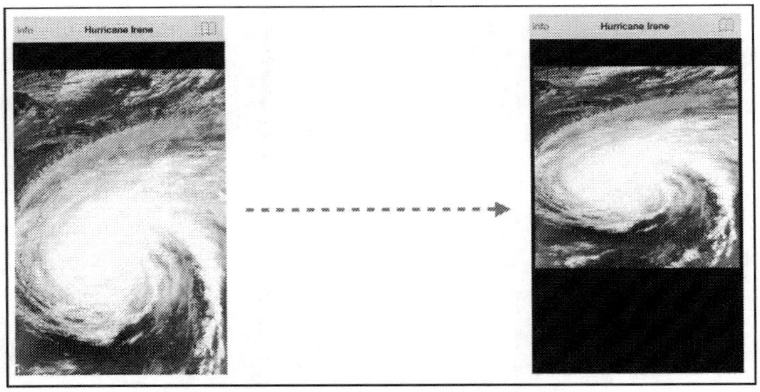

3. Finally you use `CATransform3DRotate` to rotate the image by `22.5` degrees to give it some perspective distortion as shown below:

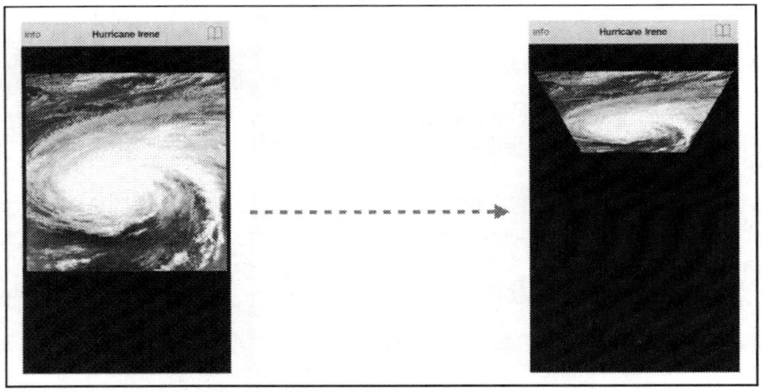

Remember, you already set the anchor point so the image rotates around its top edge.

Now you see the value of setting the `m34` value above via `view.layer.sublayerTransform`; your rotation transform simply re-uses the `m34` value from the sublayer transform, without the need to apply it here. That's handy!

Now all that's left is to apply the transform to each image. Add the following line to the end of the `if` block:

```
image.layer.transform = imageTransform
```

Build and run your project; tap the Browse button to see the result of your transforms:

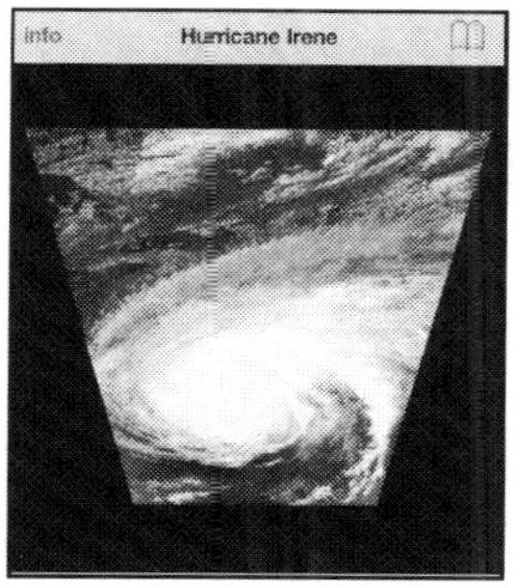

Again, you only see the top image as all other images behind it have the same transform applied. Now is a perfect opportunity to customize the transform for each image.

Add the following line to the end of the `if` block:

```
imageYOffset += view.frame.height / CGFloat(images.count)
```

This adjusts the y-offset of each image depending on where it is in the stack. You divide the screen height over the number of images so they distribute themselves evenly over the screen.

Build and run your project to see your views fan out:

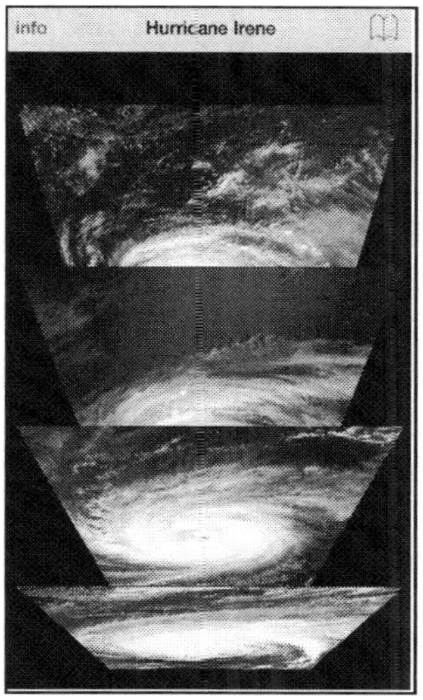

Sweet – the gallery looks just as you intended! But as this is a book about animations, it would be a shame if you didn't animate the transition to the fanned-out view, wouldn't it? :]

Animating the gallery

Find the following line in `toggleGallery()` where you set `transform` on each image:

```
image.layer.transform = imageTransform
```

Insert the following code **above that line** to animate `transform`:

```
let animation = CABasicAnimation(keyPath: "transform")
animation.fromValue = NSValue(CATransform3D:
  image.layer.transform)
animation.toValue = NSValue(CATransform3D: imageTransform)
animation.duration = 0.33

image.layer.addAnimation(animation, forKey: nil)
```

This code is definitely familiar to you: you create a layer animation on the `transform` property and animate it from its current value to the `imageTransform` you designed earlier.

Build and run your project once more; tap the Browse button and enjoy your completed animation:

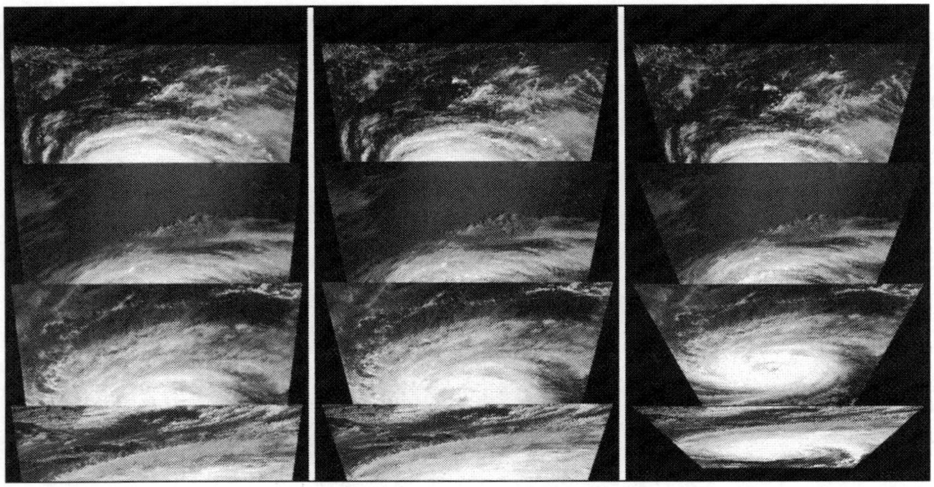

You're finished with the gallery for now; you'll revisit it in the Challenges section when you add the ability to close the fan when the user taps the Browse button.

Bringing an image to the front

In this final section, you'll add a bit of interactivity to the image gallery: tapping an image will make it jump in front of the other images so that the user can get a better look at it.

`ImageViewCard` already features a closure expression property named `didSelect`; this fires when the user taps on the image and receives the tapped image view as an input parameter.

To add this feature, you'll add a class method to `ViewController` and assign it to `didSelect` on all the image views.

First add the following code to `viewDidAppear()`, inside the `for` loop body:

```
image.didSelect = selectImage
```

Xcode will complain that `selectImage` doesn't exist, but you'll fix this in the next step.

Add the following method to `ViewController`:

```
func selectImage(selectedImage: ImageViewCard) {

  for subview in view.subviews {
    if let image = subview as? ImageViewCard {
      if image === selectedImage {
        //selected image
      } else {
        //any other image
      }
    }
  }

}
```

This is the skeleton of `selectImage()`; when the user taps one of the images, you loop over all subviews and get the `ImageViewCard` instances just like you did earlier. Then you check each `ImageViewCard` to see if it's the selected image.

Now you need two more animations: one to animate the selected image, and another to animate all the other images in the gallery.

You'll tackle this in reverse and fade out the unselected images first.

Replace the `//any other image` comment in `selectImage()` with the following code:

```
UIView.animateWithDuration(0.33, delay: 0.0,
  options: .CurveEaseIn, animations: {
    image.alpha = 0.0
```

```
    }, completion: {_ in
      image.alpha = 1.0
      image.layer.transform = CATransform3DIdentity
  })
```

This is a simple animation to fade out each image. In the `completion` block, you reset its `transform` to the identity transform and `alpha` to fully opaque. By the time the above animation is done, the selected image will be in front of all others so transparent or not, you won't see any of the unselected images. Resetting `alpha` here saves you from having to remember to reset it when you want to see the image again.

Build and run your project; open the gallery and tap on an image to see all the other unselected images fade from view:

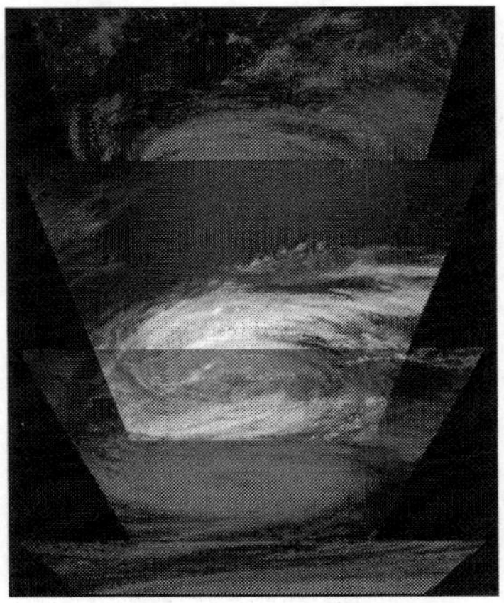

When that animation completes, the view changes back to show the top image at full-screen – because you haven't done anything with the selected image! You'll fix that now.

You'll animate the selected image's `transform` back to the identity transform and pull the image to the front when the animation completes.

Replace the `//selected image` comment in `selectImage()` with the following code:

```
UIView.animateWithDuration(0.33, delay: 0.0,
  options: .CurveEaseIn, animations: {
    image.layer.transform = CATransform3DIdentity
  }, completion: {_ in
    self.view.bringSubviewToFront(image)
})
```

Here, you're un-doing the 3D transform for the animation, and then ensuring the image is at the top of the view stack at the end so it's visible.

Finally, add the following code to the end of selectImage():

```
self.navigationItem.title = selectedImage.title
```

This will update the navigation bar with the currently selected image title.

Build and run your project; tap the various images to see how they zoom to full screen. What do you think – how does it look?

I *thought* you'd enjoy this classy little animation! :] That's a wrap; there's one small bit of functionality to clean up in the Challenge section below, but other than that, you have a really stunning animation at your fingertips. I suspect you can think of many ways to use it in your own projects!

Challenges

Challenge 1: Toggle the gallery with the Browse button

Right now the user must choose an image from the gallery once they open it. In this challenge, you'll make the Browse button work like a toggle to close the gallery view as well.

Add a new property to `ViewController` named `isGalleryOpen` and set its initial value to `false`. You need to update the value of this property in couple of places in the code:

- Set it to `true` at the end of `toggleGallery()`
- Set it to `false` at the end of `selectImage()`

At the top of `toggleGallery()`, add a check to see if the gallery is already open. If so, loop over all images and animate their `transform` back to its original value. Don't forget to reset `isGalleryOpen` and return so the rest of the method code doesn't execute as well.

That's it – if you like, play around with the animations in this project and see what other flashy elements you can add on your own!

Section V: Further Types of Animations

In the first four sections of this book, you learned about the core APIs and classes behind iOS animations.

There are two more specialized topics that don't fit in with any of the previous sections, so you get a bit of a breather from keyframes and 3D animations!

Chapter 19, "Particle Emitters" will show you how to create particle emitters and create the following snowfall effect:

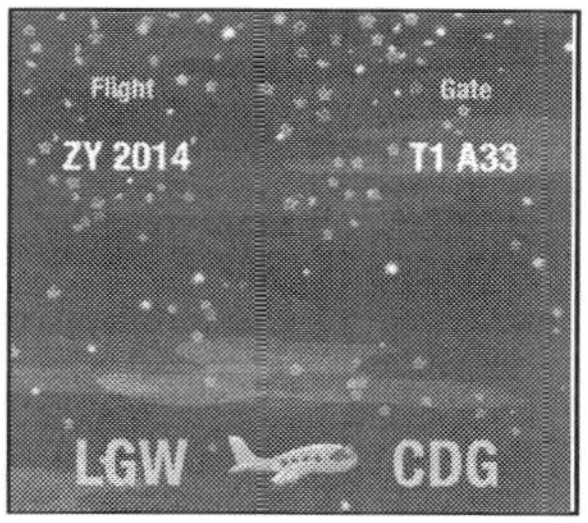

Core Animation includes a full-fledged particle emitter, which you'll use to generate a virtual blizzard full of unique snowflakes that have their own lifespan, color tint and direction.

Chapter 20, "Frame Animations with UIImageView" will walk you through sequencing multiple images together into a flipbook-style animation like so:

By combining frame animation with traditional view animations, you can create a cartoon-like effect with good old `UIImageView` and make the first steps to creating a game in UIKit.

These two chapters are the dessert after a multi-course meal of view and layer animations – dig in! :]

Chapter 19: Particle Emitters

Simulated fiery explosions, driving rain and choking smoke make us *ooh* and *aah* at the action on the big screen. In this chapter, you'll become a one-person Special Effects Team as you bring your own effects to the "small screen" and learn how to create your own special effects using particle emitters.

Waterfall, fire, smoke and rain effects all involve a large number of visual items – particles – that share common physical characteristics but may still have their own unique size, orientation, spin and trajectory.

Particles work really well to create realistic effects, as each particle can be random and unpredictable, just as objects are in nature. For example, each raindrop in a thunderstorm may have a unique size, shape, and velocity.

Here are just a few examples of the visual effects you can achieve with particle emitters:

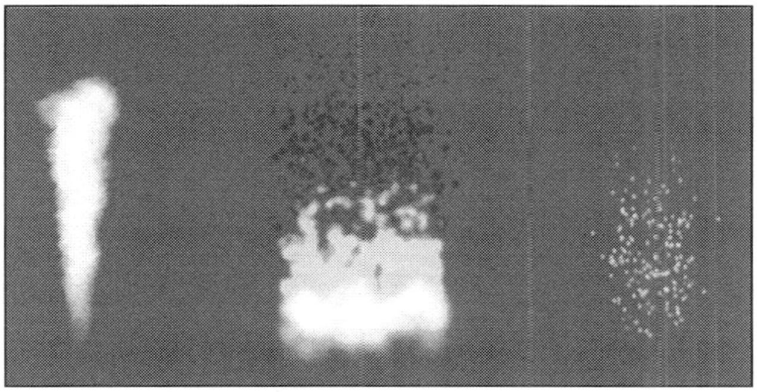

You'll revisit one of the earlier projects in this book – the Bahama Air flight info – and recreate the snow effect from Chapter 4, "View animations in practice" using particle emitters.

You'll learn how particle systems work as you experiment with different emitter properties and observe the effect they have on the resulting animation.

By the time you're done you'll be putting on your hat and gloves after seeing your particle emitter snow effect as shown below:

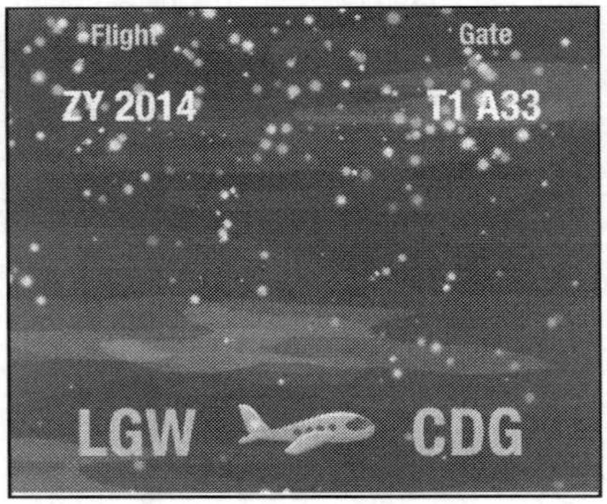

This chapter will be a lot of fun; read on to get started!

Creating your emitter layer

Although by this point in the book you've covered a lot of animation topics, there's a layer class for creating animations that you haven't seen yet: `CAEmitterLayer`. You can use this class to create particle effects natively in Core Animation.

> **Note**: There are a number of third-party classes for creating particle effects, but they're usually targeted towards integration with game frameworks. For particle animations in your UIKit apps, `CAEmitterLayer` is a great choice since it's built in and simple to use.

Open the starter project and run the app to see what you've been given to start with:

There's your London-Paris flight information screen with a gloomy weather background. The flight information on this version of the screen doesn't change; this way, you can focus on the snow effect alone.

Open **ViewController.swift** and add the following code to the bottom of `viewDidLoad()`:

```
let rect = CGRect(x: 0.0, y: 100.0, width: view.bounds.width,
  height: 50.0)
let emitter = CAEmitterLayer()
emitter.frame = rect
view.layer.addSublayer(emitter)
```

This code creates a new `CAEmitterLayer`, sets the layers's frame to take up the full width of the screen and positions the layer near the top of the screen.

Next you need to set the type of emitter to use with your particle effect.

Add the following code to `viewDidLoad()`:

```
emitter.emitterShape = kCAEmitterLayerRectangle
```

The shape of your emitter generally affects the area where new particles are being created, but it also can affect their z-position in situations where you're creating 3D-like particle systems.

Here's a look at the three simplest emitter shapes:

Point shape

An emitter shape of `kCAEmitterLayerPoint` causes all particles to be created at the same point: the emitter's position. This is a good choice for effects that involve sparks or fireworks:

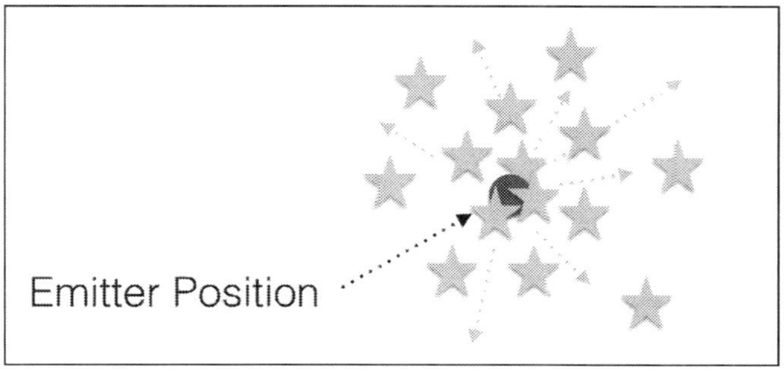

As an example, you could create a spark effect by creating all particles at the same point and making them fly in different directions before they disappear.

Line shape

An emitter shape of `kCAEmitterLayerLine` creates all particles along the top of the emitter frame.

This is an emitter shape useful for waterfall effects; the water particles appear at the top edge of the waterfall and cascade down like so:

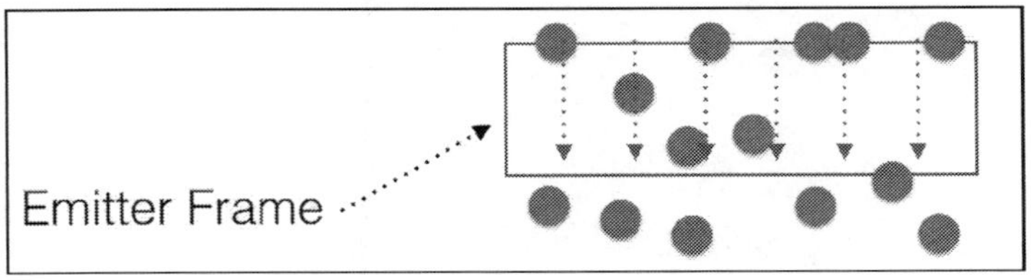

Rectangle shape

Finally, an emitter shape of `kCAEmitterLayerRectangle` creates particles randomly through a given rectangular area:

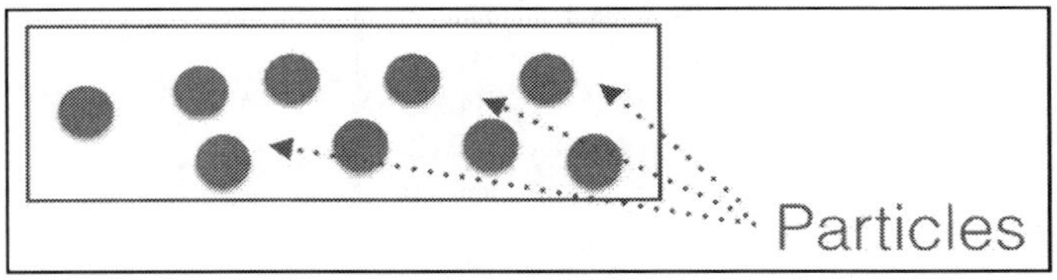

This emitter shape is great for many different effects, including bubbles in a carbonated drink and popping popcorn.

Since snow appears randomly from the whole sky, the rectangle emitter shape is a good choice for your project.

> **Note:** There are a few more emitter shapes—cuboid, circle and sphere—but these are out of the scope of this chapter. Check out the *CAEmitterLayer Class Reference* in Apple's documentation for more information.

Adding an emitter frame

Add the following code to the end of `viewDidLoad`:

```
emitter.emitterPosition = CGPoint(x: rect.width/2,
  y: rect.height/2)
emitter.emitterSize = rect.size
```

Combining the shape, position and size properties defines the emitter frame. Here you set the position of the emitter to the center of the layer and set the emitter size equal to the size of the layer.

This means the emitter takes up the entire layer frame like so:

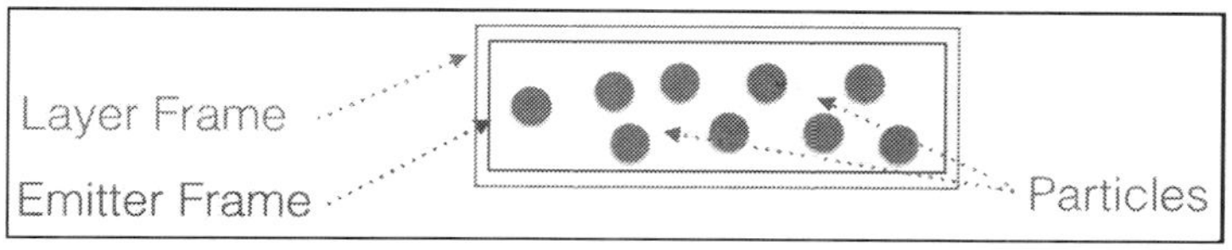

Creating an emitter cell

Now that you have configured the location and size of the emitter, you can move on to adding an **emitter cell**.

An emitter cell is the data model representing one source of particles. It's a separate class from `CAEmitterLayer` because a single emitter layer can contain one or more cells.

For example, in a popcorn animation you can have three different cells that represent the different states of a popcorn kernel: fully popped, half popped and those stubborn unpopped kernels:

In this chapter you will use only one emitter cell; you'll have an opportunity to work with multiple cells in the Challenges section of this tutorial.

Add the following code to the bottom of `viewDidLoad()`:

```
let emitterCell = CAEmitterCell()
emitterCell.contents = UIImage(named: "flake.png")!.CGImage
```

In the code above, you create a new cell and set **flake.png** as its `contents`. The `contents` property holds the template from which new particles will be created.

Below is a scaled up flake.png screenshot on a dark background:

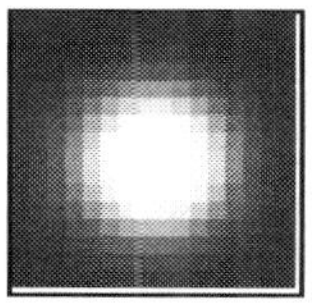

Your emitter will create multiple varying copies of this image to mimic real snowflakes.

Add the following code to the bottom of `viewDidLoad()`:

```
emitterCell.birthRate = 20
emitterCell.lifetime = 3.5
emitter.emitterCells = [emitterCell]
```

The above code instructs your cell to create `20` snowflakes every second and keep them on the screen for `3.5` seconds. This means there will be `70` snowflakes on the screen at any given time, except for the first few seconds of the animation before the oldest particles start to disappear.

Finally, you set the `emitterCells` property with an array of all your emitter cells. Remember, you can have multiple emitter cells but you're starting with one so the array has as a single value. The emitter will begin to create particles as soon as you set the list of emitter cells.

Build and run your app; check out the pseudo-snowflake effect you have so far:

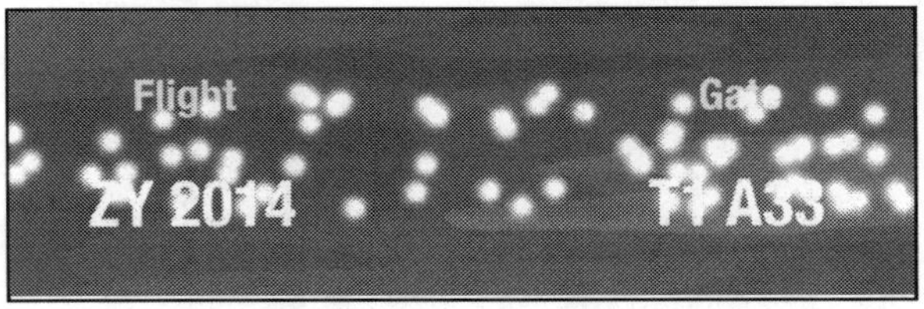

Multiple copies of flake.png show up and disappear after `3.5` seconds. However, the snow is oddly static – it's not falling anywhere. Do you have the development chops to turn this into a believable snow scene?

Great – time to investigate some more properties of `CAEmitterCell`.

Controlling your particles

At this point in the chapter the snow particles appear, float in space for a few seconds, then disappear. That's incredibly boring – even for a particle with a lifespan of `3.5` seconds! Your next task is to give these aimless particles some direction in their lives.

Changing particle direction

Add the following code to the bottom of `viewDidLoad()`:

```
emitterCell.yAcceleration = 70.0
```

This will add a little acceleration in the y-direction so the particles will drift downwards like real snow.

Build and run your project to see the effect:

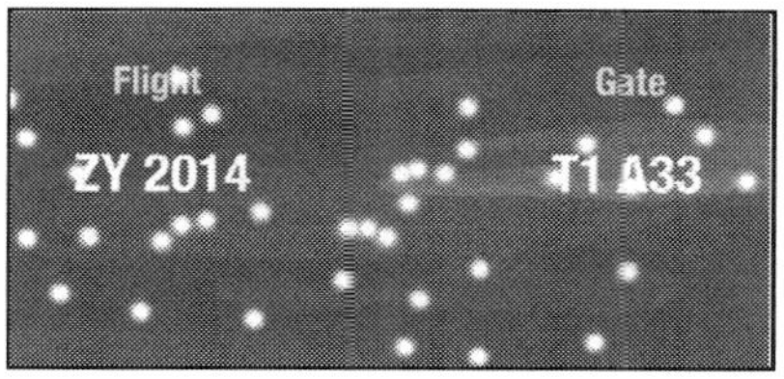

That looks a little more like snow – but snow seldom falls straight down.

To fix this, add the following bit of horizontal acceleration to your particles:

```
emitterCell.xAcceleration = 10.0
```

Build and run your project again; the snowflakes should be moving in a downward diagonal direction:

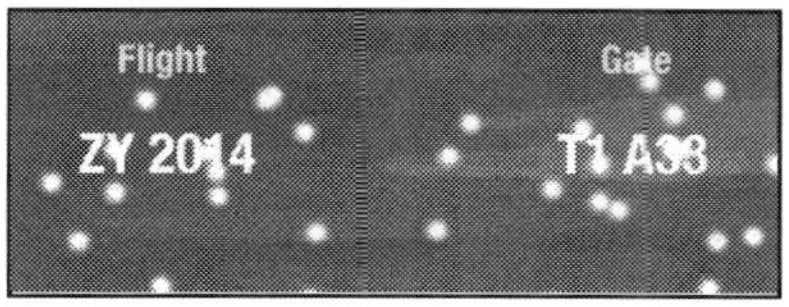

To create a gentle falling effect, you'll shoot the particles straight up and let the `yAcceleration` pull them down.

Add the following code:

```
emitterCell.velocity = 20.0
emitterCell.emissionLongitude = CGFloat(-M_PI_2)
```

The emission longitude is the initial angle of the particles, and the velocity parameter sets the initial speed of the particle like so:

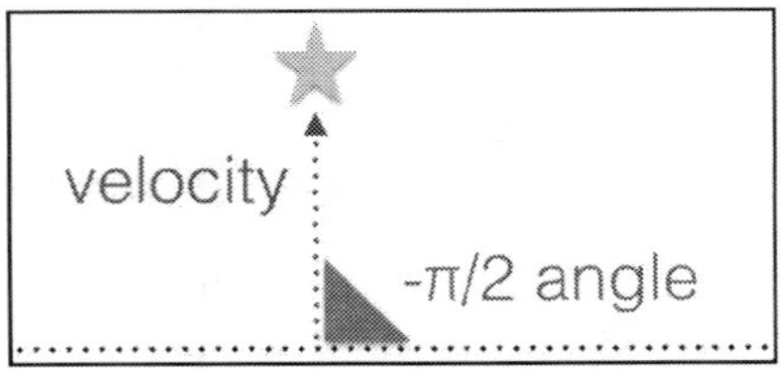

Build and run your project again to see the result:

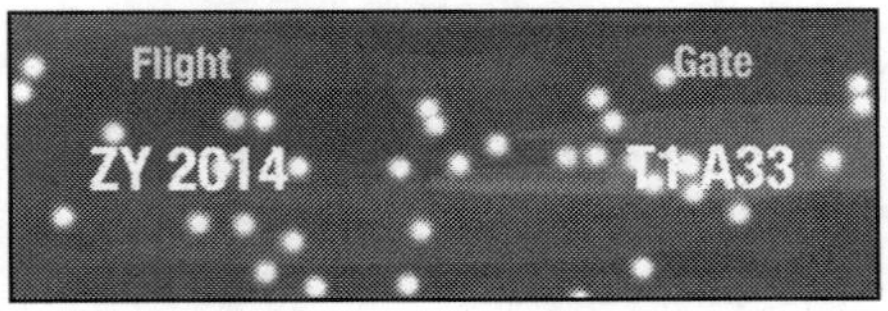

Your animation looks better and better with each change. But these particles look like snowflake-sized kill-bots moving in mechanical unison. This is because each particle has the exact same initial angle, velocity, and acceleration. You need to add some randomness to the particle creation process.

Adding randomness to your particles

Add the following code to `viewDidLoad()`:

```
emitterCell.velocityRange = 200.0
```

This tells the emitter what the randomized range of values should be. Since random ranges for particle animations are used frequently throughout this chapter, it's worth taking a bit of time to explain how they work.

All of your particles have the same initial velocity of `20`; adding a velocity range assigns a random velocity to each particle as illustrated below:

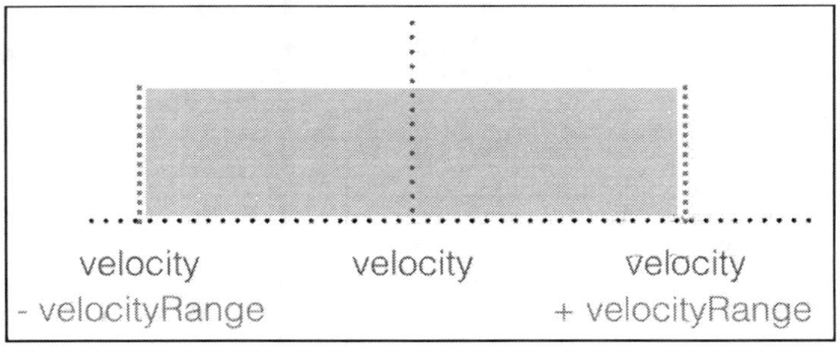

Each particle's velocity will be a random value between `(20-200)` `= -180` and `(20+200)` `= 220`. The particles with negative initial velocity will not fly up at all – they'll start floating down as soon as they appear on the screen. The particles with positive velocity will fly up first, then float down.

Build and run your project to see what your changes have wrought:

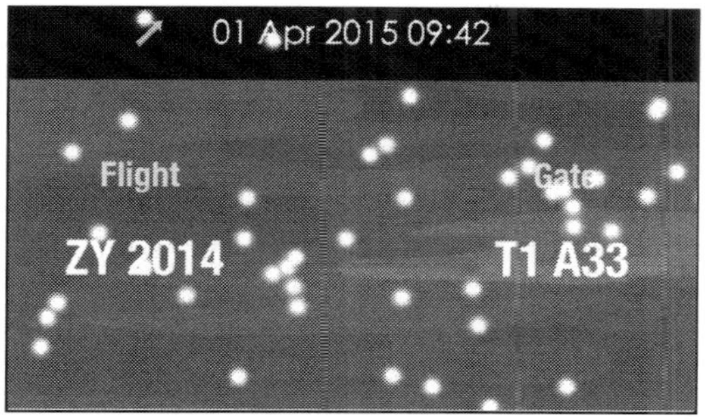

Okay, things are definitely random: some snowflakes jump as high as the top edge of the screen, while others appear, hang around for a moment, and fall down.

The initial particle direction is the next thing to randomize.

Add the following code to `viewDidLoad()`:

```
emitterCell.emissionRange = CGFloat(M_PI_2)
```

Originally, you configured all particles to shoot straight up (at a `-π/2` angle) as they appear. The above line of code instructs the emitter to pick a random angle for each particle within the range of `(-π/2 - π/2) = 180` degrees and `(-π/2 + π/2) = 0` degrees as illustrated below:

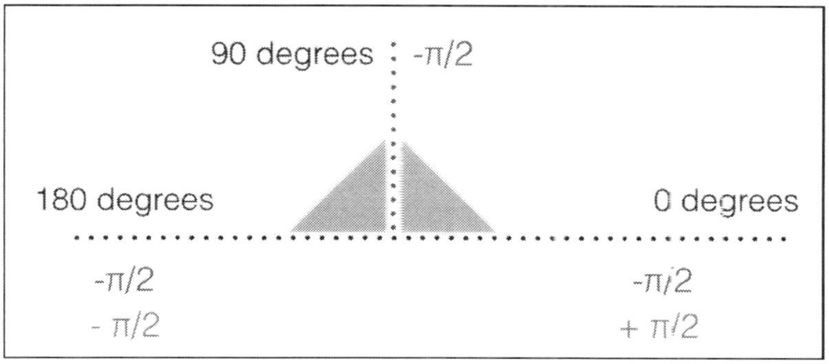

The particles will end up moving up from the x-axis in different angles rather than straight up.

Run the project again to see how the animation has changed:

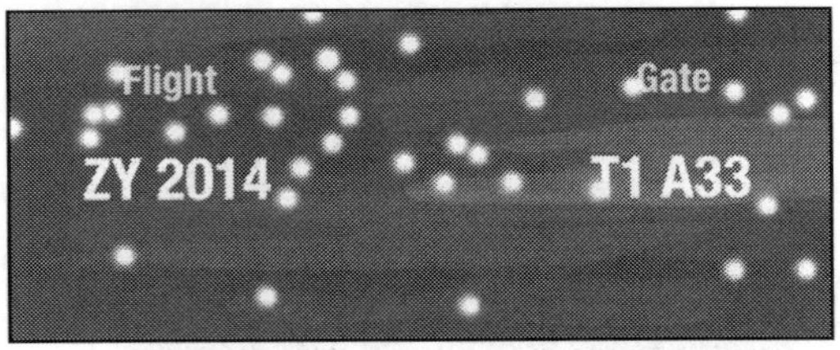

Now THAT's random! :] Your virtual snowstorm has really come to life.

Changing particle color

One of the handy features of `CAEmitterLayer` is the ability to set a tint color for your particles. For example, you could tint your snowflakes light blue instead of stark white, as the color blue is often associated with rain, water, snow or ice.

Add the following code to the bottom of `viewDidLoad()`:

```
emitterCell.color = UIColor(red: 0.9, green: 1.0, blue: 1.0,
  alpha: 1.0).CGColor
```

Build and run your project to see the tint effect on your particles:

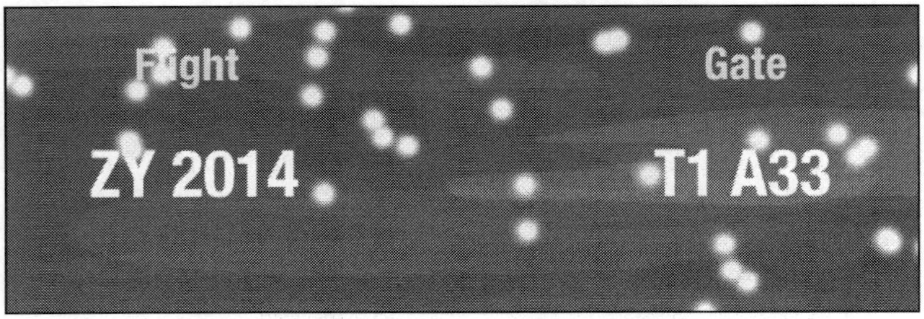

The change looks interesting, but all the snowflakes are a uniform shade of blue. Wouldn't it be great if you could randomize the color of each snowflake?

You can! All you need to do is define three separate ranges for your particle color: one each for the red, green, and blue color components.

Add the following code to the end of `viewDidLoad()`:

```
emitterCell.redRange   = 0.3
emitterCell.greenRange = 0.3
emitterCell.blueRange  = 0.3
```

This code defines the following range for each color value:

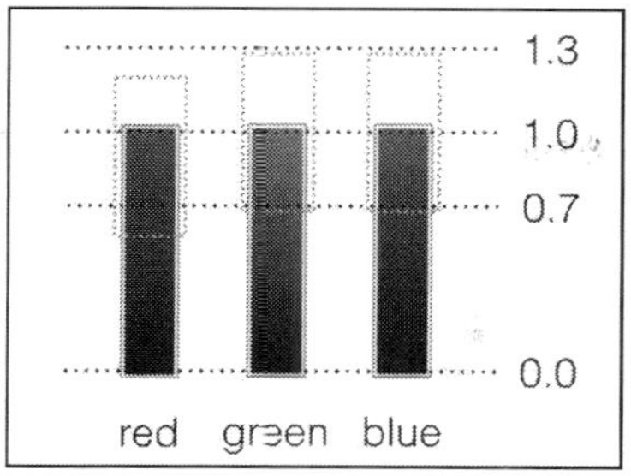

Green and blue component values will now be a random value between `0.7` and `1.3`; however, values higher than `1.0` are capped at `1.0` so the effective range is `0.7` to `1.0`. The red component will be capped between `0.6` and `1.0` since its "normal" value is `0.9`. These are relatively narrow ranges so the resulting random color will still be quite light.

Build and run your project to see the result of your snowflake dye-job:

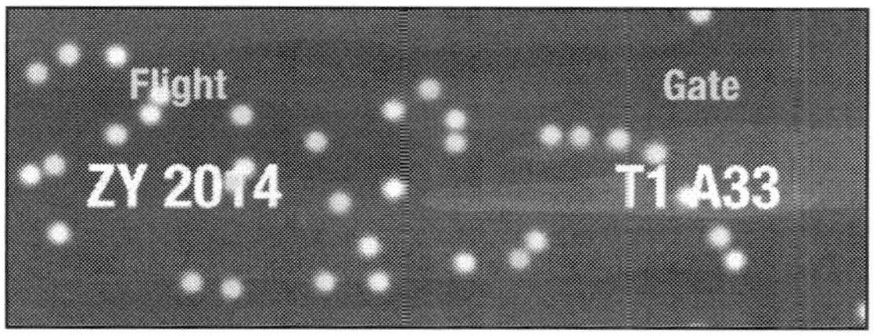

Um, well, this *is* random – but is it just me, or does it look like it's raining candy sprinkles? :]

You can experiment with the various ranges on each individual color component to bias your color towards a particular tint if you like. For now, just replace the code you added above with the following:

```
emitterCell.redRange   = 0.1
emitterCell.greenRange = 0.1
emitterCell.blueRange  = 0.1
```

Build and run to see a much more subtle color variation:

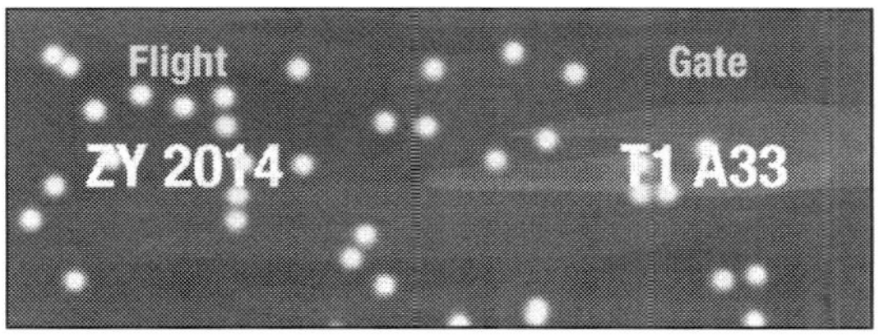

Randomizing particle appearance

Even after all the customization you've added, the snowflakes still look relatively uniform. In this section of the chapter you'll make each of your particles a beautiful and unique snowflake – and that starts with assigning a random size to each snowflake.

Add the following code to `viewDidLoad()`:

```
emitterCell.scale = 0.8
emitterCell.scaleRange = 0.8
```

Here you set the base particle size as **80%** of the original size, then you assign a wide range for the random size:

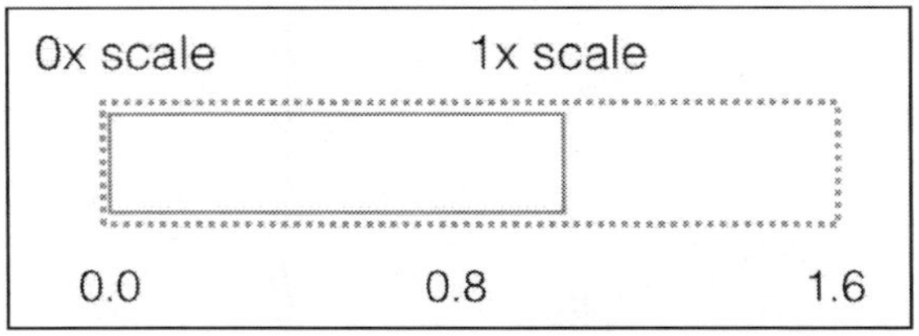

This produces big fluffy snowflakes `1.6` times the original size, all the way down to microscopic flakes with zero size that disappear as soon as you create them.

Build and run your project to see your new snowflake sizes in action:

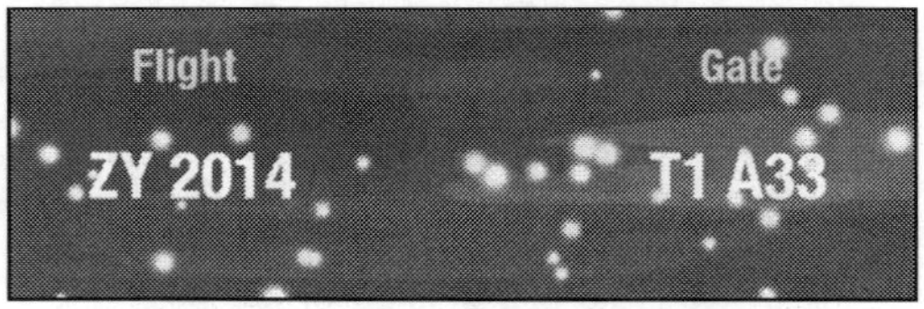

Not only can you set the initial size of your snowflakes, but you can also modify the size of the snowflake as it falls. Perhaps it's melting in the warm foggy air as it nears the ground? :]

Add the following line to `viewDidLoad()`:

```
emitterCell.scaleSpeed = -0.15
```

The `scaleSpeed` property above instructs your particles to scale down by **15%** of their original size per second.

Big particles will shrink substantially before they disappear from sight, while small particles will completely disappear before the end of their lives. Don't feel bad, it's just the snowflake circle of life.

Build and run your project to see how your snowflakes melt as they fall:

The snowflakes get smaller and smaller as they approach the bottom half of the screen. That's a neat effect – but now the bottom half of the screen looks a bit empty. I've got a fever, and the only prescription is...more snowflakes! :]

Find the line where you set `emitterCell.birthRate` and replace the value with `150` like so:

```
emitterCell.birthRate = 150
```

Build and run to see your blizzard take shape:

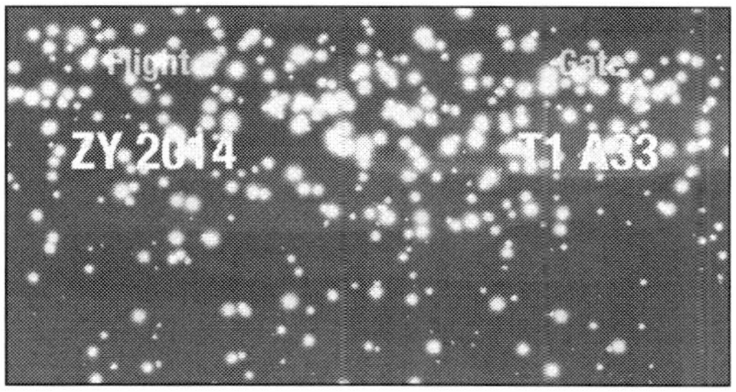

Your animation gets better and better with each iteration, but it still looks a little flat. You can add a lot of depth to the scene by randomizing the alpha value of each snowflake.

Add the following to the bottom of `viewDidLoad()`:

```
emitterCell.alphaRange = 0.75
emitterCell.alphaSpeed = -0.15
```

You set a wide alpha range, from `0.25` to a capped value of `1.0`. `alphaSpeed` works much like `scaleSpeed` to change the alpha of the particle over time.

Build and run your project again to see the depth effect that a simple alpha animation lends to your snowfall:

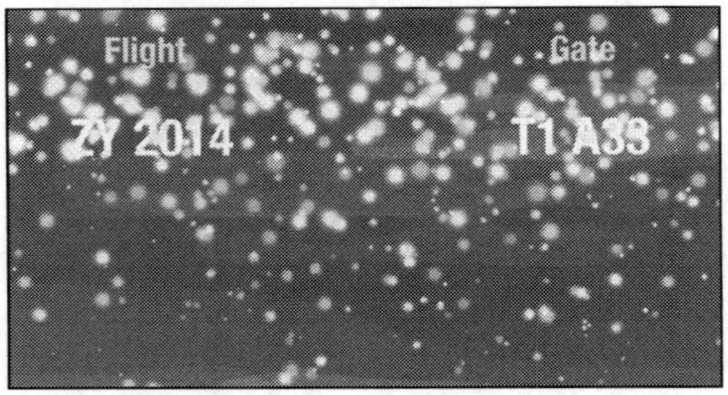

You've covered most of what `CAEmitterCell` has to offer; the rest of this chapter is about adding polish to your animation.

Adding some final polish

Find the line in `viewDidLoad()` that sets `emissionLongitude` and change it to the following:

```
emitterCell.emissionLongitude = CGFloat(-M_PI)
```

Remember, the emission longitude is the starter angle for the particles. This change will make the snowflakes swirl a bit as if pushed around by the wind.

Next, find the line in `viewDidLoad()` that declares `rect` and modify it as follows:

```
let rect = CGRect(x: 0.0, y: -70.0, width: view.bounds.width,
  height: 50.0)
```

This moves the emitter off-screen so the user doesn't see where the particles come from.

Finally, add the following bit of code to `viewDidLoad()` to randomize the length of time that a snowflake remains on the screen:

```
emitterCell.lifetimeRange = 1.0
```

This sets each snowflake's lifetime to a random value between `2.5` and `4.5` seconds.

Build and run the app to see these final bits of polish in effect.

Although this chapter was pretty heavy on the snow effect, each concept is completely applicable to other particle systems. Every particle implementation I've seen so far has worked in a similar fashion. You always have a set of features to configure per particle, and the emitter randomizes the system as it creates large amounts of copies of the original particle.

If you worked through this chapter, then you're in good shape to start exploring *any* particle system, whether it's in Sprite Kit, Unity, or any other custom particle emitter class.

Once you understand how particle systems work, it's a ton of fun to design and implement particle effects! To that end, work through the following challenge where you can customize your snowfall effect.

Challenges

Challenge 1: Add more cells to the emitter layer

This challenge is more free-form than most; your task is to add one or more cells to the emitter you just developed.

The starter project includes a number of snowflakes to choose from for your challenge cells: flake1.png, flake2.png, flake3.png and flake4.png.

Before you add more cells to the emitter, consider the effect of overcrowding on the screen. The one existing cell emits `150` snowflakes per second, which results in a dense snowfall. If you add two more cells to your emitter, you'll want to throttle back each emitter to about `50` particles per second to maintain approximately the same density of snowflakes in your system.

Play around with the properties of each cell: make some flakes swirl around, while others fall quickly to the ground. The snowflake shape flake2.png isn't symmetrical so try to set its cell's `spin` and `spinRange` properties to make those particles spin around as if blown by the wind.

There's no right or wrong solution to this challenge – just stop playing with the effect when you're satisfied. I've included one of my favorite solutions with this chapter, which you can have a look at once you're done changing your particle system:

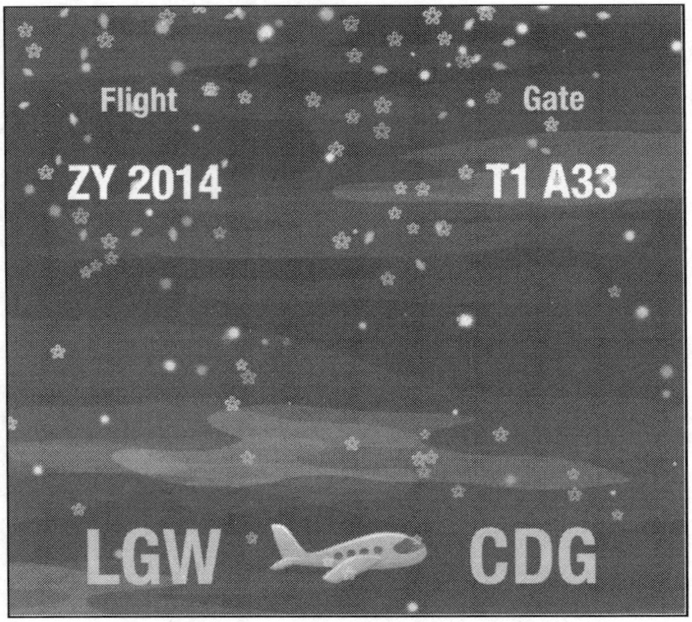

In the spirit of the snowy season, the next chapter showcases some creatures who would fully appreciate your snowfall effect: penguins!

Chapter 20: Frame Animations with UIImageView

It's finally time to learn how to create a very special type of animation. **Frame animation** is the type of animation you enjoyed as a kid and probably still adore today; it's the way Disney's *Duck Tales*, Hanna-Barbera's *Tom and Jerry* and *The Flintstones* cartoons were created.

This is also the kind of animation you use to animate characters in your games. It's not enough to simply translate your static game characters from one location to another; you need to move a character's feet or spin the aircraft's propeller to give a realistic sense of motion.

To create the effect of character movement, you break the animation into **frames**, which are still images that represent stages of the action. When you display the frames quickly, one after the other, it will look like your character is moving:

The project in this chapter is set at the South Pole and the player gets to control Pengui, the penguin. You will start with a static scene and work through the chapter to make Pengui walk and slide around his world:

Project basics

Open the starter project for this chapter and select **Main.storyboard** to see the initial game scene:

The penguin and buttons are all connected to the code in **ViewController.swift**, but nothing happens at the moment if you tap them. Open **ViewController.swift** and take a look at the guts of the code.

You'll see two outlets: one for the penguin image view (`penguin`) and one for the slide button (`slideButton`). You also have two properties, `walkFrames` and `slideFrames`, which contain the `UIImage` frames of the walking and sliding animations respectively.

The HUD buttons on the left side of the screen are connected to `actionLeft()` and `actionRight()`; you'll add some animation code to these two methods to make the penguin walk.

The HUD button on the right hand side of the screen is connected to `actionSlide()`, where you'll add some code to make the penguin jump and slide on the ice.

Open **Images.xcassets** and browse through the frame images to see the individual frames of walking and sliding animations like so:

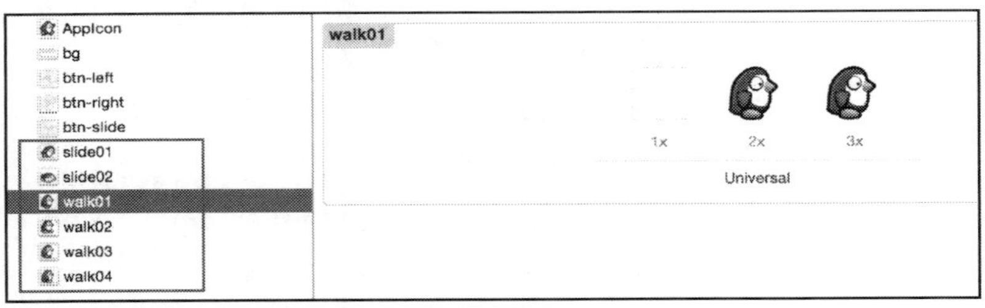

You need to walk before you can run – and in this game, your penguin needs to walk before he can slide! :] Your first task is to make the penguin walk when the player taps the HUD buttons.

Setting up your frame animation

Add the following code to the `loadWalkAnimation()` stub in **ViewController.swift:**

```
penguin.animationImages = walkFrames
penguin.animationDuration = animationDuration / 3
penguin.animationRepeatCount = 3
```

This code sets a number of properties on `UIImageView` that you might have not seen before. Here's what each of them does in turn:

- `animationImages`: This stores all the frame images of your frame animation. `walkFrames` is declared earlier in the code as an array containing `UIImage` objects, so here you just need to assign it to `penguin.animationImages` to set up the animation frames.
- `animationDuration`: This tells UIKit how long one iteration of the animation should last; since you will have the animation repeat three times (see below), you set this to one-third of the length of the total `animationDuration`.
- `animationRepeatCount`: This controls the repeat count of the animation; in this case, the animation will repeat three times.

Finally, you need to call `loadWalkAnimation()` from `viewDidLoad()` in the view controller so that the image view will be ready whenever the player taps the left arrow button.

Add the following code to the bottom of `viewDidLoad()`:

```
loadWalkAnimation()
```

Build and run the project; tap the left arrow button to set your penguin in motion:

Oh – nothing happens when you tap the left arrow button. Did you do something wrong? No; you only *configured* the image view for a frame animation – but you never started the animation. If you don't start the frame animation, the image view continues to show the contents of its `image` property.

Time to get this penguin waddling.

Add the following code to `actionLeft()`:

```
isLookingRight = false
```

To track which way the penguin faces, you'll set `isLookingRight` to `false` or `true` inside `actionLeft()` and `actionRight()` respectively.

Since you need to update the penguin's transform and the button transform every time you change the penguin's direction, you'll need to add some code to the `didSet` observer of `isLookingRight`.

Find the following property near the top of the class definition:

```
var isLookingRight: Bool = true
```

...and replace it with the code below:

```
var isLookingRight: Bool = true {
  didSet {
    let xScale: CGFloat = isLookingRight ? 1 : -1
    penguin.transform = CGAffineTransformMakeScale(xScale, 1)
    slideButton.transform = penguin.transform
  }
}
```

This code sets the x-axis scale of the penguin and the slide button to either 1 or -1 depending on the value of `isLookingRight`. Setting that transform will then flip the view so the penguin can face the correct direction:

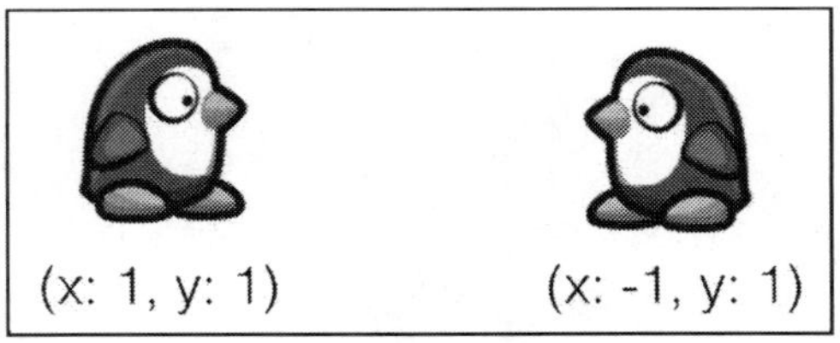

Now you need to call the animation code. Add the following to the bottom of `actionLeft()`:

```
penguin.startAnimating()
```

When you call `startAnimating()` the image view plays the animation as you configured it: each frame in the `animationImages` array displays in order for a total of three times over `1` second.

Once the animation has finished, the image view will once again display its initial contents – the `image` property.

Build and run your project; tap the left arrow button to see your penguin in action:

Your chilly friend is walking – but he's going nowhere fast! :] You'll need to move the penguin across the screen as the walking animation plays.

Translating your view

Add the following code to `actionLeft()`:

```
UIView.animateWithDuration(animationDuration, delay: 0.0, options:
.CurveEaseOut, animations: {
  self.penguin.center.x -= self.walkSize.width
}, completion: nil)
```

This is familiar code that needs little explanation by this point in the book; you simply animate your view across the screen. You use the `width` of the walking image to determine how far the penguin will move during the length the animation plays.

Run the project again; how do things look now?

That's more like it! Walking in the other direction is pretty similar code-wise.

Add the following code to `actionRight()`:

```
isLookingRight = true

penguin.startAnimating()
UIView.animateWithDuration(animationDuration, delay: 0.0, options:
.CurveEaseOut, animations: {
  self.penguin.center.x += self.walkSize.width
}, completion: nil)
```

It's almost the same code as before: you change the character orientation, play the frame animation and move it towards the right edge of the screen.

Build and run your project and play around a bit with the game. Can you think of other frame animations the character could perform?

Playing different frame animations

Now that Pengui can walk around, it's time for him to jump and slide. You'll face some new frame animation issues in this section and learn how to solve them in an elegant manner.

To make the image view play a different frame animation, you need to change the contents of the `animationImages` property. Conveniently, the `slideFrames` property of `ViewController` already contains the images for the sliding animation.

Add the following code to `loadSlideAnimation()` to load the new frame sequence:

```
penguin.animationImages = slideFrames
penguin.animationDuration = animationDuration
penguin.animationRepeatCount = 1
```

In the code above, you assign the `slideFrames` array to `animationImages`, then set the animation duration to the predefined `1` second time span. Finally, you set the repeat count to `1`.

It looks like you've taken care of everything you need above, so you can move on the code to load and play the animation.

Add the following code to `actionSlide()`:

```
loadSlideAnimation()
penguin.startAnimating()
```

Build and run your project; tap the slide button on the right hand of the screen and you'll see Pengui jumps on his tummy and bounces back to his feet:

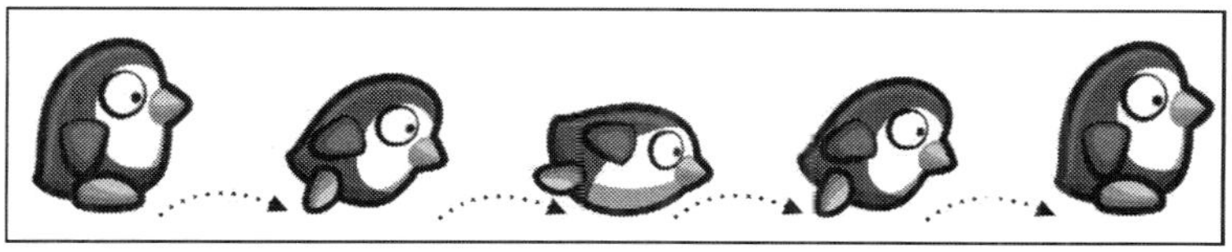

Hmm, there's something weird going on in that animation. Pengui gets real chubby as the animation runs; in fact, while he's lying on the ground he looks totally round! What gives?

Well, check the most obvious thing first: are the slide images correct? Take a peek at **slide01** and **slide02** and you'll see that the penguin is the right shape and size. So something in your project must be sabotaging Pengui's figure. Either that or he's been eating a few too many fish lately. :]

The sliding animation looks off because the frame images aren't the same between the two animations:

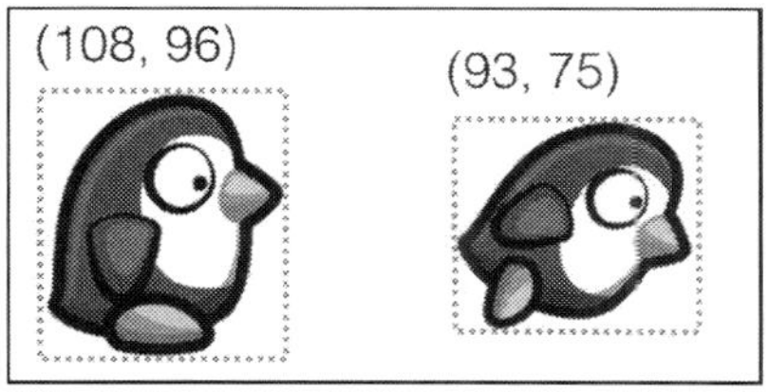

The walk frame images are `108` x `96`, while the slide images are `93` x `75`. If they were all the same size, you'd end up with a lot of empty space in each image. Imagine a character with five, six, or more frame animations; you'd end up with huge image dimensions to fit in all the possible animation frames.

> **Note**: An easy solution to this problem is to set the content mode of the image view from its default value of `Aspect Fill` to `Center` or `Top Left`. But since you're an animation ninja, you'll implement a slightly different and more flexible solution.

In this part of the chapter, you'll manually resize and reposition the image view to create a beautiful animation that flows nicely.

First, you'll need to set the desired image view frame before you play any animations; this ensures the frames are the correct size when they're visible on the screen.

Add the following code to `actionSlide()`, just before the point where you start the animations:

```
penguin.frame = CGRect(
  x: penguin.frame.origin.x,
  y: penguinY + (walkSize.height - slideSize.height),
  width: slideSize.width,
  height: slideSize.height)
```

This code moves the penguin image view down a little bit to compensate for the shorter frames of the slide animation and resizes the image view to match `slideSize`.

`slideSize` contains the size of slide01.png; `viewDidLoad()` already contains the code to fetch the image.

Now add the following code to the bottom of `actionSlide()`:

```
UIView.animateWithDuration(animationDuration - 0.02, delay: 0.0,
options: .CurveEaseOut, animations: {
  self.penguin.center.x += self.isLookingRight ?
    self.slideSize.width : -self.slideSize.width
}, completion: {_ in
  // animation is complete
})
```

In the code above, you create a view animation to move the penguin image view and simulate the jump action. You also add or subtract one penguin length – would that be a "penguimeter"? :] – depending on which way the penguin is facing.

You'll notice there's a small adjustment to the animation duration and you're making it a bit shorter – you'll see why this is necessary in just a moment.

Build and run your project; your animation should look nice and sleek at this point:

But poor Pengui is stuck on the ice; once you do a slide, all animations become slide animations, even if you tap the left and right arrow buttons.

Whoops – you didn't reset the image view frame and reload the walking frames. That's pretty easy to fix.

Replace the `// animation is complete` comment in the piece of code you added above with the following:

```
self.penguin.frame = CGRect(
  x: self.penguin.frame.origin.x,
  y: self.penguinY,
  width: self.walkSize.width,
  height: self.walkSize.height)
self.loadWalkAnimation()
```

This resets the image view frame to its initial size and loads up the walking frame sequence.

The small time interval you subtracted from the animation duration comes into play here; without it, the frame animation and the movement animation end at the same time, which sometimes results in a little glitch where the penguin returns to standing before the frame has been adjusted. Adding the little offset ensures the new frame is ready before the previous animation ends.

Build and run the project one last time; you should see that Pengui now returns to his upright position once he's done sliding.

Where to go from here?

Frame animations with `UIImageView` are simple but they are a great addition to your already impressive animation skillset.

In general, frame animations have mostly been used in games. They might gain popularity with the new WatchKit SDK – frame animations are one of the few ways to get any kind of animation on the Watch display.

You might think UIKit isn't suited for games but you'd be surprised to learn this isn't the case! If you'd like to learn a bit more about creating games with UIKit, check out the following three-part tutorial I wrote that was recently ported to Swift:

http://www.raywenderlich.com/77981/make-letter-word-game-uikit-swift-part-1.

That's it for this section of the book; in the next section you'll dive into view controller animations to bring even more excitement to your apps at a larger scale than just individual views!

Section VI: View Controller Transitions

By now you know how to create a wide range of beautiful animations for your apps. You've experimented with moving, scaling and fading views, animating different types of layers – and a whole lot more.

It's time to learn how to use these animation techniques in the broader context of app navigation and layout. You've animated multiple views and layers already, but now you'll take a bigger-picture perspective and think about animating entire view controllers!

One of the most recognizable animations of iOS is a new view controller being pushed onto the navigation stack, as shown below:

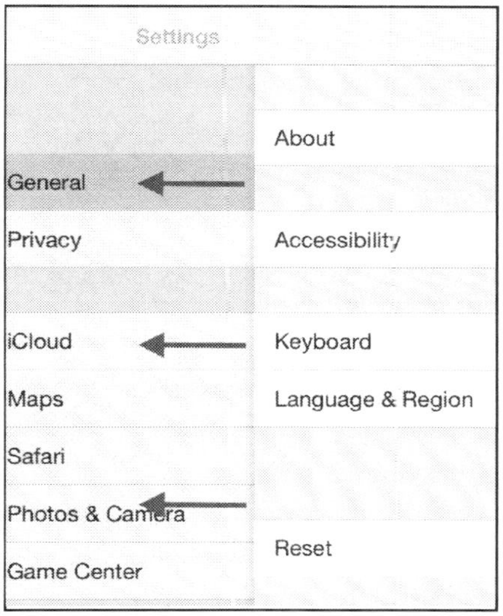

Since iOS 7, Apple added a bit of flair to that animation by adding a bit of lag before the old navigation controller starts moving away under the new one. It's a great effect – but when you're trying to build your own brand image, custom transition animations can be a big help.

In this section, you'll learn how to use animations to create your own custom view controller transitions.

You'll work on two projects in this section. In Chapter 21, you'll add transition animations to the Beginner Cook app:

- **Chapter 21, Custom Presentation Controller & Device Orientation Animations** – Learn how to present view controllers via custom animated transitions – and as a bonus, you'll create an animated transition to handle device orientation changes.

The project used in Chapters 22 and 23 – Logo Reveal – will help you learn how to create custom navigation controller transitions, including a cool effect where it appears that a logo grows to reveal the content of the next screen, like so:

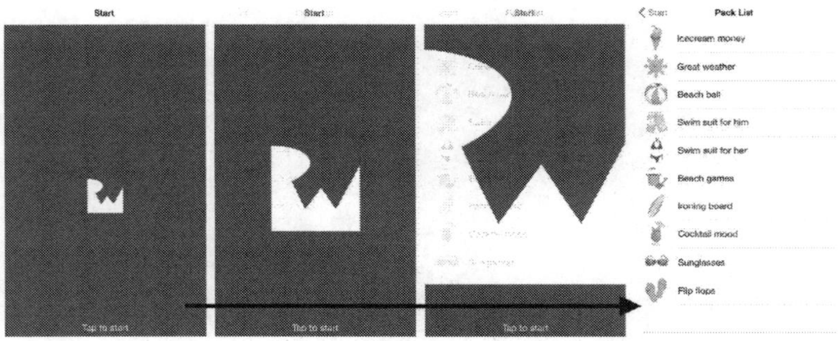

- **Chapter 22, UINavigationController Custom Transition Animations** – You'll build upon your skills with presenting view controllers and develop a really neat reveal transition for a navigation controller app.
- **Chapter 23, Interactive UINavigationController Transitions** – You'll continue on with the Logo Reveal project and make the reveal transition interactive: the user will be able to scrub back and forth through the animated transition!

Implementing custom view controller transitions takes some coding, but the results are lots of fun to look at and use. Custom transitions are an important animation technique that really makes an app stand out!

Chapter 21: Custom Presentation Controller & Device Orientation Animations

Whether you're presenting the camera view controller, the address book, or one of your own custom-designed modal screens, you call the same UIKit method every time: `presentViewController(_: animated:completion:)`. This method "gives up" the current screen to another view controller.

The default presentation animation simply slides the new view up to cover the current one. The illustration below shows a "New Contact" view controller sliding up over the list of contacts:

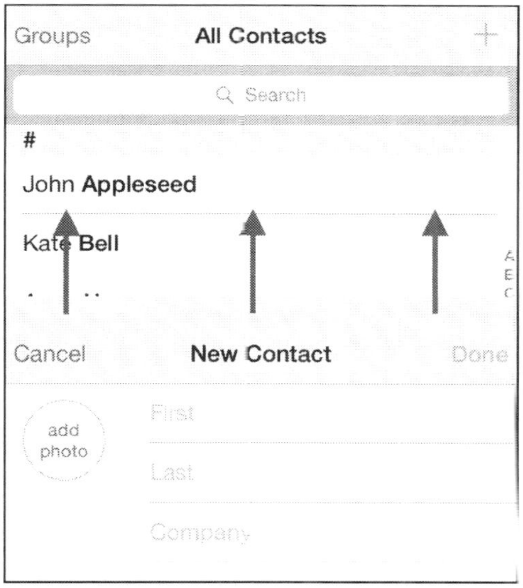

In this chapter, you'll create your own custom presentation controller animations to replace the default one and liven up this chapter's project.

Looking through the starter project

Open the starter project for this chapter, an app called Beginner Cook. Select **Main.storyboard** to begin the tour:

The first view controller (`ViewController`) contains the app's title and main description as well as a scroll view at the bottom, which shows the list of available herbs.

The main view controller presents `HerbDetailsViewController` whenever the user taps one of the images in the list; this view controller sports a background, a title, a description and some buttons to credit the image owner.

There's already enough code in `ViewController.swift` and `HerbDetailsViewController.swift` to support the basic application. Build and run the project to see how the app looks and feels:

Tap on one of the herb images, and the details screen comes up via the standard vertical cover transition. That might be OK for your garden-variety app, but your herbs deserve better!

Your job is to add some custom presentation controller animations to your app to make it blossom! You'll replace the current stock animation with one that expands the tapped herb image to a full-screen view like so:

Roll up your sleeves, put your developer apron on and get ready for the inner workings of custom presentation controllers!

Behind the scenes of custom transitions

UIKit lets you customize your view controller's presentation via the delegate pattern; you simply make your main view controller (or another class you create specifically for that purpose) adopt `UIViewControllerTransitioningDelegate`.

Every time you present a new view controller, UIKit asks its delegate whether or not it should use a custom transition. Here's what the first step of the custom transitioning dance looks like:

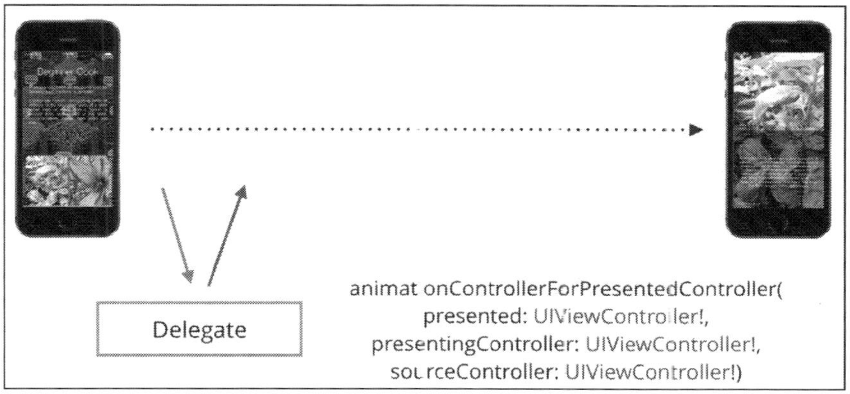

UIKit calls `animationControllerForPresentedController(:_ presentingController:sourceController:)`; if that method returns `nil` UIKit uses the built-in transition. If UIKit receives an object instead, then UIKit uses that object as the animation controller for the transition.

There are a few more steps in the dance before UIKit can use the custom animation controller:

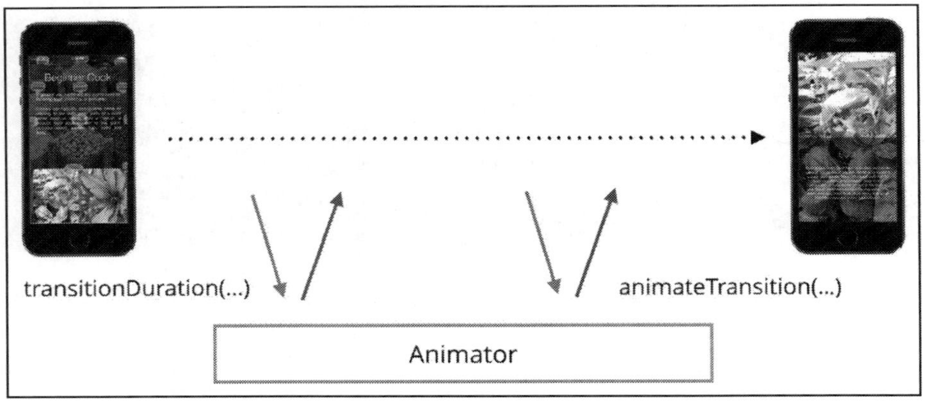

UIKit first asks your animation controller (simply known as the **animator**) for the transition duration in seconds, then calls `animateTransition()` on it. This is when your custom animation gets to take center stage.

In `animateTransition()`, you have access to both the current view controller on the screen as well as the new view controller to be presented. You can fade, scale, rotate and manipulate the existing view and the new view however you like.

Now that you've learned a bit about how custom presentation controllers work, you can start to create your own.

Implementing transition delegates

Since the delegate's task is to manage the animator object that performs the actual animations, you'll first have to create a stub for the animator class before you can write the delegate code.

From Xcode's main menu select **File\New\File...** and choose the template **iOS\Source\Cocoa Touch Class**.

Set the new class name to **PopAnimator** and make it a subclass of **NSObject**.

Open **PopAnimator.swift** and update the class definition to make it conform to the `UIViewControllerAnimatedTransitioning` protocol as follows:

```
class PopAnimator: NSObject, UIViewControllerAnimatedTransitioning
{

}
```

You'll see some complaints from Xcode since you haven't implemented the required delegate methods yet, so you'll stub those out next.

Add the following method to the class:

```
func transitionDuration(transitionContext:
UIViewControllerContextTransitioning)-> NSTimeInterval {
  return 0
}
```

The `0` value above is just a placeholder value for the duration; you'll replace this later with a real value as you work through the project.

Now add the following method stub to the class:

```
func animateTransition(transitionContext:
UIViewControllerContextTransitioning) {

}
```

The above stub will hold your animation code; adding it should have cleared the remaining errors in Xcode.

Now that you have the basic animator class, you can move on to implementing the delegate methods on the view controller side.

Open **ViewController.swift** and add the following extension to the end of the file:

```
extension ViewController: UIViewControllerTransitioningDelegate{

}
```

This code indicates the view controller conforms to the transitioning delegate protocol. You'll add some methods here in a moment.

Find `didTapImageView()` in the main body of the class. Near the bottom of that method you'll see the code that presents the details view controller. `herbDetails` is the instance of the new view controller; you'll need to set its transitioning delegate to the main controller.

Add the following code right before the last line of the method that calls `presentViewController`:

```
herbDetails.transitioningDelegate = self
```

Now UIKit will ask `ViewController` for an animator object every time you present the details view controller on the screen. However, you still haven't implemented any of `UIViewControllerTransitioningDelegate`'s methods, so UIKit will still use the default transition.

The next step is to actually create your animator object and return it to UIKit when requested.

Add the following new property to `ViewController`:

```
let transition = PopAnimator()
```

This is the instance of `PopAnimator` that will drive your animated view controller transitions. You only need one instance of `PopAnimator` since you can continue to use the same object each time you present a view controller, as the transitions are the same every time.

Now add the first delegate method to the extension in `ViewController`:

```
func animationControllerForPresentedController(
 presented: UIViewController!,
 presentingController presenting: UIViewController!,
 sourceController source: UIViewController!) ->
 UIViewControllerAnimatedTransitioning! {
  return transition
}
```

This method takes a few parameters that let you make an informed decision whether or not you want to return a custom animation. In this chapter you'll always return your single instance of `PopAnimator` since you have only one presentation transition.

You've already added the delegate method for presenting view controllers, but how will you deal with dismissing one?

Add the following delegate method to handle this:

```
func animationControllerForDismissedController(dismissed:
UIViewController!) -> UIViewControllerAnimatedTransitioning! {
  return nil
}
```

The above method does essentially the same thing as the previous one: you check which view controller was dismissed and decide whether to return `nil` and use the default animation, or return a custom transition animator and use that instead. At the moment you return `nil`, as you aren't going to implement the dismissal animation until later.

You finally have a custom animator to take care of your custom transitions. But does it work?

Build and run your project and tap one of the herb images:

Nothing happens. Why? You have a custom animator to drive the transition, but... oh, wait, you haven't added any code to the animator class! :] You'll take care of that in the next section.

Creating your transition animator

Open **PopAnimator.swift;** this is where you'll add the code to transition between the two view controllers.

First, add the following properties to this class:

```
let duration    = 1.0
var presenting  = true
var originFrame = CGRect.zero
```

You'll use `duration` in several places, such as when you tell UIKit how long the transition will take and when you create the constituent animations.

You also define `presenting` to tell the animator class whether you are presenting or dismissing a view controller. You want to keep track of this because typically, you'll run the animation forward to present and in reverse to dismiss.

Finally, you will use `originFrame` to store the original frame rect of the image the user taps – you will need that to animate from the original frame to a full screen image and vice versa. Keep an eye out for `originFrame` later on when you fetch the currently selected image and pass its frame to the animator instance.

Now you can move on to the `UIViewControllerAnimatedTransitioning` methods.

Replace the code inside `transitionDuration()` with the following:

```
return duration
```

Reusing the `duration` property lets you easily experiment with the transition animation; you can simply modify the value of the property to make the transition run faster or slower.

Setting your transition's context

It's time to add some magic to `animateTransition`. This method has one parameter of type `UIViewControllerContextTransitioning`, which gives you access to the parameters and view controllers of the transition.

Before you start working on the code itself, it's important to understand what the animation context actually *is*.

When the transition between the two view controllers begins, the existing view is added to a transition container view and the new view controller's view is created but not yet visible, as illustrated below:

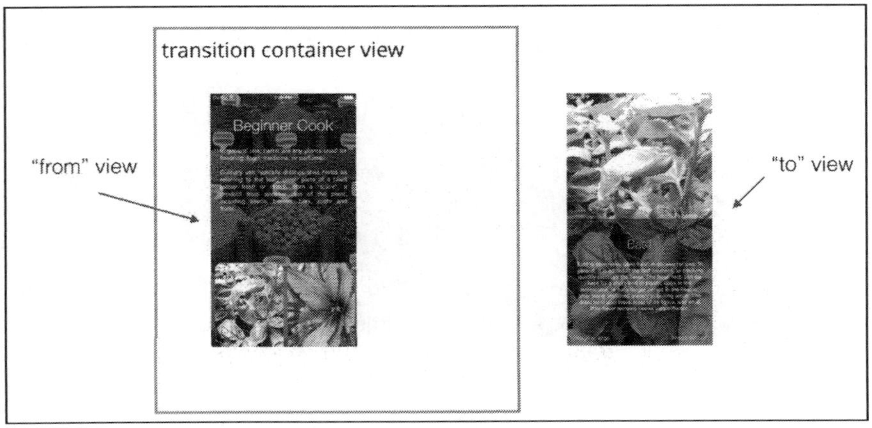

Therefore your task is to add the new view to the transition container within `animateTransition()`, "animate in" its appearance, and "animate out" the old view if required.

By default, the old view is removed from the transition container when the transition animation is done:

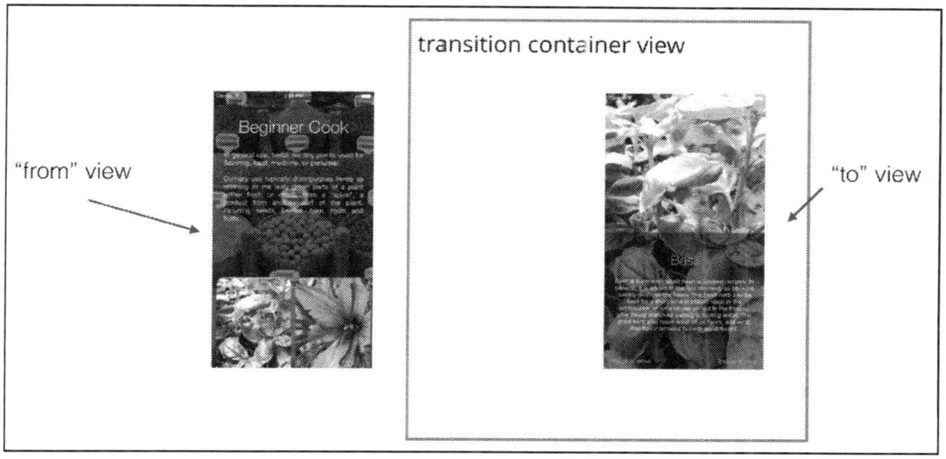

Before you get too many cooks in this kitchen, you'll create a simple transition animation to see how it works before implementing a much cooler, albeit more complicated, transition.

Adding a fade transition

You'll start with a simple fade transition to get a feel for custom transitions. Add the following code to `animateTransition()`:

```
let containerView = transitionContext.containerView()!

let toView =
  transitionContext.viewForKey(UITransitionContextToViewKey)!
```

First, you get the container view where your animations will take place, and then you fetch the new view and store it in `toView`.

The transition context object has two very handy methods that give you access to the transition players:

- `viewForKey()`: This lets you access the views of the "old" and "new" view controllers via the arguments `UITransitionContextFromViewKey` or `UITransitionContextToViewKey` respectively.

- viewControllerForKey(): This lets you access the "old and "new" view controllers via the arguments UITransitionContextFromViewControllerKey or UITransitionContextToViewControllerKey respectively.

At this point, you have both the container view and the view to be presented. Next you need to add the view to be presented as a child to the container view and animate it in some way.

Add the following to animateTransition():

```
containerView.addSubview(toView)
toView.alpha = 0.0

UIView.animateWithDuration(duration,
  animations: {
    toView.alpha = 1.0
  }, completion: { _ in
    transitionContext.completeTransition(true)
  })
```

Note that you call completeTransition() on the transition context in the animation completion block; this tells UIKit that your transition animations are done and that UIKit is free to wrap up the view controller transition.

Build and run your project; tap one of the herbs in the list and you'll see the herb overview fade in over the main view controller:

The transition is acceptable and you've seen what to do in animateTransition – but you're going to add something even better!

Adding a pop transition

You're going to structure the code for the new transition slightly differently, so replace all the code in `animateTransition()` with the following:

```
let containerView = transitionContext.containerView()!
let toView =
 transitionContext.viewForKey(UITransitionContextToViewKey)!

let herbView = presenting ? toView :
transitionContext.viewForKey(UITransitionContextFromViewKey)!
```

`containerView` is where your animations will live, while `toView` is the new view to present. If you're presenting, `herbView` is just the `toView`; otherwise it will be fetched from the context. For both presenting and dismissing, `herbView` will always be the view that you animate.

When you present the details controller view, it will grow to take up the entire screen. When dismissed, it will shrink to the image's original frame.

Add the following to `animateTransition()`:

```
let initialFrame = presenting ? originFrame : herbView.frame
let finalFrame = presenting ? herbView.frame : originFrame

let xScaleFactor = presenting ?
  initialFrame.width / finalFrame.width :
  finalFrame.width / initialFrame.width

let yScaleFactor = presenting ?
  initialFrame.height / finalFrame.height :
  finalFrame.height / initialFrame.height
```

In the code above, you detect the initial and final animation frames and then calculate the scale factor you need to apply on each axis as you animate between each view.

Now you need to carefully position the new view so it appears exactly above the tapped image; this will make it look like the tapped image expands to fill the screen.

Add the following to `animateTransition()`:

```
let scaleTransform = CGAffineTransformMakeScale(xScaleFactor,
yScaleFactor)

if presenting {
  herbView.transform = scaleTransform
  herbView.center = CGPoint(
    x: CGRectGetMidX(initialFrame),
```

```
    y: CGRectGetMidY(initialFrame))
  herbView.clipsToBounds = true
}
```

When presenting the new view, you set its scale and position so it exactly matches the size and location of the initial frame.

Now add the final bits of code to `animateTransition()`:

```
containerView.addSubview(toView)
containerView.bringSubviewToFront(herbView)

UIView.animateWithDuration(duration, delay:0.0,
  usingSpringWithDamping: 0.4,
  initialSpringVelocity: 0.0,
  options: [],
  animations: {
    herbView.transform = self.presenting ?
     CGAffineTransformIdentity : scaleTransform
    herbView.center = CGPoint(x: CGRectGetMidX(finalFrame),
                              y: CGRectGetMidY(finalFrame))

  }, completion:{_ in
    transitionContext.completeTransition(true)
})
```

This will first add `toView` to the container. Next, you need to make sure the `herbView` is on top since that's the only view you're animating. Remember that when dismissing, `toView` is the original view so in the first line, you'll be adding it *on top* of everything else and your animation will be hidden away unless you bring `herbView` to the front.

Then, you can kick off the animations – using a spring animation here will give it a bit of bounce.

Inside the `animations` expression, you change the transform and position of `herbView`. When presenting, you're going from the small size at the bottom to the full screen so the target transform is just the identity transform. When dismissing, you animate it to scale down to match the original image size.

At this point, you've set the stage by positioning the new view controller over the tapped image; you've animated between the initial and final frames; and finally, you've called `completeTransition()` to hand things back to UIKit. It's time to see your code in action!

Build and run your project; tap the first herb image to see your view controller transition in action:

Well, it's not perfect, but once you take care of a few rough edges your animation will be exactly what you wanted!

Currently your animation starts from the top-left corner; that's because the default value of `originFrame` has the origin at `(0, 0)` – and you never set it to any other value.

Open **ViewController.swift** and add the following code to the top of `animationControllerForPresentedController()`:

```
transition.originFrame =
  selectedImage!.superview!.convertRect(selectedImage!.frame,
   toView: nil)
transition.presenting = true
selectedImage!.hidden = true
```

This sets the `originFrame` of the transition to the frame of `selectedImage,` which is the image view you last tapped. Then you set `presenting` to `true` and hide the tapped image during the animation.

Build and run your project again; tap different herbs in the list and see how your transition looks for each:

Adding a dismiss transition

All that's left to do is dismiss the details controller. You've actually done most of the work in the animator already – the transition animation code does the logic juggling to set the proper initial and final frames, so you're most of the way to playing the animation both forwards and backwards. Sweet! :]

Open **ViewController.swift** and replace the body of `animationControllerForDismissedController()` with the following:

```
transition.presenting = false
return transition
```

This tells your animator object that you're dismissing a view controller so the animation code will run in the correct direction.

Build and run the project to see the result. Tap on an herb and then tap anywhere on screen to dismiss it:

The transition animation looks great, but notice the herb you picked has disappeared from the scroll view! You'll need to make sure the tapped image re-appears when you dismiss the details screen.

Open **PopAnimator.swift** and add a new closure property to the class:

```
var dismissCompletion: (()->())?
```

This will let you pass in some code to run when the dismiss transition completes.

Next, find `animateTransition()` and add the following code to the completion handler in the call to `animateWithDuration`, right before the call to `completeTransition`:

```
if !self.presenting {
  self.dismissCompletion?()
}
```

This code executes `dismissCompletion` once the dismiss animation has finished – which is the perfect spot to show the original image.

Open **ViewController.swift** and add the following code to `viewDidLoad()`:

```
transition.dismissCompletion = {
  self.selectedImage!.hidden = false
}
```

This code displays the original image to replace the herb details view controller once the transition animation completes.

Build and run your app to enjoy the transition animations both ways, now that the herbs aren't getting lost along the way!

The transition animation still looks a bit rough around the edges but you'll finish it on your own in this chapter's challenges.

Before you get to the challenges though, there's one more animation topic to deal with: view transitions for managing changes to device orientation.

Device orientation transition

> **Note**: This section of the chapter is optional; if you're not interested in learning how to handle changes in device orientation in your view controllers, skip ahead directly to the challenges.

You can think of device orientation changes as a presentation transition from a view controller to itself, just at a different size.

`viewWillTransitionToSize(_:coordinator:)`, introduced in iOS 8, gives you a simple and straightforward way to handle device orientation changes. You don't need to build separate portrait or landscape layouts; instead, you just need to react to the change to the view controller view's size.

Open **ViewController.swift** and add the following stub for `viewWillTransitionToSize(...)`:

```
override func viewWillTransitionToSize(size: CGSize,
withTransitionCoordinator coordinator:
UIViewControllerTransitionCoordinator) {
  super.viewWillTransitionToSize(size,
    withTransitionCoordinator: coordinator)

}
```

The first parameter (`size`) tells you what size your view controller is transitioning to. The second parameter (`coordinator`) is the transition coordinator object, which gives you access to a number of the transition's properties.

All you need to do in this app is reduce the alpha of the app's background image to improve the readability of the text when the device is in landscape mode.

Add the following code to `viewWillTransitionToSize`:

```
coordinator.animateAlongsideTransition({context in
  self.bgImage.alpha = (size.width>size.height) ? 0.25 : 0.55
}, completion: nil)
```

`animateAlongsideTransition` lets you specify your own custom animations to execute in parallel with the rotation animation that UIKit performs by default when you change the orientation.

Your animation closure will receive a transitioning context, just like the one you used when presenting a view controller. In this case, you don't have "from" and "to" view controllers since they're the same, but instead you can fetch properties such as the transition duration.

Inside the animation closure you check if the width of the target size is bigger than the height; if so, you reduce the alpha value of the background image to `0.25`. This makes the background fade out when transitioning to landscape mode and fade in to `0.55` alpha when transitioning to portrait orientation.

Build and run your app; rotate the device (or press Cmd + Left arrow if testing in the iPhone Simulator) to see your alpha animation in action:

You can clearly see the background dim when you rotate the screen to a landscape mode – this makes the longer lines of text easier to read.

However if you tap on a herb image you will notice that animation is somewhat messy. This happens because now the screen has a landscape orientation but the images still have portrait dimensions. Therefore the transition between the original image and the image stretched to fill up the screen is not fluid.

No fear – you can use your new friend `viewWillTransitionToSize` to fix this problem too.

There is a class method called `positionListItems()` in `ViewController` that sizes and positions the herb images. This method is called from `viewDidLoad()` when your app first starts.

Add a call to this method inside the `animateAlongsideTransition` animation block you added last, just after you set the `alpha`:

```
self.positionListItems()
```

This will animate the size and position of the herb images while the device rotates. As soon as the screen finishes re-orientating the herb images will also have resized:

And since those images will now have a landscape layout also your transition animation will work just fine – give it a try!

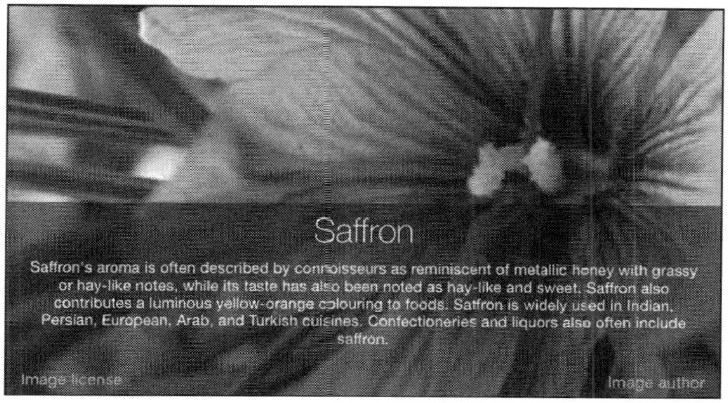

That's it for this chapter; take a look at the challenges below where you'll polish some of the remaining rough edges of your transition animations.

Challenges

There are two tiny imperfections in your presentation animation: you can see the detail view text up to the very last moment when it just disappears; in addition, the initial herb images have rounded corners, which makes the animation look jumpy at the end.

Challenge 1: Smooth the transition animation

Your first task is to fade the contents of the herb details view in or out as appropriate while transitioning. This corrects that awkward moment when the text of the detail view just disappears as it's dismissed.

Take a look at the storyboard file; you'll see the details controller already has all of its text views added to a main view connected to the `containerView` outlet.

All you need to do is fade `containerView` in or out while the transition animation takes place.

There are three steps in the solution to this challenge:

- Get a reference to the `HerbDetailsViewController` using the transition context's `viewControllerForKey` method. Remember that the key will be different depending on whether you are presenting or dismissing and that you'll need to cast the result as `HerbViewController`. The two keys to choose from are `UITransitionContextToViewControllerKey` and `UITransitionContextFromViewControllerKey`.

- Before you start the animation (the one animation already in `animateTranstion`), set the alpha of `containerView` to zero; it's an outlet property of `HerbDetailsViewController`. You only need to do this when you're presenting the view controller, not when dismissing it since it will be visible already when dismissing.
- Set the alpha of `containerView` in your `animation` closure – where you animate `herbView` – to fully opaque (`1.0`) when you're presenting and fully transparent (`0.0`) when you're dismissing.

To check the result of your changes more closely, you can increase the transition duration to `10` seconds and observe the animation in detail (or use Debug/Toggle Slow Animations in Frontmost App from the iOS Simulator main menu).

Challenge 2: Animate the corner radius

Finally you'll animate the corner radius of the details view so that it matches the rounded corners of the herb images in the main view controller.

At the end of `animateTransition` create and run a layer animation to change the corner radius of `herbView`'s layer. Animate `herbView.layer.cornerRadius` from `20.0/xScaleFactor` to `0.0` if presenting, and vice versa if dismissing. You need to take the scale factor into account because you're also transforming the view. Set the duration of the animation to `duration / 2` so that it has finished before the springing starts, otherwise it will look quite strange!

That wraps up presentation controller animations – next up, navigation controller animations. You'll notice a lot of similarities between the two, so put the herbs aside and dive right in!

Chapter 22: UINavigationController Custom Transition Animations

`UINavigationController` is one of the few built-in app navigation solutions available in iOS. You've likely used navigation controllers in your own projects – and you've certainly used them as you've worked through this book.

Pushing a new view controller onto the navigation stack or popping one off gives you sleek animation with no work on your part; a new screen comes from the right and pushes away the old one with a slight lag:

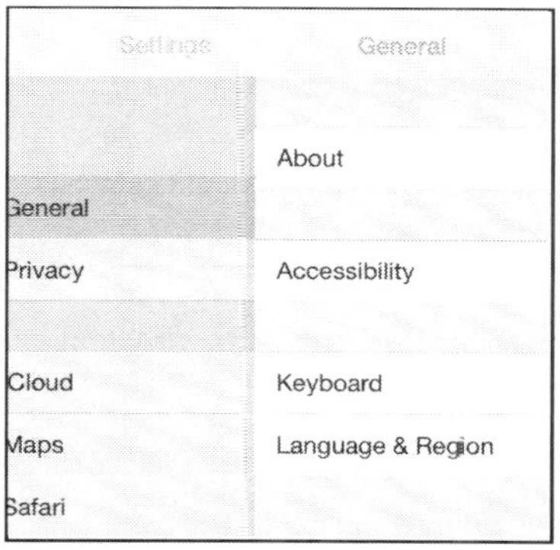

The above screenshot shows how iOS pushes a new view controller onto the navigation stack in the Settings app: the new view slides in from the right to cover the old view and the new title fades in while the old title titles fades from view.

The navigation paradigm in iOS has become old hat to users, as the same animations have been used for many years; this frees you to embellish your navigation controller transitions without throwing the user off.

In much the same way you built custom presenting view controllers in the previous chapter, you can build custom transitions to push and pop new view controllers.

You'll be working with the Logo Reveal project; in this chapter, you'll add a custom transparent view that gives the user a glimpse of the content hidden behind:

If you worked through the previous chapter, you'll find that custom navigation controller transitions feel quite similar to presenting view controllers.

Introducing Logo Reveal

Open the starter project for this chapter and select **Main.storyboard**. You'll see the project has been created from the standard Master Detail app template; it features a navigation controller, master view controller, and a detail view controller like so:

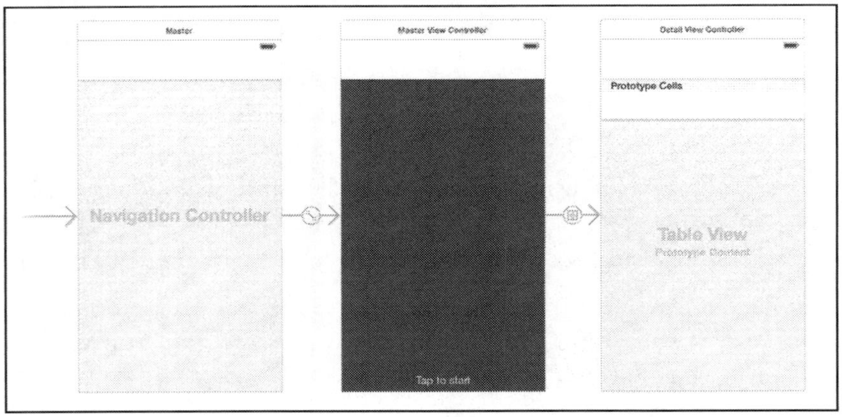

The navigation's already been hooked up for you so you can focus on customizing your navigation controllers.

Build and run your project; tap anywhere on the default screen (`MasterViewController`) to present the vacation packing list (`DetailViewController`):

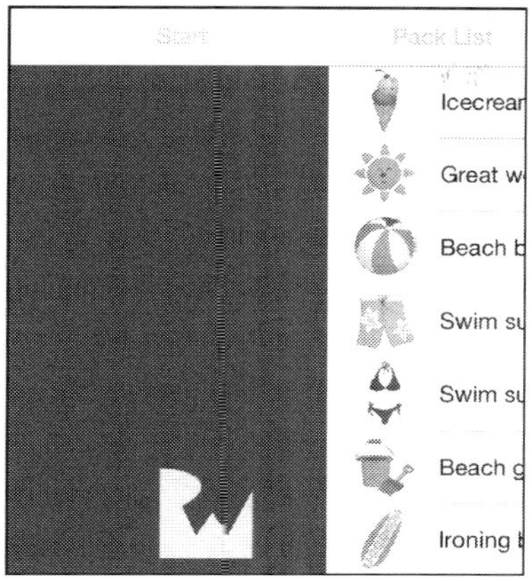

Custom navigation transitions

UIKit lets you customize navigation transitions via the delegate pattern in almost the same way you do for presenting view controllers.

You'll make your `MasterViewController` class adopt the `UINavigationControllerDelegate` protocol and set it to be the delegate to your navigation controller. Each time you push a view controller onto the navigation stack, the navigation controller will ask its delegate whether it should use the built-in transition or a custom one, as illustrated below:

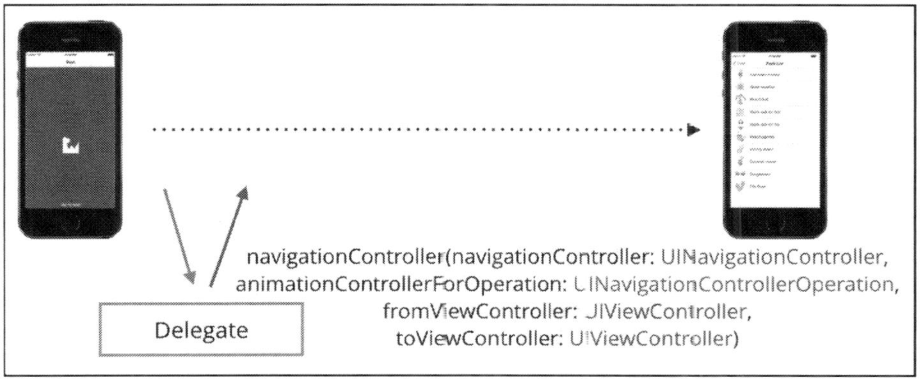

When you push or pop a view controller, the navigation controller asks its delegate to provide an animation controller for that operation.

If you return `nil` from that delegate method, the navigation controller will use the default transition. However, if you return an object, the navigation controller will use this instead as a custom transition animation controller. Yup – this sounds a *lot* like the previous chapter, doesn't it?

The animation controller should adopt the same `UIViewControllerAnimatedTransitioning` protocol you worked with in the previous chapter. Once you provide an animation controller object (or animator), the navigation controller will call the following methods on it:

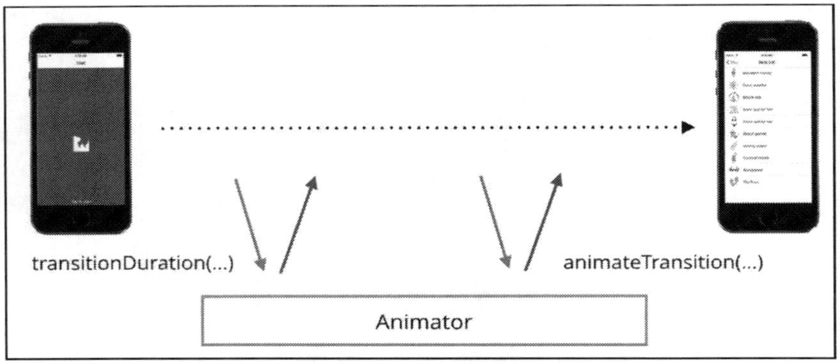

First, the navigation controller calls `transitionDuration()` to find out how long the transition will last; it then calls `animateTransition()`, which is where your custom transition animation code will live.

The navigation controller delegate

Before you can implement the delegate methods, you'll need to create the basic skeleton of the animator class.

From Xcode's main menu select **File\New\File...** and choose the template **iOS\Source\Cocoa Touch Class**.

Set the new class name to **RevealAnimator** and make it a subclass of **NSObject**.

Make the new class comply with the `UIViewControllerAnimatedTransitioning` protocol like so:

```
class RevealAnimator: NSObject,
UIViewControllerAnimatedTransitioning {

}
```

Now you need to implement the two required `UIViewControllerAnimatedTransitioning` methods to resolve Xcode's error messages.

Add the following properties to the class:

```
let animationDuration = 2.0

var operation: UINavigationControllerOperation = .Push
```

Your animation will last two seconds; that's a long time in the UI navigation world, but it will let you see your animation in minute, excruciating detail. `operation` is a property of type `UINavigationControllerOperation` that tells whether you're pushing or popping a view controller.

Now add the following two `UIViewControllerAnimatedTransitioning` methods to the class:

```
func transitionDuration(transitionContext:
UIViewControllerContextTransitioning?) -> NSTimeInterval {
    return animationDuration
}

func animateTransition(transitionContext:
UIViewControllerContextTransitioning) {
}
```

`transitionDuration()` simply returns the animation duration in seconds, while `animateTransition()` is the future home for your custom animations. You'll populate `animateTransition()` once you finish setting up your navigation controller delegate.

All your Xcode errors should have resolved by this point. Open **MasterViewController.swift**, which will serve as your navigation controller delegate.

Add the code below to the bottom of the file, outside of the class definition:

```
extension MasterViewController: UINavigationControllerDelegate {
}
```

This adopts the `UIViewNavigationControllerDelegate` protocol in a new extension; this view controller can now serve as the navigation controller delegate.

You'll need to set the navigation controller's delegate early in the view controller lifecycle, before you invoke any segues or push something onto the stack.

Add the following code to `viewDidLoad()`:

```
navigationController?.delegate = self
```

Your next task is to create an instance of `RevealAnimator` and pass it to the navigation controller when asked for an animation controller.

Add the following property to `MasterViewController`:

```
let transition = RevealAnimator()
```

This is the animator you'll use for pushing and popping view controllers.

Now that you have your animator, add the following method to the class extension:

```
func navigationController(navigationController:
UINavigationController, animationControllerForOperation operation:
UINavigationControllerOperation, fromViewController fromVC:
UIViewController, toViewController toVC: UIViewController) ->
UIViewControllerAnimatedTransitioning? {

  transition.operation = operation
  return transition
}
```

That's one monster of a method name, but if you cut through the noise you'll see that it boils down to the following parameters:

- `navigationController:` This helps to distinguish between navigation controllers in the event your object is a delegate of more than one navigation controller; this isn't likely, but you still need to protect against the possibility.
- `operation:` This is a `UINavigationControllerOperation` value, either `.Push` or `.Pop`.
- `fromVC:` This is the view controller currently visible on the screen; it's usually the last view controller in the navigation stack.
- `toVC:` This is the view controller you'll transition to.

If you support different transitions for different view controllers, this is where you'll choose what kind of animator object to return. To keep things simple in this project, you'll always return your `RevealAnimator` object after you set the animator's `operation` property to indicate either a push or pop transition.

Build and run your project; tap the first view controller and you'll see the navigation bar animate over two seconds:

Note that the update to the navigation bar lasts for the duration you specified in `RevealAnimator` – but at this point nothing else will happen. Your animator takes control of the transition, but since you didn't write any code in `animateTransition()`, no animation of the content takes place.

However, at least this indicates that the navigation controller is calling through to your custom transition properly. Now it's time to get animating!

Adding a custom reveal animation

The plan for your custom transition animation is relatively simple. You'll simply animate a mask on `DetailViewController` to make it look like the transparent part of the RW logo reveals the contents of the underlying view controller.

You'll have to juggle layers and some animation tasks, but it's nothing you haven't done so far in the book. Creating the transition animation will be an easy feat for an animation pro like you! :]

Open **RevealAnimator.swift** and add the following property:

```
weak var storedContext: UIViewControllerContextTransitioning?
```

Since you're going to create some layer animations for your transition, you'll need to store the animation context somewhere until the animation ends and the delegate method `animationDidStop(_:finished:)` executes. At that point, you'll call `completeTransition()` from within `animationDidStop()` to wrap up the transition.

Add the following code to `animateTransition()` to store the transition context for later use:

```
storedContext = transitionContext
```

> **Note**: You'll find more detail on how you fetch transition view controllers from the context and animation container views in Chapter 21, "Custom Presentation Controller & Device Orientation Animations".

Now add the following initial transition code to `animateTransition()`:

```
let fromVC = transitionContext.viewControllerForKey(
  UITransitionContextFromViewControllerKey) as!
  MasterViewController

let toVC = transitionContext.viewControllerForKey(
  UITransitionContextToViewControllerKey) as!
  DetailViewController

transitionContext.containerView()?.addSubview(toVC.view)
```

Since you'll work on the push transition initially, you can make an assumption about the identity of the "from" and "to" view controllers of the transition.

First, you fetch the "from" view controller (`fromVC`) and cast it to a `MasterViewController`; you then fetch `toVC` as a `DetailViewController`.

Finally, you simply add `toVC.view` to the transition container view. This places the vacation packing list in its final location over the main screen.

Now you're going to create the reveal animation. The secret to a reveal animation is to have an object – in your case the RW logo – grow to cover the entire area of the screen.

This sounds like a job for a scale transformation! Add the following to `animateTransition()`:

```
let animation = CABasicAnimation(keyPath: "transform")

animation.fromValue = NSValue(CATransform3D:
  CATransform3DIdentity)

animation.toValue = NSValue(CATransform3D:
  CATransform3DConcat(
    CATransform3DMakeTranslation(0.0, -10.0, 0.0),
    CATransform3DMakeScale(150.0, 150.0, 1.0)
  )
)
```

This animation grows the logo `150` times in size and moves it up a little at the same time. Why? The logo is uneven in shape and you want the view controller behind to show through the "hole" of the RW shape. Moving it up a little bit means the bottom of the zoomed image will cover the screen much faster.

The image below shows how your zoom animation will work:

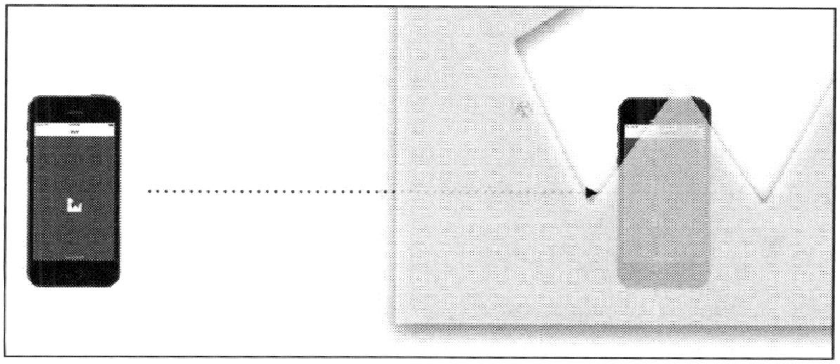

If you used a symmetrical shape like a circle or ellipse, you wouldn't have this problem – but your animation wouldn't be nearly as cool. :]

Now add the following lines to animateTransition() to refine the animation a bit:

```
animation.duration = animationDuration
animation.delegate = self
animation.fillMode = kCAFillModeForwards
animation.removedOnCompletion = false
animation.timingFunction = CAMediaTimingFunction(name:
  kCAMediaTimingFunctionEaseIn)
```

First, you set the duration of the animation to match the transition duration. You then set the animator as the delegate and configure the animation model to leave the animation on screen; this avoids glitches when the transition wraps up since the RW logo will be hidden away anyway. Finally, you add easing to make the reveal effect accelerate over time.

Your animation is complete – but to which layer should it be applied?

Open **DetailViewController.swift** and look at the maskLayer property; it contains the shape of the RW logo and is ready to be used as a mask.

Add the following code to the end of viewDidLoad():

```
maskLayer.position = CGPoint(x: view.layer.bounds.size.width/2,
  y: view.layer.bounds.size.height/2)
view.layer.mask = maskLayer
```

This positions maskLayer in the very center of the view's layer. Then you simply set maskLayer as the mask of the view controller's view.

Since the only time you need to mask the contents of the view controller is during push transitions, you can safely remove the mask once the view controller finishes transitioning.

Add the following to the end of `viewDidAppear()`:

```
view.layer.mask = nil
```

This will remove the mask after the view has appeared and the transition is complete.

Now that you have your mask layer set up, open again **RevealAnimator.swift** and add the following code to the end of `animateTransition()`:

```
toVC.maskLayer.addAnimation(animation, forKey: nil)
```

This adds the animation to the mask layer – which means you can test out the current state of your transition.

Build and run your project to see how things look so far:

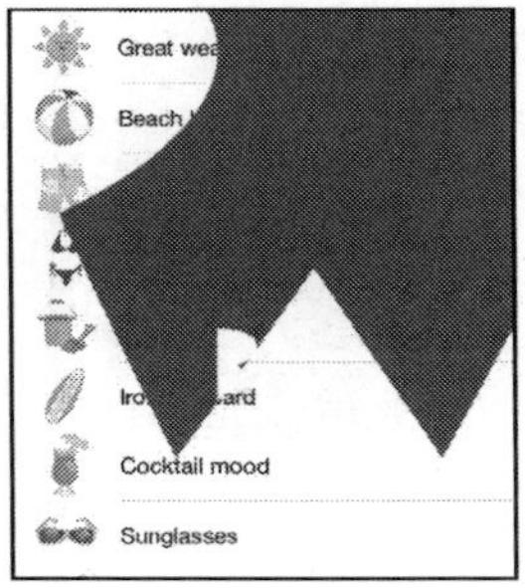

Not bad, not bad; your reveal is running, but the animation is somewhat clunky and you can't go back to the main screen once you push the pack list on top. Time to fix those issues!

Taking care of the rough edges

You likely noticed you can still see the original logo behind the zooming reveal logo. The easiest way to handle this is to run the reveal animation on the original logo as well; you already have the animation, so it's no matter to reuse it. This will make the original logo grow with the mask, matching its shape exactly so it won't be in the way.

Add the following to `animateTransition()`:

```
fromVC.logo.addAnimation(animation, forKey: nil)
```

Build and run your project again to verify that the original logo is no longer hanging around:

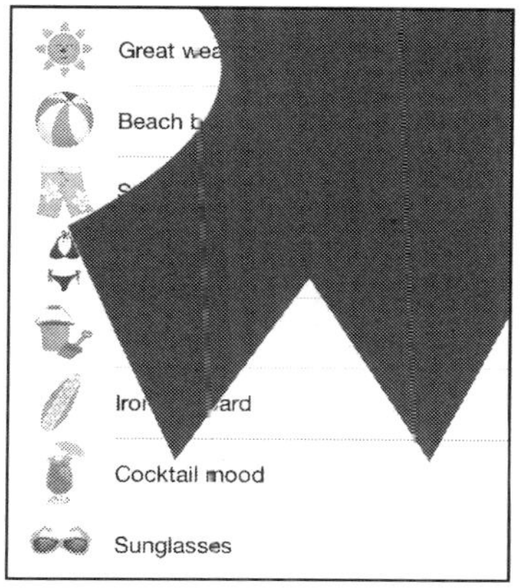

Now, a slightly harder problem – what's up with the navigation not working any more after the first push transition?

If you take a look at what you've done so far, you'll see that you never really wrap up the transition. You planned to call `completeTransition()` when the animation ended – but never got around to implementing that code.

`RevealAnimator` is set as the delegate of your reveal animation. Therefore, you need to override `animationDidStop(_:finished:)` and complete the transition within that method.

Add the following code to `RevealAnimator`:

```
override func animationDidStop(anim: CAAnimation,
  finished flag: Bool) {

  if let context = storedContext {
   context.completeTransition(!context.transitionWasCancelled())

   //reset logo
  }

  storedContext = nil
}
```

Here you check whether you have a stored transition context; if so, you call `completeTransition()` on it. This passes the ball back to the navigation controller to wrap up with the transition on UIKit's side.

At the end of the method, you simply set the reference to the transition context to `nil`.

Since the reveal animation won't be removed automagically upon completion, you'll need to handle things yourself.

Replace the `//reset logo` comment in `animationDidStop()`with the following:

```
let fromVC = context.viewControllerForKey(
  UITransitionContextFromViewControllerKey) as!
  MasterViewController

fromVC.logo.removeAllAnimations()
```

That should do it. Build and run your project; push the packing list view controller onto the screen, then tap **Start** to return to the original view. The proof that you're calling your custom transition is shown by the following spectacular crash:

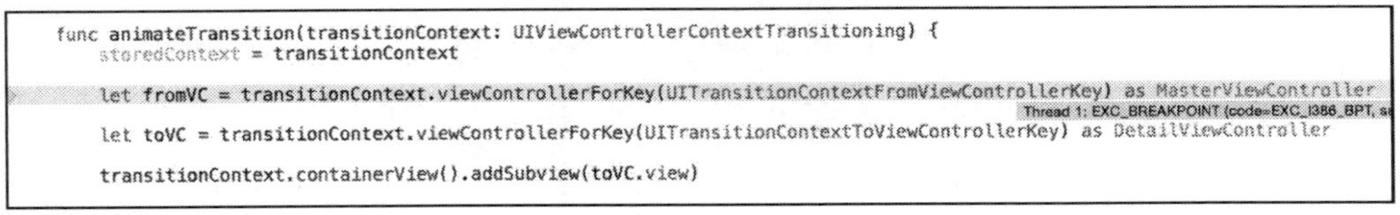

You're trying to cast the "from" view controller to a `MasterViewController` instance – which is true only for the push transition, but not for the pop transition. Whoops.

Open **RevealAnimator.swift** and find `animateTransition()`. You'll need to wrap most of the code here in a conditional. Add the following line just after the first line where you set `storedContext`:

```
if operation == .Push {
```

Then, scroll all the way to the end of the method and add a closing brace for the `if` at the very end of the method.

The condition checks whether you're dealing with a push transition before you try to cast it. This should take care of that crashing piece of code.

Build and run to try it out again – your push transition is working, but your pop transition won't do anything yet since you don't have any code in `animateTransition()` to handle it.

This is where you get to flex your ninja coding muscles; you'll create the pop transition on your own in the Challenges section below – and add a bit of elegance to the reveal animation along the way.

Challenges

Challenge 1: Fade in the new view controller

Right now the transition looks like a sharp cutout; the contents of the new view controller are visible instantly and make the whole animation look a bit clunky.

Your challenge is to fade in the new view controller as the reveal animation runs.

To do this, create a fade in `CABasicAnimation` and add it to the layer of `toVC.view`. Use the same transition duration for this new animation and set `fromValue` and `toValue` to animate from fully transparent to fully opaque.

Call your new animation just after the point where you add the reveal animation to both the logo and the mask layers.

When you are finished, your transition should look like the following:

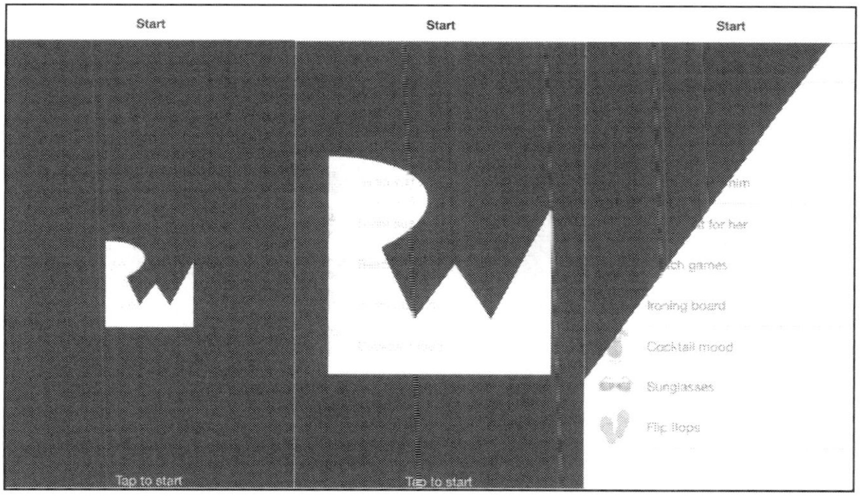

It appears as if your cutout becomes progressively more transparent as it grows; this gives the transition a mysterious effect.

Challenge 2: Add pop transition

To create a pop transition, you'll simply add a complementary `else` branch to the `if` statement inside `animateTransition()` of `RevealAnimator`. Inside the `else` branch you can add any animations you want, but don't forget to call `completeTransition()` when you're finished.

Here's how to create a simple shrink transition:

1. Add an `else` branch to the `if` inside `animateTransition()`.
2. Fetch the "from" and "to" views using the `viewForKey` method on the context. Because you're not doing anything with the properties of the view controller this time, you can just fetch the views alone.
3. Work with the transition `containerView` and insert the `toView` **below** `fromView`. Tip: use `insertSubview(_:belowSubview:_)`.
4. Use an animation to scale `fromView` to `0.01x` . Don't use `0.0` for scaling – this will confuse UIKit. For this animation you can use an ordinary view animation – there's no need to create a layer animation.
5. When the animation finishes, call `completeTransition()` on the transition context just as you did before.

This will result in the following tasteful shrinking transition:

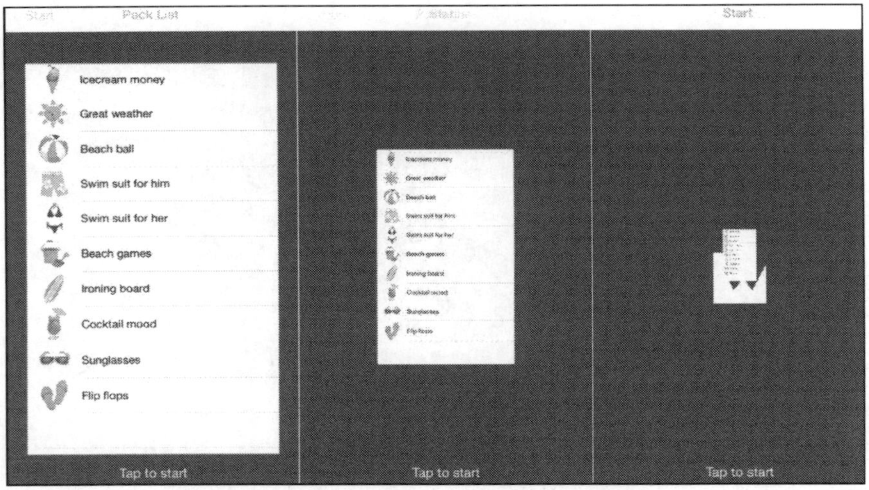

How did you do with the challenges? If you created your own custom pop transition – good on you; that's the true spirit of development!

As you might have guessed, you can create custom transitions for `UITabBarController` too. You won't cover them here, but they work in a similar way to navigation controller transitions so you can easily figure them out based on what you've learned so far.

The next chapter takes transitions to the next level, and shows you how to let your user *interact* with the transitions themselves!

Chapter 23: Interactive UINavigationController Transitions

The reveal transition you created in the previous chapter looks pretty neat, but custom animations are only half the story. You've been sheltered from the truth, dear friend, but no more; as your reward for making your way to the end of this book, you're about to become privy to the secrets of the iOS ancients.

Not only can you create a custom animation for your transition – you can also make it *interactive* and respond to the actions of the user. Typically, you'd drive this action through a pan gesture, which is the approach you're going to take in this chapter.

When you're done, your users will be able to scrub back and forth through the reveal transition by sliding their finger across the screen. How cool would that be?

Yeah, I thought you'd be interested! :] Read on to see how it's done!

Creating an interactive transition

When your navigation controller asks its delegate for an animation controller, two things can happen. You can return `nil`, in which case the navigation controller runs the standard transition animation. You know that much already.

However – if you *do* return an animation controller then the navigation controller asks its delegate for an interaction controller like so:

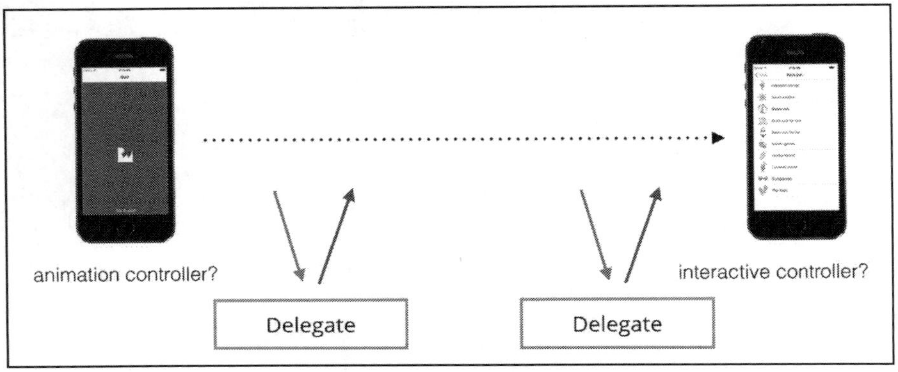

The interaction controller moves the transition along based on the user's actions, instead of simply animating the changes from start to finish. The interaction controller does not necessarily need to be a separate class from the animation controller; in fact, performing some tasks is a little easier when both controllers are in the same class. You just need to make sure that said class conforms to both `UIViewControllerAnimatedTransitioning` and `UIViewControllerInteractiveTransitioning`.

`UIViewControllerInteractiveTransitioning` has only one required method – `startInteractiveTransition(_:)` – that takes a transitioning context as its parameter. The interaction controller then regularly calls `updateInteractiveTransition(_:)` to move the transition along. To begin, you'll need to change how you handle your user input.

Handling the pan gesture

First of all, the tap gesture recognizer in `MasterViewController` just won't cut it anymore. A tap happens momentarily and then it's gone; you can't track its progress and use it to drive a transition. On the other hand, a pan gesture has clear states for the starting, progressing, and ending phases of the transition.

Open the starter project for this chapter; alternatively, you can use your completed project (including the challenges) from the previous chapter.

Open **Main.storyboard**; go to the master view controller and change the text of the label towards the bottom of the screen to "**Slide to start**" like so:

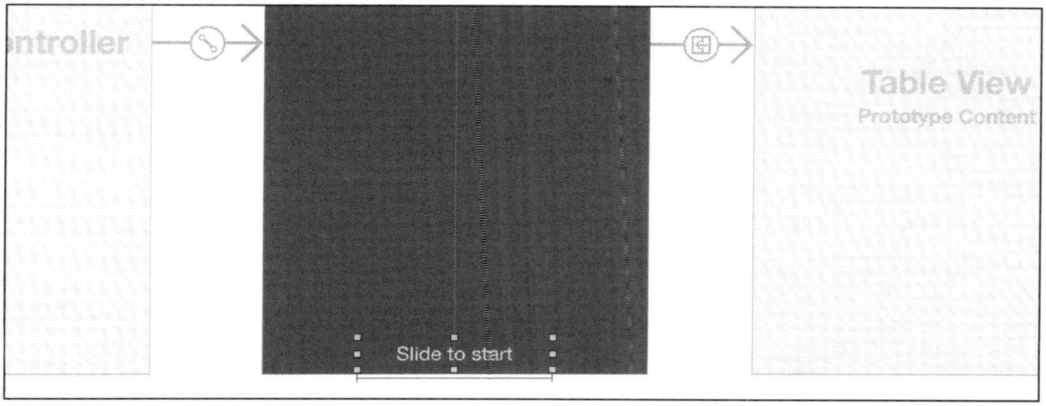

This will reflect the action you expect from the user.

Next, open **MasterViewController.swift** and remove the following code that creates the tap gesture recognizer:

```
override func viewDidAppear(animated: Bool) {
  super.viewDidAppear(animated)

  // add the tap gesture recognizer
  let tap = UITapGestureRecognizer(target: self, action:
Selector("didTap"))
  view.addGestureRecognizer(tap)
```

In its place, insert the following pan recognizer code:

```
let pan = UIPanGestureRecognizer(target: self, action:
  Selector("didPan:"))
view.addGestureRecognizer(pan)
```

As the user pans across the screen, the recognizer invokes `didPan()` on your `MasterViewController` class.

You'll need to modify your `RevealAnimator` class quite a bit to handle the new, interactive transition; you'll take care of this in the next section.

Using interactive animator classes

To manage your transition, you'll use one of Apple's built-in interactive animator classes: `UIPercentDrivenInteractiveTransition`. This class conforms to `UIViewControllerInteractiveTransitioning` and lets you get and set your transition's progress as a value representing the percentage complete.

This makes your life a little easier, as you can use this class to adjust the `percentComplete` property accordingly and call `updateInteractiveTransition()` to set the current visible progress of the transition. This will skip through the transition animation to the point that corresponds to the calculated transition progress.

You'll learn more about how `UIPercentDrivenInteractiveTransition` works as you work through the rest of this chapter.

Open **RevealAnimator.swift** and update the class definition at the top of the file as follows:

```
class RevealAnimator: UIPercentDrivenInteractiveTransition,
UIViewControllerAnimatedTransitioning {
```

Now the super class of `RevealAnimator` will be `UIPercentDrivenInteractiveTransition`.

Next, add the following property to tell the animator whether or not it should drive the transition in an interactive fashion:

```
var interactive = false
```

Now add the following method to `RevealAnimator`:

```
func handlePan(recognizer: UIPanGestureRecognizer) {

}
```

When the user pans across the screen, you'll pass the recognizer to `handlePan()` in `RevealAnimator`, at which point you'll update the current progress of the transition.

You'll populate `handlePan()` in just a bit, but first you'll need to set up the gesture handling.

Open **MasterViewController.swift** and add the following delegate method to provide an interaction controller to the `MasterViewController` extension in that file:

```
func navigationController(navigationController:
UINavigationController,
```

```
interactionControllerForAnimationController animationController:
UIViewControllerAnimatedTransitioning) ->
UIViewControllerInteractiveTransitioning? {

  if !transition.interactive {
    return nil
  }
  return transition
}
```

You only return an interaction controller when you want the transition to be interactive. For example, in your Logo Reveal project the reveal transition is interactive, but the custom pop transition will remain as-is.

Now you need to hook up your pan gesture recognizer to the interaction controller. Add the following method to `MasterViewController`:

```
func didPan(recognizer: UIPanGestureRecognizer) {
  switch recognizer.state {
  case .Began:
    transition.interactive = true
    performSegueWithIdentifier("details", sender: nil)
  default:
    transition.handlePan(recognizer)
  }
}
```

As the pan gesture starts, you ensure `interactive` is set to `true` and then begin the segue to the next view controller. Performing the segue kicks off the transition as detailed in the previous chapter; the delegate methods you've added return `transition` for the animation controller *and* for the interaction controller.

In all cases, if the gesture has already started you simply hand things over to the interaction controller as illustrated below:

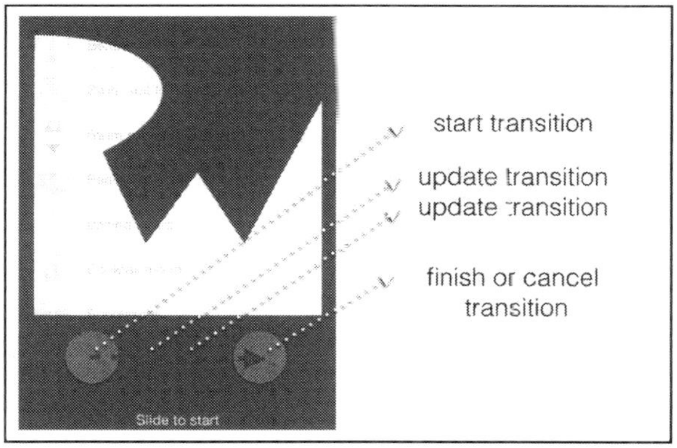

Calculating your animation's progress

The most important bit of your pan gesture handler is to figure out how far along the transition should be.

Open **RevealAnimator.swift** and add the following code to `handlePan()`:

```
let translation = recognizer.translationInView(
  recognizer.view!.superview!)
var progress: CGFloat = abs(translation.x / 200.0)
progress = min(max(progress, 0.01), 0.99)
```

First, you get the translation from the pan gesture recognizer; the translation lets you know how many points the user moved their finger/stylus/appendage/whatever on both the X and Y axes. Logically, the further the user pans from the initial location, the greater the progress of the transition.

To calculate the current progress, you take the translation on the X axis and divide it by `200` points. For example, if the user's finger is `100` points away from the initial pan location, the transition will be `50%` complete. `200` points is a bit of an arbitrary number, but it's a good starting point for the total distance the user needs to pan to complete the transition.

You shouldn't care whether the user pans to the right or to the left – that's why you use `abs()` to get the absolute value of the pan distance.

Finally, you cap the `progress` variable between `0.01` and `0.99`; my testing shows that interaction controllers behave better if you don't let the user finish or revert the transition from the pan gesture alone.

Now that you know the progress of the transition animation, you can update the transition animation as well.

Add the following code to `handlePan()`:

```
switch recognizer.state {
  case .Changed:
    updateInteractiveTransition(progress)
  default:
    break
}
```

`updateInteractiveTransition()` inherits from the `UIPercentDrivenInteractiveTransition` class and sets the current progress of the transition animation.

As the user pans across the screen, the gesture recognizer repeatedly calls `didPan()` in `MasterViewController`, which in turn forwards the recognizer to `handlePan()` in `RevealAnimator`.

Build and run your project; pan across the screen to see what your transition looks like:

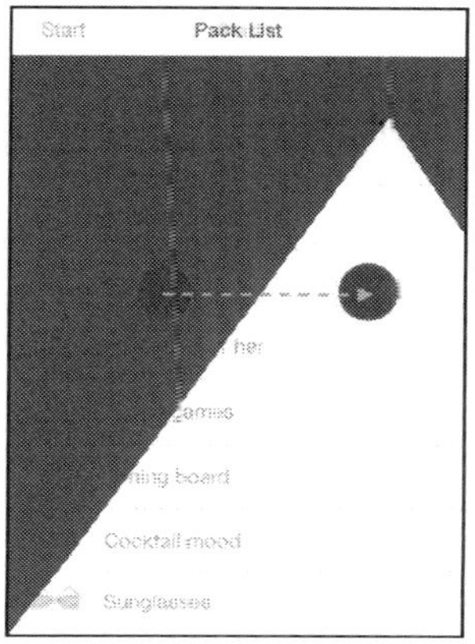

Since your transition isn't quite complete, the whole navigation breaks as soon as you lift your finger. However, you can see that the reveal animation followed your pan gesture – you're getting close to completing your interactive transition!

`updateInteractiveTransition()` smoothly handled your transition's progress and displayed the correct frame of the transition animation for you; your code didn't need to lift a finger. :] It's sometimes surprising to see how advanced some of Apple's UI features can be right out of the box!

All that's left is to handle the end state of your interactive transition.

Handling early termination

Here you face a totally new problem: the user might lift their finger before they've panned `200` points on the X axis. This leaves the transition in an unfinished state.

Luckily, `UIPercentDrivenInteractiveTransition` gives you a couple of methods for free that you can use to revert, or complete, the transition depending on the user's actions.

Add the following two cases inside the `switch` statement you added above, just before the `default` case:

```
case .Cancelled, .Ended:
  let transitionLayer = storedContext!.containerView()!.layer
```

```
transitionLayer.beginTime = CACurrentMediaTime()

if progress < 0.5 {
  completionSpeed = -1.0
  cancelInteractiveTransition()
} else {
  completionSpeed = 1.0
  finishInteractiveTransition()
}
```

The `.Cancelled` and `.Ended` cases are effectively the same thing as far as your project is concerned. Before doing anything else, you fetch the layer of the `containerView` for the transition and set its `beginTime` to the current Core Animation time.

If the user panned far enough before they released, you fully present the new view controller; if not, you simply roll back the animation progress. In both cases, you set the completion speed to make the animation run in the correct direction.

> **Note**: Setting the time and speed is a workaround for what seems like a UIKit bug; if you *don't* use layer animations in the transition, you don't have to set the layer's begin time and the completion speed.

If the user pans through less than `50%` of the required distance, you call `cancelInteractiveTransition()` – an inherited method – to animate the transition back to its initial state. If the user pans through more than `50%` of the distance, you call `finishInteractiveTransition()`, which plays the animation the rest of the way through. These two states are illustrated below:

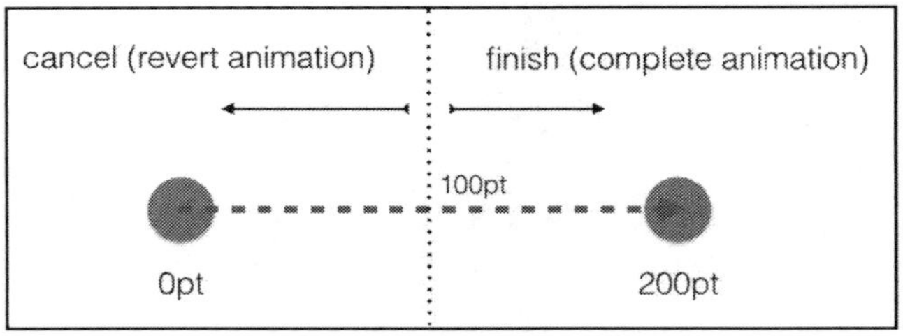

Build and run the app, and try panning part way and most of the way to see the difference.

Did you notice that when you panned through the reveal animation, you couldn't go *back* to the list? That's because you set `interactive` to `true` in `handlePan()` – and you never reset it to `false`! Therefore, when you pop the view controller, you return an interaction controller from the delegate method that's never updated – and your pop transition gets stuck at `0%` progress.

The correct spot to reset the `interactive` property is when the pan gesture ends.

Add the following code to the `.Ended` case:

```
interactive = false
```

This should let you pop back to the initial screen.

Build and run again, and you should be able to move back and forth.

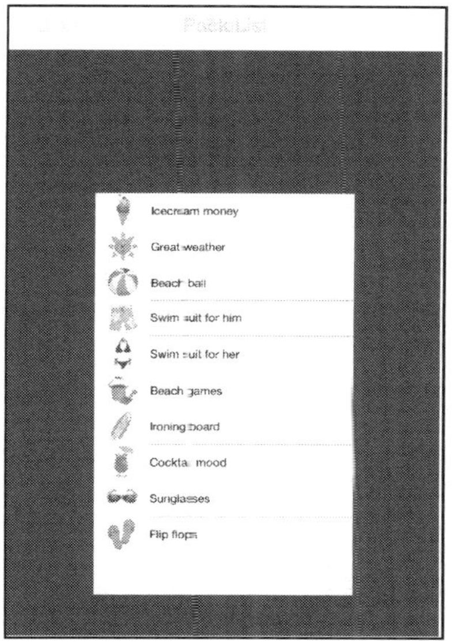

You've completed your Logo Reveal project; `RevealAnimator` is now performing two *different* transition animations, including one that's interactive! Great job!

This wraps up the section on view controller transitions. Congratulations on working through this section; these transition APIs are not easy to learn; but all the effort has been worth it.

Challenges

Challenge 1: Make the pop transition interactive

The final challenge is a bit more difficult than usual, but by now you're an animation ninja, and I know you can handle anything I throw at you!

Your task in this challenge is to make the pop transition interactive. That's not as easy as it sounds, as you'll need to change code in a number of places throughout the project.

The challenge directions below are just broad strokes, so you'll need to plan your approach before you start coding.

First, in `DetailViewController`; make a `weak` property to hold the animator and fetch the animator object from `MasterViewController`. You can access `MasterViewController` from the navigation controller stack.

Once you do that, add a pan gesture handler to `DetailViewController`. Your handler should be almost identical to the method in `MasterViewController` with one small difference: it should pop the current view controller rather than invoke a segue.

At this point the custom pop transition should be mostly functional. You are using view animations for your pop transition, but view animations don't need `beginTime` or `completionSpeed` to be adjusted. Ensure you don't modify these properties when the animator operation is `.Pop`.

You'll end up with a cool interactive pop transition – and don't forget to make sure that tapping the **Back** button in the navigation bar still works! :]

Section VII: Third-Party Animation Libraries

So far you've seen how powerful the built-in animation APIs can be and you've used them to create all sorts of animations and visual effects.

Like any good tour guide, I've only shown you my personal, favorite elements of UIKit and Core Animation throughout this book. There are still more things to discover about Core Animation: transactions, discrete animations, and other neat iOS animation features.

However – there is also a lot to explore outside of Apple's walled garden. There are a number of open source animation libraries that can help you achieve easily tasks like custom timings, chaining animations, drawing on screen, and much more.

In this section of the book you will learn about two open source animation libraries.

Easy Animation

In the following **Chapter 24, Easy Animation** you are going to try out a library I've created while I was writing the first edition of this book.

As the name suggests, **Easy Animation** allows you to quickly create and experiment with layer animations and animation sequences.

You know and love `CABasicAnimation` but you have to admit, the code you need to create animations with it is a bit verbose.

For example if you want to round the corners of a layer called `myLayer` in the span of `1.0` second with `0.5` seconds delay and ease the beginning of the animation you need all these lines of code:

```
let round = CABasicAnimation(keyPath: "cornerRadius")
round.fromValue = 0.0
round.toValue = 50.0
round.duration = 1.0
round.beginTime = CACurrentMediaTime() + 0.5
round.fillMode = kCAFillModeBackwards
round.timingFunction = CAMediaTimingFunction(name:
  kCAMediaTimingFunctionEaseIn)
myLayer.addAnimation(round, key: nil)
myLayer.cornerRadius = 50.0
```

More code means more possibility to introduce bugs and less time to experiment and polish. Easy Animation allows you to animate layers by using the standard UIKit animation methods.

To create precisely the same animation from the example above you only need to write this:

```
UIView.animateWithDuration(1.0, delay: 0.5, options: .CurveEaseIn,
animations: {
  myLayer.cornerRadius = 50.0
}, completion: nil)
```

You can freely mix and match view and layer animations in the same `animations` block, use the `completion` blocks, create joint view-layer spring animations, and much more.

Facebook Pop

Pop is the most widely re-used library in Facebook's own iOS apps; this means the library is mature, robust, extensively tested and pretty much feature-complete.

Pop lets you create animations just like the ones you've learned about in this book – but with a twist. Pop gives you a few more animation features that you don't get with Core Animation out of the box, such as spring and decay animations.

Finally, the library itself is easily extensible so you can quickly make it work with just about *any* property you'd like animate on *any* object – and not just a layer or view class.

In this section you'll work on a simple UIKit game and explore many of Pop's features in the process:

That's a familiar sight to many of you. A ball, a field, and a goal; time to let your inner hooligan out, paint yourself in your favorite club's colors and get ready to bring this game to life in the following three chapters:

- **Chapter 25, Getting Started with Pop** – You'll learn how to install Pop via CocoaPods and will look into the benefits of using Pop in your project.
- **Chapter 26, Decay Animations with Pop** – You'll create an animation whose speed decays over time. You'll also see how easy it can be to create interactive animations with Pop.
- **Chapter 27, Spring Animations with Pop** – Finally, you'll explore Pop's implementation of spring animations. Boiiing! :]

Installing and integrating Pop takes a little bit of effort, but it's well worth it in the end and brings your animation's fun factor to a whole new level. Time to join the game – and hopefully you'll avoid any red cards along the way! :]

Chapter 24: Easy Animation

This chapter shows you how to use Easy Animation to build powerful view and layer animations quickly and easily. Easy Animation builds upon the solid foundation of Core Animation and gives you more mileage from the same APIs you've been using throughout this book.

Easy Animation extends the existing `animateWithDuration(_:animations:)` APIs and introduces a couple of new ones that follow the same naming pattern. And since Easy Animation is an open source library written in Swift, you can always peek inside and see how it works.

In the first section of this chapter, you'll play around with a few simple animations to get a sense of what you can do.

Then you'll move on and convert the project from Chapter 16, "Replicating Animations" to use Easy Animation. This project is a perfect playground to work with since it features a lot of animations and you'll get to see first-hand how many lines of code Easy Animation saves you in a real-life project.

Intro to Easy Animation

Open the **AddItem** starter project for this chapter and select **Main.storyboard**. Pay attention to which one you're opening since there are two starter projects for this chapter.

The storyboard features a table view in the lower half of the initial view controller and a big + button in the upper half.

The table view is already wired to the `ViewController` class so you can run up the project immediately check out what the app looks like:

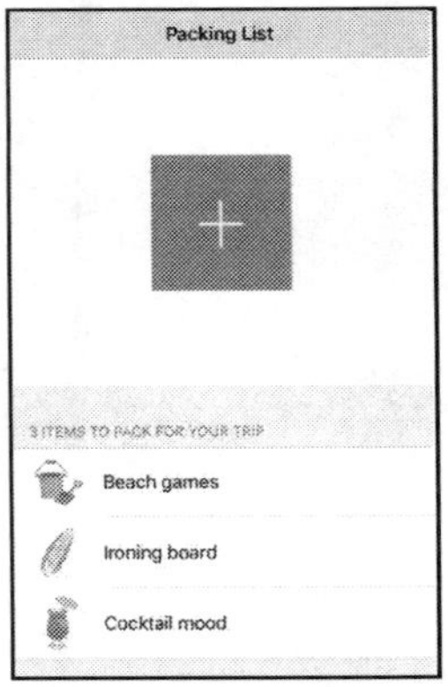

This packing app is more fun than similar ones in the previous chapters of the book: when the app's finished, the big plus button on top will add a random item to the packing list no matter what the user actually wants in their luggage! :]

Installation

First and foremost, you need a copy of Easy Animation. Open the GitHub page for version 1.0: https://github.com/icanzilb/EasyAnimation/releases/tag/1.0.0 and click the **Source code (zip)** button on the right to download the library source code.

> **Note**: If you are familiar with CocoaPods you can get Easy Animation by adding `pod 'EasyAnimation', '1.0.0'` to your Podfile. If you don't know what CocoaPods is, the next chapter covers this in more detail.

Unzip the downloaded archive file and drag the sub-folder called **EasyAnimation** onto Xcode's project navigator. In the dialog that pops up, check the **Copy Items if Needed** checkbox:

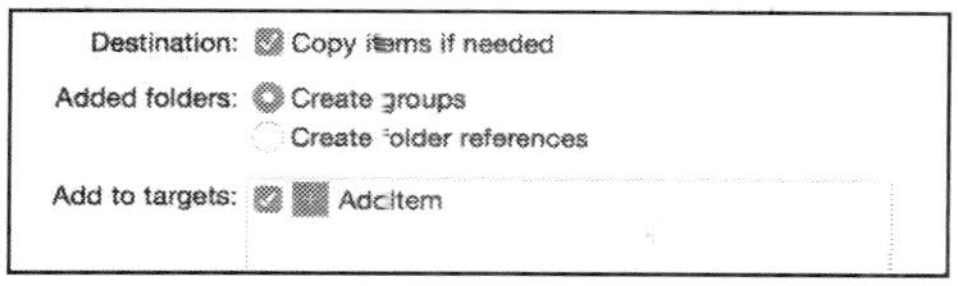

Verify that you see the **EasyAnimation** folder and the files in your project like so:

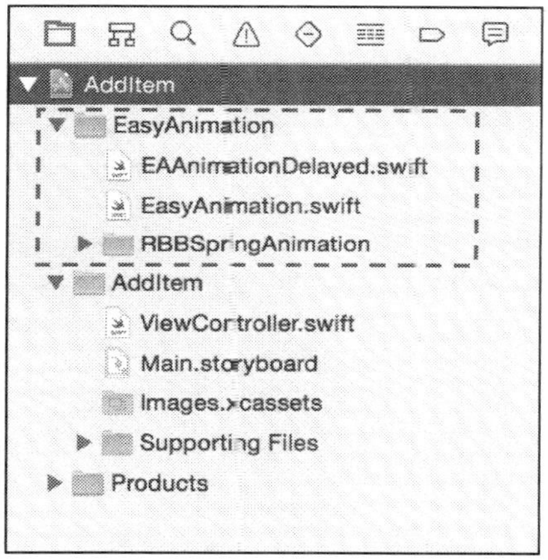

As soon as you've imported the files, you can start creating Easy Animation powered animations.

> **Note**: If you use CocoaPods with frameworks enabled, don't forget to import the framework by adding `import EasyAnimation` to the top of your source files.

Easy Layer Animations

First, you'll add a playful rotation animation to the plus button. Open **ViewController.swift** and add the following to `actionAddItem()`:

```
UIView.animateWithDuration(1.0, delay: 0.0,
usingSpringWithDamping: 0.33, initialSpringVelocity: 0.0, options:
[], animations: {
  self.plusButton.transform = CGAffineTransformRotate(
    self.plusButton.transform, CGFloat(-M_PI_2))
}, completion: nil)
```

You've created animations just like this one in previous chapters, so you probably aren't terribly impressed. Nevertheless, run the project and make sure the button rotates playfully when you tap it:

Next, you'll animate the corner radius of the button's layer. To liven up the animation, you'll combine the rotation and the corner radius animations in a group so it looks like the button transforms into a circle as it rotates.

The usual approach for a combo animation like this would be to create a `CAAnimationGroup` and two separate `CABasicAnimation` instances: one to animate the layer's `transform` property and the other its corner radius.

However, you have Easy Animation on your side. Simply add the following underlined bit of code to adjust the `cornerRadius` property from within the `animations` closure, just as you would for any view property:

```
UIView.animateWithDuration(1.0, delay: 0.0,
usingSpringWithDamping: 0.33, initialSpringVelocity: 0.0, options:
[], animations: {
  self.plusButton.transform = CGAffineTransformRotate(
    self.plusButton.transform, CGFloat(-M_PI_2))
  self.plusButton.layer.cornerRadius = 62.5
}, completion: nil)
```

You've appended a single line, which simply sets the button's corner radius to half the length of its side. This ought to round its corners to the point where the square becomes a circle.

Run the project again and check the resulting animation:

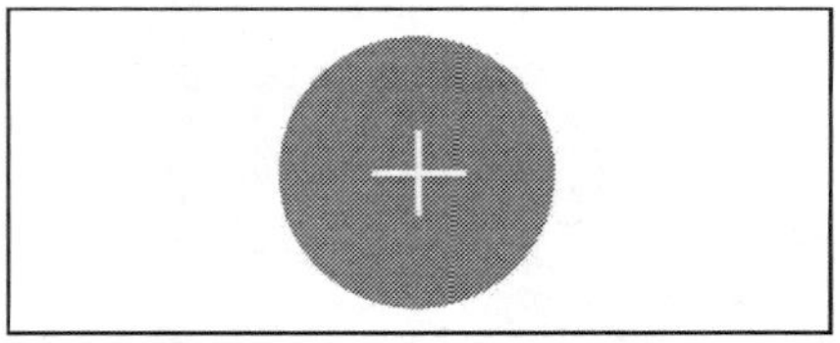

The square smoothly animates into a circle, and not only that — it does so with a spring animation. The corners jiggle around a bit and then come to rest.

But... how? So far you've only used using `CABasicAnimation` and `CASpringAnimation` for layer animations. How can a view animation include a change to a layer property?

Easy Animation extends the existing UIKit animation APIs just a little and picks up any changes to animatable layer properties. It creates the respective animations automatically for you.

Even more – Easy Animation groups the view and layer animations together in a group so you don't need to create a group yourself.

Add two more lines to the `animations` closure:

```
self.plusButton.layer.borderWidth = 2.0
self.plusButton.layer.borderColor = UIColor.grayColor().CGColor
```

These two lines animate the button border width and color respectively, just as you would for your view animations:

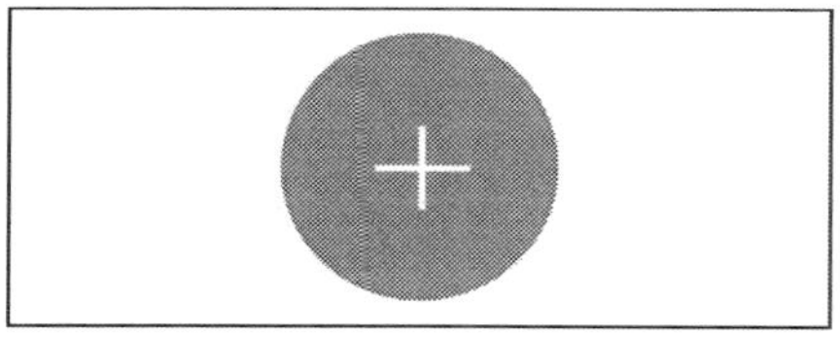

Easy Animation Sequences

Now you'll add a second animation that runs after the button has rotated to animate all changed properties back to their initial values.

In the first section of the book you learned how to start a second animation from within the `completion` block of another animation. Later, you embraced view keyframe animations to build more complex animation sequences.

Even further in the book you learned how to use animation delegates for your layer animations so you can detect when your animations have completed.

Even though *all* those approaches have their advantages, Easy Animation makes building animation sequences – well, just *easier!* :]

Easy Animation introduces two new methods you can use to start a sequence of animations:

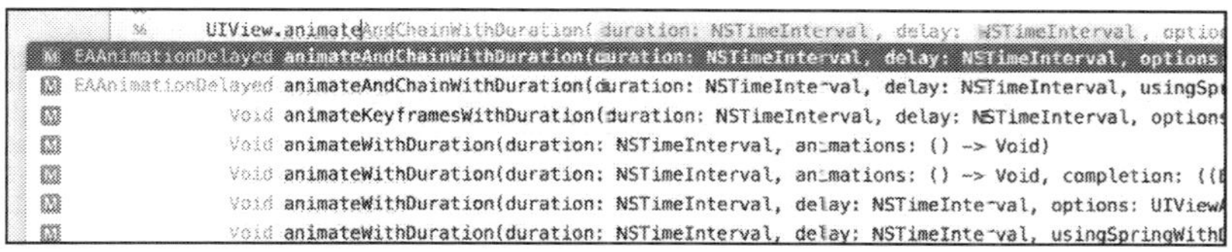

`animateAndChainWithDuration(_:delay:options:animations:completion:)` lets you create an animation sequence by providing exactly the same initial parameters as you would for its original UIKit counterpart.

`animateAndChainWithDuration(_:delay:usingSpringWithDamping: initialSpringVelocity:options:animations:completion:)` starts an animation chain with a spring animation as the first animation. It takes the same parameters as its original UIKit counterpart.

Starting an animation sequence is very simple – replace the method name in your code:

```
UIView.animateWithDuration(…
```

with:

```
UIView.animateAndChainWithDuration(…
```

Since the parameter count and names are the same, you can run and test your project right away. Nothing has changed though – you've created an animation sequence consisting of a single animation.

To add a second animation to the sequence, just place the cursor after the closing parenthesis of the first animation call, and type a "." (a period or full stop); Xcode's autocomplete feature will offer more animations for you to add:

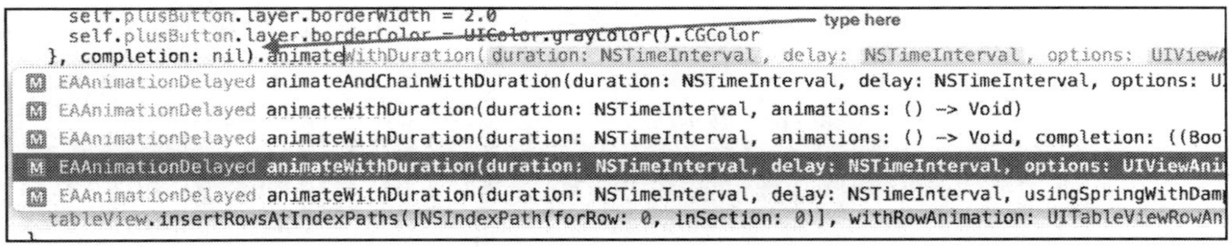

Choose the third `animateWithDuration` option from the suggested list – the one that lets you specify animation options — and set `cornerRadius` and `borderWidth` to their initial values. Use `0.15` seconds for the animation duration, `0.5` seconds of delay, and `.CurveEaseOut` for the options.

The complete code should now look like this:

```
UIView.animateAndChainWithDuration(1.0, delay: 0.0,
usingSpringWithDamping: 0.33, initialSpringVelocity: 0.0, options:
[], animations: {
  self.plusButton.transform = CGAffineTransformRotate(
    self.plusButton.transform, CGFloat(-M_PI_2))
  self.plusButton.layer.cornerRadius = 62.5
  self.plusButton.layer.borderWidth = 2.0
```

```
    self.plusButton.layer.borderColor =
      UIColor.grayColor().CGColor
  }, completion: nil)
    .animateWithDuration(0.15, delay: 0.5, options: .CurveEaseOut,
  animations: {
    self.plusButton.layer.cornerRadius = 0.0
    self.plusButton.layer.borderWidth = 0.0
  }, completion: nil)
```

Run your project again, tap the button and you'll see it rotate, pause for half a second, then grow its corners back. At the end of the animation, the button will look the same as it did before you tapped it:

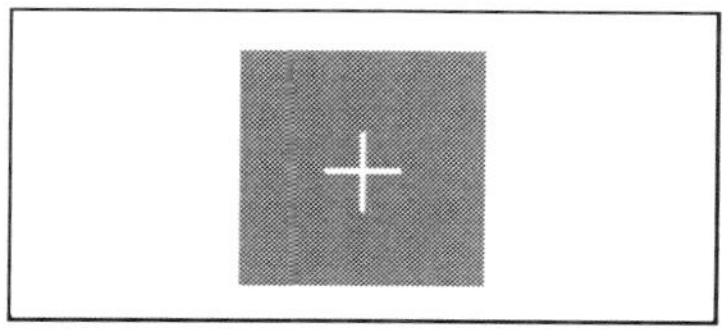

You can tap the button again and again and it will run the animation sequence each time.

> **Note**: To have a little fun at the button's expense, add the `.Repeat` option to the *second* animation call. Run the project, tap the button and watch it go! :] Don't forget to remove `.Repeat` option before continuing working trough the chapter.

Completion closures

With Easy Animation, chaining animations is easy and doesn't require the use of the `completion` parameter. However, they're still available; you can use the `completion` closures to execute custom code at the end of the animation or in between the different animations of a sequence.

In this section, you are going to disable the button while it animates so the user cannot tap it again during the current animation.

Insert the following to the *top* of `actionAddItem()`:

```
plusButton.enabled = false
```

Then replace the `nil` value of the completion block of the *second* animation with:

```
{_ in
  self.plusButton.enabled = true
}
```

This code will disable the button and re-enable it when the second animation in the sequence has finished running. If you tap repeatedly on the button it won't react while it's animating.

Finally replace the `nil` value of the `completion` parameter of the *first* animation with the following:

```
{_ in
  self.addRandomItem()
}
```

This code will add a random item to the list once the first leg of the button animation has completed. Run and enjoy the finished app:

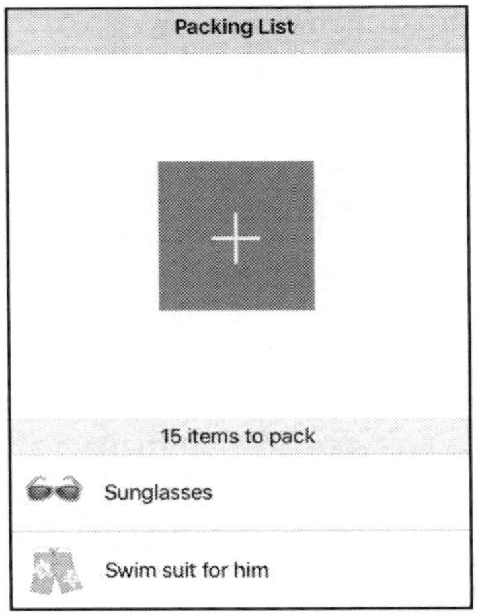

Converting an existing project

In this second half of the chapter, instead of building a new project from scratch, you'll revisit the Iris app from **Chapter 16, "Replicating Animations"** and will convert some of its many layer animations to Easy Animation.

Doing that will give you a good understanding how vanilla Core Animation code compares to Easy Animation.

Open the Iris starter project for this chapter and play a bit with the app – ask Iris a couple of questions and listen to the answers.

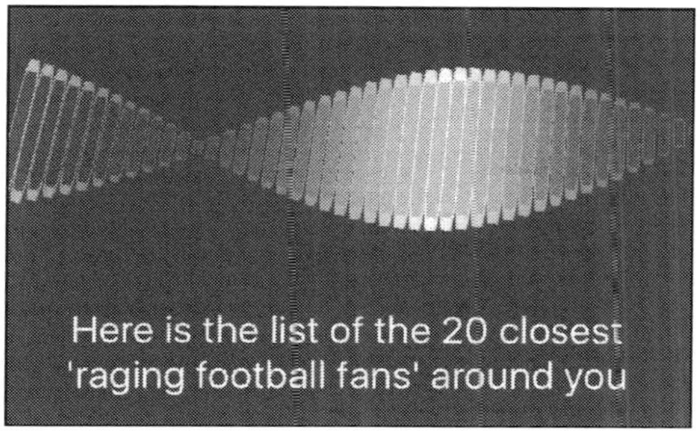

Depending on your coding style, you should have about 180 – 200 lines of code in **ViewController.swift**. Let's see if you can get that number down significantly by using Easy Animation!

Before you start coding, drag the **EasyAnimation** source code folder onto the Xcode project navigator to import the library; alternatively, if you're using CocoaPods add `pod 'EasyAnimation', '1.0.0'` to your pod file.

Now open **ViewController.swift** and scroll to the `startSpeaking()` method. Look for the `scale animation` and remove the following code that creates that animation:

```
let scale = CABasicAnimation(keyPath: "transform")
scale.fromValue = NSValue(CATransform3D: CATransform3DIdentity)
scale.toValue = NSValue(CATransform3D:
  CATransform3DMakeScale(1.4, 15, 1.0))
scale.duration = 0.33
scale.repeatCount = Float.infinity
scale.autoreverses = true
scale.timingFunction = CAMediaTimingFunction(name:
  kCAMediaTimingFunctionEaseOut)
dot.addAnimation(scale, forKey: "dotScale")
```

In its place, insert the Easy Animation code to create an identical animation:

```
UIView.animateWithDuration(0.33, delay: 0.0, options: [.Repeat,
.Autoreverse, .CurveEaseOut], animations: {
  self.dot.transform = CATransform3DMakeScale(1.4, 15, 1.0)
}, completion: nil)
```

That's much less code, isn't it? And it's easier to read too!

Run the project to make sure the animation looks exactly the same:

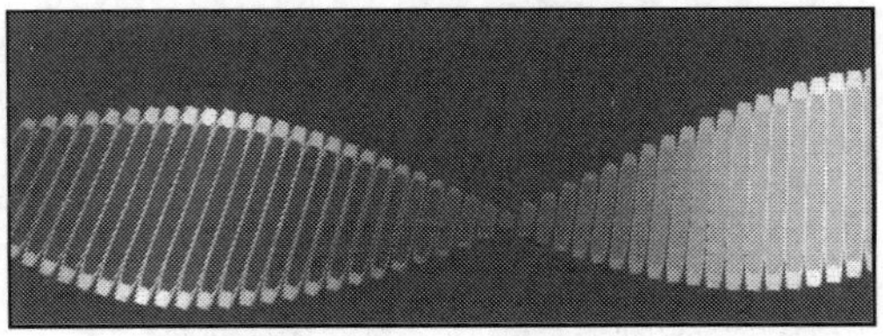

Don't lose momentum; convert the next animation in the code under the `//opacity animation comment`. Delete the following lines:

```
let fade = CABasicAnimation(keyPath: "opacity")
fade.fromValue = 1.0
fade.toValue = 0.2
fade.duration = 0.33
fade.beginTime = CACurrentMediaTime() + 0.33
fade.repeatCount = Float.infinity
fade.autoreverses = true
fade.timingFunction = CAMediaTimingFunction(name:
  kCAMediaTimingFunctionEaseOut)
dot.addAnimation(fade, forKey: "dotOpacity")
```

And insert in its place:

```
UIView.animateWithDuration(0.33, delay: 0.33, options: [.Repeat,
.Autoreverse, .CurveEaseOut], animations: {
  self.dot.opacity = 0.2
}, completion: nil)
```

You created exactly the same animation as the one you removed, but used the simpler Easy Animation syntax.

You can probably convert the next animation in the code all by yourself. If you don't need directions, simply skip over the instructions below and do it on your own.

Delete the following lines below the `//tint animation` comment:

```
let tint = CABasicAnimation(keyPath: "backgroundColor")
tint.fromValue = UIColor.magentaColor().CGColor
tint.toValue = UIColor.cyanColor().CGColor
tint.duration = 0.66
tint.beginTime = CACurrentMediaTime() + 0.28
tint.fillMode = kCAFillModeBackwards
tint.repeatCount = Float.infinity
tint.autoreverses = true
tint.timingFunction = CAMediaTimingFunction(name:
  kCAMediaTimingFunctionEaseInEaseOut)
dot.addAnimation(tint, forKey: "dotColor")
```

And in their place insert:

```
UIView.animateWithDuration(0.66, delay: 0.28, options: [.Repeat,
.Autoreverse, .CurveEaseInOut], animations: {
  self.dot.backgroundColor = UIColor.cyanColor().CGColor
}, completion: nil)
```

Note that unlike your view animations, where you can use `UIColor` objects when animating colors, your layer animations still need `CGColor` values; it's a small price to pay on the whole for being able to save yourself lots of typing.

Another peek at the running app will show you no change in the running animations; exactly what you want for this exercise:

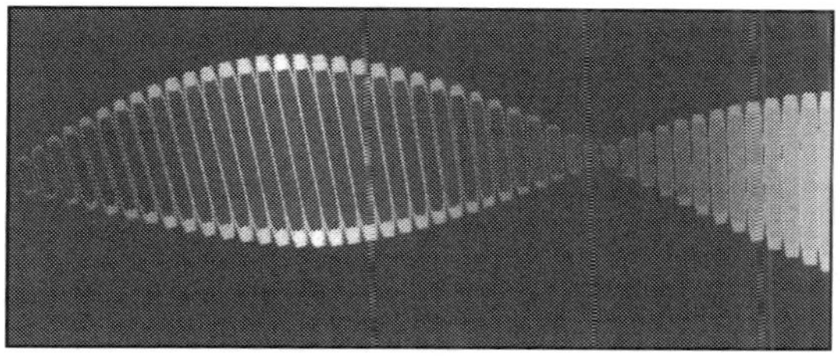

By now you've cut about 20 lines of code from **ViewController.swift**. And if you scan the source code you will quickly realize you can strip a lot more!

Next you will create a chain animation to reproduce the wave movement. For this you will need a new class instance property. Scroll to the top of `ViewController` and add the following below the other properties:

```
var waveAnimation: EAAnimationDelayed?
```

`EAAnimationDelayed` is the class Easy Animation uses to store animation sequences. If you check the two methods you use to create animation sequences, you'll see they return an `EAAnimationDelayed` instance.

Scroll down to `startSpeaking()` and delete this whole chunk of code:

```
//initial rotation
let initialRotation = CABasicAnimation(keyPath:
  "instanceTransform.rotation")
initialRotation.fromValue = 0.0
initialRotation.toValue   = 0.01
initialRotation.duration = 0.33
initialRotation.removedOnCompletion = false
initialRotation.fillMode = kCAFillModeForwards
initialRotation.timingFunction = CAMediaTimingFunction(name:
  kCAMediaTimingFunctionEaseOut)
```

```
replicator.addAnimation(initialRotation, forKey:
  "initialRotation")

//instance rotation
let rotation = CABasicAnimation(keyPath:
  "instanceTransform.rotation")
rotation.fromValue = 0.01
rotation.toValue    = -0.01
rotation.duration = 0.99
rotation.beginTime = CACurrentMediaTime() + 0.33
rotation.repeatCount = Float.infinity
rotation.autoreverses = true
rotation.timingFunction = CAMediaTimingFunction(name:
  kCAMediaTimingFunctionEaseInEaseOut)
replicator.addAnimation(rotation, forKey: "replicatorRotation")
```

In its place add:

```
waveAnimation = UIView.animateAndChainWithDuration(0.5,
 delay: 0.0, options: .CurveEaseInOut, animations: {
  self.replicator.instanceTransform = CATransform3DConcat(
    CATransform3DMakeTranslation(-self.dotOffset, 0.0, 0.0),
    CATransform3DMakeRotation(0.01, 0.0, 0.0, 1.0)
  )
}, completion: nil)
  .animateWithDuration(0.5, delay: 0.0, options: [.CurveEaseInOut,
.Repeat], animations: {
  self.replicator.instanceTransform = CATransform3DConcat(
    CATransform3DMakeTranslation(-self.dotOffset, 0.0, 0.0),
    CATransform3DMakeRotation(-0.01, 0.0, 0.0, 1.0)
  )
}, completion: nil)
```

This code, so much shorter than the original, is much easier to read through and understand.

First, you run an animation that sets the `replicator`'s `instanceTransform` to a compound transform of the original translation and a `0.01` radian rotation on the Z axis. The first leg of the sequence bends the replicator down:

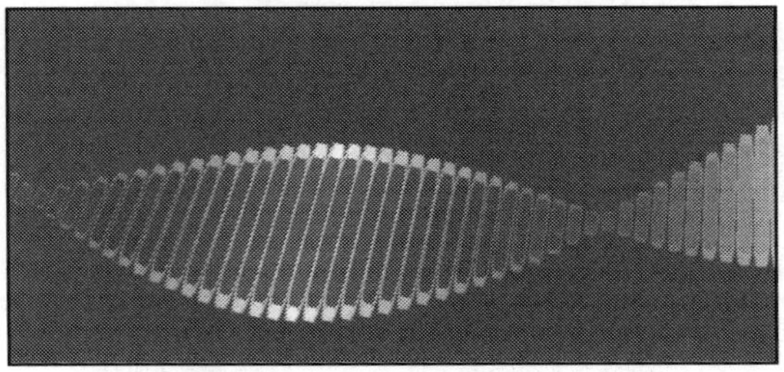

Then the second animation in the sequence animates the `replicator`'s `instanceTransform` to the same translation plus rotation combination, but using `-0.01` radians instead. The second animation bends the replicator upwards like so:

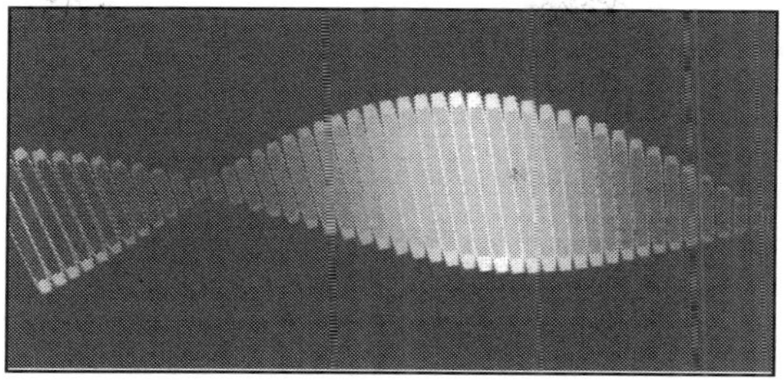

Finally you add the `.Repeat` option to the second animation; when you create a sequence with Easy Animation this repeats the complete animation sequence. As a result, the two animations keep running one after the other forever.

All of this is now stored in `waveAnimation`. You're keeping a reference to it so you can use it later to stop the sequence.

Now scroll down to `endSpeaking()` and delete all the code inside that method. You will need to re-structure the code, so it's better to start off fresh.

First of all, you will need to cancel the wave animation sequence. Insert the following into `endSpeaking()`:

```
waveAnimation?.cancelAnimationChain {

}
```

`cancelAnimationChain()` lets the currently running animation from the sequence finish, then executes the completion closure you provide as a parameter. This is your chance to do cleanup after your animation, which is necessary because you don't know which part of the sequence last executed.

Reset the `dot` layer first. Insert into the `completion` closure:

```
self.dot.removeAllAnimations()

self.dot.transform = CATransform3DIdentity
self.dot.opacity = 1.0
self.dot.backgroundColor = UIColor.lightGrayColor().CGColor
```

This removes all running animations; once that's done you reset the properties affected by those animations.

Next you need to reset the instance transform on the replicator layer itself to its initial value. Add the following code to the closure:

```
self.replicator.instanceTransform =
  CATransform3DMakeTranslation(-self.dotOffset, 0.0, 0.0)
```

This will reset the rotation on the replicator instances and keep the translation as you'll still need it.

Finally show the speak button and reset the label text with the following code:

```
self.speakButton.hidden = false
self.meterLabel.text = "Hold to speak"
```

Give the app another try to make sure all looks good after Iris finishes speaking:

You will notice that you've lost the nice transition between the two animations. In some rare cases like this one you can't reproduce all Core Animation animations with Easy Animation.

By now you have all the knowledge needed to decide between Core Animation layer animations and the simpler and less verbose Easy Animation APIs.

So far you've dumped 30 to 40 lines of code from the starter project. And you're not yet finished! In the challenge section, you'll look into converting a couple more animations to further improve the code.

If you'd like to read more about Easy Animation, check out its page on GitHub and peek into the demo app that comes with the library:

https://github.com/icanzilb/EasyAnimation

Challenges

Challenge 1: Try an animation sequence on your own

Create an animation sequence on your own that animates the border color of the speak button from *white* to *green* to *orange* and back to *white*. Start the animation when the app launches and let it repeat indefinitely.

In the final chapters of the book, you'll take on another animation library: the well-known Pop library created by Facebook and used across a multitude of apps including Instagram, Paper and Facebook itself.

Chapter 25: Getting Started with Pop

In this chapter you'll learn how to install Pop and take it for a quick test drive by creating a few simple animations.

Since Pop is written in super-efficient C++ code, not Swift, you can't use the library as-is in your projects. However, it's easy to integrate Objective-C/C++ libraries into your Swift projects using CocoaPods. Don't worry – if you're not familiar with CocoaPods you'll walk through the process in a step-by-step fashion.

Once you have Pop installed and running, you'll have a chance to work with Pop a little and see where Pop animations really shine compared to their UIKit counterparts.

Open the starter project for this chapter and run it. You'll see the initial setup of the game – a field, a goal, and a ball:

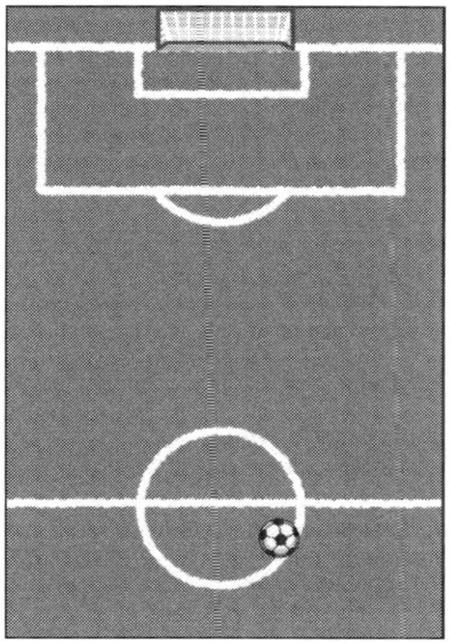

The ball appears at a random position each time you run the app, so don't worry if your app looks a little different than the screenshot above.

Put your finger on the ball and swipe; you'll see a message appear in the Xcode console, showing that a pan recognizer is already attached to the ball image view. All you need to do is add some cool animations to the project using Pop.

> **Note:** If you're already familiar with CocoaPods and it's installed on your machine, you can simply install the pod using `pod 'pop', '~> 1.0'` and skip directly to **Creating a Bridging Header**.
>
> If you're not interested in CocoaPods, or the steps below don't work for you for some reason, the resources for this chapter include a version of the project with Pop already installed. If you use that version, skip straight to **Your First Pop Animation**.

Installing CocoaPods and Pop

Without getting into a lot of detail, CocoaPods is a code dependency manager for iOS and OS X that helps keep your third-party open source libraries up-to-date. Whenever a new version of a library is available, it's a simple task to get the updated version – and ensure that it doesn't break your project!

Start **Terminal** from the Applications/Utilities folder; you'll see the command-line interface of OS X like so:

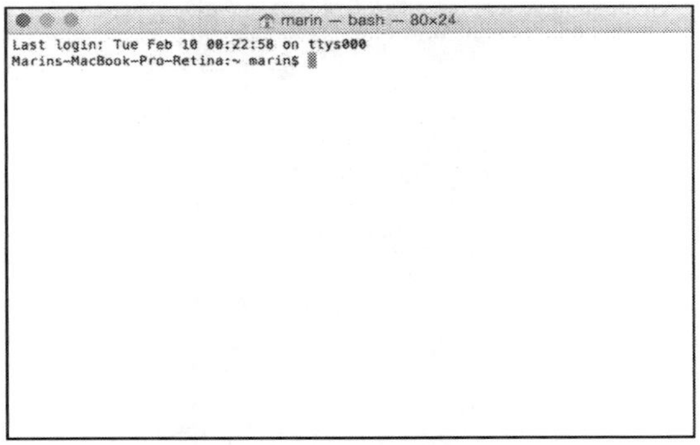

On the bottom line you'll see, by default, your computer's name and your own user name. It's time to enter some commands!

Type the command below and press Enter:

```
sudo gem install cocoapods
```

The above command installs CocoaPods for you. If Terminal prompts you for your password, input it and press Enter to authorize the installation of CocoaPods on your computer.

You won't see any activity for a few moments (up to couple of minutes in rare cases) while the installation initializes, but after a bit you'll see your screen fill with output:

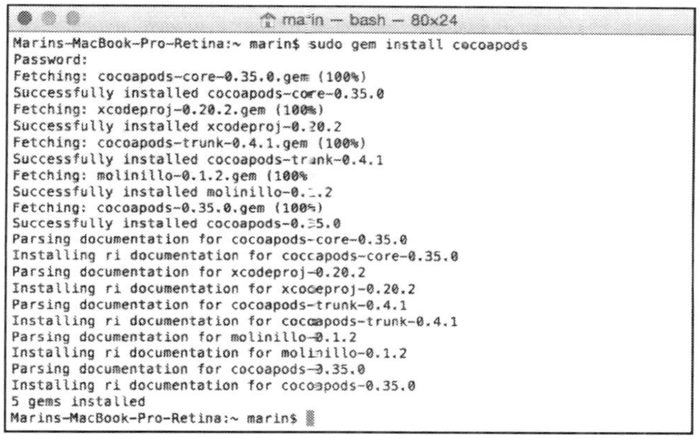

The output should end with a line like `x gems installed` – this means that your install of CocoaPods succeeded.

Long live automated software delivery! :]

> **Note:** In rare cases, you might see error messages pop up instead of the output from the screenshot above. If that happens, take a look at the CocoaPods troubleshooting guide for the best advice on how to proceed:
> http://guides.cocoapods.org/using/troubleshooting#installing-cocoapods

Now that you've taken care of the CocoaPods installation, you can proceed to adding the Pop library to your project.

Head back to Xcode and the starter project. From Xcode's main menu select **File\New\File...** then choose the **iOS\Other\Empty** template for the new file. Enter **Podfile** as the name of the new file and save it within the root folder of the project – that is, in the same folder as the **Popsoccer.xcodeproj** file.

Podfile will contain the list of CocoaPods you want to manage in your project; it's just a simple plaintext file. At this point, it will be empty, as shown below:

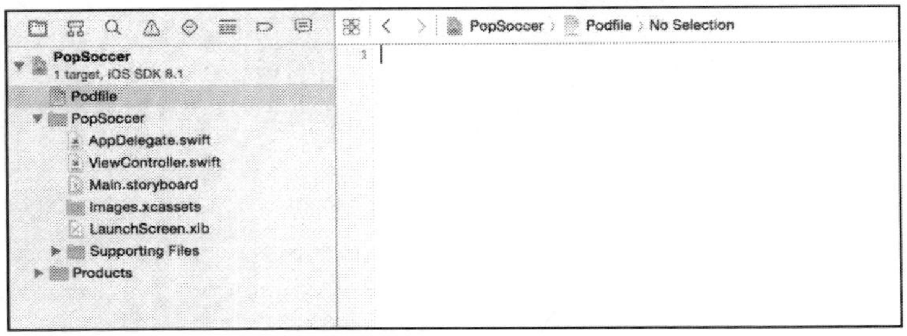

For your project, you only need to manage one library – Pop. Enter the following line at the top of the file:

```
pod 'pop', '~> 1.0'
```

The above line tells CocoaPods that you want to use the pod named **pop** and you want to use the latest `1.0.x` version of the pod. For example, at the time this chapter was written `1.0.7` was the latest release available, but there will undoubtedly be a version `1.0.8` or `1.0.9` in the near future.

Why not just grab the latest version available, you ask? A minor version upgrade such as `1.1` could be the first version to introduce breaking changes – so you use the `~> 1.0` notation to tell CocoaPods you want to automatically get the newest available version up to, but not including, `1.1`.

Using this approach ensures you'll benefit from the latest bug fixes and feature updates without worrying about version updates breaking your own code.

> **Note:** For a more detailed look into CocoaPods, check out www.cocoapods.org or read through our "Introduction to CocoaPods" tutorial here: http://www.raywenderlich.com/64546/introduction-to-cocoapods-2.

Save your changes to **Podfile**, then quit Xcode entirely. The next step changes the whole project structure so you'll have to restart Xcode eventually anyway.

Switch to Terminal and navigate to the root folder of your project where **Podfile** lives.

> **Note:** Use the `cd` command to change directories in Terminal. A handy shortcut is to type `cd` followed by a space, and then drag the project's root folder from Finder into Terminal, which will fill in the directory path for you.

To check that you're in the right folder, enter the following command:

```
ls -al
```

This command lists the files in the folder as shown below:

```
drwxr-xr-x  6 marin  staff   204 Feb 10 23:53 .
drwxr-xr-x  4 marin  staff   136 Feb 10 19:15 ..
-rw-r--r--@ 1 marin  staff  6148 Feb 10 19:13 .DS_Store
-rw-r--r--@ 1 marin  staff    19 Feb 10 23:53 Podfile
drwxr-xr-x  8 marin  staff   272 Feb 10 19:16 PopSoccer
drwxr-xr-x  5 marin  staff   170 Feb 10 23:49 PopSoccer.xcodeproj
```

Make sure you see **Podfile** in the list of files. If not, then either you're in the wrong directory, or Podfile isn't in the right directory. Either that or some ninja internet hamsters are eating your files at random. :]

Type the following command to install all libraries listed in **Podfile**:

```
pod install
```

This will spit out the following in Terminal:

```
Analyzing dependencies
Downloading dependencies
Installing pop (1.0.7)
Generating Pods project
Integrating client project

[!] From now on use `PopSoccer.xcworkspace`.
```

This shows you that CocoaPods fetched the latest version of Pop from GitHub and installed it in your Xcode project.

Note the last line shown above; from now on you will have to use **the newly created workspace instead of your original project file**. This is important since the workspace includes your project + the selected pods; if you open the **.xcodeproj** file instead, you won't have Pop available.

Open **PopSoccer.xcworkspace** (again, not your **.xcodeproj** file!) and look at the files CocoaPods created automatically for you:

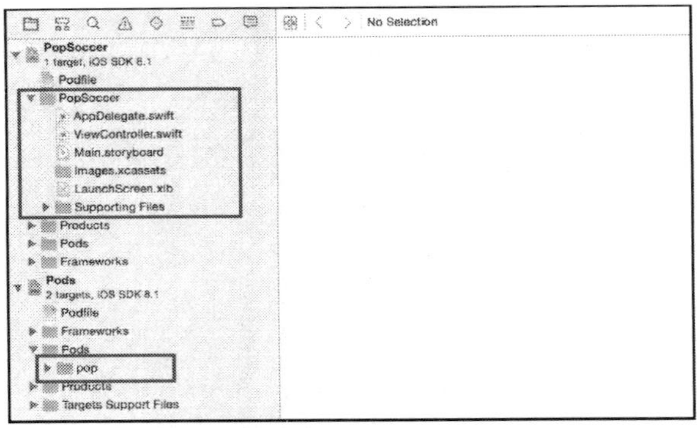

There are two projects in your workspace: the first is your original project with such files as **AppDelegate.swift** and **ViewController.swift**, while the second project has been generated automatically and it's expected that you won't change any of the files inside yourself. However, if you're interested, browse through the source files and you'll see the source code for Pop in **Pods/pop**.

> **Note**: If you *do* change any of the files in the Pods project, you'll lose those changes the next time you update your pods via the CocoaPods command line interface.

Okay, you've installed Pop – the next step is to create a bridging header to use the C++ Pop interface in your Swift project. Onward!

Creating a bridging header

Since Pop is an Objective-C/C++ library and PopSoccer is a nice, clean Swift project, you'll need something to make them play nicely together – a bridging header.

Ensure the **PopSoccer** project is selected in the Project Navigator, then from Xcode's main menu select **File\New\File...** and then **iOS\Source\Objective-C file for** the file template. Name the new file **DeleteMe**, choose File Type **Empty File** and click **Next** to continue.

Then simply click **Create Bridging Header** and you'll see the following dialog appear:

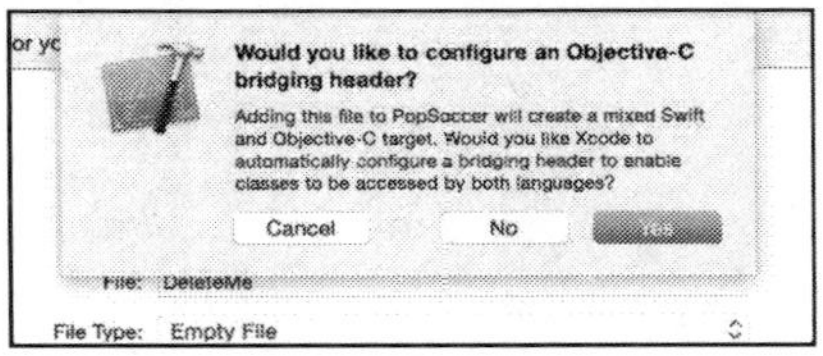

A bridging header is just what you need to use Pop from your Swift source files. Click **Yes** and Xcode happily creates and configures one for you: **PopSoccer-Bridging-Header.h**

Delete **DeleteMe.m** at this point – it's played its role in creating the bridging header and you won't need it any longer.

> **Note**: Although a bit unorthodox, I've found that the above method of adding a dummy Objective-C file to the project to get Xcode to set up a bridging header to your Swift project with CocoaPods is the safest, most coherent way to do it.

Open the newly created **PopSoccer-Bridging-Header.h** and the following line to the bottom of the file:

```
#import <pop/POP.h>
```

This imports the Pop library automatically into **all** of your Swift files. Build your project just to make everything compiles nicely.

All good? Then you're finally ready to try out some Pop animations!

Your first Pop animation

Since you know so much about creating animations with Core Animation and `CABasicAnimation`, you'll find Pop is quite easy to learn. Just take a look at the following two identical animations created with Core Animation and Pop respectively:

```
let fade =
  CABasicAnimation(keyPath:
  "opacity")

fade.fromValue = 1.0
fade.toValue   = 0.0
fade.duration  = 2.0
view.layer.addAnimation(fade,
  forKey: nil)
```

```
let fade =
  POPBasicAnimation(
  propertyNamed:
  kPOPLayerOpacity)
fade.fromValue = 1.0
fade.toValue   = 0.0
fade.duration  = 2.0
view.pop_addAnimation(fade,
  forKey: nil)
```

Pop has its own animation class and its own method to add animations to views or layers, but the principle of animating a given property between two values over a period of time remains the same.

You might be wondering, then, why you would use Pop over good old `CABasicAnimation`, if they're so close in nature. Pop has a number of advantages over plain old layer animations:

No model vs. presentation separation

One significant benefit of Pop is the lack of separation between the model and presentation of your animation. Remember when you ended up with inactive text fields when you were learning about layer animations with the Bahama Air login project?

This issue doesn't exist in Pop, as Pop animates the presentation layer directly so you don't need to worry about fill modes or updating the animated property once the animation completes. In general, you need to worry less about animating views or layers in Pop.

Animations are mutable

In Core Animation you create an animation and then send it off to the rendering server to display on screen, where you don't have much control over the animation beyond cancelling it outright. With Pop you can change your mind mid-way through the animation and modify the end value of the animation; the animation will simply continue from its current state and animate to the new end value.

Built for interactivity

In Facebook's own apps you often fling UI elements around, such as images you want off the screen and articles you wish to open.

With that in mind, the Pop team built a special animation that integrates seamlessly with pan gesture recognizers. You can create animations that are a natural continuation of a pan gesture with only few lines of code.

Are you now convinced that Pop has something to offer, even to an animation pro like yourself? :] The rest of this chapter will get you started with Pop and give you a taste of some of its benefits.

Fade in with Core Animation

In this section, you'll animate the soccer ball so it fades in when the game starts.

Open **ViewController.swift** and add the following line to the bottom of `viewWillAppear(_:)`:

```
ball.alpha = 0.0
```

This code hides the ball at the start so you can fade it in.

Now you need a helper method that fades in a view so you can reuse the same animation code multiple times. Add the following method to `ViewController`:

```
func fadeInView(view: UIView) {
  UIView.animateWithDuration(1.0, animations: {
    view.alpha = 1.0
  })
}
```

This code should look quite familiar since you've created countless fade animations in this book. The method above simply takes a view as its parameter and fades it in by animating the `alpha` value.

To animate the appearance of the ball, add the following to `viewDidAppear(_:)`:

```
fadeInView(ball)
```

Build and run your project; you'll see the ball fade in as soon as the game starts. Okay, this isn't earth-shattering code, but trust me – I'm going somewhere with this. :]

Now you'll add some code to observe the `alpha` property of the soccer ball as it animates on screen. Add the following line to the top of `viewDidLoad`:

```
ball.addObserver(self, forKeyPath: "alpha", options: .New,
context: nil)
```

Whenever `alpha` changes, `ViewController` will receive a message about the change. To handle all the change messages, override the built-in observer method as follows:

```
override func observeValueForKeyPath(keyPath: String?, ofObject
object: AnyObject?, change: [String : AnyObject]?, context:
UnsafeMutablePointer<Void>) {
  if object === ball && keyPath == "alpha" {
    print(ball.alpha)
  } else {
    super.observeValueForKeyPath(keyPath, ofObject: object,
      change: change, context: context)
  }
}
```

`observeValueForKey(_:ofObject:change:context:)` receives *all* changes for *all* observed properties. So, just to be safe, you check that the object being changed is `ball` and that the changed property is `alpha`. Once you're sure you have the right property, simply print the new value of `alpha` to the console.

Build and run your project; you should see the following output appear in the Xcode console:

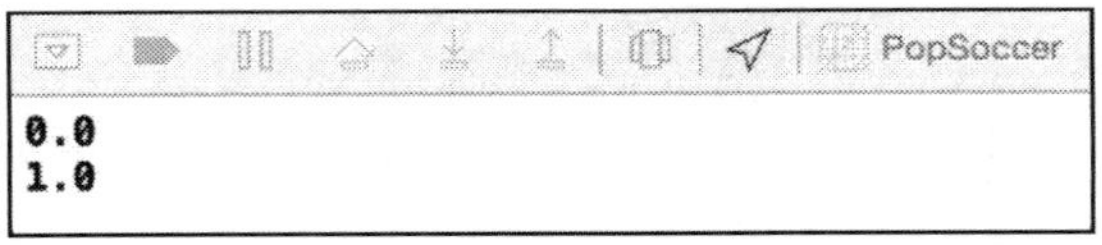

Here, `alpha` only changes twice: first when you set its alpha to `0.0` in `viewWillAppear(_:)` and then when you set it to `1.0` in `viewDidAppear(_:)`.

With Core Animation, the properties of the view or layer you're working with change only when they're referenced in code – you cannot observe the changes as the animation progresses.

Now – check out how Pop handles this same issue.

Fade in animation with Pop

Replace all the code in `fadeInView(_:)` with the following:

```
let fade = POPBasicAnimation(propertyNamed: kPOPViewAlpha)
fade.fromValue = 0.0
fade.toValue = 1.0
fade.duration = 1.0
```

The code above creates a `POPBasicAnimation` animation. The syntax is almost identical to the original animation, where the only difference is you need to use the pre-defined constant `kPOPViewAlpha` to tell Pop you want to animate the `alpha` property. This approach is a bit safer than passing around strings as you do in Core Animation.

Just as you did with `CABasicAnimation`, you've created an animation instance that describes a *possible* animation. Nothing will happen on the screen until you add this animation to a visible view or layer.

Add the following to the end of `fadeInView(_:)`:

```
view.pop_addAnimation(fade, forKey: nil)
```

Pop adds a few extra methods to all objects that allow you to add and remove animations in a similar fashion to Core Animation. Besides `pop_addAnimation(_:forKey:)` you'll find useful and familiar sounding methods like `pop_removeAnimationForKey(_:)`, `pop_removeAllAnimations()`, and `pop_animationKeys()`. You'll get a chance to use these in the next two chapters.

Build and run your project; the ball fades in as usual but this time the console also fills rapidly with output:

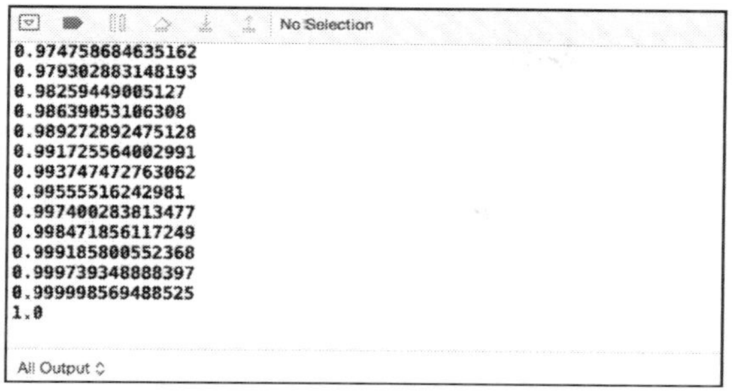

Whoa! Where did all those values come from? When you use Pop to animate the ball's `alpha` property, you can observe the intermediate steps of the fade animation.

I'll bet that getting started with Pop was easier than you expected. In the next chapter, you'll move beyond the basics and get to score some goals!

Challenges

Challenge 1: Learning more about POPBasicAnimation

Since `POPBasicAnimation` is designed to behave as closely as possible to `CABasicAnimation`, in this challenge you will simply experiment with a few properties on your own.

For your fade animation, try setting the properties `autoreverses` and `repeatCount`; these two properties behave in Pop the same as they do in Core Animation. `POPBasicAnimation` also features the boolean `repeatForever` for those cases when you simply want an animation to run forever.

Another useful property is `timingFunction`, which accepts a `CAMediaTimingFunction` just as `CABasicAnimation` does. Try an ease-in and an ease-out timing function in your fade animation.

Finally, `POPBasicAnimation` features a `String` property called `name`. As you know from earlier chapters, being able to assign a name to your animation is superbly useful. Give that a try and set the animation name to `ballAnimation`.

Once you feel at home with `POPBasicAnimation`, move on to the next chapter where you'll learn more about Pop, including how to create interactive animations with decaying movement.

Chapter 26: Decay Animations wth Pop

Up to this point in the book, you've only dealt with animations that animate a property from a start value to a predefined end point. Even in spring animations, where a fair amount of jiggling happens, you still set the exact end value upfront.

Pop provides you with a totally new kind of animation – a **decay** animation – that takes an initial velocity vector along with a deceleration rate and calculates the final animation value on its own.

This comes in very handy with animations based on user input, such as the one that drives a scroll view: the content scrolls up and down based on the user's pan gestures.

If the user swipes faster, the scroll view scrolls further; if the user swipes fast initially but slows down just before lifting their finger from the screen, then the scroll view also scrolls slowly and comes to rest.

Animations that feel like natural continuations of the user's gestures really make your UI feel alive. In this chapter you'll learn how to create such animations easily with Pop.

Adding pan interactivity

You'll continue your explorations of Pop in the Pop Soccer project from the previous chapter. If you didn't work through the complete chapter or want to start off fresh, simply open the starter project provided for this chapter, since it picks up where the previous chapter left off.

> **Note**: Don't forget you need to open the Xcode workspace file **PopSoccer.xcworkspace** and not the Xcode project file.

Build and run your project; as soon as the game launches you'll see the ball appear on the screen via the Pop fade animation you created in the previous chapter:

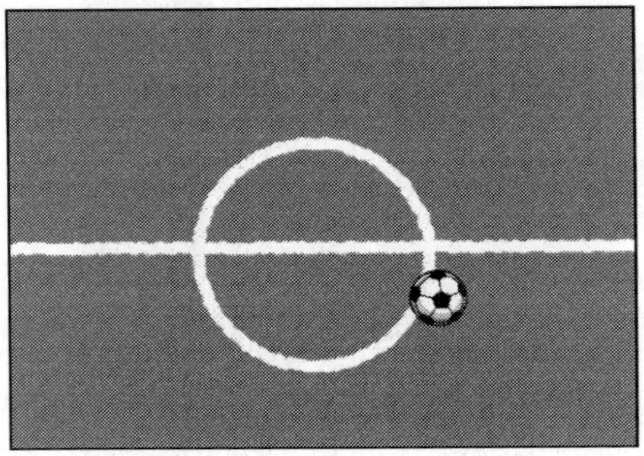

That ball looks great – but it would be nice if you could *do* something with it! :] You'll add some functionality to your game to let the player shoot the ball – but the first step is to let the player drag the ball around. This is relatively easy to do thanks to the pan gesture recognizer that is already attached to the ball.

Open **ViewController.swift** and find `didPan(_:)`; this is the method that the pan recognizer calls repeatedly as the player moves their finger over the ball image view.

Add the following code to `didPan(_:)`:

```
switch pan.state {
  case .Changed:
    ball.center = pan.locationInView(view)
  default: break
}
```

This code checks if the gesture is in progress (i.e. the player's finger is sliding) and if so, it updates the ball position. Just as in previous chapters, you fetch the current gesture position within the view controller's view by using `locationInView(_:)`.

That's all you need to let the player drag the ball around. Build and run your project and try it yourself:

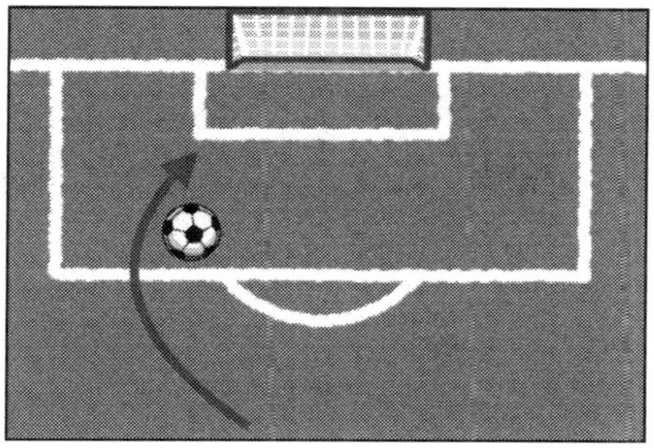

You can drag the ball anywhere you want – even straight into the goal. But that's cheating – so don't do that! :]

One interesting aspect of a pan gesture recognizer is that it also gives you the velocity of the gesture at any given moment. This makes it easy to check how fast the user is swiping. You can even check if they are swiping *too* fast – over the iOS speed limit!

Add the following code to `didPan(_:)`:

```
print(pan.velocityInView(view))
```

This simply lets you see the current velocity of your pan gesture.

Build and run the game once more; drag the ball around and you'll see the velocity changes reflected in the console:

```
Panning...
(5.1409329217276,-68.8996945742672)
Panning...
(26.3135602335488,-10.890761468366)
Panning...
(42.1376950661903,-32.6722844050979)
Panning...
(42.1376950661903,-32.6722844050979)
```

This is just an example of what your output might look like. You can see that the velocity is a 2D vector; the value tells you the speed in points per second over both the x- and y-axes. Try swiping horizontally; you'll see the second value (the velocity on the y-axis) hover around zero. Try swiping vertically to see the same effect on the x-axis.

Remember what I told you at the beginning of this chapter: that decay animations take an initial velocity, instead of a start and end value. I wonder if you could use the pan velocity in your decay animations. Hmmm! :]

Decay animations

To make the ball movement fluid, you'll need to start the decay animation as soon as the pan gesture completes. There's no better place to do that than the `.Ended` case of the recognizer's state.

Add the following `case` to the `switch` statement in `didPan(_:)`:

```
case .Ended:
  let velocity = pan.velocityInView(view)

  let animation = POPDecayAnimation(propertyNamed:
    kPOPViewCenter)
  animation.fromValue = NSValue(CGPoint: ball.center)
  animation.velocity = NSValue(CGPoint: velocity)

  ball.pop_addAnimation(animation, forKey: nil)
```

As soon as the gesture ends, you take a few steps to build the decay animation:

- First you fetch the velocity of the gesture and store it as a local constant named `velocity`.
- Then you create a `PopDecayAnimation` animation. You animate the view's `center` (you use `kPOPViewCenter` for the property name) and set the animation's start value to the view's current center position. Then you set the animation's velocity to the value you received from the pan recognizer.
- Finally, you simply add the animation as you did before for your basic Pop animations by calling `pop_addAnimation(_:forKey:)` on the `ball` image view.

This takes care of your decay animation, but there's one case you haven't covered yet. Add the following `case` to the same `switch` block:

```
case .Began:
  ball.pop_removeAllAnimations()
```

This will remove all ongoing animations when you start a new pan gesture and will ensure your animations and gestures don't clash over control of the ball.

Build and run your project; nudge the ball gently in one direction and you'll see how it magically carries on until it reaches its final resting point, like so:

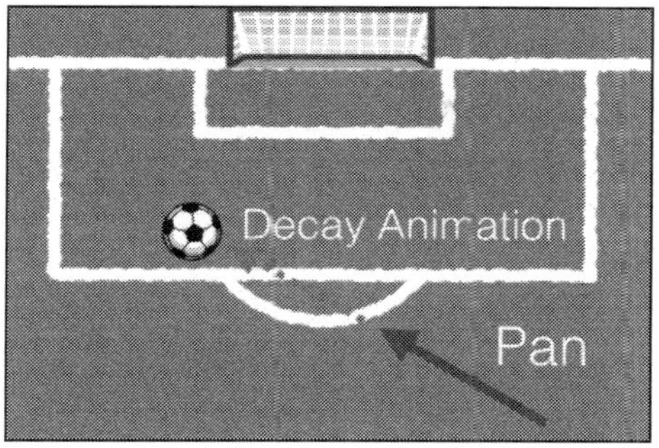

If you flick the ball outside of the screen (and into your virtual neighbor's rosebush :]), you'll have to restart the game since there's currently no way to bring the ball back on the screen.

That would get quite tiresome very quickly; the next section will show you how to use an animation delegate to bring the ball back on the field after each shot.

Pop animation delegate

The animation delegate protocol looks pretty similar to the native Core Animation protocol, but it offers a few more methods.

Two methods match Core Animation exactly:

- `pop_animationDidStart(_:)`: Pop calls this method on your delegate when the animation starts.
- `pop_animationDidStop(_:finished:)`: called when the animation completes or has been cancelled.

Pop introduces the following two extra methods to the delegate protocol:

- `pop_animationDidApply(_:)`: Pop calls this method after it applies each frame of the animation; this gives you a lot of precise control over the animation and lets you hook into animation events at just the right moment.

- `pop_animationDidReachToValue(_:)`: Pop calls this method when the animation reaches its `toValue`.

To see how Pop delegation works, you're going to hook into the animation completion callback.

Animation stopped callback

Scroll to `didPan(_:)` and find the `.Ended` case. Add the following line just before the line where you add the animation to the ball:

```
animation.delegate = self
```

Next, add a class extension at the end of the file to hold the `POPAnimationDelegate` methods, like so:

```
extension ViewController: POPAnimationDelegate {

}
```

That should take care of setting up the animation delegate.

Next, add one of the optional delegate methods to react to the animation completion:

```
func pop_animationDidStop(anim: POPAnimation!, finished: Bool) {
  print("animation did stop")
}
```

Build and run your project; this time, shoot the ball and wait a few moments for the ball to fully settle. You should see the `animation did stop` message in the console:

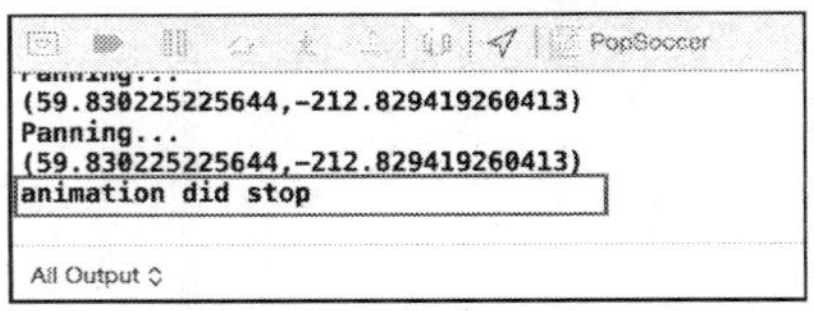

Now that you know the delegate is wired properly, you can hook into the delegate method to reset the ball position once the ball comes to rest.

Since you don't know in advance how much time the decay animation will take to complete, `pop_animationDidStop(_:)` is just the right spot to add your code.

Add the following code just below the line where you print `animation did stop`:

```
if finished {
  resetBall()
}
```

In the case where the animation hasn't been cancelled mid-way through and it completed successfully, you call `resetBall()` to make the ball re-appear somewhere mid-field so the player can take another shot.

To make the transition look a little nicer, add the following line at the bottom of `resetBall()`:

```
fadeInView(ball)
```

This makes the ball fade in as it re-appears in its new position.

The game is starting to look and feel quite good! However, as much fun as it is kicking a virtual ball around, you can't score even if you make a beautiful shot straight into the goal. You'll fix this in the next section.

Animation progress callback

You can use `pop_animationDidApply(_:)` to tap into the animation after each frame is rendered; this allows you to track the progress with very high precision without using key-value observing.

To let the player score on the goal, you'll implement `pop_animationDidApply(_:)` and at each step of the animation check if the ball's position is within the goal's bounding frame.

Add the following new method to your class extension:

```
func pop_animationDidApply(anim: POPAnimation!) {
  if goal.frame.contains(ball.center) {
    ball.pop_removeAllAnimations()
    print("GOAL")
  }
}
```

You use `contains()` to check if the ball's center is within the goal frame – if that's true, then you remove all animations from the ball.

This will result in a fun effect – try shooting the ball into the goal. As soon as the ball is inside it will just freeze there, sometimes right on the goal line, waiting for the referee's decision!

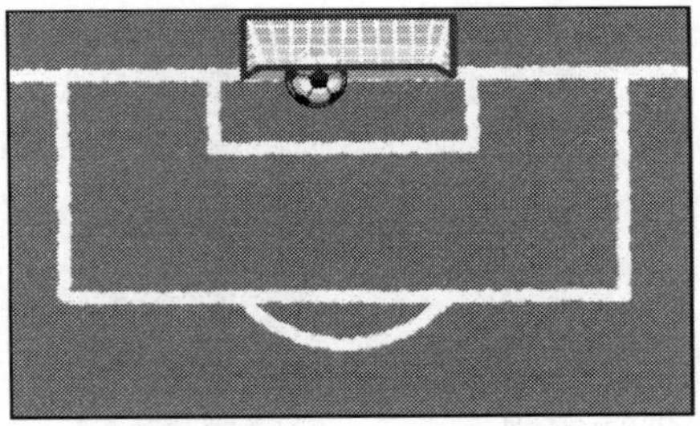

The player can finally score on the goal, but to take another shot they have to pick the ball out of the goal manually. That's no fun. To wrap up this chapter, you'll add some code to reset the ball after a goal.

Add the following code inside the `if` statement that you just added above:

```
resetBall()
return
```

This will reset the ball position after the player scores so they can take another shot. Nice!

Challenges

Challenge 1: Experiment with decay animations

As in the previous chapter, you will get to experiment a bit on your own in this challenge.

To understand decay animations a little better, try setting different values for the `deceleration` property on your ball decay animation. `deceleration` takes values ranging from `0.0` (faster deceleration) to `1.0` (slowest deceleration). The default value is `0.998`, so there's not much room to make your animation decay slower.

An interesting feature of Pop's decay animation is that it still has a `duration` property like all other animations – but this property is read-only. It comes in handy when you want to know upfront how much time it's going to take the decay animation to complete.

As soon as you set the velocity and potentially the deceleration on your decay animation, you can inspect duration to see the animation completion time.

When you feel comfortable with decay animations, move on to the next chapter and work through the final Pop topic in this book – spring animations.

Oh yes, I almost forgot – the next section also includes a master challenge for the entire Pop section of this book! See you there! :]

Chapter 27: Spring Animations with Pop

Spring animations are a great way to add some bounciness to your app – or to simply make your animations look a bit snappier. You created some spring animations earlier in the book while you were learning about view animations in UIKit.

Pop's spring animations have a similar look and feel to the ones in UIKit, but the way you create them is slightly different. In the UIView API, UIKit tries to work the specific damping and velocity values into the specified duration of your animation.

In contrast, Pop lets you set the spring "bounciness" and a velocity; the Pop animation engine then calculates the effect and determines on its own what the duration of the animation should be.

In this chapter, you'll assemble some spring animations and look into few more Pop features like animation completion blocks and animation dynamism.

By the end of the chapter, you'll have completed your Pop project with more advanced ball handling and some bouncy in-game messages as well:

Ready? Players, take the field! :]

Spring animations

If you followed through the tutorial in the previous chapter, you can simply keep working from where you left off. Otherwise, you can use the starter project for this chapter if you skipped a few parts or simply want to start fresh.

> **Note**: Don't forget you need to open the Xcode workspace file **PopSoccer.xcworkspace** and not the Xcode project file.

For your first spring animation, you'll add a new method to `ViewController` that will display springy in-game messages.

Open **ViewController.swift** and add the initial version of this new method:

```
func animateMessage(text: String) {
  let offScreenFrame = CGRect(x: -view.frame.size.width,
    y: 200.0, width: view.frame.size.width, height: 50.0)
  let label = UILabel(frame: offScreenFrame)
}
```

Here you define the frame for the label (`offScreenFrame`). In your spring animation, the initial frame of the label is to the left of the visible area of the screen, like so:

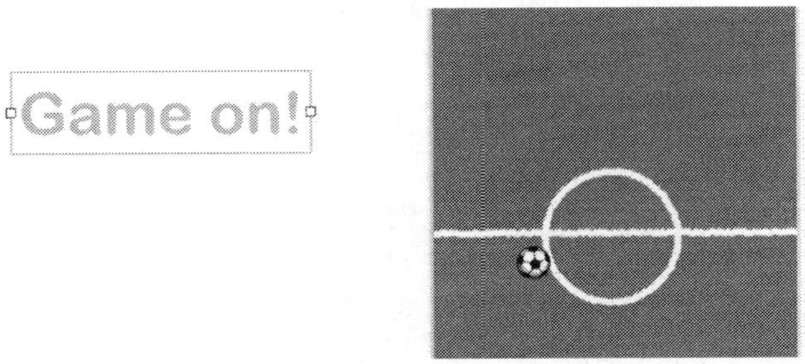

You then create the label using the supplied frame. At this point, you can customize the appearance of the label.

Add the following code to the end of `animateMessage(_:)`:

```
label.font = UIFont(name: "ArialRoundedMTBold", size: 52.0)
label.textAlignment = .Center
label.textColor = UIColor.yellowColor()
label.text = text
label.shadowColor = UIColor.darkGrayColor()
label.shadowOffset = CGSize(width: 2.0, height: 2.0)
```

```
view.addSubview(label)
```

You use the Arial Rounded font for the message; it's a nice rounded font, which is suitable for games and comes with OS X. You then set the color of the text to yellow and add just a bit of shadow to make the text stand out.

Finally, you add the newly created label to the view controller's view. This will make the text look playful yet polished:

Now that your label is complete, you can animate it. Add the following to the end of animateMessage(_:):

```
let bounce = POPSpringAnimation(propertyNamed: kPOPViewCenter)
bounce.fromValue = NSValue(CGPoint: label.center)
bounce.toValue = NSValue(CGPoint: view.center)
```

In the code above, you create a new instance of POPSpringAnimation. Since this animation animates the view's center property, you use kPOPViewCenter as the name of the animation property.

You then set the start and end positions for the animation: the label moves its initial position off-screen to the center of the view controller's view. The message then snaps into its final location with the following bouncy effect:

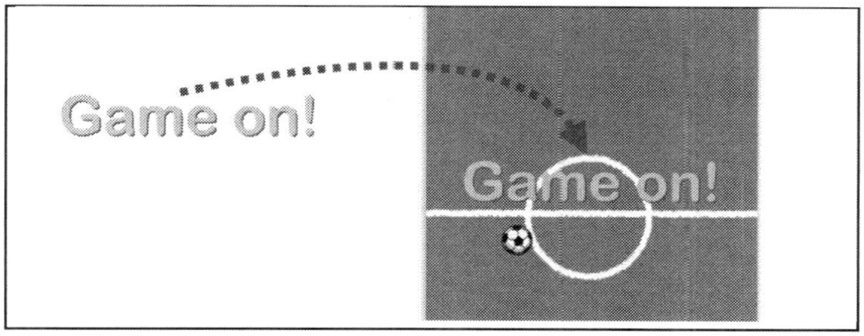

Note that you need to use NSValue boxing just as you do with CABasicAnimation, since fromValue and toValue are of type AnyObject and need a class instance rather than a struct.

POPSpringAnimation provides you with several properties that you'll use to control the springy behavior of the animation:

- springBounciness sets the "bounciness" of your spring animation. It takes a value between 0.0 (no bouncing at all) and 20.0 (a lot of bouncing). The default value of this property is 4.0; if you don't set springBounciness explicitly, the default value makes your spring animation jiggle just a little.
- springSpeed sets the speed of the animation. This property also takes a value between 0.0 (very slow) and 20.0 (very fast). The spring speed defaults to 12.0.

You want the messages in your game to appear with a playful snap; to do this you'll have to increase the speed of your animation and make it bounce as much as possible.

Add the following code to animateMessage(_:):

```
bounce.springSpeed = 15.0
bounce.springBounciness = 20.0

label.pop_addAnimation(bounce, forKey: nil)
```

This will set the spring parameters and then add the animation to the label view.

All that's left is to call animateMessage(_:) from somewhere in your code with an appropriate message.

Scroll up to viewDidAppear(_:); this is a good place to add some code to show a welcome message to the player as soon as the game starts.

Append the following to viewDidAppear(_:):

```
animateMessage("Game on!")
```

Build and run your project; as soon as the game starts you'll see your bouncy message appear:

You can easily speed up or slow down the effect by adjusting `springSpeed` to produce an awesome animation exactly to your liking.

For example, if you don't want the animation to be quite so snappy, try setting `springSpeed` to `1.0` – that will give you a nice wide bounce. If you want to see the animation in even more detail, try `0.15` instead.

Believe it or not, that covers the basics of spring animations in Pop! That was probably easier than you thought! :]

You can dig through the library header files in **Pods/pop/POPSpringAnimation.h** if you'd like to learn a bit more about the abilities of Pop spring animations. However, there's still more to learn about Pop so you'll move on to yet another feature – completion blocks and delegates in Pop.

Animation completion block

Discussions between iOS developers over delegates and blocks/closures can get heated pretty fast. However, Pop is a special case; it's almost a hybrid of both.

Pop gives you the best of both worlds: it gives you a very powerful delegate protocol that you learned about in the previous chapter, but if you only need to perform an action when the animation completes you can do that as well via the `completionBlock` property.

Head back to your Pop Soccer game; right now your "Game On!" message remains on the screen indefinitely. You'd like that message to remain in place for a moment once the animation completes, but then disappear from view.

This sounds like a perfect opportunity to use an animation completion block.

Head back to `animateMessage(_:)` and insert the following code just **before** the line where you call `pop_addAnimation(_:key:)`:

```
bounce.completionBlock = { animation, finished in

}
```

Before writing the actual code, take a look at the two parameters here and think about what to do once the animation finishes. The two parameters are the same as the ones that you have in the `animationDidStop(_:finished:)` delegate method you've already learned about.

First, you get back your own animation object; this helps you avoid strongly capturing your original variable by mistake.

The second parameter is a Boolean telling you whether the animation finished successfully or if it was cancelled in some way.

Now you'll add the code to fade out the label. To make things a bit more interesting you will do that Inception-style.

Add the following code inside the closure you added above:

```
let fadeOut = POPBasicAnimation(propertyNamed: kPOPViewAlpha)
fadeOut.toValue = 0.0
fadeOut.duration = 0.5
fadeOut.completionBlock = {_, _ in
  label.removeFromSuperview()
}
label.pop_addAnimation(fadeOut, forKey: nil)
```

Here you create a fade animation and add it to `label`. In this new fade animation's completion block you remove `label` from the view hierarchy.

Build and run your project and see what it looks like:

One of the benefits of Pop is that you can change an animation mid-flight. You'll add a feature to let the user tap on the screen while the animation is running and change the bounce target location on the fly.

Dynamic animations

Changing the final property value while an animation is running is only possible with Pop, not Core Animation, since Pop owns its animation objects and works directly with the presentation layer.

Start by adding the tap gesture recognizer that will drive the dynamic changes to the spring animation. Scroll to `viewDidLoad()` and add the following code to the end of the method:

```
let tap = UITapGestureRecognizer(target: self,
  action: Selector("didTap:"))
view.addGestureRecognizer(tap)
```

Your gesture recognizer calls `didTap(_:)` when the player taps anywhere on the screen. In `didTap(_:)` you first find out if there's a message on the screen.

Add the following new property to the `ViewController` class:

```
weak var currentMessage: UILabel?
```

This is a weak variable since you don't need a strong reference and it's possible the label has already been removed from the view.

Then scroll to `animateMessage(_:)` and insert the following code just before the line where you add `label` to the view controller's view:

```
currentMessage = label
```

This simply assigns the new label to your new variable.

The final preparation step is to assign a key to the spring animation; assigning a key gives the animation a name that you can use to access the animation while it's running).

Find the line where you add the `bounce` animation to the `label` and replace `nil` with `"bounce"` to name the animation:

```
label.pop_addAnimation(bounce, forKey: "bounce")
```

Now that your animation has a key, you can access and modify it from within `didTap(_:)`. And speaking of `didTap(_:)`, now would be a great time to finally add that method:

```
func didTap(tap: UITapGestureRecognizer) {
  if let label = currentMessage {

  }
}
```

As your first task in `didTap(_:)`, you check if there's a message currently visible on the screen. If so, you can then proceed to check if Pop is currently displaying a spring animation on the label.

To do that, insert the following code inside the `if` block:

```
if let bounce = label.pop_animationForKey("bounce") as?
POPSpringAnimation {

}
```

In the code above, you look for an animation that's running on `label` with a key of `"bounce"`. Just to make doubly sure it's the right animation, you add a conditional cast to `POPSpringAnimation`.

Now you can modify `bounce` to immediately alter the currently running animation.

Add the following line inside the inner `if` block:

```
bounce.toValue = NSValue(CGPoint: tap.locationInView(view))
```

Here you simply grab the tapped location, box it as an `NSValue`, and set it as the `toValue` of the animation. "Really?" you ask. "Could it be that easy to modify a running animation?"

Give it a try and see! :]

Build and run your project; tap the screen when the message appears and you'll see the label change its direction mid-flight and finish its bounce animation at the location you tapped:

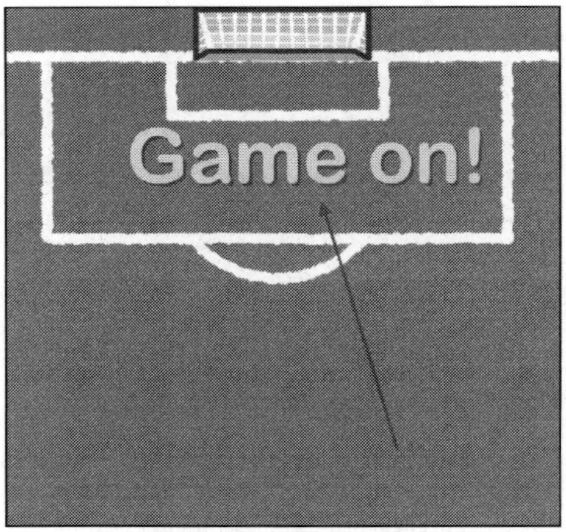

Now *that's* an incredibly cool feature, isn't it? :]

Thanks to Pop, you can build these interactive features backed by animations to respond to user events.

Challenges

As you've seen, Pop is incredibly useful for creating animations and will serve as an invaluable addition to your animation tool belt – especially if you need to create interactive live UIs with organic and playful animations.

Challenge 1: Promote the "Goal" message to the screen

This challenge is rather simple, but the game won't feel complete if you don't take care of this detail.

When the player scores a goal you print a message in the console –that's not terribly rewarding. Display the "Goal!" message using your new and shiny `animateMessage(_:)` method, like so:

Challenge 2: Reset the ball when it gets outside of the field

When the ball goes off the screen, you should reset it for another try. To start, you can add a key to the ball decay animation. Then in `pop_animationDidApply(_:)` check if the current ball position is out of the screen. If so, remove the decay animation from the ball and reset the ball position.

Über haxx0r challenge: Make the ball bounce off the sides of the field

For this final challenge, make the ball bounce off the left and right sides of the screen. The ball should maintain its forward momentum when it reaches the left or right margin, but invert its horizontal velocity, like so:

You can decide the exact details for your solution on your own, but if you need a bit more direction consider the following design:

- Define minimum and maximum X coordinates for the ball animation. The minimum acceptable value would be half the width of the ball and the maximum would be the width of the screen minus half the width of the ball.
- Add a new check in `pop_animationDidApply(_:)` to see if the ball's X coordinate is currently less than the minimum acceptable X coordinate, or greater than the maximum one. You need this check to happen *before* the out of bounds check in the previous challenge!
- If the ball is outside of the allowed range, store the animation's velocity (it's an `NSValue`, which you can unbox by calling its `CGPointValue()` method) and remove the animation from the ball.
- Before kicking off the new animation, move the ball back into the allowed space; you can do that with one line of code by setting its X coordinate to: `min(max(minX, ball.center.x), maxX)`
- Create and run a new decay animation starting from the current ball position that has the same Y velocity as the previous velocity, but a new inverted X velocity.
- Don't forget to set the animation delegate and give the animation the same key as the one you just removed.

This wraps up the Pop Soccer project – you've created a fun little game and learned a lot about Pop along the way.

If you like what you've seen so far with the Pop library, check out their page on GitHub (https://github.com/facebook/pop) and let the team know you appreciate their efforts by starring their repository or checking out the rest of their open source projects https://code.facebook.com/projects.

Conclusion

We hope you're excited about the breadth of animations available to you in iOS! Animations bring life and playfulness to touch-based interfaces; this makes people feel more connected to your interface and creates memorable app experiences for your users.

You're now equipped to use and understand the animation tools available to you, from layers to 3D effects and beyond. It's up to you now to couple your creativity with the things you've learned in this book and create some impressive effects of your own!

If you have any questions or comments about the projects in this book or in your own animations, please stop by our forums at http://www.raywenderlich.com/forums.

If you want to follow Marin's continuing experiments with iOS animations check out his monthly newsletter:
http://www.ios-animations-by-emails.com.

Thank you again for purchasing this book. Your continued support is what makes the books, tutorials, videos and other things we do at raywenderlich.com possible—we truly appreciate it!

May all your animations be fun and fluid, with furiously high frame rates!

– Marin, Richard, Chris, Greg and Vicki

The *iOS Animations by Tutorials* team

47099237R00216

Made in the USA
Charleston, SC
29 September 2015